HISTORY OF CHRISTIANITY IN KOREA

| In Soo Kim, Ph.D. |

QUMRAN
Publishing House

To the English Readers

Around twenty years ago, I wrote this book to be used as a textbook at the Presbyterian College and Theological Seminary (Seoul, South Korea) where I had taught for many years. Among several of my books, written about the history of the Korean Church, this book was my very first. During my years lecturing at the Seminary, many people who were interested in the rapid growth of the Korean Church asked me what the reasons were for the Korean Church to grow so rapidly and become very large. They wanted to know how the Korean Church could expand so quickly compared to other churches of Asian countries.

Surveying books that are written in English on the history of the Korean Church, I knew that there was no single book except one small book that was written by an American missionary who worked in Korea a generation ago.

To answer those who asked me the reason for the rapid growth of the Church, I thought it better to translate one of my books on the Korean Church history rather than provide a fragmented answer. I hope that one can survey the entire history of the Korean Church through this book. Even though I had written several volumes on this topic, I decided to translate this shorter version of those books to lessen the burden of the reader.

It is my desire for those who read this book that you may have a greater understanding of the Korean Church and pray for the Church to carry out her responsibilities in which the Lord has charged.

I would like to give my sincere thanks and appreciation to those who have contributed to the publishing of this book, and may God bless those who read this small piece.

In Christ
June 2011

Los Angeles, CA
The Author

Preface

Studying history is not an easy thing, and writing the history even harder. Perhaps that is the reason why there are not many people studying history nor many good history books. Nations with lack of knowledge of history fail to learn the lesson of their history and are bound to repeat their tragedies.

There are already a good number of books on the history of the Korean church. While many of these are highly academic and difficult in content and are indispensable guides to scholars and history experts, the general public found it difficult to comprehend them. And some publications merely contain brief summaries of history and serve as nothing but simple lists of historical events.

As I spent many years lecturing the "History of the Korean Church" at the Presbyterian College and Theological Seminary(Seoul, Korea), I had been thinking of consolidating my lecture notes and publish them as a single volume for the benefit of history students, when I was contacted by the Presbyterian Church in Korea Publishing about writing History of the Korean Church as one of the volumes for their theological research book series.

I would like to emphasize that this book has been written for those reading and studying the history of the Korean church for the first time. Special efforts have been made to facilitate an easy and comprehensive bird's-eye view of the Korean church. Consequently annotations were kept to an absolute minimum: maximum of two or three per page.

Writing history always involves a view of history. Representative views of history for the history of the Korean church include Dr. Nak Jun Paik's mission view of history (sungyo sagwan) and Prof Kyeong Bae Min's nationalist view of history (minjok sagwan), which are the most evident of all, and the popularist (minjung sagwan), which emerged in the 1970s for writing history from the viewpoint of Minjung, and the positivist view of history, which was attempted by the history lecturers at ordinary universities for using verified materials and fusing the Korean history and the history of the Korean church as one. It seems that the latter two have not yet fully been established as valid view of history and will require more efforts and time for their full acceptance.

Fundamentally speaking, any church history should be written with the redemption view of history or the divine providence view of history. History of the world may be written in all sorts of historical views, but the history of church must always be written in a way that reflects the divine providence for salvation of mankind and God's redemptive works. It should therefore be regarded that an account of church history is true and valid only if it has been written according to the historical view of divine providence. I am a strong advocate of the historical view of divine providence, and I have made every effort to abide by that view throughout this book.

Time constraints played a major factor in limiting the quality and scope of this book's content. Please bear with me for the mean while until I produce a better piece of work when time permits.

Summer of 1993
The Author

CONTENTS

PART I

Chapter 1

Possibility of Contacts with Christianity before the Catholic Mission

1. Nestorian Mission to the East

Scholars largely disagree as to when Christianity was first introduced to Korea. In this section we will briefly discuss the question of when Nestorianism was first introduced to Korea, since this is directly related to the question of when Christianity was introduced to Korea.

First of all, what is Nestorianism? Nestorianism was established as a Christian sect when Nestorius, the Patriarch of Constantinople, the capital of the Eastern Roman Empire, was condemned as a herecy for calling the Virgin Mary "Mother of Christ" (Christotokos) at the Council of Ephesus in A.D. 431.[1] When all the churches

---

1 Kenneth S. Laourette, *A History of Christianity* (New York: Harper and Row Publishers, 1953), 169.

were recognizing the Virgin Mary as the "Mother of God"(Theotok os), Cyril of Alexandria was highly displeased with Nestorius who claimed it to be right to call the Virgin Mary "Mother of Christ" rather than "Mother of God" because she gave birth to the Christ. Thus a council was held in Ephesus and Nestorius was eventually condemned and removed as a heresy.

Nestorius was then sent in exile to Egypt. But his disciples built monasteries in Persia(present Iran), trained missionaries and sent them to various regions. One of the missionary groups traveled through India and arrived in China.[2] It was in A.D. 635(the ninth year of the Emperor Taizong of Tang dynasty) when Alopen and his Nestorian missionaries arrived in China. By "unanticipated rovidence,"[3] Alopen's group was given a warm welcome and was permitted by Emperor Taizong to undertake missionary activitics. In 638, they were given a lot of land and built the Persian Temple with the sponsorship of the Tang dynasty. They were also involved in translation of the Scripture and were active in missions.

The Tang Chinese called this new religion from the West the "Religion of Persia" because it came from Persia. But the religion was later renamed as the "Religion of Daegin (Rome)" when they learned that it actually originated from Rome. However, it was latcalled the "Luminous Religion." Thus the Nestorianism in Tang

---

2 The event of Nestorianism coming into China was known by the discovery of the monument of Nestorianism that was found near Shian in 1625. Jang Sik Lee, *Asia Godae Gidogiosa* (History of the Ancient Christian History in Asia (Gidokgiomoonsa, 1993), 230.

3 S. H. Moffett, *A History of Christianity in Asia* (San Francisco: Harper, 1992), 292. Cf. 288-314 of this book about the coming of Nestorianism into China.

was called either the "Luminous Religion" or the "Luminous Religion of Daegin." Under the protection of Taizong and many other successive emperors, Nestorianism gained strength and its missions were actively carried out. In Tang China, Nestorianism grew steadily under the protection of the royal courts and popularity of the people for about 200 years.

However, Nestorianism in China was faced with an exceedingly difficult situation. This was because Wuzong began to persecute all foreign religions as he came to the throne. Being a devout Taoist, Wuzong was not happy with foreign religions flourishing in his own country. In 845, he decreed that all foreign religions be scraped out, especially Buddhism. This was primarily to restrict and control the Buddhist temples which were holding a large portion of farm lands and properties, and the Buddhist monks who enjoyed a luxurious lifestyle despite the under performing economy.[4] But this decree did not concern Buddhism alone. With all foreign religions under the royal pressure, Nestorianism was not spared from the whips of persecution. As a result, Nestorianism could not survive in Tang China any longer and was left to fade away by itself. Let us now examine the possibility of Nestorianism reaching Korea.

2. Possibility of Nestorian Mission to Korea

When Nestorianism was actively propagating itself in Tang China, Silla was in the process of unifying the three kingdoms in Korea

---

4 At that time, the 4,600 Buddhist temples were shut down and the 265,000 monks returned to secular life.

(A.D. 66).[5] It is a well-known fact that Tang China assisted Silla for unifying the three kingdoms; the Silla-Tang joint forces destroyed Goguryo and Baekje and established Unified Silla. Besides the military relationship, Silla was closely associated with Tang in various ways. In particular, it was common for Silla Buddhist monks to study abroad in Tang and return to Silla with the newly learned doctrines because Silla and Tang China shared the same national religion of Buddhism. Since Silla and Tang China were frequently in touch with one another through many channels, it is more than reasonable to suppose that Nestorianism, which was quite popular in Tang, was introduced to Silla.

The possibility of Nestorianism being introduced to Silla was also raised by a British scholar. It was E. A. Gordon, a woman archaeologist. Gordon concentrated in the studies of the introduction of Christianity to the East and exchanges between Christianity and Buddhism. She also stayed a number of years in Korea, studying the possibility of introduction of Nestorianism into Korea and published reasonable explanations for this.[6] Gordon stated that traces of Nestorianism are visible in the Gwaneumbosal(Buddhist saint) statue, Nahan(Buddhist saint) statue and so on at Bulguk Buddhist Temple in Gyoungju, Kyongbuk Province. She also claimed that similar traces of Nestorianism could be found in warrior statues placed in front of royal and civilian tombs of the Unified Silla period.

---

5 Three Kingdoms were Goguryo(37B.C.-A.D.668), Baekje(18B.C.-A.D.663), and Silla(57B.C.-A.D.935).

6 Cf. E. A. Gordon, *Christianity and the Mahayana* (Tokyo: Maruzen, 1921).

Gordon even built a replica of the Nestorian Monument at Jangan Buddhist Temple on Mt. Geumgang(Diamond) in commemoration of her work. Such claims of Gordon were accepted by several scholars of the history of the Korean church.[7] Among them, Rev. Yang Sun Kim, one of the pioneers of the history of the Korean church, advocated this the most. As items proving the arrival of Nestorianism in Korea, Kim mentions the stone cross found in Bulguk Temple in 1956, the Gwaneum(Buddhist saint) statue that looks like the Virgin Mary, and the bronze cross at Daeheung Temple in Haenam, South Jeolla.[8]

Despite such indications of possibility, however, arrival of Nestorianism in Korea still remains only as a question of probability until concrete historical document are discovered. Therefore, we are left with no choice but to leave the introduction of Nestorian Christianity to Korea as "one of the romantic issues."[9]

3. Possibility of Contacts with Christianity in Koryo

Although the possibility of Nestorianism reaching Korea during Unified Silla, we could not prove this due to inadequate historical documents. Instead, history clearly presents us with the traces of Roman Catholicism in Korea after Silla was defeated by Goryo

---

7 Those who insisted on this view were Yoon Tae Oh , Kwang Soo Kim, and Jang Sik Lee.
8 Yang Sun Kim, *Ganchoorin Hanguk Giohoesa* (Brief History of the Korean Church) (Daehan Yesugio Jangrohoe Chonghoe Gioyookboo, 1962), 8.
9 Kyong Bae Min, *Hanguk Gidokgiohoesa* (History of the Christian Church in Korea) (Seoul: Yonsei University Press, 1993), 29.

and when Goryo was established as the owner of the Korean Peninsula.

In China, Genghis Khan defeated Song dynasty established the Yuan Dynasty. With his bellicose character, Genghis Khan began to advance toward the West and became a strong threat to West Europe by overrunning Persia and stretching his territories all the way to Poland. The Holy See was both worried and pleased with such Mongol aggression. This was because Islam, which emerged in the middle of the seventh century, grew in power and took possession of four out of the five dioceses of the early church of Jerusalem, Antioch, Alexandria and Constantinople, except Rome which was located in the West. Although Pope Urban II and his successors staged the Crusades in order to scrape out the Muslims who attacked and robbed the Christian pilgrims and to take back the holy land from the pagans, the campaigns failed repeatedly and Islam was gaining more power than ever.

Seeing the Mongolia advancing toward the West, the Holy See had two different attitudes. While the Holy See was afraid of this warlike race invading Europe, it hoped that the Mongols would weaken its age-long enemy of the Islamic states and further prevent westward aggression of Islam by plundering and overrunning the territory. Consequently, the Holy See was both afraid and in favor of the Mongols. The Holy See decided that it could defeat Islam by partnering with the Mongols, and more than that, was determined to evangelize this gentile people.

In 1245, Pope Innocent IV summoned a general council in Lyons,

France, where it was decided to dispatch envoys and missionaries for amity with Mongolia and its missions. Around this time, a number of orders with missionary passion emerged within the Catholic Church. The most well-known among them were the Franciscans, established in 1209 by St. Francisco of Assisi in Italy, and the Dominicans, established in 1216 by St. Dominic in Spain. It was the Franciscans who were the first to volunteer as missionaries to the Mongols, and Giovanni di Pian de Carpini, one of Francisco's disciples, was appointed as the chief envoy. Giovanni and his envoys departed from Lyons in April 1245 and arrived in then capital of Mongolia, Karakorum, in July of the following year.[10] Here, they participated in the coronation ceremony of Emperor Dingzong, presented the Pope's letter, obtained Dingzong's reply, and returned to Europe in Autumn of 1247.

Thus, Roman Catholic's official envoy visited China, and since then, the Roman Catholic Church and China maintained a friendly relationship for some time. In middle of all these, there is an interesting incident in regards to Korea. When William de Rubruck, a Franciscan, came to Mongolia in the second mission from the Holy See in 1253, he introduced Korea to Europe. When Louis IX of France launched the sixth Crusade in order to conquer the Holy Land and was staying in Cyprus on his campaign, he learned that Sartach, one of the generals of Batu Khan of Mongolia, was a Nestorian Christian. Perceiving that the Mongolian mission would

---

10 Cf. Kenneth S. Latourette, *A History of the Expansion of Christianity*, vol. II (New York: Harper and Brothers, 1978), 280.

be successful with Sartach's assistance, Louis IX sent Rubruck to Sartach who was camping near the Volga River in 1253. Upon meeting with Sartach, Rubruck was disappointed to discover that Sartach was not a Nestorian Christian. Nevertheless, Rubruck recognized that a royal approval was necessary for the Mongolian mission. He set out for Karakorum, then-capital of Mongolia, arrived there in January of 1253, and met with Emperor Dingzong. Emperor Dingzong showed hospitability toward Rubruck and asked him to go back after spending the winter in Mongolia. Meanwhile Rubruck met with Dingzong several times in an attempt to evangelize him, but his efforts were in vain and he returned home in July 1253.[11]

On his visit to Mongolia, Rubruck made tremendous impacts on the history of Korea by introducing her to the Western world. When Mongolia demanded Goryo of stupendous funds for raising military and forced Goryo to build numerous battleships in order to conquer Japan, Rubruck reached the riverside the Yalu river. In his travel records, Rubruck named the country across the river as Caulei. This name was introduced to Europe and was later became known as Korea in English. Thus, Rubruck became the very person who used the earliest form of the name "Korea" and introduced Korea to the West for the first time.

It can be said that Roman Catholic Church's mission to China was full-fledged when the Franciscan missionary John of Monte

---

11 W. W. Rockhill, *The Journey of William of Rubruck to the Eastern Part of the World, 1253-1255* (London: The Hekluyt Society, 1900), 21-26. Kenneth S. Latourette, *A History of the Expansion of Christianity.* vol. II (New York: Harper and Brothers, 1978), 333.

Corvino, sent by Pope Nicholas IV, arrived in Beijing in 1294. This was when Mongolia defeated Song dynasty, renamed the dynasty as Yuan, and moved its capital from Karakorum to Beijing. Emperor Chengzong of Yuan showed hospitality to Corvino and allowed his missionary works. Consequently, Corvino's mission works were exceedingly successful with the Emperor's support. In his letter to the Holy See in 1305, he reported that there were two cathedrals in Beijing, there were more than 6,000 believers, more than 150 boys were taught Latin hymns, and a children's choir were formed and they sang hymns in services.[12]

Encouraged by Corvino's achievements of the Roman Catholic mission in China, Pope Clement V further committed to the Chinese mission by founding a diocese in China in 1307. He appointed Corvino as Archbishop of Cambaluc and sent seven bishops as Corvino's assistants. When Corvino passed away in China in 1328, the Holy See appointed and sent Nicolas, a professor in the University of Paris, as his successor but he died on his way to China. Again, John of Marignolli was sent and he arrived in Beijing in 1342, but he was forced to go back after three years due to the political unrest. Consequently, more successors were appointed but most of them died on the way even before reaching the mission field. In effect, the Roman Catholic mission in China that Corvino pioneered was left to fade away into history after about a century of survival. One important reason for this was that the Yuan Dynasty,

---

12 A. C. Moule, *Christians in China before the Year 1550* (London: Society for Promoting Christian Knowledge, 1930), 177-180. C. Dawson, ed., *Mission to Asia* (New York: Harper and Row Publishing Co., 1966), 225-229.

which guaranteed freedom of religions and was favorable to Catholic missions, collapsed. Thus, in the same way that Nestorianism died out along with the collapse of Tang China, Roman Catholicism disappeared into history as the Yuan Dynasty fell. China then would have to wait another two long centuries before Catholic missions reach her again.

Chapter 2

Pre-Mission Contacts with Catholicism

1. The Hideyoshi Invasion and Catholicism

Once a Catholic priest visited Korea, before the Catholic mission to Korea was launched. This took place during one of the most tragic wars of Korean history, the Hideyoshi Invasion.

Following Columbus's discovery of the New World in 1492, Pope Alexander VI issued a bull in May, 1493, decreeing Catholic nations to propagate the Catholic faith in their expeditions. Also, in order to prevent conflicts between the great naval powers Spain and Portugal in their expeditions and colonial rules, the Pope divided the world into two parts and allocated them each portion. In other words, the Pope spread out the atlas of the world, drew a line from the North Pole through Azores all the way to the South Pole, and commissioned Spain and Portugal to carry out missionary works to the west and to the east of the line respectively.[13]

Following Martin Luther's staging of Reformation in 1517, the Protestant power spread like wildfire, essentially challenging the Holy See and its millennium-long authority. Naturally, the corrupt Rome was perplexed at the rise of the new church but was also awakened to its internal renewal movement. At this time, Society of Jesus emerged as an organization that raised high the banner of Roman Catholicism. Founded by Ignatius Loyola from Spain in 1534, this religious order possessed a fervent passion for missions.

World mission of the Society of Jesus was heavily concentrated toward the East. The hero of the Eastern mission was Francis Xavier, one of the founders of the order. Sponsored by the Portuguese king, he embarked on Eastern mission and arrived in Goa of India in 1541. After a considerably successful ministry for 8 years there, he set out for his next destination, Japan. He arrived in Kyushu in 1549 and firmly established a foundation for the Catholic Church in Japan after three years. Catholics in Japan numbered about 300, 000 at the time.[14] He then left for China for further mission works, but he died of a fever on an island before reaching China.

The Catholic mission in Japan, started by Xavier, could expand greatly due to the lenient religious policy of Oda Nobunaga, one of the rulers of Japan at that time. Oda is also known to have

---

13 This is why even within South America, Brazil uses Portuguese while other countries use Spanish. See Stephen Neill, *A History of Christian Missions*, 2nd ed. (New York: Penguin Books, 1986), ch. 5.

14 See Charles Dallet, *The History of the Catholic Church in Korea*, trans. Charles Messenger (New Heaven: 1952), translated and annotated by Eung Yeol Ahn and Seok Woo Choi (Bundo Publishing, 1979-1980), vol. 1, 279, footnote 1.

given a plot of land to the Catholic Church for the building of a seminary. Of course, Oda's reciprocal policy did not attribute to his dedication in the Christian faith. On the contrary, it is implied that he intended to use Christianity as a new restraining threat against the Buddhist dominance which was exercising tremendous political and social influence in Japan. Toyotomi Hideyoshi, Oda's successor, also exercised a lenient policy toward Christianity and guaranteed protection of the mission work. History has it that he met with the Jesuit priests in Osaka before launching the Hideyoshi Invasion against Korea. He told them his plan to invade Ming China and Korea, and he also pledged to build Christian churches in Korea and convert the people into Catholic believers.[15] Thus it could be deduced that he had a favorable view of Catholicism in the beginning.

However, there are some interpretations suggesting that Hideyoshi intended to weaken the Catholic Church by sending a large number of Catholics to war. While there are no concrete evidence supporting or defying such possibility, various historical materials show that one of Hideyoshi's leading generals, Konishi Yukinaga, was a devout Catholic with the Christian name Augustino, and that many of his soldiers were Catholics. According to one record, approximately 10 percent of the Japanese soldiers landed in Busan, South Kyongsang Province during the Invasion were Catholics,[16] and some claim that a majority of soldiers under Konishi's command were Catholics.

---

15 R. Storry, *A History of Modern Japan* (New York: Penguin Books, 1961), 47.
16 F. Blinkley, *A History of the Japanese People* (London: The Encyclopedia Britannica Press, 1915), 509.

Even if some of these claims are somewhat exaggerated, we can safely assume that a large number of the Japanese soldiers sent for the invasion of Korea were Catholics.

2. The First Catholic Priest to Enter Korea - G. de Cespedes

The Hideyoshi Invasion was a gruesome war that left a deep scar in the history of Korea. The sufferings of the Korean people over the seven years of turmoil were simply beyond description. In his book, *A History of Korea in Biblical Perspective*, Seok Hun Ham described the horrible scene of the time. "When a drunken Ming soldier threw up on the street, everyone ran toward it and wrestled against each other to eat the vomit and those who could not eat it were wailing."[17] This statement alone is more than sufficient to tell us the hardship of the Korean people at that time.

In such a situation, Father Gregorio de Cespedes was brought into Korea to serve as a chaplain to the Catholic soldiers under the command of Konishi. In essence, Father Cespedes was the very first Christian priest to set foot in Korea in the four-millennium history of the Korean people. He was commended by Father Pedro Gomez, the parish priest of the Society of Jesus in Japan, to come to Korea.

Cespedes was born in Madrid, Spain, in 1511, joined the Jesuits at the age of 18, and was ordained a father in 1575 when he

---

17 Seok Hun Ham, *Seongseojeok Ipjangesuhbon Chosunyeoksa* (A History of Korea in Biblical Perspective) (Seoul: Sinsaenggwan, 1961), 162-163.

was serving as a missionary in Goa, India. Consequently, he moved to Japan and undertook successful mission works, baptizing about a hundred people. His extraordinary fluency in Japanese was very much favored by the Japanese. He gradually extended his social contacts with high ranking officials and Konishi was one of them. In 1585, he was appointed as the principal of a seminary in Osaka, where he concentrated on teaching priest candidates.

No doubt Cespedes' linguistic ability was an important factor for being selected as the chaplain to the Catholic soldiers fighting in Korea, but his close relationship with Konishi should be viewed as equally important, if not more. One day in December of 1593,[18] he arrived in Korea with Foucan Eion, a young Japanese friar. Cespedes's activities in Korea were fairly regular for a chaplain, such as conducting mass, hearing confessions, and anointing the wounded soldiers immediately before their deaths.

One important point for us to consider is whether he carried out any missionary work among the Korean people here. Unfortunately there are no records of Cespedes preaching to the Korean people. The reason is simple. He stayed within the Japanese army garrison, where it would be impossible for him to meet any Korean citizens. Furthermore, he could not speak any Korean, and he was not commissioned to evangelize Korea. In his book, *Histoire de l'Eglise de Coree*, Father C. Dallet also defies the possibility of Cespedes preaching to the Korean citizens.

---

18 While scholars largely disagree on the exact year and date, this is generally thought to be the year after the Hideyoshi Invasion. C. Dallet, *The History of the Catholic Church in Korea*, vol. 1, 281.

During Cespedes stayed in Korea, he did not have any chance to contact Koreans except those who will bring to Japan as slaves. The Korean army strategy was to evacuate the Korean people not staying surround the castle where the Japanese troops. Thus the Japanese troops were isolated. Most of the people fled to the North and if the Japanese troops approached then they fled into forests or valley. The Korean people has strong hostile feeling to the foreigners, and it is strong enough to make vain about conversion to Christianity due to hostility to the invaders.[19]

Let alone Dallet's records, it is more than natural to understandable that no Korean would respond positively to the preaching of a westerner who came with the invasion army who savaged the country under detestable banners.

Although there are no records that clearly indicate how long Cespedes stayed in Korea, it is known that he had to return to Japan after several months due to conflicts with other generals who were devout Buddhists. Nevertheless, it is interesting to note that the region where Cespedes stayed for a several months, Ungcheon in South Gyoungsang is home to Rev. Kee Cheol Joo, the celebrated Protestant martyr of Korea. It is by far ironic to see that the very place with traces of the first Roman Catholic priest who came with an invasion army is the birthplace of Rev. Kee Cheol Joo who stood against the Japanese during the Japanese

---

19 Ibid., 284-285.

Occupation(A.D. 1910-1945).

Although Cespedes, as the first Christian priest to set foot in Korea, could not achieve anything significant in the Christian history of Korea, he did great things for Koreans after returning to Japan. During the war, Koreans were captured as slaves and were sold to inhumane slave traders for raising military funds. Cespedes worked in various ways to put an end to such inhumane practices. Although he even ordered the immoral traders involved in human trafficking to be excommunicated, but such religious chastisements were neither binding and were nor quite effective. He had catechisms translated into Korean for the Koreans brought into Japan, he cultivated the Christian faith in them by teaching doctrines, and he gave rest to the homesick souls who were suffering as prisoners of war in the foreign land.[20]

Among the Koreans who embraced the Catholic faith in the foreign land, many were martyred away from home when Tokugawa launched the eradication policy of Christianity. According one record, as many as 25 were exiled or jailed and 21 were martyred. Nine of the martyrs were included among the 205 Japanese martyrs when Pope Pius IX beatified[21] them as Blessed Martyrs in July 1867.[22]

The tragedy suffered by Koreans during the Hideyoshi Invasion was so tremendous that the Korea Dynasty later had to adopt

---

20 *Ibid.*, 283.
21 In Catholicism, this is performed to recognize dead believers as the Blessed.
22 C. H. Robinson, *History of Christian Missions* (Edinburgh: T. & T. Clark, 1915), 248.

the isolationist policy. The continual attempts of Korean mission by the Catholic Church inevitably resulted in much conflict, marking the early history of Christianity in Korea with the blood of countless martyrs.

It became less and less likely that the Roman Catholicism would successfully reach Korea through Japan. Just like all other forms of exchanges at that time, it began to seem better that Christianity be introduced to Korea via China. In the next section, we will see the introduction of the Catholic Church to Korea through China.

3. Crown Prince Sohyon's Contact with Catholicism in China

Destined to be hustled and disrupted by the three major powers of China, Japan and Russia, Korea suffered unprecedented wars of the Hideyoshi Invasion, and she was attacked from the north after a generation passed since the Hideyoshi Invasion. In 1636, Jurchens of Manchuria extended their power, took possession of China, and established Qing China. Not withholding the military momentum of establishing a new dynasty, their 100,000 troops showed no mercy in devastating Korea, which has not even restored itself from the turmoil by the Japanese. King Injo escaped to Namhansan fortress, but was forced to walk out with a white flag after 45 days in the first lunar month of 1637, leaving irreversible disgrace in history. Such a disgrace took place at Samjeondo(present Songpa, Seoul) where King Injo knelt and bowed three times, touched his forehead on the ground nine times to pay honor to Emperor Taizong and submitted Korea as a vassal kingdom to Qing China, which had been despised as barbarians over the years.[23]

After accomplishing conquest of Korea, Emperor Taizong of Qing took with him Crown Prince Sohyon and some of the loyal retainers as hostages on his way back to China. This happened in the first lunar month of 1637. Qing officially overran the fallen Ming Dynasty. It conquered Beijing as its new capital and began to establish Qing as a new dynasty of China. Thus, Crown Prince Sohyon, who had been staying at Shenyang for 8 years, was transferred to Beijing. Here, Crown Prince Sohyon came in contact with the Catholic Church.

It was quite natural for him to come in contact with Father Adam Schall, commonly called Adam Schall,[24] a German Jesuit who was the bishop of the Diocese of Beijing at that time. Since Catholicism has traditionally had the mission strategy of moving from the top to the bottom, the Catholic priest could not overlook the importance of the Crown Prince who would later become the king of Korea. As for Crown Prince Sohyon, he had spent dull eight years in the cold wilderness of Manchuria, and he was exposed to the advanced Western civilization when he arrived in Beijing. Being a highly academic person, he began have curiosity over many of the new things around him. In addition, he was strongly attracted to the Westerners since they were different in many ways

---

23 Hong Yeol Ryu, *Hanguk Cheonjugiohoesa* (History of the Catholic Church in Korea) vol. 1, Revised (Seoul: Catholic Publishing Co., 1962), 41.
24 His full name was Johann Adam Schall von Bell(1591-1666).

from the Chinese who were around him at all times. Moreover, Adam Schall's residence was close to Crown Prince Sohyon's place. The Crown Prince was further attracted to the priest who approached him in a very friendly manner, and he frequently visited the South Church in Beijing, which was supervised by Adam Schall. Adam Schall showed and explained various Western books on science, astronomy, geography, and almanac to the Crown Prince and he gave him Catholic catechisms, encourage him to read them through. Thus, the Crown Prince was naturally exposed not only to various scientific publications of the West but also to the Catholic doctrines.

When the Crown Prince was returning home in the first lunar month of 1645, Adam Schall gave him various Western books, Catholic catechisms and a statue of the Crucified Christ and ask him to take home those. But the Crown Prince only accepted non-religious books and declined to take the catechisms and the statue by speaking these words:

······I would like to take the western religious books and statue of heavenly God, but there is no anyone who knows the Roman Catholic Church, thus it might defile these sacred things. Therefore, I return the statue of heavenly God.[25]

Here, we can see that Korea was not quite ready to receive

25 Hong Yeol Ryu, *Hanguk Cheonjugiohoesa* (History of the Catholic Church in Korea) vol. 1, 44.

the Christian faith at this time. The Crown Prince unfortunately suffered a fever and passed away merely two months after arriving in his home country.[26] And thus, the Catholic faith that Crown Prince Sohyon came in contact with while he was held as hostage could not be introduced into Korea.

4. The Confucian Literati's Contact with Western Learning

Korea's academia could not extend beyond the boundaries of Confucianism. Literati of the time believed that doctrines of Confucius and Mencius were the greatest knowledge in the world and that there could be no higher learning than Confucianism itself. Unlike the original intent, Confucianism was exhausted by causing people to get entangled in idle debates and form useless factions. These numerous factions eventually wore out the national strength, exposing Korea to the brutality of Japan and China.

In progress of such national disasters, some literati began to reflect upon themselves and search for means to regain the national strength. Deciding that the traditional doctrines of Confucius and Mencius would not be useful in this cause, they began to search for new learning and new school of thoughts. Such new learning and thoughts could be found only from those of the West, and these were made available to them only through the Christian missionaries and their Western science and technology.

At that time Korea sent several delegations to China each year.[27]

---

26 *Ibid.*, 46.

Many literati were involved in the expeditions and they frequently engaged with Western missionaries to satisfy their academic curiosity. Thus the literati were able to see and learn new knowledge and technology.

Among them was Du Won Chung who enthusiastically brought the Western civilization into Korea. On his way to Beijing in 1631, Chung met with the Italian Jesuit J. Rodriquez in Dengzhou and received from him various books on astronomy, almanac, and geography as well as on the production of cannons. In particular, he brought a cannon into the country and test fired it in the presence of King Injo and all the government officials, both surprising them and demonstrating to them the firepower of the Western weaponry. At this time, some Catholic books were brought in as well, but were not distributed and were hoarded in palace storerooms.[28]

In 1720 (46th year of King Sookjong), Yi Myoung Lee, who went to Beijing on an expedition, met the German priest I. Goegler at the South Church and learned from him astronomy and almanac. And in 1766 (42nd year of King Youngjo), Dae Yong Hong also met Catholic priests at the South Church, learning astronomy and almanac and also discussing Western Learning with them. Nevertheless, their interests were confined to the Western scientific kno-

---

27 Major delegations include Suhngjeolsa (King's birthday), Wondansa (New Year), Dongjisa (Winter), and Cheonchusa (Fall). Some large missions with about 300 to 500 envoy, such as Jungsa(Chief), Busa(vice-chief), Seojanggwan (officer for documents) and Sangtongsa (translator) traveled as far as China. *Ibid.*, 49.

28 Gwang Soo Kim, *Hanguk Gidokgio Jeollaesa* (A History of Introduction of Christianity to Korea) (Seoul: Korea Christian Institute, 1984), 72.

wledge, not on religious aspects of the Catholic doctrines.[29]

While the interest in science was increasing among the literati, a few literati among those who studied Western books and Western sciences began to show interest in Catholicism itself. They were mainly Southern literati in the Gyounggi and Chungcheong regions, namely Cheol Sin Kwon, Il Sin Kwon, Yak Yong Chung, Yak Jeon Chung, Ga Hwan Lee, Beok Lee, and Seung Hoon Lee. Especially, Cheol Sin Kwon, Yak Jeon Chung and Beok Lee were the central figures who read and studied the books on doctrines of the Western Learning and applied their teachings in everyday life. In 1777 (1st year of King Jeongjo), they traveled around Cheonjinam(Buddist hermitage) and Jueo Temple on Mt. Aengja near Yangsuri in Mahyeon, Yangjugun (present east of Seoul), and held meetings for Study. They studied the Catholic doctrines and put them into practice as far as possible, such as by forbidding any labor on the Lord's Day, praying in the morning and in the evening, and setting aside a weekday for meat-free diet.[30] Some records still remain documenting their activities at the meetings for the Study:

During the winter, we studied doctrine at the Jueo-temple, ⋯⋯following the rule which were made by Nokam(Cheol

---

29 Among them were also Ik Lee, Soo Gwang Lee, Mong In Ryu, and Gyoon Huh. See Neung Hwa Lee, *Korea Gidokgiogeup Oegiosa* (A History of Christianity and Diplomacy in Korea), vol. 1 (Korea Gidokgio Changmunsa, 1928), 23-24.

30 Hong Yeol Ryu, *Hanguk Cheonjugiohoesa* (History of the Catholic Church in Korea) vol. 1, 80.

Sin Kwon), they got up at early morning and washed face with cold water, and recited Bonjajam, at sunrise-Kyongjaejam, at noon-Saholjam, and at sunset-Seomyong. The ceremonies were solemnity and prudence. From then, they observed the rule and laws without violation.[31]

Therefore, the Catholic Church in Korea was founded as a result of the academic studies of literati, and it was bound to be complicated with politics as the literati were appointed into or removed from government offices.

---

31 Won Soon Lee, "Cheonjinam, Jueosa Ganghakhoe Nonbyeon (Discussion of the Study Meeting at Cheonjin Hermitage and Jueo Temple)," *Hanguk Cheonjugiohoesa Yongu* (A Study of the History of Catholicism in Korea), (Korea Catholic History Institute, 1986), 85-87.

Chapter 3

Establishment of the Catholic Church in Korea

1. Seung Hoon Lee's Baptism

Seung Hoon Lee's baptism is considered as the starting point of the Catholic Church in Korea. This is because Lee was the first Korean to get baptized. Baptism is an act of public announcement of one's faith in God and is also the first of the seven sacraments in the Catholic Church. Therefore, Seung Hoon Lee's baptism was the most significant event in the history of the Catholic Church in Korea, and it is also the starting point of Christianity in Korea.

Lee was born in 1756 (32nd year of King Youngjo) in Pyongchang, Gangwon Province. He grew up as a brilliant boy and he became famous for his academic excellence and intelligence around the age of 20. He passed the Jinsa examination at age of 25 and served as hyungam(Magistrate) in the Pyoungtaek region in Kyo-

ngki Province. He became Yak Yong Chung's brother-in-law, and
he became related to Byeok Lee by marriage. Therefore, the literati
all belonged to Southerners and were progressives deeply involved
in studying the Western Learning.[32]

Around this period, Seung Hoon Lee's father Dong Wook Lee
accompanied In Jeom Hwang, both a Dongjisa(Winter delegates)
and a Saeunsa(delegates of expression for gratitude), to Beijing
as a Seojanggwan(Officer for documents). Taking advantage of
this opportunity, the literati, who were already engaged in studying
of the Western Learning, sent Seung Hoon Lee on the Dongjisa
mission in order for him to get books on the Western Learning
from China. Their leader, Byeok Lee, instructed Seung Hoon Lee
with the following words:

> I believe that you have a chance to visit Beizing due
> to a God's special provision to save this small and miserable
> country. When you enter Peiking go to the Roman Catholic
> Church and meet fathers to ask and pursuit the deep doctrines.
> Observe the liturgy and bring doctrinal books a lot. Be
> careful because you have great duties.[33]

From these statements, it can be seen that, unlike the preceding
literati, they had much more interest and passion in the doctrines
of Catholicism than they were interested in Western sciences. Arri-

---

32 Hong Yeol Ryu, *Hanguk Cheonjugiohoesa* (History of the Catholic Church
   in Korea), vol. 1, 81.
33 C. Dallet, *The History of the Catholic Church in Korea*, vol. 1, 303-304.

ving in Beijing, Seung Hoon Lee interacted with Catholic priests there, studied many aspects of Western sciences, and received instructions on Catholic doctrines. While learning the doctrines, Lee fully realized that Catholicism was the real truth. Before returning from Beijing in February 1784, he publicly confessed his faith and was baptized by the Jesuit Father Louis de Grammont at the North Church in Beijing. Thus at the age of 27, he became the first Korean ever to get baptized.[34]

Seung Hoon Lee's baptism was breaking news and the focal point of interest for many Catholic missionaries in Beijing at that time. Father de Ventabon wrote of this incident in a report to his home country.

> I inform you with great joyfulness that God made a convert to light of Gospel into a kingdom where no single priest entered at al······the people who came last winter······when they would like to see our church building, we gave them several doctrinal books. One of them at the age of 27 who was learned person read these booklets and opened his mind with God's help, he confessed the faith······We asked him if the king ordered him to give up faith, how you do. He answered immediately without hesitation that rather I give up what I believe the truth, I am ready to supper of any torture even death······He was given the name of Peter as christen name.[35]

34 Ibid., 306.
35 Ibid.

Seung Hoon Lee was christened "Peter", which means "Rock", signifying that he would become the foundation a stone for the Korean Church. In the following month, he returned home with many Catholic doctrine books, Crucifixes, paintings, rosaries, and other Catholic items and was welcomed by the eager literati of the Western Learning. Instead of missionaries entering the country and propagating the religion among the potential believers, Catholicism in Korea started off as a man seeking out a priest outside the country, confessing his faith, and getting baptized. This is how the Catholic Church started in Korea.

Seung Hoon Lee's baptism took place in 1784 which was exactly 100 years before the arrival of the first Protestant missionary, Horace N. Allen, M.D. Thus Catholicism was recorded in the history as entering Korea a century earlier than Protestantism.

2. Dawn of Catholicism and Period of Pseudo-Priests

After receiving Catholic books from Seung Hoon Lee, Byeok Lee carefully read the books on doctrine and came to an understanding of the Christian truth. Much inspired, he decided to own the faith, was christened John by Seung Hoon Lee.[36] Byeok Lee could not hold this new truth within himself and preached to Cheol Sin Kwon in Yanggeun, Kyounggi Province and converted him. He also preached to Kwon's younger brother, Il Sin Kwon, and won him over. Moreover, he converted the three Chung brothers Yak

---

36 *Ibid.*, 312.

Jeon, Yak Jong, and Yak Yong who greatly contributed to the history of early Catholic missions. They were all baptized by Seung Hoon Lee.

This group of new converts started meeting in the Jungin(middle class) Beom Woo Kim's house in Myoung-dong in Seoul from the spring of 1785, conducting services and studying doctrine. Since none of them was an ordained priest, they decided Byeok Lee as a father[37] on their own for carried out the activities. They also performed sacraments, like confirmation and penance. But before long, they realized what they were doing was not right. In 1787, while studying many books on doctrine, they realized that it was wrong for a layman to conduct sacraments. In order to further investigate this matter, they decided to send Yu Il Yoon to China. Hearing Yoon's report, the priests in Beijing were amazed and inspired by the development of the Catholic Church in Korea. C. Dallet recorded of this in the following statement:

> It was great pleasure for us especially for bishop de Gouvea
> that one came from country that no single priest entered.
> He reported how the gospel spreaded mysteriously.[38]

Yu Il Yoon returned to Korea with Bishop A. de Gouvea's letter. The bishop made it clear that it was illegal for a layman

---

37 In his famous book, *A History of the Christian Missions*, 2nd ed. (New York: Penguin Books, 1986), Stephen Neill referred to Byeok Lee as a "Bishop", 414.
38 C. Dallet, *The History of the Catholic Church in Korea*, vol. 1, 327.

to conduct sacraments and such must not be done by all means. Therefore Byeok Lee and the followers stopped conducting sacraments and decided to request a priest from Beijing. But things did not turn out to be as easy as they hoped.

3. Eulsachujo Jeokbalsageon(Persecution of 1785-Incident of the Year of Eul-sa, 1785)

In terms of the characteristics of the time and encounter with the existing culture, it was inevitable for Catholicism in Korea to experience persecutions in its establishment and development. The entire nation had been accustomed to conservative and traditional customs for a very long time, and it had become more than difficult for the people to accommodate foreign cultures and religions.

As Catholics began meeting at Beom Woo Kim's home in Myoungdong, Seoul, they multiplied in number as time passed by. Then, in the spring of 1785 (9th year of King Jeongjo), petty town officials were passing by Beom Woo Kim's house, which was full of people. Suspecting the crowd as gamblers, they went inside and started investigating. When they saw Catholic books and portraits, they confiscated them and arrested everyone in the house for further investigation by the Ministry of Justice. At that time the Minister of Justice of that time, Hwa Jin Kim, kept a low profile of the case, dismissing the 'yangbans'(nobility) with a caution and sending Beom Woo Kim in exile to Danyang, Chungcheong Province. Kim passed away there after a year; he was the first martyr in the history of the Catholic Church in Korea.[39] It must also be noted that Myoungdong Cathedral, which is essentially the center of the Catholic Church in Korea today, stands not far from where Kim's house used to be.

This incident is called Eulsachujo Jeokbal Incident (Persecution of 1785-Incident of the Year of Eul-sa). This incident was in effect a foretaste of more difficult fights between the Catholic Church in Korea and the government. Also, this incident served as a turning point in history where the existence of a strange religion, Catholicism, became known to the government, and Confucian scholars began to join together in acute protests against the religion.

4. Renegades of the Early Catholic Church

As soon as the Catholic Church started rooting in Korea, it was placed in the center of heavy storms. Barely knowing the doctrine of the church and void of a priest shepherding them, it was perhaps nearly impossible to cultivate a strong faith. Voices of impeachment against this new religion were heard through out the government and from parts of the society. First of all, Confucian literati began to raise their voices. And as the persecution gained momentum, some of the early believers began to abandon the faith one by one. The most pitiful of all was that the first Korean ever to get baptized into Catholicism, Seung Hoon Lee, lost his faith.

Seung Hoon Lee, who was serving as the Hyungam(Magistrate

---

39 Seok Woo Choi, *Hanguk Cheonjugiohoeui Yeoksa* (History of the Catholic Church in Korea) (Korea Church History Institute, 1982), 27.

of county) of Pyoungtaek since the autumn of 1789, was persistently persuaded by his younger brother, Chi Hoon Lee, and was won over. In 1791, he eventually wrote a statement of denunciation and declared his negation.[40] When he was accused for the so-called "Seung Hoon Lee's Guseo Incident" (purchasing books) with the charge of printing books on the Western Learning in 1791, he wrote in his public document, "since it was a heresy,……I burned all the books and articles brought in (from Beijing)……and I denounced (the Western Learning)."[41] This was how Seung Hoon Lee, who was christened Peter so that he would be come the rock for the Catholic Church in Korea, ended up being a renegade. Lee later repented on his act and tried to receive the sacrament of forgiveness from the Chinese Father Wen Mo Zhou. But this never happened, and he passed away as a renegade during the Persecution of 1801.[42]

Likewise, Yak Yong Chung built a Jamyoungso (a letter for stating one's innocence) to prove his denunciation. On the other hand, four years before Seung Hoon Lee's negation, Byeok Lee declared that he would excommunicate himself from the Catholics and abandon the faith when his father intended to hang himself if Byeok Lee did not denounce the Catholic faith. Since the incident

40 Hong Yeol Ryu, *Hanguk Cheonjugiohoesa* (History of the Catholic Church in Korea), vol. 1, 144.
41 Compiled by Man Chae Lee, "Pyoungtaek Hyungam Seung Hoon Lee Gongseo" (Pyoungtaek Hyungam Seung Hoon Lee's Public Statements), *Byeogwipyeon*, vol. 3, Photographic Edition (Seoul: Yeolhwadang, 1972), 199.
42 Hong Yeol Ryu, *Hanguk Cheonjugiohoesa* (History of the Catholic Church in Korea), vol. 1, 144.

Byeok Lee suffered a great distress and died as a renegade within three days. Such negation of the two pioneers of the Early Catholic Church in Korea was a sign of more troubles to come against Catholicism and its followers.

Chapter 4

The Persevering Catholic Church in Persecution

1. Persecution of 1785: Catholicism was Perceived as Denying the Kingship and Parentage

There are indeed many reasons for the harsh persecution the Catholic Church has suffered in its initial periods in Korea. The most devastating among them was the misconception that Catholicism was a religion that denied the kingship and parentage. In the fourth lunar month of 1785, Jangnyoung (Prosecutor) Ha Won Yoo wrote in his memorial to the King, "Catholicism only recognizes the Heaven and denies the existence of the King and parents. It is deceiving the people and confusing the society with the notion that there are heaven and hell. It is more destructive than floods or beasts."[43]

---

43 Hong Yeol Ryu, *Hanguk Cheonjugiohoesa* (History of the Catholic Church in Korea), vol. 1, 92.

Then, Ha Won Yoo's argument of Catholicism denying the king ship and parentage was quite sufficiently proven by an incident. It was the Jinsan Incident that took place at Jinsan, Chungcheong Province. A maternal relative of Yak Yong Chung, Ji Chung Yoon was a Honam scholar who passed the Jinsa examination (1783). When he moved to Seoul in 1784, he visited Beom Woo Kim and had a chance to read the True Doctrine of God and the Seven conquests[44] at his place. And when he returned to his hometown, he was deeply involved in studying of the Western Learning with his maternal cousin Sang Yeon Kwon and became a Catholic convert. Meanwhile, when Ji Chung Yoon's mother Kwon passed away, he put on the mourning dress and wailed for her, but he neither kept the ancestral tablets nor conducted memorial worship for her. In essence, he was abolishing ancestral worship, which was one of the fundamental virtues of Confucianism.

The issue of ancestral worship had already been at the center of serious arguments in China for nearly a century as Catholicism was first introduced. When the Jesuit missionary Matteo Ricci came to China and began the missionary work, he recognized ancestral worship as a simple political rite and did not place any restrictions on it. By stating that Christianity was a developed form of Confucianism and that the 'Heaven'(天) in Confucianism

---

44 The Seven Conquests are the laws Catholics should keep, in addition to the Ten Commandments. They included: ① humility for overcoming pride, ② love for overcoming envy, ③ patience for overcoming anger, ④ charity for overcoming greed, ⑤ self-control for overcoming appetite, ⑥ control of passion for overcoming adultery, and ⑦ diligence for overcoming idleness. *Ibid.*, 101.

was identical to the Christian God, Ricci became highly successful in his missionary work. But when the Franciscan missionaries came to China, they found that Catholicism and Confucianism were syncretized into a strange form of Christianity. Consequently, the Franciscan missionaries reported this to the Holy See and as a result, Pope Clement XI issued the "Ex illa die" in 1715 against ancestral worship, and Pope Benedict XIV also decreed the "Ex quo singulari" in 1742 and banned all ancestral worship practices.[45] And finally in 1773, Pope Clement XIV dismissed the Society of Jesus for approving ancestral worship.

Abiding by such ruling of Rome, the Franciscan bishop of Beijing, A. de Gouvea, also forbade the Catholics in Korea from ancestral worship and the believers followed his instruction. Of course, prohibition of ancestral worship was undoubtedly an antisocial behavior intolerable by the traditionally Confucian society. Nevertheless, this issue was not merely a problem of religious matter but was also closely related to the political context of the time.

In this period, the majority of yangban(nobility) in Honam were Southerners, who were again divided into two factions. One was the Sinseo(believing Western faith) faction led by Jae Gong Chae, and the other the Gongseo(attacking Western faith) faction led by Nak An Hong . In an attempt to weaken the power of Jwauijung(second position of the cabinet) Jae Gong Chae, Gongseo faction raised up the issue of Catholicism and accused Ji Chung Yoon and Sang Yeon Kwon of abolishing ancestral worship. Although King Jeong

---

45 *Ibid.*, 97.

jo had been in favor of Jae Gong Chae, he was pressured to behead both of them for the cause of Byeoksawijung (upholding Confucianism as the only study of highest value). He also burned many Western books kept in Hongmungwan (Royal library) and gave strict order for those who kept Western books in private homes to surrender the books and burn them.[46]

From the fact that the Catholic Church in Korea started off from academic inquiries of yangban scholars and that yangban officials joined in the faith, we can easily see that it was unavoidable for the Catholic faith to be manipulated as an important tool of attacks against political oppositions in the bloody inter-faction fights. Therefore we cannot deny that the acute persecution against the Catholic Church in Korea was based more on reasons of political clashes than on purely doctrinal elements.

2. Persecution of 1801 Martyrdom of the First Priest, Father James Wen Mo Zhou

By its very nature, the Catholic Church is incomplete without priests. The church cannot be established unless one or more priests must serve in masses and sacraments. Therefore, unlike the Protest ant Church, priests are an absolute requirement for the Catholic Church. Having persevered without a priest for about a decade, the early Catholic Church in Korea had requested the bishop in Beijing for a priest and was eagerly waiting for a positive response.

---

46 *Jeongjo Sillok* (Chronicles of King Jeongjo), vol. 33, Gyemijo, 11th Month of 15th Year of King Jeongjo.

Even though the government's acute persecution against the shepherd-less flock resulted in some renegades, the number kept increasing for those who abode by the ways of the faith and suffered the honor of martyrdom.

Having received the request from Korea for a priest, in February 1791 the bishop in Beijing dispatched Father Johanne dos Remedios, a Portuguese who grew up in Macau. But by the time he made it to the bank of Yalu River, the Jinsan Incident(Persecution of 1791) took place and persecution against the Western Learning (Catholicism) was acute. Security force along the border was heavy, making it difficult for him to enter the country secretly. Moreover, the guide could not make it to the other side of the border, and he had no choice but to return.

Again, Catholics in Korea sent to Beijing Yu Il Yoon and Hwang Ji, who met Bishop A. de Gouvea and requested him to send a priest to Korea. This request was accepted, and for the first time, a priest secretly entered Korea and arrived in Seoul in the beginning of 1795. This was the Chinese priest Father James Wen Mo Zhou.

Father Zhou was a learned and capable priest who was born in Suzhou, Jiangsu, he grew up as an orphan, was ordained after graduating from Beijing Catholic Seminary. He was selected as a priest to Korea especially because of his appearance was extremely close to that of Korean people.[47]

---

47 Hong Yeol Ryu, *Hanguk Cheonjugiohoesa* (History of the Catholic Church in Korea), vol. 1, 110.

Guided by Yu Il Yoon and Hwang Ji, Father James Wen Mo Zhou disguised himself as a station employee. He hid in the forests during the day and he travelled during the night. He secretly entered Seoul in January 1795. Ten years after Seung Hoon Lee's baptism, Korea Catholics finally had an official priest among them. Father Zhou learned Korean secretly, and baptized the shepherd-less believers and conducted masses for them. Thus, the Catholic Church in Korea began to lay the foundation as an official church.[48]

Around this period, there was a drastic change within the Royal Court and this change had a tremendous impact on the Catholic Church. King Jeongjo passed away and King Soonjo was enthroned at the age of 11. Due to his young age, King Jeongjo's second wife, Queen Jeongsoon acted as a regent, and this resulted in shifting of powers.[49] The Court at that time was divided into two factions: Sipa, which showed a sympathetic toward Crown Prince Sado, King Jeongjo's father, when he was killed by being locked in a grain box; and Byeokpa, which was not in favor of the Crown Prince. Therefore, King Jeongjo employed Sipa officials, who were sympathetic to his father, kept Byeokpa officials at bay. Ironically, many Catholics belonged to Sipa and the Court's persecution against Catholicism naturally subsided.

However, Queen Jeongsoon, who became King Soonjo's regent, was a sister of Gwi Ju Kim who was accused of a violation and died in exile during the reign of King Jeongjo. Unsurprisingly,

---

48 C. Dallet, *The History of the Catholic Church in Korea*, vol. 1 (1990), 397.
49 Hong Yeol Ryu, *Hanguk Cheonjugiohoesa* (The History of the Catholic Church in Korea), vol. 1, 123.

she held a grudge against Sipa, and using the close relationship between Sipa and Catholicism, she began to flame the fire of persecution for the purpose of eliminating Sipa. In 1801, the first year of King Soonjo, Queen Jeongsoon issued the following message that commands Jae Gong Chae, the dead leader of Sipa, to be post-mortem removed from the government office post-mortem and Catholicism be eradicated.

The ex-king said that the right science [confusicanism] is bright, then false science [Roman Catholicism] will be decreased. However, I heard that the false science flourished from Seoul to countries. The governors and magistrates must try to convert the follower from false science······After forbidden, someone not obeyed, then convict him or her as treason. The governors and magistrates must execute 'Ogajaktongbeop'(the rule of five-home-system). If there is a follower within the system, let the head of the system report to district office and punish him or her. Let never be single follower of false science.[50]

Such policy of eradicating Catholicism resulted in execution of many Catholics. Cheol Sin Kwon was beaten to death in February 1801. Yak Jong Chung, Pil Gong Choi, Kyo Man Hong, and Nak Min Hong were beheaded outside the Seoso Gate in the same month, and Seung Hoon Lee was also beheaded around this time.

---

50 Jae Mun Chung and Jae Seon Chung, *Hanguk Catollik Eojewa Oneul* (Catholicism in Korea, Yesterday and Today), (Catholic Publishing Co., 1963), 50.

Yak Jeon Chung and Yak Yong Chung negated and were sent in exile to Heuksan Island in Jeolla Province and Janggi in Gyounggi Province, respectively. At this time, the royal family member Prince Euneon's wife Song Maria and her daughter-in-law Shin Maria, who were baptized by Father James Wen Mo Zhou, were bestowed poison as a death penalty. And not long after this, King Jeongjo's half brother Prince Euneon was also bestowed poison. In addition, Sa Young Hwang, who is famous for his "Baeksuh"(silk letter) and Sim Hwang, who was arrested on his way to deliver the Baeksuh, both joined the throng of martyrs by getting beheaded.[51]

Among those martyred during the Persecution of 1801 was also Father James Wen Mo Zhou, who was the first priest in Korea. While Father Zhou was carrying out his activities in Korea secretly, Young Ik Han, a believer, negated and reported Father Zhou's activities to the district office. Aided by other believers who suspected Young Ik Han of strange activities, Father Zhou managed to escape, but Yu Il Yoon and Ji Hwang, who escorted Father Zhou, were taken to the district office and were martyred the following day after a series of torture and flogging. Assisted again by Wan Sook Kang, a female believer, Father Zhou secretly carried out propagation activities for about six years, drastically increasing the number of Catholics from 4,000 at the time of his arrival to more than 10,000.[52]

But this time too, there was a renegade who turned Wan Suk

---

51 For detailed information on the martyrs, see Hong Yeol Ryu, *Hanguk Cheonjugiohoesa* (History of the Catholic Church in Korea), vol. I, 128-136.
52 *Ibid.*, 137.

Kang over, and she was tortured for information on Father Zhou's whereabouts. Kang admitted that he had stayed at her place but she did not provide any other information saying that she did not know where he was now. Left with no other choice, the district office posted Father Zhou's portraits in various places and offered rewards for information leading to him. Although Father Zhou once thought of crossing the border and returning to China, seeing that many believers were tortured and killed because of him, he eventually turned himself in to the Uigeumbu (office for interrogating serious criminals).

The government handled Father Zhou with care in the beginning since he was Chinese. But they decided to execute him on the charge of his secret entry to the country. Thus, in April 1801 in Saenamteo(execution place), Father Zhou was beheaded with arrows pushed through the ears, and his head was hung up on a pole. After Father James Wen Mo Zhou's death, the Catholic Church in Korea became like a flock without a shepherd again and had to wait another 30 years before the arrival of the next priest.

3. Sa Young Hwang's Baeksuh (Silk Letter) Incident - Question of Mission Methodology

Around the time that Catholicism was ruled out as a false learning and as a religion that denies the kingship and parentage, an unfortunate event took place to further reinforce such intolerant stance of the Royal Court. This was the "Sa Young Hwang's Baeksuh"(silk letter) incident.

Sa Young Hwang was Yak Yong Chung's elder brother Yak Hyeon's son-in-law. A strong-willed Catholic, he was christened Alexander by Father James Wen Mo Zhou. Born in Changwon, Gyoungsang Province, he passed the jinsa examination at the age of 17 and his brilliance was well known. When the Persecution of 1801 broke out, he hid himself in a potter's cave in Baeron in Jecheon, Chungcheong Province. During this time, Sa Young Hwang and his friend Sim Hwang intended to put an end to the persecution by reporting the acute persecution of the Korea Royal Court against Catholicism to the bishop in Beijing. Thus, Sa Young Hwang took a piece of white silk, 62cm wide and 38cm long, and wrote an incredibly long letter of 13,000 chinese characters with a very small brush. This letter was written on silk, and thus it was called "the Baeksuh"(silk letter).[53]

Sim Hwang, with the Baeksuh hidden under his clothes, was arrested on a shore in Hwanghae Province by a government official immediately before boarding on the ship headed to Qing China and was transferred to Seoul with several other Catholics accompanying him. The author of the letter, Sa Young Hwang, was also arrested in Jecheon in September of the same year, and the content of the letter was made public. At the public exposure of the letter, the entire Royal Court and the people were struck by its content, and the Royal Court further became confident of the validity of its persecution.

---

53 *Ibid.*, 165.

The letter was basically divided into three parts: the first part contained details on the condition of Catholicism, activities of Father James Wen Mo Zhou, and the martyrs during the Persecution of 1801, the second part described Father Zhou's execution, and the third part contained a few proposals concerning the Royal Court and the freedom of propagation in Korea. However, this Baeksuh had a serious problem with the proposals put forth by Sa Young Hwang. A summary of the proposals are as follows.[54]

First, Korea has no economic power whatsoever and thus it intends to attain sympathy of the Western Empire, follow the Holy Religion, and receive funds for relieving the people.

Second, since Korea abides by the commands of Emperor of Qing, its suzerain state, a Western priest should be sent to Korea with the consent of the Emperor of Qing.

Third, since the Korea Dynasty has become weak and is at the verge of its collapse, Korea should be put under the rule of Qing, and an administrator should be dispatched to the area between Anju and Pyoungyang in Pyoungan Province so that one of the Emperor's sons or brothers[55] can oversea and protect this country.

Fourth, since there has been peace in Korea for 200 years and the people do not know to fight in wars, a several hundred ships and strong Western troops of 50,000 to 60,000 should be sent over for easy propagation of the missionaries. Also, since the King of Korea is still young and has not yet married a Queen, Korea

---

54 *Ibid.*
55 Emperor's sons or brothers were often appointed as kings over certain regions.

will eventually become faithful to the Qing Dynasty if a Qing Princess is sent in marriage to the King and he is taken as a royal son-in-law because the next King will be the Qing Emperor's grandson.

Lastly, he was blamed by all as the worst traitor in the history for having written, "even if this country falls, no harm will be done to the outward appearance of the Holy Religion."

Although Sa Young Hwang's intention of writing the letter might have been good willed for putting an end to the persecution by the Royal Court, securing the freedom of propagation, and leading all the people to God in heaven, his proposals were unmistakably unforgivable by the Royal Court and the people.

This Baeksuh incident became a good example for discerning the methodology for missions. Looking back on the history, it is true that the Catholic Church has often employed physical force in its methods for missions. This naturally led them to the conclusion that it was all right to involve physical force as long as the cause was good. Nevertheless, just like the Western saying, "You must not steal a candle to read the scriptures," it must not be overlooked that no matter how good a cause it cannot be tolerated if its method is unethical or unevangelical. Missions must be carried out only through evangelical methods.

As mentioned above, Sa Young Hwang was hacked into pieces on a charge of high treason during the Persecution of 1801 and his properties were confiscated. Heavy punishment also befell on all of his family members; his mother was sent in exile to Geoje

Island, his wife to Jeju Island, and his children to Chuja Island. During this persecution, the number of martyrs totaled more than 300.[56]

The Baeksuh was kept in Uigeumbu until Bishop G. C. Mutel, the bishop of the Seoul diocese, acquired it in 1894. It was then delivered to Pope Pius XI in July 1925 when 79 of Korea martyrs were beatified in Rome.[57] While translating the Baeksuh into French, Bishop Mutel was recorded as stating that most of the contents were fanciful and extremely dangerous and that its link to persecution was understandable.

---

56 Sinyuchisa, *Byeokwipyeon*, vol. 5.
57 Hong Yeol Ryu, *Hanguk Cheonjugiohoesa* (History of the Catholic Church in Korea), vol. I, 167.

Chapter 5

Establishment of the Vicariate Apostolic of Korea and Continuing Persecutions

1. Establishment of the Apostolic Vicariate of Korea

In his book *The History of the Catholic Church in Korea*, C. Dallet recorded about the Korean Royal Court's Persecution against Catholicism with the following words.

······Reviewing persecution with faithful eyes, it brought much valuable results. There are many new elected persons in the heaven and the Korea Catholic Church sent powerful seekers in front of God. In spite of much difficulties, plentiful fruits of missionaries message is due to martyrs' prayers.[58]

---

58 C. Dallet, *The History of the Catholic Church in Korea*, vol. 1, 619. # 1

The Royal Court might have thought that physical force would be an effective tool for uprooting Catholicism, the true nature of the Christian Church is that it is built to expand under persecutions and grow even stronger with the shedding of martyrs' blood. Although he Catholic Church in Korea was much disturbed by the acute persecution against it, its growth was not slowed down. Such persistency of the faith was made known both in and out of Korea, and this finally led to the establishment of the independent Apostolic Vicariate of Korea. Korea had served China as its suzerain, and Korea had been interferred with by Qing in all aspects, and Korea activities. Thus the independence of the Church in Korea, well ahead of the full independence of the state, was highly significant. But this, too, was fulfilled after much complications.

Catholics were dispersed by the acute persecution of the Royal Court and they continued to keep their faith secretly in small groups. By this time, the first generation pioneers of the Catholic Church in Korea either were martyred or negated, and Yak Jong Chung's son Ha Sang Chung and others began to emerge as so-called second generation leaders of the Church in Korea. The highest priority for them was to get hold of a priest who could tend the shepherd-less flock of believers. They needed to get in touch with the Bishop in Beijing, but this was not easy at all because the selection criteria for the diplomatic mission to Beijing were very difficult. But the chance finally came ten years after the persecution.

Yeo Jin Lee barely made it to the Dongjisa(Winter delegates) mission to Beijing in 1811, and he carried a letter each to be delivered to the Bishop in Beijing and to the Holy See.[59] The former bishop A. de Gouvea had passed away in 1808, and the Nazarene priest Pres was the Bishop there. Pres warmly welcomed Yeo Jin Lee and company. He was moved by the heroic struggles of Catholics in Korea and was grateful for the request for a priest, but the Diocese of Beijing was also going through a difficult time. In China, a persecution also broke out against Catholicism in 1805, slaying priests and destroying seminaries. Moreover, France, which had been sponsoring the Diocese of Beijing, underwent the Revolution(1789) and the Diocese had experienced much financial difficulty since then.[60] Therefore, an immediate dispatching of a priest was not possible.

Five years later in 1816, the priest acquisition movement was started again by Ha Sang Chung. After successfully obtaining an opportunity to visit Beijing, Ha Sang Chung went and requested the Bishop for a priest, and he persistently pushed this request each time he had a chance. Jin Gil Yoo, a former interpreter, joined Chung in this task. He wrote an earnest letter to the Holy See. This letter was translated into Latin in the diocese office in Beijing and was delivered to Pope Leo XII in 1827. The Pope read this letter and was greatly by moved. Thus he issued an encyclical, whereby, "it was decided that an independent mission field be established in Korea under direct control of the Holy See, and the Paris Foreign Missions Society be mandated for its missionary

---

59 Hong Yeol Ryu, *Hanguk Cheonjugiohoesa* (History of the Catholic Church in Korea), vol. I, 182.
60 C. Dallet, *The History of the Catholic Church in Korea*, vol. 2, 37-39.

work." This decision was not for establishing Korea as an entirely independent diocese.[61]

Following this decision, the Paris Foreign Missions Society chose to send to Korea the French priest Father B. Bruguiere, a missionary in Thailand who volunteered for the work.[62] Consequently, Pope Gregory XVI appointed B. Bruguiere as the father for the Korea Apostolic Vicariate and declared the establishment of the Apostolic Vicariate. This took place in September 1831, nearly half a century after Seung Hoon Lee's baptism. Thus the Catholic Church in Korea was affirmed as a separate mission field, completely independent from China.

One thing we must take note here is that Father Fang Chi Liu, a Qing Chinese, persistently worked against the establishment of the independent diocese in Korea. He disturbed the independence of the Church in Korea by claiming that the Church must be subject to the Diocese of Beijing because Korea was subject to Qing China. Nevertheless, his intension was short-lived, and perseverance of the Korean Catholics was materialized in independence of the Vicariate Apostolic of Korea.

However, there was a paradox here. Those Korean believers who were enticed by Fang Chi Liu's deceitful schemes wrote a

61 This was a vicariate apostolic and was led by a vicar apostolic. Seok Woo Choi, "Chosungiogu Seolchungui Giohoesajeok Uimi," (Significance of Establishment of the Apostolic Vicariate of Korea in the Perspective of the Church History), *Giohoesa Youngu* (A Study on the Church History), vol. 4, 79.

62 Hong Yeol Ryu, *Hanguk Cheonjugiohoesa* (History of the Catholic Church in Korea), vol. I, 245.

letter to Bruguiere, saying that it was not possible for them to accept Bruguiere as the first bishop of the Vicariate Apostolic of Korea. In spite of this, he embarked on his journey to Korea in order to accomplish the mission given him. But disturbed by the thought that he would not be welcomed in Korea, he wandered around in Manchuria for four years and passed away without ever reaching Korea. Alas, how can this paradox be explained that the Korean Church had so longed for a shepherd and yet she turned the willing one away at the doorstep?[63]

After Bruguiere's unfulfilled death, in January 1836, Father Pierre P. Maubant became the first Western priest to cross the Yalu and reach Seoul secretly, wearing a reed hat and a mourning dress.[64] This was 36 years after Father James Wen Mo Zhou's martyrdom. Following Maubant's lead, Father Laurent M.J. Imbert, who had been working in Sichuan in China and was appointed as the second bishop of the Vicariate Apostolic of Korea, and the French priest Jacques H. Chastan secretly entered Seoul in the following year. Thus the believers in Korea were greatly encouraged and the missionary work visibly expanded, raising the number of Catholics to 9,000.[65] Realizing that Korean priests would be necessary in the near future, they began seeking priest candidates. And thus, theological training was given to Ha Sang Chung, who at age the of 42 was still single with the hope of becoming a priest, Mun Woo Lee, Seung Hoon Lee's son Sin Gyu Lee, and a few others. But

---

63 *Ibid.*, 248-255.
64 *Ibid.*, 293.
65 C. Dallet, *The History of the Catholic Church in Korea*, vol. 2, 238, 253-254.

none of them would become the first Korean priest; he was prepared some other place.

2. Continuing Persecutions - Persecution of 1839 (The Year of Geehae, 1839)

Martyrs' blood was the fuel for the growth of the Catholic Church in Korea. It would be no exaggeration to say that the Catholic Church of today would not have come into being without the precious blood of the forerunners. Just around the time the priests entered Korea secretly and the Church began to grow slowly, anot her wind of persecutions was about to blow. As always, the persecution against Catholicism took place during shifting of political powers.

After Queen Jeongsoon Kim, led the Persecution of 1801, died in 1805, her political power was turned over to Jo Soon Kim, King Soonjo's father-in-law. This would later lead to emergence of the Andong Kim clan, the King's maternal relation, as a major power toward the end of the Korea Dynasty. Jo Soon Kim was a member of Sipa, who were in favor of Catholicism, and he naturally favored Catholicism. This gave Catholics a chance to relax for a while. But the history repeats itself in that there would always be an opposing power rising against the newly emerging authority. Now, the Andong Kim power was opposed by the Pung yang Cho clan. Emergence of the Pungyang Cho clan was possible because King Soonjo's son Crown Prince Hyo Myoung, was married to a daughter of Man Young Cho of the Pungyang Cho clan.

After Jo Soon Kim, the central figure of the Andong Kim power, died in 1832 and King Soonjo passed away two years later, Pungyang Cho's power expanded rapidly. Following King Soonjo's death, the dead Hyomyoung's son was enthroned as King Heonjong. However, Queen Soonwon, who was King Soonjo's wife, began to rule as a regent because King Heonjong was a mere 8-year-old.[66] Even though Queen Soonwon of the Andong Kim clan became a regent, Andong Kim's power continued to weaken as major posts in the Royal Court were dominated by Pungyang Cho.

In order to completely eradicate the weakened Andong Kim power, the Pungyang Cho officials continually requested Queen Soonwon to uproot Catholicism. Persuaded that this could not be delayed any longer, in April 1839, Queen Soonwon issued 'Sahaktochiryoung,' an ordinance for exterminating Catholics. This was the beginning of the Persecution of 1839. Intended to be a reinforcement measure to the already practiced Ogajaktongbeop (one band of five household), this ordinance led to a nationwide arrest of Catholics, the majority of who would be taken through the procedures of arrest, imprisonment, and then execution. Including the execution of Myoung Hyuk Nam, Deuk In Kwon, Gwang Heon Lee, Hee Soon Park, Agada Lee and others outside the Seoso Gate in May, execution of countless Catholics followed in every corner of the country.[67]

As persecutions almost always produce renegades, further damage

---

66 Hong Yeol Ryu, *Hanguk Cheonjugiohoesa* (History of the Catholic Church in Korea), vol. I, 273.
67 C. Dallet, *The History of the Catholic Church in Korea*, vol. 2, 406-421.

was inflicted by those renegades. Most of the leadership was arrested because of the information provided by one of the renegades, Soon Seong Kim. Those arrested included Ha Sang Chung, Jin Gil Yoo, and Sin Cheol Cho. Soon Seong Kim's negation further led to the arrest of Bishop Imbert in August. Father Maubant and Father Chastan, who were hiding away, also received the bishop's letter urging them to surrender and turned themselves in. The three French priests were taken to Uigeumbu and were charged for disturbing the national security, were beheaded in Saenamteo on September 21 of the same year, and their heads hung on a city gate. They were the first Western priests to get martyred in Korea, a mission field thousands of miles away from home. Ha Sang Chung and Jin Gil Yoo were also beheaded on the following day. Record has it that as many as 54 were martyred, about 60 died in prison, and about 50 were released after renouncing the faith.[68]

Not relenting the lash of persecution, the Royal Court issued 'Cheoksayooneum.'[69] Here, this was manipulated for proclaiming persecution against Catholicism, justifying its eradication of Catholics. The Court commanded the people to stay away from the temptations of the pagan religion and made it clear that anyone who joins it would not be spared.

---

68 Seok Mun Hyeon, *Gihaeilgi* (Kihae Annals), ch. 1-2.
69 'Yooneum' refers to the royal message that the King issued in the New Year to the people in eight provinces for encouraging farming activities.

3. Ha Sang Chung's Letter to the Minister - the First Letter in Defense of Catholicism

Seeing the countless innocent lives taken away as Catholicism was viewed as a pagan religion, Ha Sang Chung wrote the 'Sangje-sangsuh'(letter to the minister) the very first letter written by a Korean in defense of Catholicism in which he explained the basic doctrine of Catholicism to the Royal Court so that it would come to an accurate understanding of the religion. This letter was addressed to Wooichung(the third rank in the cabinet) In Young Cho who at that time was acting as the frontline leader in the eradication of Catholicism.

Containing approximately 3,400 Chinese characters, this letter was much shorter than Sa Young Hwang's Baeksuh(silk letter) had about 13,000 characters, but Prof. Kyoung Bae Min evaluated that,

> the literary style and rhetorics as well as the logics and apologetical points dwelled upon were so mighty and overwhelming that it was published by the Bishop Kao-Yakmang of Hong-Kong to be used as a text book of systematic theology at seminaries throughout China proper and South East Asia.[70]

The letter to the minister attempted to explain the Christian

---

70 Kyong Bae Min, *Hanguk Gidokgiohoesa* (History of Christian Church in Korea) (Seoul: Yonsei University Press, 2005), 58.

truth, show misconceptions, and plead for the King's mercy. In one aspect, while Sa Young Hwang's Baeksuh(silk letter) was complaining of the King's physical force against the freedom of propa-gation, Ha Sang Chung's 'Sangjesangsuh' was an earnest plea that wish the Royal Court to withdraw the persecution on its own people. It is interesting to note that these significant documents written by two early Catholics had very different perspectives of achieving freedom for propagation. The Baeksuh(silk letter) by Sa Young Hwang and 'Sangjesangsuh' by Ha Sang Chung were brothers-in-law are highly appraised as important documents written by Koreans of the Early Catholic Church in Korea.[71]

4. The First Korean Priest Andrew Tae Gun Kim's Martyrdom: Persecution of the Year of Byongo, 1846

Although there were occasional negations in mild of acute persecutions by the Royal Court, the Catholic Church in Korea faithfully continued her missionary work. For a long time the Church had persevered without a priest and waited for one to come from outside of the country, but now the Catholic Church in Korea was about to have a priest from its own people.

The person to receive the honor of being ordained as the first Korean priest was Andrew Tae Gun Kim. Kim was born in August

---

71 Korean translation of 'Sangjesangseo' is in Yoon Tae Oh, "Catolik Giohoeui Bakhaesawa Singio Jeonsa," (History of Persecution of the Catholic Church and Pre-Protestant History), *Hanguk Giohoesa* (History of the Korean Church) (Hyeseonmunhwasa, 1979), 315-327.

1821 in Ugang-myeon, Gangjin-gun, in Chungcheong Province. He grew up in a devout Catholic home where both his grandfather and father were martyred during persecutions. When he reached the age of 16, he was selected by Father Maubant as a priest candidate along with Yang Yeop Choi(Franscis Choi), and a few others. He was sent to Macau, where he received theological training and was ordained as the first Korean priest in August 1845.[72] After his ordination, he looked for a chance to return to his homeland.

Now that the priests secretly working in Korea were all martyred and Korea was left without any priest, the Paris Foreign Missions Society sent Father Jean J. Ferreol as the third bishop of Korea along with Father Ambroise Maistre. Andrew Tae Gun Kim hired a ship and managed to enter Korea secretly through Ganggyoung in Chungcheong Province in October 1845 with Bishop Ferreol and the newly appointed father, M.N.A. Daveluy. They carried out missionary work in Seoul and Chungcheong Province. Then Bishop Ferreol sent Andrew Tae Gun Kim to Manchuria so that he could assist Father Maistre and Yang Yeop Choi who were looking for an opportunity to enter Korea from there. Kim decided that entering by land would not be a good option. Instead, he took the route by the Yellow Sea because it was at the height of the croaker fishing season in Yeongpyung Island, but he was arrested by government officials at Deungsan Cape on the shore of Hwanghae Province and was sent to Seoul.

Fortunately, Father Ferreol and Father Daveluy were not arrested

---

72 C. Dallet, *The History of the Catholic Church in Korea*, vol. 3, 80.

at this time. However, when a French fleet came to the open sea off the shore of Hongju in Chungcheong Province and protested regarding the responsibility over the death of the three French priests, the Royal Court was provoked by it and beheaded Father Andrew Tae Gun Kim along with Seok Mu Hyeon, Gyoung Mun Nam, and Yi Hyong Han in July 1846. Father Kim was 25 years old at that time.[73] Thus, the first Korean priest Andrew Tae Gun Kim shed his blood for the furtherance of the Early Catholic Church in Korea.

This took place in the year of Byoungo (1846) and thus is also called the Byoungo Persecution. Andrew Tae Gun Kim was named a Venerable in 1857 by Pope Pius IX, was named a Blessed in July 1925, and his head is now kept in the chapel at the Seoul Catholic Theological Seminary.

5. Persecution of the Year of Byeongin, 1866

In the heat of persecutions, time passed by and major changes took place in the Royal Court. When King Heonjong passed away without a successor in 1844, the right to appoint the next king was handed over to Queen Soonwon who had been restrained by the Punyang Cho dominance. Queen Soonwon instated King Cheoljong, who was then known as the Ganghwa (island) Boy. It must be noted here that King Cheoljong's grandfather was Prince Euneon who was martyred in midst of persecution against Catholicism.

---

73 *Ibid.*, 118-120.

This in effect meant that the politically influential Pungyang Cho clan was to be pushed away from the epicenter and that Catholic-friendly Andong Kim clan would resume the power. King Cheoljong granted the petition for pardoning Prince Euneon, his wife, his daughter-in-law Shin, Seung Hoon Lee, and others who had been killed during the Persecution of 1801.[74]

Under this sun shining climate, the Catholic Church began to undergo unprecedented development. After the third bishop, Ferreol, died of a disease, Father Simon F. Berneux was appointed as the fourth bishop and entered Korea with four other missionaries. Their missionary work resulted in a rapid growth of the Church, raising the membership to 13,000 by 1857 and, in less than a decade, to 23,000 by 1865 (the 2nd year of King Gojong). The number of priests also increased accordingly; there were as many as 12 Western missionaries who worked in secret.[75]

However, such rapid revival of the Catholic Church was not viewed as an ordinary matter by the people. The Catholic Church in Korea always under the direct influence of political changes in the Royal Court was faced with yet another circumstance when King Cheoljong suddenly passed away in December 1863 and Heungseongun's son was enthroned as King Gojong. Heungseongun had been acting as a madman for his own survival. He took up the post of Daewongun as a regent for the young King. His regency was fated for a tragedy for both the modern history of Korea

---

74 Hong Yeol Ryu, *Hanguk Cheonjugiohoesa* (History of the Catholic Church in Korea), vol. I, 515.
75 C. Dallet, *The History of the Catholic Church in Korea*, vol. 3, 213, 273, 327.

and the history of the Catholic Church.

Around this period, all the ports in Russia would freeze in the winter, and thus Russia was betting all its efforts securing ice-free ports that would allow them sea transport in the winter. For this cause, Russia was looking to East Asia. Peter the Great conquered Siberia, the Treaty of Beijing was signed in 1860, and Russia began to threaten Korea by opening the port at Vladivostok. A Russian fleet approached Youngil Bay in the East Sea to survey the coast in April of 1853, and another Russian fleet appeared in the open sea off the coast of Deogwon, Youngheung in Hamgyoung Province to demand initiation of trades. In January 1866, a Russian warship came to Wonsan demanding trades and even put pressure that Russians be allowed to reside there.[76]

The super power Russia was a great threat to the Royal Court, and Daewongun began to search for ways to tackle this problem. Perhaps it was only natural for Catholic leaders, such as Bong Ju Hong, Gi Ho Kim and Jong Sam Nam, to reason that an alliance between Korea, France, and Britain could prove politically useful against the southward advancing Russians and also allow freedom

---

[76] In the spring of 1895, Nicholas II wrote, "Russia is in an absolute need of an ice-free port where ships can freely sail all throughout the year. This port must be located on the continent (Southeast of Korea) and at the same time be linked to our territory via Siberia." F. H. Harrington, *God, Mammon, and the Japanese*, translated by Gwang Rin Lee, *Gaehwagiui Hanmigwangye* (Seoul: Iljogak, 1991), 298. Won Soon Lee, "Cheonjugio Bakhaeui Yeoksajeok Baegyoung" (Historical Background of the Catholic Persecution), *Hanguk Cheonjugiohoesa Youngu* (A Study on the History of the Catholic Church in Korea), 133. Russia acquired the Manchuria region through the Treaty of 1860 between Russia and China.

of the Catholic mission. The time was also ripe for this, not only because Daewongun had no reason to be hostile toward Catholicism, but also because Daewongun's wife, Min, was highly interested in Catholicism, studied doctrine books, memorized prayers daily, and had even asked Bishop Berneux to conduct a thanksgiving mass when her son, King Gojong, was enthroned.[77] Another factor working in favor of Catholics was that King Gojong's nurse, Park, was a devout Catholic with the Christian name Martha and would provide an easy access to Daewongun.

Jong Sam Nam met with Daewongun, who was absorbed in seeking out ways to fend off the southward advancing Russians, and proposed the idea of the alliance between Korea, France, and Britain as protection against Russia. To this, Daewongun responded positively and asked Jong Sam Nam to arrange a meeting with Bishop Berneux for further discussion on the matter. However, Bishop Berneux did not take this matter lightly. He doubted that the Court of Korea that had cruelly massacred so many Catholics all along would show such favor to Catholicism all of a sudden. Moreover, involvement in this matter was definitely going to result in the involvement of the Church in complicated political issues. Should the plan fail, it was very clear that the Court would not be easy on the Catholic Church. Consequently, it was not a simple matter for the bishop to respond to Daewongun's request for a meeting. After having to wait a long time for Bishop Berneux's reply, Daewongun became displeased, and he slowly changed his

---

77 *The Edinburg Review* (1872), 327.

mind as the Russian threat subsided.

Now, factional conflicts in the political circles were draining the national strength and corrupt officials' abuse of the people reached its peak. Commoners were suffering in devastating poverty, and popular uprisings continually took place nationwide. In an attempt to resolve the national distress and reinforce his position, Daewongun began to join hands with anti-Catholic and conservative Confucian literati for persecution against the Church. This decision was inevitable because Britain, Germany, France, America, Russia, and other imperialistic nations of the 19th century were threatening Korea with their dominating military power. The Court had but to undermine the Catholic Church, which was constantly in touch with France and other Western nations. Even though it was once planned to ward off the Russians by relying on France and Britain, such plan was no longer useful now that Russia did not continue to present any threat.

Unlike previous persecutions that lasted a year or two each, this persecution led by Daewongun continued on for about 7 to 8 years, from 1866 to 1873, when Daewongun was dethroned, and its damage inflicted on the Church was beyond description.[78] During the short period of peace, the Catholic Church developed rapidly. There were 12 foreign priests besides Bishop Berneux

---

78 While the exact number of martyrs during this period is unobtainable due to a lack of any accurate census, C. Dallet numbered it as about 8,000 and Hyeon Hwang recorded it as 20,000 in his *Maecheonyarok* (Maecheon's History Review). Jong Soon Yoo, "Byounginbakhae Sungyojaui Sibok Susokjaryo" (Materials for Beatification of Martyrs of Persecution of 1866), *Giohoesa Youngu* (A Study on the Church History), vol. 6, 312.

and more than 20,000 believers. There was also a preparatory seminary for training priests in Baeron, Chungcheong Province, and two woodblock printing workshops in Seoul were printing doctrine books.

After arresting Bishop Berneux, other priests, and central figures, Daewongun realized that Catholicism had a large following all across the country and was further determined to eradicate the root of evil. Among the twelve foreign priests, nine were arrested, were beheaded along with their Korean followers, and their martyrly blood was poured on this land once again. Among those not arrested, Father Felix C. Ridel was assisted by the believers to get out of the country and arrived at Qufu in Shandong, China. Ridel immediately reported to Admiral P. G. Rose, the French fleet who was stationed there, about the persecution against Catholicism and terrible death of the French priests in Korea. Ridel also asserted that the two French priests not yet arrested, Stanislas Feron and Alphonse N. Calai, must be rescued.

Consequently, in October of the same year(1866), Rose took seven heavily armed warships and left Qufu for Korea. Accompanying this fleet were Father Ridel acting as a guide and interpreter and three other Korean Catholics. Rose's fleet sailed in the Yellow Sea, conquered Ganghwa Island, and traveled up the Han River to Yanghwajin. But in November, the fleet was forced by Korean troops to retreat. The battle between Rose's fleet and the Korean army is called the "French Disturbance of 1866."[79] While retreating,

---

79 Hong Yeol Ryu, *Hanguk Cheonjugiohoesa* (History of the Catholic Church

Rose and his fleet landed on Ganghwa Island again, captured 19 boxes of silver bars (approx. 900kg) and plundered various materials of historical significance kept in the depository. This incident was certainly a representation of typical Western imperialist exploitation of powerless nations. After this, Daewongun's fury burned even greater against Catholicism and even killing young children.

6. Violation of Namyoungun's Tomb - Cause for Another Persecution

It is common that incidents that take away many lives start with the wrong ideas or decisions of a few. One of them was Father S. Feron who violated the tomb of Namyoungun, Daewongun's father. Anxious for putting an end to the persecution against Catholics and for securing freedom of propagating Catholicism in Korea, Feron a totally absurd idea from some Korean Catholics who were setting away from harms of persecution. The idea was that they could dig up the tomb of Daewongun's father and take the ashes and tomb articles as a security for negotiation with Daewongun. In short, the plan was that Daewongun would grant freedom for propagation of Catholicism for getting his father's ashes and other articles back.

Feron shared this plan with the Jewish German merchant E. Oppert and requested his involvement.[80] Absolutely convinced that tombs of royal family members in the Orient are full of gold

---

in Korea), vol. II, 125.
80 E. Oppert, *A Forbidden Land, Voyage to Corea* (London: 1880), 315.

and jewelry, Oppert could not resist this offer. Fully motivated, in May 1868, they hired a boat. Along with several Korean people and laborers, they arrived in Deoksan-myeon, Yesan-gun in Chungcheong Province where Namyoungun's tomb was located. Nearly after ten hours of digging the solid tomb with various tools from China, they found the coffin. However, they had to stop their mission and return because the night was nearly over, the village residents began to move around, and the boat would not be able to sail out at low tide. On the way back, they raided civilian homes at Harihupo, stole their belongings, and exercised violence over them.[81]

After they withdrew, their deeds were reported to the Royal Court. We can easily imagine the gravity of the ferocity and vehemence when Daewongun was told that Catholics were involved in the incident. Another wave of massacre against Catholics was more than inevitable.

A few years later in June 1871, another persecution took place. In 1866, an American trading ship, the General Sherman, sailed up the Daedong River, Pyungyang and demanded trading. In the process, the ship engaged in a battle with Korean troops, and the Sherman was eventually burned down.[82] In order to demand an explanation for this incident, Admiral J. Rogers of the U.S.

---

81 Hong Yeol Ryu, *Hanguk Cheonjugiohoesa* (History of the Catholic Church in Korea), vol. II, 156.
82 On board the General Sherman was Robert Thomas, who became the first Protestant missionary martyred in Korea. Details on this will be discussed in the later chapter on Protestantism.

Asiatic Squadron led five warships to Ganghwa Island. The American fleet inflicted heavy casualties on the Korean troops for about a month and retreated. This incident is called the "Sinmee-yangyo" (Western Disturbance of the Year of Sinmee, 1871). After the Americans withdrew, Daewongun erected 'Cheokhwabi,' monuments marking his determination to seclude foreigners, across the country and strengthened the isolation policy. This unfortunately delayed Korea's commercial trades with other nations and acceptance of advanced foreign civilization, which eventually led to the occupation by the Japanese.

It was perhaps still not the time for the Catholic Church in Korea to be vested full freedom. They were given freedom for propagation only after Korea was forced to sign trade agreements with powerful nations. The concept of freedom of religion was gradually accepted by leaders and commoners of Korea as Western consulates opened in Korea and they freely conducted services. Therefore, the Catholic Church had to wait until the 1880s, when treaties with foreign countries were signed, in order to carry out her missionary and religious activities in total freedom.

7. Publications by the Catholic Church Contribution to Popularization of Hangeul (Korean native letters)

As mentioned earlier, Catholicism was introduced to Korea largely because of the scholastic curiosity of the Confucian literati. Moreover, doctrine books and other Western books were imported from China and it was natural that they were written in Chinese characters.

Therefore, only those literate in Chinese, i.e., yangban(nobility) and jungin(middleclass), were capable of reading the doctrine books and study them. The merchants and lowly people were virtually excluded from the Western learning. Although the number was few for those who could read Chinese, more and more commoners began to join in the Catholic faith, and there was an increasing need for doctrine books written in Hangeul. So in the initial stage, doctrine books brought in from China, such as *Seonggyo Jeolyo* (Doctrine of the Holy Religion) and *Seonggyo Yori Mundap*(The Holy Religion Catechism), were translated and published in Hangeul.

On the other hand, Korean Catholics of certain level of faith began to author a number of doctrine books. For instance, Byeok Lee's *Seonggyo Yoji*(Essentials of the Holy Religion) summarized important points of Catholic doctrine in its own right, and Yak Jong Chung's *Jugyo Yoji*(Essentials of the Lord's Teaching) was indeed a high-level doctrine book that was even approved by Father James Wen Mo Zhou.[83]

Unequipped with printers, these books were usually hand-copied for dissemination. Bishop Imbert, who entered Korea in 1837, decided that printing was the only way for effective distribution of doctrine books among the Korean Catholics. Thus, in 1864 when the wind of persecution was briefly softened, two printers were installed in Taepyoung-dong in Seoul and various doctrine books were printed for distribution.[84]

---

83 Seok Woo Choi, "Hangukgiohoe Gyoriseoui Byeoncheonsa" (Changes in Doctrine Books of the Korea Church), *Hanguk Giohoesaui Tamsaek* (Inquiry of the History of the Korean Church), 356.

The priests of the Early Catholic Church decided that missionary activities in Korea should not be short-term but carried out with more permanency. Even during the time when death followed the m so close like a shadow, they dedicated themselves in writing of grammar books and dictionaries for Korean education and translating of various doctrine books were come by the priests who to came to Korea later. After arduously labor for over ten years, Father Pourthie published *The Korea Grammar* and *The Latin-Korea-Chinese Dictionary*, but unfortunately he was beheaded during the Persecution of 1866 and these titles were burned without having put into any meaningful use. In 1891, Father M.N.A. Daveluy completed The Korea-Latin Dictionary and Father Redel, who escaped from persecution to China, toiled for ten years in writing of The Korea Grammar and The Korea-French Dictionary. The latter was published in Yokohama, Japan, in 1880.

No applause is sufficient for their hard work in midst of the acute persecution. In particular, although their efforts of translating and publishing the doctrine books in Hangeul were geared toward propagation of Catholicism, the effects were far reaching. The excellent and highly scientific Hangeul alphabet invented by King

---

84 Doctrine books printed at this time include *Seonggyo Yori Mundap* (The Holy Religion Catechism), *Cheonju Seonggio Gonggwa* (Teachings of the Holy Religion of the Heaven Lord), *Cheonju Seonggio Yegiu* (Principles of the Holy Religion of the Heaven Lord), *Seongchal Giryak* (The Holy Survey), *Ryoungse Daeui* (Baptism Essentials), *Hoejoe Jikji* (Repentance and Righteousness), *Sinmyoung Chohaeng* (Introduction to the Divine Life), *Cheondang Jikro* (Straight Way to Heaven), and *Syounggio Jeolio* (Doctrine of the Holy Religion). See Kyoung Bae Min, *Hanguk Gidokgiohoesa* (History of the Christian Church in Korea), 64.

Sejong was looked down by yangbans who regarded the Chinese characters as the only writing of value, and it was considered as an inferior method of writing that was employed only by commoners. Against this backdrop, the Catholic priests not only published doctrine books and popularized Hangeul, but also undertook the honorable work of eradicating illiteracy of the public and educating them as well-informed people by teaching them how to write.

At this point, let us withdraw from descriptions of the establishment of the Early Catholic Church and its history of persecution, and examine the introduction and accommodation of the Protestant Church in Korea.

PART II

Chapter 1

Pre-Mission Contacts with Protestantism

1. First Protestants to Korea

(1) Jan J. Weltevree

Identifying the first Westerner to Korea is not quite an important matter but is certainly interesting. Should he be a Christian, this matter will pose a great importance to the history of the Korean Protestant Church. Records suggest that the first Westerner to set foot in Korea was Ma Ri-I who had drifted to Jeju Island.[85] Following him, as mentioned earlier, the Catholic priest Cespedes came to Korea during the Hideyoshi Invasion as a chaplain for the Japanese troops.

---

85 Gwang Soo Kim, "Weltevreewa Hamelui Urinara Pyodoe Gwanhan Giohoesajeok Gochal" (Examination of Drifting of Weltevree and Hamel to Korea in the Perspective of the Church History), *Giohoewa Sinhak* (Church and Theology), vol. 6 (1973), 94.

However, here, we want to identify the first Western Protestant to Korea. Presently available records indicate that the first Western Protestants to Korea were Jan J. Weltevree (Korean name: Yeon Park) and three other Dutchmen who drifted to a shore in Jeolla Province in 1627. In the modern times, the Netherlands had gained much control over the oceans of the world; she was dominating the world trades with about 30,000 ships which constituted nearly 75% of all European merchant vessels. Therefore it was common for Dutch sailors to experience shipwrecks in unfamiliar waters. Weltevree, too, was caught in a storm on his trading route to Japan and was shipwrecked after having drifted to the open sea off the coast of Gyeongju, South Kyongsang Providence.

Arrested by government officials, Weltevree and his peers were transferred to Seoul, where they were assigned to the army for the Byongja Horan (Manchu Invasion of 1636). Two of Weltevree's peers perished in the war, while Weltevree survived was recognized for his military merit as well as permitted to marry a Koean woman with whom he had a son and a daughter. Thus he became the first Westerner to be naturalized as a Korean citizen and to be the father of interracial children.[86] He also worked as an interpreter for foreigners who drifted to Korea from time to time. Unfortunately no direct record exists to imply that Weltevree was a Protestant. Nevertheless, because Netherlands was a Protestant state and most of her people were Christians, it is not difficult to believe that

---

86 Jae Ryun Chung, *Hangeo Manrok* (Random Notes) vol. 2, *Yeongyeong Jeonjip* (The Yeongyeong Collection), vol. 56.

he was also a Christian. Various records about him also further confirm that he was a Christian.[87] However, he was not missionary and there are no traces of him involved in evangelistic efforts. History has it that he passed away after having lived his full life in Korea.

(2) Hendrick Hamel

The second Protestants to Korea after Weltevree were Hendrick Hamel and his company who were caught in a storm and drifted to Jeju Island in 1653 (the 4th year of King Hyojong) on their way to Nagasaki, Japan, to discover new markets in East Asia. Their ship wrecked off the shore of Jeju Island; 28 drowned and 36 made it to Hwasunpo. They were soon detained in the Jeju local government office, and Weltevree was sent as an interpreter after their arrival was reported to Seoul. Hamel and his company, who were frightened and anxious in the unfamiliar land, rejoiced with tears upon founding out that the interpreter was from their own home country. After being transferred to Seoul, they were assigned to the military training unit and then were sent to Yeosu, Jeolla Province. Hamel was delighted to be stationed by the sea and looked for a chance to escape to Japan.

The chance finally came in September 1666 when Hamel and his eight peers escaped in the darkness of night and arrived in Nagasaki; this was after 13 years of detention. They were assisted

---

87 Gwang Soo Kim, *Hanguk Gidokgio Jeollaesa* (History of the Introduction of Christianity in Korea) (Korea Christianity Institute, 1984), 152-153.

by a Dutch trading firm there and finally returned home in July 1668. After his return, Hamel wrote *An Account of the Shipwreck of a Dutch Vessel on the Coast of the Isle of Quelpart and The Description of the Kingdom of Corea.*

An Account of the Shipwreck of a Dutch Vessel on the Coast of the Isle of Quelpart contained accounts of Hamel and his company's drifting at sea, life in Korea, their escape and return to the homeland while *The Description of the Kingdom of Corea* documented the geography, climate, products, politics, religions and social customs of Korea. Just around the time when Europeans were increasingly interested in the Orient, these books were published and became quite popular. Therefore, Hamel's books played a crucial role in introducing Korea to many Europeans.

The question of whether Hamel was a Protestant is clearly answered in the ending portion of his *An Account of the Shipwreck of a Dutch Vessel on the Coast of the Isle of Quelpart.*

We nine persons, who returned alive, thanked God for His grace for protecting us for 13 years, 28 days of a long captive life. We also prayed to God for the great grace of those who were still there [Korea].[88]

(3) Murray Maxwell and Basil Hall

Two captains of the Royal Navy of the United Kingdom, Murray

88 Quoted from *ibid.*, 185.

Maxwell and Basil Hall, were assigned to the task of exploring the West coast of Korea. In 1816, they led a warship to the West coast of Korea, explored the shoreline, drafted marine charts and anchored at Maryangjin in Gunsan Bay, Chungcheong Province. There they gave a Chinese Bible to Cheomsa(local officer) Dae Bok Cho who welcomed them. Thus, Dae Bok Cho became the first Korean ever to hold a Bible in his hands.

After returning to Britain, Basil Hall wrote *A Voyage of Disco-very to the West Coast of Corea and the Great Loochoo Island* and published it in 1818. Along with Hamel's voyage journal, this book greatly contributed in introducing Korea to Europe. In particular, this book contained drawings of Korean people that were more than enough for arousing the curiosity of Europeans. The Canadian missionary James S. Gale, who undertook missionary work in Korea, wrote that Napoleon looked at these pictures and had many questions when Hall showed them to him at St. Helena.[89]

These early Protestants came to Korea not on Christian missions but through shipwrecks while on their duties or carrying out their assignments. Accordingly, their early arrivals in Korea carry no significant important in view of the Christian history in Korea.

---

89 James S. Gale, "History of Korea," *The Korea Mission Field* (June 1927), 126.

2. First Protestant Ministers to Korea - Knocking on the Door of Mission

(1) Karl A. F. Gützlaff's Missionary Journey[90]

Half a century before resident missionaries came to Korea, there were a few missionaries who visited Korea for ascertaining the feasibility of missionary work. In principle they were neither sent as missionaries to Korea nor did they carry out any missionary work by living here. Nonetheless, these are people of great significance in the history of the Korean Church for having entered the country in order to sow the seed of the Good News.

The first missionary to set foot in Korea was Karl A.F.Gützlaff, who was a medical doctor and pastor. He was born as a Jewish German at Pyriz in Pomerania, Germany in July 1803. He studied theology at Halle, the birthplace of German Pietism, and was ordained there. Owning the ambition to be a missionary since young age, during his trip to England he met Robert Morrison, the English missionary who pioneered missions in China. Gützlaff listened to Morrison's report of missions there and was thus determined to become a missionary to China.

Sent by the Netherlands Missionary Society, he arrived at Batavia in Southeast Asia in January 1727 and was received by Walter H. Medhurst, an English Congregationalist missionary working

---

90 For a detailed account of Gützlaff's life, see his *Journal of Three Voyages along the Coast of China, in 1831, 1832, and 1833, with Notices of Siam, Corea, and the Loo-Choo Islands* (London: Frederick Westley and A.H. Davis, 1834).

there. In response to Medhurst's suggestion, Gützlaff attempted missionary work in Thailand twice. But his efforts did not yield much fruits and his wife passed away. Much disappointed, he departed for China back to his original plan.

In 1831, he traveled through the Liaodong Peninsula and arrived in Macau, where he joined Morrison who was preparing to secure a foothold for missionary work. By the time Gützlaff arrived in Macau in June 1831, he had spent about six months on a missionary journey that stretched over most of the Western coast of China and Manchuria. It was through this missionary journey that he achieved many things and ascertained the feasibility of further missionary work. This journey would also later serve as a reason for him to come to Korea.

Gützlaff's journey to Korea was a part of a business plan for the East India Company, which served as an advance army for the colonization of India, secured its monopoly over China, and was now intending to expand its trading network to other countries in the East Asia. Accordingly, the East India Company was preparing the Lord Amherst, a one-ton class trading ship, for sail to Korea, Japan, Okinawa and Taiwan. At this time, Captain Hugh H. Lindsay was familiar with Gützlaff, and asked Gützlaff, who by now rendered various assistance for missions in China, to board the ship as an interpreter, medical doctor and chaplain. Gützlaff was more than willing to accept this request and thus he was recorded as the first missionary to come to Korea.

The Lord Amherst left Macau in February 1832, sailed along

the coast of Shandong and landed on an island near Paiknyeong Island off the West coast of Korea in Hwanghae Province in July. Those onboard the Lord Amherst attempted to get in contact with the local officials in the island through conversations by writing but were unsuccessful. Leaving the island, Gützlaff and company sailed southward and arrived at Godae Island off of the Hongju Bay in Chungcheong Province and managed to meet a local official there. They gave the official a petition and gifts for the King (Soonjo) for granting trades. Gützlaff also gave the official a copy of the Chinese Bible as suggested by Captain Lindsay.[91] While waiting for a reply from Seoul, Gützlaff attempted to get in contact with Koreans in the area. When supervision of the officials relaxed, he set foot on the island, met with the locals and gave them Chinese Bibles and medicine. In his journal he recorded his giving away of Bibles to Koreans with the following words:

As the boatmen were under no restraint from the observation of their countrymen, they showed us great deal of cordiality. Unable to repay a present of books which we made them, they gave us tobacco leaves, highly delighted that we condescended to accept them.[92]

While Gützlaff was staying here, he was created for two major

---

91 Yang Sun Kim, *Hanguk Gidokgiohoesa Yongu* (A Study of History of the Korean Church) (Seoul: Christian Publishing Co., 1971), 42.

92 K. Gützlaff, *Journal of Three Voyages along the Coast of China, in 1831, 1832, and 1833, with Notices of Siam, Corea, and the Loo-Choo Islands* (London: Frederick Westley and A.H. Davis, 1834), 326.

accomplishments in the history of the Korean Church and the history of Korea herself. The most significant accomplishment for the history of the Korean Church was that he translated the Lord's prayer into Korean. When the Lord Amherst arrived at Godae Island, officials from Maryangjin came aboard the ship to inquire of the reasons for the visit and status of the ship. However, due to the inclement weather, they were forced to spend the night on the ship. Gützlaff took this opportunity to have the Chinese version of the Lord's Prayer translated into Korean. He wrote the Lord's Prayer in Chinese characters, showed it to Mr. Yang, Hongju Moksa(deputy) Min Hoe Lee's pupil, and had him write the Korean meanings next to the Chinese characters. This was the very first instance of translating a portion of the Bible being translated into Korean.

One other remarkable thing was that Gützlaff gave potato seeds to the islanders and taught them now to plant and grow potatoes. He planted the potatoes along the beach and gave them planting directions written in Chinese. Thus, potatoes began to be distributed across Chungcheong Province.[93] Gützlaff's contribution was especially significant for the hunger and famine-struck people who were now able to rely on potatoes for an alternative food source. This is why Gützlaff should all the more be remembered as a great missionary who gave to Koreans the bread of life, the Bible and the bread of the body, potatoes.

In August, a special envoy and an interpreter came from Seoul.

---

93 *Ibid.*, 341.

They explained that Korea was in no place to engage foreign countries in commercial and trading practices without the consent of the Chinese Emperor and that Gützlaff and his company should leave immediately. The gifts and the Bible that the captain sent to the King were also returned. The captain and Gützlaff realized that they were left with no choice, and thus they gave up initiating trades with Korea and left the island. As he watched the ship sail further and further away from the Korea shore, Gützlaff knelt on the deck and offered a sincere prayer to God.

> In the great plan of the eternal God, there will be a time of merciful visitation for them. While we look for this, we ought to be very anxious to hasten its approach, by diffusing the glorious doctrines of the cross by all means in our power······The scripture teaches us to believe that God can bless even these feeble beginnings. Let us hope that better days will soon dawn for Corea.[94]

Even though the first missionary to Korea had to depart in this way, Korea later received the Gospel, just as he prayed, and became a mission field with unprecedented achievements due to the dedication successive missionaries. Although Korea was not quite read y at this moment to yield any visible fruits immediately, the seed of the Gospel that Gützlaff sowed was taking root deep in the ground.

---

94 *Ibid.*, 355.

(2) Rev. Robert J. Thomas' Martyrdom

Among the many missionaries who visited Korea to survey the feasibility of missionary work before launching full-scale missionary campaigns, the first Protestant martyr to shed blood in Korea was Rev. Robert J. Thomas.

Robert J. Thomas was born at Rhayada in Wales as a son of a Congregationalist pastor in September 1840. He completed his undergraduate and theological education at New College, London University, and was ordained in 1859. With an extraordinary interest in missions, he and his wife were sent by the London Missionary Society to China in the same year he was ordained. But unfortunately, his wife died immediately after arriving in Shanghai in the autumn of that year.

Saddened by his wife's death, Thomas further experienced conflicts with the leadership of the London Missionary Society. Consequently, he quit his assignment and instead started working for the customs office at Qufu in Shandong. While working there, he met Alexander Williamson, a missionary from the Bible Society of Scotland, and his passion for missions were rekindled. Then, by accident, he met two Korean Catholics who had escaped by a wooden boat from the persecutions in Korea.[95]

Thomas heard their account about the hardship of the Catholic Church in Korea and became even more passionate for missionary work in Korea. He resigned from the customs office and looked

---

[95] *Annual Report of the National Bible Society of Scotland for 1865*, 35-37.

for an opportunity to become involved in missions in Korea. In September 1865, he was able to board a ship bound for the West coast of Korea with Chinese Bibles that Williamson provided.

After arriving at Changlin Island off the coast of Hwanghae Province, he spent about two and a half months distributing Bibles to the islanders, learning Korean, and evangelizing the people.[96] Although he intended to meet the King and receive a royal permission for missions, he was caught in a sudden storm, was drifted to a shore of Manchuria, and finally made it to Beijing in January 1866 after much difficulties. In Beijing, he worked as a deputy for the president of Beijing University, which was under the management of the London Missionary Society, but his focus remained on missionary work in Korea.

At this time Korea was undergoing the Persecution of 1866, a full-scale oppression against the Catholic Church. Receiving news of the persecution, the French legation in China decided to send the French Asiatic Squadron, led by Admiral P.G. Rose, to take punitive action against Korea. Thomas, who had just returned from his voyage to the West coast of Korea, was then asked to join the Squadron as a guide and interpreter and he gladly accepted the request. However, this plan was called off because a riot broke out in Indochina and the Squadron was ordered for deployment there instead.

Looking for yet another chance, Thomas was informed that from

---

96 A Letters of Rev. R. J. Thomas, January 12 1866. *The Missionary Magazine and Chronicle* (July 1866), 200-201.

Tianjin, the General Sherman, a trading ship owned by an American named Preston, was leaving for Korea. In July 1866, he boarded the ship as an interpreter and guide, and sailed toward Korea, the land of his missionary dream. His last letter to the London Missionary Society contained detailed description of the situation at that time.

> I resolved to proceed······I take a good supply of (Christian) books with Bibles and am quite sanguine that I shall be welcomed by the people······Trusting the Directors will approve of our efforts to spread the doctrines of the Bible unmixed with human error, in this unknown land.[97]

About a week later, the General Sherman reached Yonggang-gun, at the mouth of the Daedong River, and began to sail up the river toward Pyongyang. Munjeonggwan (Inspector) came to where the ship was anchoring and asked for the destination and objectives of the ship, and Thomas interpreted the conversation in unpolished Korean. To the reply that the ship came to trade with Korea, the Munjeonggwan told that the law forbade any trading with foreign countries and that they should leave. But the General Sherman ignored the instructions and continued sailing.

The General Sherman was actually armed, something not to

---

97 A Letter of Thomas, August 1, 1886, sent from Qufu. Quoted from Kyoung Bae Min, *Daehan Yesugio Jangnohoe 100 Yonsa* (Centennial History of the Korean Presbyterian Church) (The Board of Education Department of the Korean Presbyterian Church, 1984), 37.

be expected of a trading ship. As the ship ignored the instructions for withdrawal and continued to sail up the river, Koreans could not relax their vigilance. Moreover, when the sailors detained and forcefully handled Junggun(Military officer) Hyeon Ik Lee who went aboard to investigate the ship, the soldiers and the residents along the river banks started throwing stones and shooting arrows and guns. The crew members of the General Sherman were also frightened and began to shoot guns and cannons at the soldiers and the residents. While all this was happening, the Daedong river, which had been flooded, began to become shallower, and the General Sherman became stuck in the riverbed. The soldiers then joined several small boats together, loaded it with wood, set it on fire then let it flow down toward the ship. As soon as the boats on fire hit the General Sherman, she began to burn.[98]

When the ship was set on fire, the sailors jumped into the river, swam to the river bank, while the waiting soldiers began to kill them with swords one by one. Rev. Thomas too could not also remain on the ship and thus swam in the Daedong river with a few Bibles tucked in side his jacket. When Rev. Thomas swam out of the Daedong, a soldier, Chun Gwon Park killed him with a sword; and thus Rev. Thomas became the very first Protestant missionary to be martyred in Korea. Before his death, Rev. Thomas handed Chun Gwon Park a Bible. Although Park did not initially accept the Bible, he picked it up before returning home. Park

---

98 Yang Sun Kim, *Hanguk Gidokgiohoesa Yongu* (A Study of the History of the Korean Church) (Seoul: Christian Publishing Co., 1971), 45.

later became a Christian and a leader of Anju Church. Furthermore, the home of Young Sik Park, barrack gate officer, who used the Bible pages as wallpaper, later became the site of the first church in Pyongyang, Neoldarikkol Chapel.[99] Young Tae Park, Chun Gwon Park's nephew, who also became a Christian, worked as an assistant to a Southern Presbyterian (U.S.) missionary, William Reynolds, and contributed greatly as a member of the Korean Bible Translation Committee.[100]

Rev. Thomas was killed as the first Protestant martyr in Korea on September 2, 1866. He was 27 years old.[101] Even though he died in an instance, the Gospel that he passed to one soldier became the foundation stone for the Korean Church, and Pyongyang, where Rev. Thomas's blood flowed through the Daedong river, became the epicenter of the Korean Church and was dubbed the Jerusalem of the East Asia. In memory of his death, a thousand Korean believers gathered at Ssuk Island, where Rev. Thomas was thought to have been buried, for a memorial service in 1927. There a chapel was built in the shape of a T, the first letter of his name, and was dedicated as the Rev. Thomas Memorial Chapel in 1932.[102]

---

99 *Ibid.*, 49.

100 Young Hun Lee, *Hanguk Gidokgiohoesa* (History of the Korean Church) (Concordia, 1978), 62-63.

101 *Annual Report of the London Missionary Society for 1867*, 80.

102 Harry A. Rhodes, ed., *History of the Korea Mission Presbyterian Church U.S.A. 1884-1934*, vol. I (Korea Mission, Presbyterian Church, U.S.A., 1934), 72-73.

3. Korean Converts outside Korea

(1) Uiju Youths Converted in Manchuria

While foreign missionaries continually passed by the coast of Korea for missionary work in Korea, there began to emergence of some Koreans who accepted the Protestant faith by coming in contact with missionaries in Manchuria and Japan.

The Presbyterian Church of Scotland began its missionary work in China in 1862, and the Bible Society of Scotland had been undertaking its missionary activities from its center at Shandong. In 1812, the Scotland Missionary Society sent John Ross and his brother-in-law John McIntyre as missionaries to China. These two missionaries contributed to the Protestant missions in Korea before permanent missionaries arrived in Korea. According to the decision made by the Missionary Society, they chose Yingkou, Manchuria as their place of appointment and commenced missionary work there.

After hearing from A. Williamson about the martyrdom of the British missionary Thomas, Ross's passion began to burn for Korea, which had yet to hear the Good News. Driven by the thought of approaching the Korean border as close as possible, he left Yingkou in 1874 and visited the Koryomun(Korean Gate) located on the opposite side of Uiju, North Pyeongan Province on the lower Yalu river.[103] Inhabited by about 3,000 Koreans, the Korean

---

103 J. Ross, "The Christian Dawn in Korea," *The Missionary Review of the World,*

Gate was the center of trades between Korea and Manchuria. Here, Ross met a Korean merchant and learned about some basic facts about Korea and few simple Korean. This merchant was the father of Hong Joon Paik, who would be the first Korean Protestant to get baptized.

During this trip, Ross acquired a general knowledge about Korea. By seeing the strict control of entry of foreigners, he also realized that entering Korea would not be easy as foreign religions were subject to tight supervision.

After the short survey, Ross visited the Korean Gate again in 1874. This time, he met several youths from Uiju, North Pyeongan Province. They were Hong Joon Paik, Eung Chan Lee, Suhng Ha Lee, and Jin Gee Kim who came to the Korean Gate for trading and met Ross's secretary there. Accepting Ross' of proposal of his paying them generously and teaching them Western civilization, these young men signed a contract to teach Korean to Ross, McIntyre and other Western missionaries before departing for Yingkou.

At Yingkou, the four youths taught the Westerners Korean and had close fellowship with them, but they persistently refused to accept or confess the Christian faith. Needless to say, this was because the Royal Court was practicing a very strict law that subjected anyone who believed in foreign religions to the court's maximum possible punishments. But the dedication of the missionaries and the power of the Gospel eventually won them over, and they accepted the Christian faith in 1876. After spending two

---

III-4 (April 1890), 241.

years in Yingkou as language instructors, they were baptized by McIntyre.[104] They became the first Korean Protestants, and thus the Protestant Church in Korea started off. Ross accounts this incident with following words:

> McIntyre baptized four scholarly Korean youngsters. I am sure that these young men are the first fruits of a future harvest······I think that the Korean people are more simple and religious than the Chinese, thus, I expect that Christianity will spread out broadly and rapidly among the Koreans.[105]

After this, two Uiju youths, Sang Yoon Suh and his younger brother Gyeong Jo, came to Yingkou to sell red ginseng. In Yingkou, however, Sang Yoon Suh caught a high fever and his life became endangered. Ross met with the youths and admitted Sang Yoon Suh to the hospital managed by the missions there, where he nursed him with much care. Deeply touched and grateful, Sang Yoon Suh was baptized by Ross in 1879, the same year he was discharged from the hospital.[106]

---

104 Yang Sun Kim, *Hanguk Gidokgiohoesa Yongu* (A Study of the History of the Korean Church), 50.
105 John Ross, "Manchuria Mission," *United Presbyterian Magazine* (October 1880), 333-334.
106 Yang Sun Kim, *Hanguk Gidokgiohoesa Yongu* (A Study of the History of the Korean Church), 50. Cf. Yang Sun Kim, "Ross Buhsiongwa Hanguk Protestantism" (The Ross Version and the Korean Protestantism), *Baeksan Hakbo* (The Baeksan Gazette), no. 3.

(2) Korean Bible Translation in Manchuria

Another historical accomplishment by the Uiju youths who became Christians in Manchuria was their role in the Korean translation of the Bible. Ross had a grand plan for translating a Korean Bible. First, Ross felt the need for systematic learning of Hangeul and thus published *A Korean Primer* in 1877 with the help of the Uiju youths. He continued his effort of learning Korean culture and history, and published *History of Corea, Ancient and Modern* in 1879. However, these were merely the preparatory works for Bible translation and were not his ultimate goals. Despite the difficult circumstance, Ross utilized the help of the Uiju youths for the Bible translation. Finally in the spring of 1882, he published *Yesu-syeonggyo Nugabogeumjeonsuh* (Gospel of Luke) as a 51-page long Hanji(Korean traditional paper) volume. And in May of the same year, he published 3,000 copies of *Yesusuhonggyo Yohanne Bogeumjeonsuh* (Gospel of John).[107] Thus the first work of Korean Bible translation was commenced. In 1882, the year that these two books were published, a USA-Korea treaty was signed, the US legation was installed in Korea, and trades between Korea and the USA began to take place in official terms.

Following the publication of the Gospel of Matthew and the Gospel of Mark in 1884, other books of the Bible were translated and *Yesusuhonggyojeonsuh* (Bible of the Holy Religion of Jesus), containing the entire New Testament, was published in 1887. The

---

107 *Ibid.,* 50-51.

fact that the Bible was translated and published outside Korea even before permanent missionaries entered the country was certainly a noticeable achievement in the entire history of world missions.

(3) Works of Colporteurs

In early history of the Korean Church, colporteurs played an important role of selling Bibles and evangelizing people across the country.

The Uiju youths who helped Bible translation in Manchuria were now given the responsibilities of carrying the Bibles around, preaching the Good News and planting churches. Even though Chinese Bibles were previously distributed through various channels, they were confined to the elite class who could read Chinese, and were out of reach of the general public. But now could read them and, that Hangeul Bibles were published, any literate person naturally, the number of believers began to increase.

However, bringing in the Bibles to Korea was not so easy because the law strictly prohibited such an act. One day on his missionary journey of transporting the Gospels, Suhng Ha Lee had to stay at an inn near the bank of the Yalu river. When he walked out for a while, the suspecting innkeeper opened Lee's luggage. Seeing the forbidden books, he threw some into the Yalu river and burned the rest. When informed of this incident, Ross stated, "The water into which the Bibles were thrown will become the 'water of life' to the Koreans and the ashes will be fertilizer, bringing about a great growth in the Korean Church."[108]

Following Suhng Ha Lee's failure to take Bibles into Korea, Hong Joon Paik attempted to take the Bible across the border, he realized that taking in the Bibles was almost impossible and he devised an idea. He went out to the market and bought some books of low value. He then tore out the Bible page by page, twisted them together into strings and tied the newly bought books with the strings. Then he crossed the river carrying the books. Officials examined the books and, finding nothing unusual, let him pass through the border. Reaching his home, Hong Joon Paik threw the books away, untied the strings and rebound the Bible for use in evangelization.[109]

After returning to their homes, the Uiju youths vigorously under took evangelization activities and a number of believers began to emerge. As Hong Joon Paik held doctrine catechism classes, the number continued to grow, and by 1885 there was a congregation of about 18 people.

Later Sang Yoon Suh also came home and joined in the evangelist work. But the district office was informed of his activities and issued an order for his arrest. Consequently, he fled to his uncle's home at Songcheon (also called Sollae), an estuary village in Jangye-on, Hwanghae Province. He continued to evangelize the people

---

108 H. A. Rhodes, ed., *History of the Korea Mission Presbyterian Church U.S.A. 1884-1934*, vol. I (Korea Mission, Presbyterian Church, U.S.A., 1934), 74.
109 Yang Sun Kim, "Hangukui Sungsuh Beonyeoksa" (The History of Bible Translation in Korea), *Sungsuh Hanguk* (Scriptures Korea) (Bible Society of Korea, 1967), 20-21.

here and won a number of converts. Under the leadership of Sang Yoon Suh, a small thatched cottage in Sollae was used as a chapel and became the first Protestant church in Korea.[110] Sollae later became a village of an astonishing accomplishment whereby 50 out of the 58 families were Christians.

To aid in the supply of Bibles, Ross shipped 6,000 Bible portions to Incheon Port in 1884. Fortunately, the German adviser at the Incheon customs office, P.G. von Mölendorf, helped in the process and the Bibles entered the country safely. As the Bibles were further distributed, the evangelist movement expanded gradually and there were Christians even in Seoul.[111]

Thus, the pioneers who accepted the Protestant faith in the foreign land helped in translation and publication of Korean Bibles. The Bibles were then used in evangelism, producing converts and planting churches. This was remarkable, especially for the fact that the Korean converts established the Early Protestant Church in Korea without depending on the help of foreign missionaries.

(4) Soo Jeong Lee's Conversion and Bible Translation in Japan

We can see that God has prepared many things in order to save the Korean people. While the Scottish missionaries were actively engaged in Bible translation projects with the newly converte

---

110 Nak Jun Paik, *Hanguk Gaesingiosa* (The History of Protestantism in Korea) (Yonsei University Press, 1973), 51.
111 Yang Sun Kim, *Hanguk Gidokgiohoesa Yongu* (A Study of the History of the Korean Church), 52.

d youths from Uiju, a steady preparation for Protestant missions in Korea was also carried out in Japan. In 1881, King Gojong sent a study delegation named the Gentlemen's Observation Mission to Japan to inspect the foreign world. Among the delegates was Jong Soo Ahn. In Japan he met various people, including Dr. Tsudasen, a famous Japanese agriculturist. While Jong Soo Ahn attained much agricultural knowledge from him, he was particularly more drawn to the writing on the hanging scroll in Tsudasen's study room. It was the Sermon on the Mount and it gave Ahn a deep sensation.[112]

Upon his return, Ahn met his friend Soo Jeong Lee and told him about Tsudasen, recommending him to meet Tsudasen when he went to Japan. As a reward for rescuing Queen Min during the Imogunran (the Soldiers' Riot of the year of Imo, 1882), Soo Jeong Lee was given a chance to accompany Young Hyo Park as his unofficial attendant on his mission to Japan in September 1882. As soon as they arrived in Japan, Lee went to meet Dr. Tsudasen as recommended by Jong Soo Ahn. Tsudasen warmly welcomed Soo Jeong Lee, briefly explained the Christian doctrine, and gave him a Chinese Bible. Back at his lodge, Lee read the Chinese Bible, was deeply touched and began to take great interest in Christianity. Assisted by Tsudasen, he undertook a systematic study of the Bible, confessed the faith, and was baptized by an American missionary, G.W. Knox, at Rogetsuchou Church in April 1883.[113] Thus Lee became the first Korean Protestant in Japan,

---

112 *Ibid.*, 54.

following the Uiju youths in Manchuria. The third Japan National Christian Fellowship Conference was held in Tokyo in May of the year that Lee was baptized. Lee participated in the conference, offered a public prayer in Korean, and even confessed his faith in public.[114] Lee evangelized various Korean students in Japan; the number was added to those evangelized and baptized by Lee, and there was even a Bible study class for Korean students in Japan.

After possessing the faith, Lee decided that he could not keep the joy and passion within himself. Determined that missionaries must be sent to evangelize Korea, he requested for the American Mission Board to send missionaries. Soo Jeong Lee's petition was featured in the children's section of the 1883 Christmas edition of *The Missionary Review of the World*.[115] He also wrote petitions to other missionary magazines. Knox, who baptized Lee, positively responded to his appeal, referring to him as "a Macedonian from Corea."[116]

At this point the Japanese Church had indicated its intension to help in missionary work in Korea, but Lee decided that it would be better for the American Church to take the call considering

---

113 G. W. Knox, "Affair in Corea," *The Foreign Missionary* (1883), 17.

114 A translation of Lee, Sujeong's testimony can be found on Yun Tae Oh, "Suhnguja Lee Soo Jeong," (Soo Jeong Lee the Pioneer), *Hanguk Gidokgiosa* (History of Christianity in Korea), vol. 4 (Hye Suhn Publishing Co., 1983), 64-67.

115 Yang Sun Kim, *Hanguk Gidokgiohoesa Yongu* (A Study of the History of the Korean Church), 58.

116 "A Macedonian from Corea" *The Foreign Missionary* (June 1883).

the age-long anti-Japanese attitude of Koreans. In December 1883, he sent the following public appeal to the American Church.

> Your country is well known to us as a Christian land; but if you do not send the gospel to us, I am afraid other nations will hasten to send their teachers, and I fear that such teachings are not in accordance with the will of the Lord. Although I am a man of no influence, I will do my utmost to aid such missionaries as you may send.[117]

Soo Jeong Lee's proposal for missionary work caused the American Church to have much interest in missions in Korea, and it served as a foundation for future missionary work.

Lee's conversion was definitely big news to the missionaries who had been working in Japan and at the same time exploring the feasibility of missions in Korea. Among them, H. Loomis, Director of the American Bible Society in Japan, showed great interest toward Lee. He met Lee and requested his help for translating the Bible into Korean, and Lee accepted the offer with gladness. Loomis described this as below.

> His(Rijutei) most concern is to give numerous Bibles to his people. He knows that the works of the American Bible Society for other counties. He is very glad that the ABS is going to work for his country……he began with

---

117 Ri, Jutei, "Ri Jutei to the Christian of America, Greeting," *The Missionary Review* (March 1884), 145-146.

enthusiasm this work. When I visited him yesterday, he finished the translation of the Gospel according to Matthew and Mark qutite much.[118]

Taking Bible translation as his inevitable divine assignment, Lee started off with simple tasks. His first tasks involved annotating the Chinese Bible with Korean pronunciations and meanings for easier reading and understanding. This work was not taxing, so he was able to complete the entire New Testament within a few months. So-called Hyeonto Sungsuh was published with *Sinyak Suhngsuh Magajeon*(Gospel of Mark) as the first portion in November 1884, followed by other books. However, this Chinese-annotated Bible was accessible to the elite class. Realizing the urgent need for a Hangeul Bible, he undertook the work without any delays.

Lee immediately started translating the Gospel of Mark, the shortest among the four Gospels. This work was initiated in June 1883 and was completed in April the following year. Despite much difficulties, the American Bible Society in Yokohama published 1,000 copies of this translation in February 1885.[119] Therefore it was possible for Underwood, the first permanent missionary to set foot in Korea in the same year, to bring this Gospel of Mark. Lee continued on with translating the Gospel of Luke, but this was not published. By the request of a Methodist missionary,

---

118 A Letter of H. Loomis to Dr. Gilman, May 30, 1883.
119 Historical Catalogues of Printed Editions of the Holy Scriptures, In the *Library of the British and Foreign Bible Society*, vol. II. Ser. no. 5991 (London: The Bible House, Co., 1903), 887.

R. S. Maclay, he also translated the Methodist catechism, 1,000 copies of which were published and read widely across Korea.

Unfortunately Soo Jeong Lee's work in Japan could not last long. When Ok Gyun Kim, one of the leaders of the Coup d'Etat of 1884, defected to Japan, the Royal Court summoned the leaders and supporters of the coup to return to Korea and even attempted to assassinate them. While keeping a distance from Ok Gyun Kim, Lee decided that it would be wise for him to end his four-year-long stay in Japan and return to Korea, especially considering his past relationship with Young Ik Min. But, unfortunately Dr. Nak Jun Paik suggests evidence that Lee denounced the Christian faith just before returning to Korea.[120] If he really did denounce the Christian faith, this is a true tragedy. However, even if he had negated, his accomplishments in the history of the Korean Church will never be underrated.

---

120 Nak Jun Paik, *Hanguk Gaesingiosa* (History of Protestantism in Korea) (Seoul: Yonsei University Press, 1973), 94-95.

Chapter 2

Arrival of Missionaries

1 . Steps Leading up to Arrival of Missionaries

(1) Signing of the Korea－U.S.A. Treaty

The seclusion policy of the Korea Royal Court was put to an end and the country opened its door to foreign nations as a result of the Unyang (warship named Unyang) Incident in 1875 (1st year of King Gojong). In order to force a commercial treaty on the tightly shut Korea, Japan deliberately sent three navy vessels, including the Unyang, into the waters off of Ganghwa Island and prompted the Korea troops to fire on them. To this, the Japanese fleet shelled several fortresses on Ganghwa Island, and the Korea troops suffered heavy casualties by the superior firepower of the Japanese. The immobilized Korea inevitably signed the Treaty of

Ganghwa with Japan in February 1876. This was the first treaty ever to be signed with a foreign country for the modern Korea, and Korea's age long seclusion policy was finally put to an end.[121]

Many treaties with other imperialist states followed the treaty with Japan. The first to sign a treaty with Korea from the Western world was the United States of America. Since 1867, the USA attempted to investigate and call Korea to account of the destruction of the General Sherman, which had carried Rev. Thomas as mentioned earlier. In January of the same year, the Wachusett, led by Captain R. W. Shufeldt, came to the West coast and investigated eyewitnesses about the last moments of the General Sherman. Also in April, the U.S.S. Shenandoah appeared at the mouth of the Daedong river and staged a violent demonstration.

While the U.S. was clearly determined to get the Korean Government to compensate and apologize for the destruction of the General Sherman, they were also interested in opening up the closed doors of Korea and establish trades with her. The U. S. Government delegated this task to John Rodgers, the commander of the Asiatic Squadron of the United States Navy. In May 1871, Rodgers led five of the Asiatic Squadron warships in the shelling of Ganghwa Island, causing the first and probably the last battle between Korea and the U. S. A. The U. S. navy dominated the initial stage of the battle with the superior firepower, but Rodgers's objectives could not be accomplished with just one small battle. His mission

---

121 Woo Keun Han, *Hanguk Tongsa*(Entire History of Korea) (Seoul: Eulyumunhwasa, 1983), 412.

eventually failed, and he had to retreat.[122]

The trade agreement with the U. S. was signed primarily to act as a restraint against Japan and for Qing China, who was becoming anxious of the Japanese expansion into Korea since the Treaty of Ganghwa in 1876 and had urged the Korea Government to sign the agreement with the U. S. Around this period, the U. S. had sent the Ticonderoga for a tour around the world for expanding the American market in various regions of the globe. The Ticonderoga left the U. S. A. in December 1878 and it arrived at Nagasaki, Japan in April 1880 after traveling to many parts of the world. After persistent persuasion by Yuan Shikai of Qing China, Korea's Hong Jip Kim and America's Shufeldt signed the historic "Treaty of Amity and Commerce between the United States of America and Corea" in a tent on the Jemulpo beach.[123] With this treaty, Korea and the U. S. newly established a blood-tied alliance and the U. S. could also now take significant actions for missions in Korea. The fact that the Korean-American Treaty was signed just around the time when American missionaries were entering Korea clearly demonstrates God's divine appointment of saving the Korean people. The Korean-American Treaty also cleared away Korea's disgrace of having to obtain the Chinese government's consent on every major decision. Korea was finally able to take its stand as a fully independent state.

After the signing of the treaty, it was assented by the U. S.

---

122 *Woman's Work for Woman* XII-8 (August 1896), 208.
123 Guksa Pyeonchan Wiwonhoe, *Hanguksa* 16 (History of Korea, 16) (Eulyu Editorial Committee of National History, 1975), 226.

Congress and ratified by President C. A. Arthur. Accordingly in May 1883, L. H. Foote arrived in Korea as a minister plenipotentiary the exchanged instruments of ratification, and commenced his service as the first American diplomatic minister in Seoul. In response to the U. S. actions, the Korea Government also dispatched to the United States an eight-man diplomatic mission comprising of Chief Envoy Young Ik Min, Deputy Envoy Young Sik Hong, and attendants such as Gwang Beom Suh and Gil Joon Yoo. They left Jemulpo in July 1883 on a U.S. navy vessel, stopped at Yokohama, and finally arrived at San Francisco in September. They crossed the continent by train and arrived at Washington D. C. in September. There they met the President, and returned to Korea in December.

(2) John F. Goucher and R. S. Maclay - Preparing for Missions in Korea

While the diplomatic mission to the United States was traveling from San Francisco to Washington D. C. on the pan continental train, they encountered a man who would become one of the most important central figures in the history of missions in Korea. This man was Dr. John F. Goucher,[124] Methodist pastor, who founded the Goucher College in 1885 in Baltimore, Maryland. While traveling together on the train for three days, Dr. Goucher began to take much interest in Korea. Sensing the feasibility of missions in Korea, he wrote a letter to the Methodist Foreign Mission Board in Nove-

---

124 Goucher College was founded in 1885, and Goucher served as its president from 1890 through 1908.

mber 1883. He sent 2,000 dollars along with the letter, stating that it would be good to start missionary work in Korea.[125] However, the American Methodist Church did not yet have plans for missionary work in Korea and did not respond positively. As a result, Goucher wrote directly to R. S. Maclay, the representative of Methodist missionaries in Japan, and instructed, "it would be good to go and visit Korea, examine the country and start missionary work there."[126]

Receiving Goucher's letter, Maclay immediately decided to go to Korea, and in June 1884 he departed for Korea for a two-week tour with his wife. Fortunately he shared a close friendship with Ok Kyun Kim while he was in Japan, and therefore he went to meet Ok Kyun Kim. Since Kim was a high-level government official at that time, Maclay handed him a petition asking the King to allow him to carry out medical and educational services in Korea. A few days later, Ok Kyun Kim relayed the King's reply to Maclay, "the King carefully read my letter last night and he has decided to allow the Missionary Society to start hospital and education services in Korea as per my request."[127] Having secured the king's permission, Maclay requested Foote, the American minister in Korea, to find a piece of land near the legation to start the missionary work before he returned to Japan.

After returning to Japan, he immediately wrote a letter to the

---

125 R. S. Maclay, "Korea's Permit to Christianity," *The Missionary Review of the World* (August 1895), 287.
126 *Ibid.*, 289.
127 *Ibid.*

Mission Board in the U.S. saying, "Dr. Mcclay believes it better to begin in educational and medical work, using no disguise as to the ultimate object being evangelization! Schools would be welcomed, and hospitals are a necessity."[128]

The Mission Board read Maclay's letter, deeply realized the need of missionary work in Korea, and published in its missionary magazine *The Gospel in All Lands* various articles by missionaries in Japan that called for support of missionary work in Korea. Readers of the magazine gave mission funds and Dr. Goucher's offering was added to this funds. The following series of events resulted in the Methodist Episcopal (North) Church taking the first step in sending missionaries to Korea. At the end of 1884, William B. Scranton, who was a pastor and medical doctor, his mother Mary F. Scranton, and Rev. Henry G. Appenzeller were appointed as missionaries to Korea.

Behind the initial success of missions in Korea was God's amazing divine providence that involved the signing of the Korean-American Treaty, Young Ik Min's encounter with Dr. Goucher on the train, and Maclay's securing the King's royal permission for missionary work in Korea.

(3) David W. McWilliams Makes Presbyterian Mission Possible

While the U.S. Methodist Church was well into missionary work for Korea, the U.S. Presbyterian Church(Northern branch) was

---

128 *Annual Report of the Missionary Society of the Methodist Episcopal Church for 1884*, 204-205.

also quietly laying its foundation stones for missionary work in Korea. As mentioned earlier, Soo Jeong Lee's Macedonian call for Korean missions aroused much interest for many people. However, members of mission boards had opposing views, as some thought that it was still too early to get involved with Korea while others thought that the work must start without any delay. For instance, the general secretary of the Foreign Mission Board of the U.S. Congregationalist wrote an article that it was too early for Korean missions. On the other hand, F. F. Ellinwood, the general secretary of the Foreign Mission Board of the U.S. Presbyterian Church (Northern branch), had the foresight that Korean missions had to be carried out immediately.

Then, a man prepared by God for Korean missions read article about Korean missions and inquired of his mission board. David W. McWilliams was a member of the Lafayette Presbyterian Church in New York, a member of the Foreign Mission Board of the Presbyterian Church (Northern branch) and the administrator of properties for Frederick Marquand. He read a petition for Korean missions in a missionary magazine and began to have much interest in the matter. He inquired F.F. Ellinwood, the general secretary of the Foreign Mission Board of the Northern Presbyterian Church, on the feasibility of missionary work in Korea, and Ellinwood confirmed the urgency of missions in Korea. With Ellinwood's reply, McWilliams wrote him that he was willing to donate 5,000 dollars[129] to cover the expenses of two missionaries' work for

---

129 David W. McWilliams to F. F. Ellinwood, February 8, 1884. The Presbyterian

two years provided that missionary work would immediately start in Korea.

Much encouraged by this offer, the Mission Board committed itself in setting up the plan for missions in Korea. The plan was further solidified as many others sent in mission funds, and John W. Heron, a "young doctor with excellent medical skills and sacrificial dedication," was appointed as the first missionary to Korea in the spring of 1884. However, the Mission Board decided that circumstances in Korea were not evaluated sufficiently and an immediate entry was too risky. Thus Heron was called to go to Japan first and study Korean language while waiting for a good tim to enter Korea. While Heron was first to be appointed as a missionary to Korea, he was only able to enter Korea in June 1885 after a long wait in Japan. This meant that Horace N. Allen, who arrived in Korea as a medical missionary in September 1884, and Horace G. Underwood, who arrived in April 1885, came to Korea a little earlier than Heron. Although he was the first to be appointed as a missionary to Korea, Heron was not given the honor of being the first missionary to arrive in Korea.

Historical Society (PHS hereafter) in Philadelphia. Regarding the amount of money McWilliams sent, Lillias Underwood wrote it as 6,000 dollars in her biography of her husband, Underwood of Korea (New York: Fleming H. Revell, 1918), 35. Thus many books, which quoted from Lillias' Book, wrote as $6,000, but it is $5,000. It is clearly written in McWilliams' letter to Ellinwood.

2. Arrival of the First Missionary, Horace N. Allen, M.D.

The long and tedious preparation period was over, and the first Protestant missionary finally arrived in Korea in September 1884. This was exactly one hundred years after Seung Hoon Lee was baptized in Beijing as the first Korean Catholic. The year 1884 naturally became recognized as the starting point of the Mission of the Protestant Church in Korea.[130] The honor of being the first Protestant missionary to Korea was given to Horace N. Allen, a medical doctor sent by the Northern Presbyterian Church in the U.S.A.[131]

Allen was born in Delaware, Ohio in April 1858 as a descendant of Ithan Allen, a hero during the Independence War of the U.S.A. After graduated from Ohio Wesleyan University, he graduated from Miami Medical College at Cincinnati and became a medical doctor in 1883. Allen was a college student just around the time when the Second Great Awakening swept across America and many college students were volunteering to foreign missions. Allen was also much influenced by this movement and enrolled in the medical college with the intension to become a missionary. As a result,

---

130 There are different views about recognizing 1884 as the starting year of Protestant missions in Korea. However, the Korean Church had its Jubilee celebration of Protestant missions in 1934 and held a grand festival in celebration of the 100th anniversary of Protestant missions in 1984.
131 For more information on Allen's life, see F. H. Harrington, *God, Mammon, and the Japanese* (Madison: Univ. of Wisconsin, 1944). Also, Kyoung Bae Min, *Allenui Suhngiowa Geundae Hanmioegio* (Allen's Missionary Work and Modern Korean-American Diplomacy) (Seoul: Yonsei University Press, 1991).

after obtaining the M.D. license, he submitted a medical missionary application to the Northern Presbyterian Church in the spring of 1883. The application was accepted, and Allen was appointed as a missionary to China. Soon after, he got married and left for China at age of 25 in 1883.

When he arrived in Shanghai in October 1883, he lost a large sum of his money, quarreled with some missionaries there over minuscule issues and his wife fell into poor health. Therefore, he began to consider moving his station to a warmer place. It was then that, his medical missionary friends suggested he go to Korea. So, Allen wrote to the Mission Board in New York stating that there were no doctors in Korea and foreign legations and customs offices were in urgent need of doctors and also that he wished to go to Korea if the board would grant him to do so.[132]

While the board in New York gave him the green light, and Allen departed for Korea while leaving his wife in Shanghai. He arrived at Jemulpo on September 20, 1884. Thus, in the four-mille nnium Korean history, Allen arrived in Korea as the first Protestant missionary (albeit his religious status had to remain hidden) and the era of Protestant missions commenced in Korea. Two days after arriving at Jemulpo, he rode a donkey with a Chinese language teacher that came with him from Shanghai and entered Seoul. He then met the U.S. minister Lucius Foote at the U.S. legation, and Foote appointed Allen as an unpaid doctor for the

---

132 H. N. Allen to F. F. Ellinwood, Shanghai, June 9, 1884, PHS.

U.S. legation. This was the most suitable job for him given the circumstance that no open missionary activities could be carried out. This office also gave him a legitimate reason to reside in Korea. Later on when Foote was granted an audience with King Gojong, he introduced Allen as a doctor belonging to the legation.

In the following month, Allen went to Shanghai and brought his family back to move into a new home in Seoul. Allen did not just serve as a doctor for the U.S. legation but day-by-day he was on a busy schedule, attending to various foreign residents as well as the British and other legations. He also held prayer meetings and services on a daily basis. Then, Korea Royal Court dramatically realized Allen's importance when the Kapsin-Jungby on(Coup d'Etat of 1884) took place in December 1884. This was one of the key transitions in the Protestant Church in Korea; Underwood once referred to it as God's "providentially just previous to the emeute of 1884."[133]

At that time, the Royal Court of Korea was divided by a power struggle between the Conservatives and the Progressives. The Progressives planned a drastic conspiracy against the Conservatives. In December 1884, a banquet was planned in celebration of the opening of the new Postal Administration that would introduce the modern postal system to Korea for the first time. The Progressives conspired to take this opportunity to kill all the Conservatives, structure a new cabinet and pave the way for liberal politics. At

---

133 Horace G. Underwood, *The Call of Korea, Political-Social-Religious* (New York: Fleming H. Revell, 1908), 100.

the height of the evening banquet on December 4, they shouted that the building was on fire and indiscriminately killed the Conservatives as they rushed out one by one. At this time, Young Ik Min, the head of the Conservatives and also Queen Min's nephew, was stabbed with daggers at seven points. He was at the verge of losing his life as his major vessels were cut and his body was severely wounded. The U.S. minister Foote and the customs adviser S.A. Möllendorf gave Young Ik Min a first-aid treatment and carried him to Möllendorf's home, while Allen was summoned for immediate attendance.

In the meantime Allen was on his way, several royal Oriental medical doctors attempted to save Min's life, but Oriental medicine was not effective for cut vessels and body wounds. Finally Allen arrived. At a glance Allen was able to assess the severity of Min's condition. Allen hesitated for a minute. Should he fail to save this patient's life, he certainly had to bear the heavy responsibility of being accountable for Min's life. At the same time, it was not a doctor's duty to say no to any patient. He took courage and began treating Min. He used silk strings to sew together the cut and torn parts of the body and applied medicine on the wounds. With God's boundless grace, Allen's treatments yielded dramatic effects, and Young Ik Min was fully recovered in a short period of time. Young Ik Min later said to Allen, "Our people think you are a great doctor, they won't believe you came from America, but think you dropped down from Heaven for this occasion."[134]

---

134 H. N. Allen to F. F. Ellinwood, February 4, 1885, PHS.

This incident served as an opportunity for Allen to introduce Western medicine to royal officials and high-level officials; the excellence of Western technology was demonstrated to the people. Moreover, Allen earned proximity to the Court. Soon Allen was appointed as King Gojong's physician, and the King also appointed him to the office of 'Champan'(vice minister) as a reward for saving Young Ik Min. Allen was awarded with the office of 'Gasu-hndaebu' (jeong 2pum-second level in the cabinet).[135] This was a "very material advantage to out whole work."[136] to the Protestant missionary work that would follow.

Being a doctor, Allen had thought of opening a hospital from the beginning, and he decided that the time had come for him to obtain a royal permission for the work. Therefore, Allen submitted a letter to the Government through the U.S. minister G.C. Foulk in the Spring of 1885, explaining the necessity for a hospital. The King and the government officials had no reason to oppose Allen's request since they were already well aware of Allen's excellent medical skills and his love for Koreans. The Government accepted Allen's petition with no problem.

As a result, Allen opened a clinic named "Gwanghyewon" on April 9, 1885. Its name signified Allen's aim to bestow grace

---

135 Allen was rewarded "Gasundaeboo" *Allen's Diary*, October 25, 1886. *Seungjeongwonilgee* (Diary of Seungjeongwon) King Kojong Year of 23, Sep. 27.

136 O. R. Avison, "History of the Medical Work in Korea, Under the Mission of the Presbyterian Church in the U.S.A. from 1884 to 1909," *Quarto Centennial Papers, read before the Korea Mission of the Presbyterian Church in the U.S.A. at the Annual Meeting in Pyeng Yang: 1909*, 31.

on all the people. The venue was the home of Young Sik Hong who was beaten to death during the Postal Administration Incident. The Government assigned a few officials to this clinic and about two weeks after its opening its door, on April 23, Gwangyewon was renamed "Jejungwon," which meant "saving many people." It was only natural that Underwood started working here when he arrived as the first Protestant minister in Korea because freedom was not granted for any missionary work yet. Consequently, Jejungwon served as a waiting place for newly arriving missionaries and also a legitimate hiding and acting place when there was no religious freedom. God's abundant love for Korea is fully reflected on the fact that Jejungwon later became the Severance Hospital, along with the Yonhee College of Medicine, would the invaluable fore leader of medicine in modern Korea.

3. Horace G. Underwood Arrives

The first ordained pastor missionary to set foot in Korea was Horace G. Underwood. Underwood was born in London, England, in July 1859 as the fourth child of six brothers and sisters between John and Elizabeth Underwood. His father John was a chemist and inventor. He invented a safety check that could not be altered after being written and a carbon paper that could be used up to 75 times. He also improved the ribbon of the type writer.[137] John was a devout Christian and his faith had an absolute influence

---

137 Lillias Underwood, *Underwood of Korea* (New York: Fleming H. Revell, 1918), 25.

over his children. Horace Underwood also grew up learning the deep meanings of his faith from his father. When Horace Underwood was six years old, his mother died and his stepmother raised him. For a while he studied in France with his elder brother Fred, but his entire family eventually moved to the New World after his father was betrayed by a partner and was forced to close the business. The family moved to the United States and settled down at New Durham in New Jersey, when Horace was twelve years old. There the family attended a Dutch Reformed Church.

Recalling Underwood's childhood ambitions of becoming a pastor and missionary, his father enrolled him in New York University in 1877 in order to provide him with a college education and later send him to a seminary. As his family was not wealthy by any terms, he had to walk daily to his university, which was about 12 kilometers (7.5 miles) away from home.

In 1881, the year of his father's death, Underwood graduated from New York University and enrolled in New Brunswick Seminary of the Dutch Reformed Church. While at the seminary, he slept no more than five hours every night and invested the remaining 19 hours in studies and various religious activities.[138] Such vigorous drive in his life continued on even when he serve as a missionary in Korea and it facilitate as one of the reasons for his relatively early death. When he was in his second year at the seminary, the Korean-American Treaty was signed. Underwood happened to read an article on this, which one of his classmates had cut

138 *Ibid.*, 27.

out from a newspaper and posted on the classroom wall. This was the first moment when Underwood was introduced to the country of his destiny.

In October 1883, Underwood attended the United States Theological Seminary Alliance Conference at Hartford in Connecticut where he was deeply inspired by many great speakers and was further determined to become a missionary. At the Conference, he also met Henry Appenzeller, who would go to Korea on the same ship as Underwood and become a lifetime friend.

Underwood graduated from the seminary in the spring of 1884, and shortly after, he also received his Masters in Literature from New York University. In November of the same year, he was ordained as a pastor at the Classis of New Brunswick of the Dutch Reformed Church. Several churches invited him for pastoral ministry, but he had to turn them down and explore opportunities to serve as a missionary. When Horace was still at the seminary, Rev. Albert Altmann, a missionary in Japan at that time, had once visited Underwood's seminary and challenged the students to serve as missionaries for the 1.3 million dying souls in Korea.[139] At that time, Underwood was not bothered much because he was determined to be a missionary to India. But when he began exploring opportunities to go out as a missionary, he learned that no missionary work had started in Korea because there were no volunteers. At that moment, he heard a voice within his heart, "Why not go yourself?"[140]

---

139 *Ibid.*, 34.

So he went to the Dutch Reformed Church where he was associated with and undertook two separate instances to indicate his desire to serve as a missionary to Korea. But the Denomination Board replied that the church was unable to pioneer a new mission field due to lack of resources. So he visited the Northern Presbyterian Church twice and asked them to send him to Korea. They, too, answered that it was not possible. But fortunately, around the same time McWilliams pledged mission funds, and the Northern Presbyterian Church officially appointed Underwood as a missionary to Korea in July 1884.

The 25-year-old Underwood departed from San Francisco in December 1884, and arrived in Yokohama, Japan in January 1885 where he was given a warm welcome by Northern Presbyterian missionaries there. While waiting for ships bound for Korea, he started learning the Korean language from Koreans studying there. Finally, there was a ship sailing to Korea. Underwood got on the ship, and arrived at Jemulpo on Easter, April 5, 1885. Also aboard this ship were Appenzeller, whom Underwood had met earlier at the United States Theological Seminary Alliance Conference, and his wife who were sent by the Northern Methodist Church of the United States. As a result, the Appenzellers and Underwood set foot in Korea simultaneously. In other words, Presbyterian and Methodist missionaries arrived in Korea on the same day. Having arrived at Jemulpo, Rev. Appenzeller recorded of this day

---

140 H. G. Underwood, "Reminiscences," In *Quarto Centennial Papers* (1909), 98-99.

with the following words:

> We came here on Easter. May He who on that day burst
> asunder the bars of death, break the bands that bind this
> people, and bring them to the light and liberty of God's
> children.[141]

Foulk,[142] the United States Chargé d'Affaires in Korea approved
Underwood's entry to the country but turned the Appenzellers
back. This was not only because Mrs. Appenzeller was pregnant,
but also because the political situation was very much unstable
due to the aftermath of the 'Kapsin Jungbyon'(Coup d'Etat of
1884) that had taken place just a few months ago. Given the unpre-
dictable political situation, Foulk decided that it was not safe for
a foreign woman to enter the country and instead ordered them
to return to Japan. Left with no choice, the Appenzellers returned
to Japan, and Underwood entered Seoul alone after spending two
days at Jemulpo. As a result, a permanent Protestant minister finally
arrived in Korea, and the era of Protestant missions was officially
started.

Underwood was received warmly by Allen, and he began his
first ministry by working at Jejungwon which Allen had just opened.
About two months after returning to Japan, the Appenzellers came

---

141 *The Annual Report of the Missionary Society of the Methodist Episcopal Church*
(1885), 237.
142 The first U.S. Minister L. Foote was back in the U.S., and G. C. Foulk,
who escorted the diplomatic mission to the U.S. back to Korea, was
serving as the chargé d'affaires.

back to Korea again. Just a month and a half before his arrival, Scranton, a Methodist pastor and doctor, had arrived in May 1885, and Scranton's mother, Mary Scranton, and the Appenzellers arrived in June. The Northern Presbyterian medical missionary J. W. Heron, who had been learning the language in Japan, also arrived in Korea at this time and started working at Allen's Jejungwon. As there was no freedom of missionary work and no direct evangelism could be carried out in Korea at the time, it was truly God's divine providence to allow the missionary work to start through medical missions.

Chapter 3

Activities of Missionaries

1. Medical Missions

Activities that missionaries undertake in mission fields could be categorized into three areas. The first is evangelization, the second civilization and the third modernization. In terms of missiological theory, missionaries emphasized evangelization only at times.[143] However, evangelization to uncivilized and underdeveloped peoples always required efforts of civilization and modernization. As seen in the Christian history of Korea, medical and educational services, which represent civilization and modernization as a whole, prove to be most useful tools when the freedom of evangelization is not fully granted. We discussed in earlier chapters that Allen

---

[143] This theory was advocated by various mission theorists, including Rufus Anderson (1796-1880). He was a Congregationalist pastor and worked at the American Board of Commissioners for Foreign Missions (ABCFM) as an assistant secretary.

treated Young Ik Min during the Kapsin Jungbyon(Postal Adminis
tration Incident) and opened Jejungwon. Protestant mission work
in Korea started with the medical service as Underwood, Heron
and the Methodist medical missionary and pastor Scranton joined
Allen here at Jejungwon.

Jejungwon was initially set up in the modified living room of
Young Sik Hong's home and later it moved to Gurigae in 1887
with the support from Northern Presbyterian Church. Later in 1900,
L.H.Severance, a businessman in Cleveland, Ohio, donated a large
sum (15,000 dollars), which was used for purchasing a plot of
land just outside South Gate in front of Seoul Station. This moved
Jejungwon into a new modern building constructed on that plot.

Medical mission work accompanied many difficulties. While
the clinic was open to everyone in need, patients continued to
crowd it. At the beginning Allen had to look after the patients
all alone without a nurse or helper. Fortunately Underwood was
able to help in the pharmacy and Heron and Scranton gave extra
helping hands, but medicines and medical supplies were simply
insufficient. Contagious diseases would break out whenever the
weather became warmer. Virtually untrained in matters of hygiene,
Koreans would drink water without boiling even in the summer
and it was common for an entire family or a village to be wiped
out by contagious diseases.

After helping out at Jejungwon for some time, Scranton parted
with it in September 1885 and started a private clinic at his residence
in Jeong-dong. This clinic too became crowded quickly, forcing

him to secure a new building in June the following year, and open a full-scale hospital with a new name "Sibyeongwon(Si hospital)."[144] This hospital consequently moved to Sang-dong inside South Gate, where many poor people were given the benefits of quality medical services.

Treating patients, however, posed another problem. The problem was about treating female patients. The Korean society at that time was governed by traditional Confucius values, one of which dictates that boys and girls of ages older than 7 must not sit next to each other. Given the cultural context, it was unacceptable for women to come to clinics crowded by men, and it was quite problematic for male doctors to touch and treat female patients. This called for a need of female doctors and women-only clinics. Fortunately, A. Ellers, a female doctor sent by Northern Presbyterian Church, arrived in 1886 and was given the "task of overseeing all important matters pertaining to women of all classes."[145] One point we must not overlook is the term "regardless of status." This clearly displays the mission policy of Northern Presbyterian Church. This means that missions must not be dictated by certain class of people and that status or class should not be a problem in any manner. Thus, a new phase in Protestant missions began as medical services and evangelization efforts were expanded to women, who were among the many oppressed and neglected low

144 *The Annual Report, Methodist Episcopal Church, North, for 1886,* 268.
145 *The Annual Report of the Board of the Foreign Missions of the Presbyterian Church, U.S.A., 1887,* 155. (hereinafter shorted as The Annual Report, Presbyterian Church, North).

class members of the society. Immediately upon her arrival, Ellers became the Queen's physician and served as a doctor for high-class ladies. In addition, a women's section was installed in Jejungwon, where Ellers served as the Chief of Women's Section and treated many female patients.[146]

There was also a women-only hospital. After spending some-time at Sibyeongwon since October 1887, M. Howard opened a women-only hospital, "Boguyeogwan," in the following year in Jeong-dong and concentrated in treating of women.[147] More and more clinics were established in Seoul, namely in Dongdaemun(the East Gate), Aeogae outside Suhdaemun(the West Gate), and Mohwa-gwan. The Anglican Church also later bought a piece of land in Nak-dong in South of Seoul and built Nakdong Hospital. As medical missionaries increased in number, many Christian hospitals were established across the peninsula and became important venues of evangelization activities and mission works.

2. Educational Projects

(1) Underwood's Orphanage

In almost every mission field, medical services and educational projects go hand in hand for securing the bridgehead for mission works in the initial stage. Although hospitals and schools were once excluded from mission works in accordance to Rufus Ande-

---

146 Ibid.
147 The Annual Report, Methodist Episcopal Church, North, for 1888, 340-341.

rson's missiological theory, these two arms of activities are undoubtedly the paramount of initial mission works and they served as excellent tool of evangelization in themselves. These two forms of ministries played crucial roles in Korea as well. While medical services are targeted at the sick only, education is meant for all children and even less learned adults. By design, education is more inclusive and facilitates more direct contact points for evangelization as compared to medical services.

Just before the missionaries began education works, there already a Western-style school in Korea. Called Yugyounggongwon, this school was established in 1883 and was taught by T. E. Halifax as ordered by King Gojong. In the spring of 1885, King Gojong requested the U.S. inspector of education, General John Eaton, for three talented teachers. In response to this, three students at Union Theological Seminary, New York, G. W. Gilmore, D. A. Bunker, and H. B. Hulbert came to Korea and began teaching here. However, they witnessed the school being seriously manipulated by corrupted practices of government officials, eventually resigning from the school and returning to their homes. In spite of this, Bunker and Hulbert later came to Korea again as Methodist missionaries.

Just around the time Protestant missions began in Korea, the only effective institutes of elementary education in Korea were nothing more than the Suhdang (village schoolhouses). These Suhdangs were truly basic in their operation, only teaching Chinese writings. Moreover, these schoolhouses were open to children of wealthy

Yangban(Nobility) families; poor children were essentially deprive
d of any opportunity for education. Underwood was the first missionary to undertake education with a modern school system. As soon
as arriving in Korea, he attentively watched the neglected orphans
on the street. As he began housing them one by one, he was
soon running an orphanage. In February 1886, Underwood obtained
a government permit for accommodating and teaching orphans
in a small house. People began spreading weird rumors like Underwood was raising the children only to eat them up when they
are fully grown or Underwood was going to sell them out as
slaves. Nevertheless Underwood is seen describing to his friend
Hulbert his ambition for the orphanage to expand into a university
and theological seminary.[148] This orphanage was initially called
by various names like "Underwood Hakdang,"(school) "Yesugio
Hakdang"(1891) and "Minnoa Hakdang"(1893), and it was later
called 'Gyeongsin School"(1905), the predecessor of the present
Gyeongsin Middle and High School. However, as the missionary
board adopted the Nevius Method and emphasized the concept
of self-support, the orphanage had to be suspended because the
all-providing orphanage was deemed to be contradicting the Nevius
Method. Instead, the orphanage was converted into a vocational
school where students could study and earn a living by working.

---

148 Lillias Underwood, *Underwood of Korea*, 44-45.

(2) Ewhahakdang (Girls-school)

The very first modern girl's school in Korea was founded by Mary F. Scranton, who established Ewhahakdang. After arriving in Korea in June 1885, Mary bought about two dozen thatched cottages and empty plots of land near the Methodist Mission Head quarters in Jeong-dong, Seoul, and started building "Yeoja (girls) Hakdang" and "Bunyeowon." (center for women).[149] When these buildings were completed in November 1886, she opened the first women's school. Mary describes the situation at that time in the following manner.

School work was commenced in the house of Dr. Stanton six months previous to the removal to the new Home. It began with one scholar. She was the concubine of an official who was desirous his wife should learn English, with the hope that she might sometime become interpreter for the Queen. She remained with us only about three months. The first permanent pupil came in June, 1886, one month later than Mrs. Kim. Poverty unquestionably brought the girl to us, but not many days had passed before the mother felt it better to brave poverty rather than trust her child to a foreigner. The second pupil was a little waif who, with her sick mother, was picked up out by the city wall by Dr. Scranton and taken first to his hospital for treatment.

149 Mary Scranton, "Woman's Work in Korea," *The Korean Repository* (January 1896), 4.

Koreans watched these girls very closely. As they did not find them unhappy or ill treated, other mothers gradually gained little confidence, and at the time of removal to the Home on the hill, the school members four, and the following January we counted seven.[150]

On the purpose of this school, G. W. Gilmore stated, "It is to educate them as exemplary housewives in their place of daily living and to train them as messengers of the Way of the Cross to their relatives and friends."[151] It can be seen here that this school's ultimate purpose is to train messengers of the Way of the Cross and that this is indeed a school with a Christian heart. Scranton also pointed out this important truth about the school's purpose.

We are not going to propose that the Korean young girls follow the foreign life style, or style of clothes. It is an misunderstanding that we are going to totally change them. We only hope that they become better Koreans. We also hope that they are proud of being Koreans, and Korea will be better country through Christ and His teachings.[152]

Here, the school's purpose of "producing Korean leaders for

---

150 *Ibid.*, 4-5.
151 G. W. Gilmore, *Korea from Its Capital* (Philadelphia: Presbyterian Board of Publication and Sabbath School Work, 1892), 300.
152 *The Gospel in All Lands for 1888*, 373.

Koreans" is clearly displayed. They made significant efforts in retaining Korean tradition and culture in terms of lifestyle and clothing.

Taking the name of Ewha (pear blossom) that represented the flower of Chosun(Korea) Dynasty, Queen Min named this school "Ewhahakdang." Thus was the beginning of Ewha Girls' Middle and High Schools and Ewha Women's University which trained and produced so many women leaders in the modern history of Korea.

(3) Baejaehakdang(Boys-school)

Unlike Underwood who started working at Jejungwon, Appenzeller's heart was on education. He showed extraordinary interest in English education which we found to be most needed in Korea at that time. In fact, this was one of the easiest tasks he could get himself involved. He sent a letter through Chargé d'Affaires Foulk to the Korean Government, requesting permission for setting up an English school. The Government acceded to this request, allowing a school to open in June 1886 with 6 students. The number increased and there were 20 students by October. King Gojong bestowed a name to this school in 1887. He named it "Baejaehakdang" for the meaning of training many good leaders.[153] In the same year, an independent school building was constructed with a chapel, four classrooms, a library, a principal's office, and a technical

---

153 *Baejaesa* (History of Baejae) (Baejae Middle School and High School, 1955), 65.

section where they taught subjects of technology. This school also mandated its students to pay tuitions instead of studying for free of charge. Since 1888, a self-help section was set up in the school, encouraging students to earn money through various activities such as guarding the school or cleaning the school so that they could study on their own living. It is a well-known fact that this school later became the present Baejae Middle School and High School.[154]

3. Evangelization Ministries

(1) Master Noh, the First Baptized Believer

At any time, medical services and educational projects were no more than complementary support to evangelization ministries. Missionaries came to Korea for no other purpose but to evangelize the country. Evangelism was definitely the first and the last goal of the missionaries. However, freedom of evangelization non-existent in Korea and it was not possible for them to preach openly. Nevertheless, we know that God works even when times people think it is impossible.

The first person to be baptized by missionaries in Korea was Choon Kyong Noh, otherwise better known as Master Noh. Living just outside Seoul, he was informed about Christianity through some documents boycotting Christianity. With his much aroused curiosity about Christianity, he visited Allen's language teacher

---

154 *The Annual Report, Methodist Episcopal Church, North, for 1885*, 239, *for 1886*, 267, 313.

to find out more about the religion. Then, in Allen's study room, he spotted the Gospel of Mark and the Gospel of Luke, both written in Chinese characters, and took them home without permission. While reading the books, he understood more of the Christian truth. Determined to deepen his understanding, Noh went to study the Bible with Underwood, borrowed the Bible and doctrine books, and even participated in worship services for foreigners.[155]

Soon, he made up his mind to accept Jesus as his Savior. After completing the baptism formula, he was baptized by Underwood on the Sunday afternoon of July 18, 1886. He was the very first baptized Protestant believer in Korea. His baptism was a direct violation of the national law. If it were to be known to the Royal Court, his life would be taken away and even Underwood could be punished for having baptized him. Nevertheless, Master Noh put his life at stake and got baptized. Underwood, too, was determined to face whatever pain and fear in doing the will of God.[156] This was indeed an action of faith and determination that overcame the fear of death.

In the next spring, Sang Yoon Suh brought his younger brother Gyeong Jo and two other young men from Sollae, Hwanghae Province, to Seoul and asked Underwood to baptize them. Underwood explained to them that baptism is a violation of the national law and it could cost them their lives. But they were already prepared and they insisted him to baptize them. Thus, Underwood had the

155 Underwood's letter from Seoul dated July 29, 1886, *The Foreign Missionary* XLV-5 (October 1886), 223-224.
156 H. G. Underwood to F. F. Ellinwood, July 9, 1889, PHS.

physically fit Yugyounggongwon teacher H. Hulbert to guard the gate and performed the baptismal ceremony in the presence of many missionaries. Allen advised that the baptism should be postponed in fear of conflict with the Korean Government, but Underwood was persistent in saying, "······and as a simple follower of Christ dare not deny it them. I can find no warrant for such action either in the history of missions, in the story of the acts of the Apostles or in the teachings of Christ."[157] Underwood's calling for missions was simply undisturbed. Although Allen's view of respecting the boundaries of the national law was important, Underwood's unrelenting attitude of going ahead with baptism even by putting his own life at stake for violation of the national law remains as our example of the martyrs in the history of the church. Following this incident, the number of baptized Korean Protestant believers increased slowly but steadily.

(2) Establishment of the First Church, Jeongdong Church (later Saemunan Church)

Underwood performed the first baptism ceremony in Korea just after a year of staying in Korea. Then just one more year later, in 1887, he is seen establishing the first organized church in Korea. Taking 14 believers, Underwood organized a church with two elders on September 27, 1887. Initially named "Jeongdong Church," it relocated to Saemunan(inside the new gate) later and was thus

---

157 H. G. Underwood to H. N. Allen, January 27, 1886: copy to F. F. Ellinwood, PHS.

renamed "Saemunan Church."[158] The founding church members were not direct results of the missionaries' evangelization efforts. They were those who read the Gospels as supplied by colporteurs and believed in Jesus even before Underwood arrived in Korea. They were baptized by Underwood much later when he arrived. Thus, this church was essentially an indigenous church established by Koreans themselves. It was also the first organized church in Korea with two appointed elders.[159] The church experienced a steady growth; the number reached 25 by end of the first year.

(3) Bible Translation Work

One of the first things a missionary undertakes upon arrival at a mission field is Bible translation. Interestingly, the Bible was already available in Hangeul(native Korean letters) when the missionaries arrived in Korea and it gave them a head start in their ministries. However, previously translated Korean Bibles were found to contain many translation errors and inappropriate terminology. It was also Underwood who was first to undertake Bible translation work in Korea. Underwood was left with no choice but to translate the Bible from the scratch again because the previously translated versions were "The version⋯⋯so full of Chinese terms, so badly spelt and badly printed."[160]

---

158 H. G. Underwood to F. F. Ellinwood, September 27, October 7, 1887, PHS.

159 J. Ross, "The Christian Dawn in Korea," *The Missionary Review of the World* III-4 (April 1890), 247.

160 H. G. Underwood to F. F. Ellinwood, November 15, 1905, PHS.

Underwood and Appenzeller worked alongside with their language teachers to translate the Gospel of Mark. The first translation draft was completed and published in 1881.

While Underwood was staying in Japan for printing the newly translated Gospel of Mark, the Chairman of Bible Translation Committee J. C. Hepburn advised him to organize a Bible Translation Committee for translating the entire Bible. Upon his return to Korea, Underwood suggested to Methodist Mission to organize a Bible Translation Committee. As a result, the Committee for Translating the Bible into the Korean Language was established in 1887. Underwood, Appenzeller, and Scranton were nominated as committee members, and Underwood was selected as the chairman. Underwood continued to serve as the chairman of the committee until his death in 1916.[161] It is then no wonder to recognize Underwood as the single greatest contributor to translation of Hangeul Bible. This committee was restructured and new members were added to it in 1893. It was accordingly renamed the Permanent Executive Bible Committee.

The Bible translation work was to go through careful and stringent deliberation processes: first, missionaries and helpers were to translate together; second, the work was to be shown to other translators for accommodating their opinions; third, yet another group of translators were to read the work and present their opinions; and last, the committee were to read each verse, open discussion on it, decide by vote if there are objections, and confirm the translati-

---

161 Lillias Underwood, *Underwood of Korea*, 48.

on.[162] With the persevering work of the translation committee, the complete New Testament was translated and published in 1900. A service of commemoration and thanksgiving for the newly translated New Testament was held in Jeongdong Methodist Church with represe-ntatives from all mission agencies and organizations.[163]

Following the completion of the New Testament, the translation committee undertook the work of translating the Old Testament. Compared to the New Testament, the Old Testament was much lengthier. Further dampened by the busy schedule of the translation committee members, the progress was very slow. Nevertheless, their dedication and sacrifice saw the completion of the Old Testament in 1910, and the complete Korean Old Testament and New Testament was published as a single volume in the following year. Finally, the complete Word of God was put into the hands of Koreans in their own tongue. Completion of the Bible translation was indeed a direct result of God's divine grace and sacrifices of the translators. Regarding the publication of the entire Bible in Korean, Presbyterian Mission sent the following report to the United States.

It will be duly written that the year of 1911 is the year of accomplishment of the Bible [both translation and publication]. This year is the 301st anniversary of the King

---

162 W. D. Reynolds, "Bible Translation in Korea," *The Korean Repository* (1896), 471.

163 W. F. Bull, "Interesting Meeting in Korea," *The Missionary* (February 1901), 78.

James Version, but the first year of the Korean Bible publication. It is so helpful for the students of the Bible classes. The Seoul Mission Station gives praise to three persons for this job: Underwood, Gale, and Pieters.[164]

This version of Korean Bible was revised cover to cover in 1937. This revised version is called the Revised Korean Version, and the earlier version is called the Original Korean Version.

(4) Literature and Hymnals

The primary publication for Christianity is of course the Bible. But if we were to choose another essential publication for worship and personal devotion, it is definitely the hymnals. As the Bible was published and distributed across the country, there was an increased need for hymnals. Methodist missionaries G. H. Jones and L. C. Rothweiler were among the first to identify this need and publish a hymnal. They edited and published *Chanmiga* in 1892. Presbyterian Mission and Methodist Mission commissioned the Methodist missionary Jones and the Presbyterian missionary Underwood to edit a hymnal that was to be used commonly for both mission boards. But Jones returned to the States for a furlough soon after the job assignment, and thus Underwood had to continue the work alone. Despite the difficulty, Underwood persevered and published *Chanyangga* in 1893. This was the first hymnal to contain

---

164 *The Report of the Korean Mission of the PCUSA to the Annual Meeting (1911)*, 6.

4-part scores.[165] However, Presbyterian Mission decided that they could not take it as an official hymnal because the work was done completely by Underwood alone. While Underwood's hymnal was put to an unofficial use for some time, in 1895, the Presbyterian missionary G. Lee and the lady M. H. Gifford edited and published *Chansuhngsi*. Thus Underwood's *Chanyangga* was used in Seoul and *Chansuhngsi* in Pyeongan Province. Then in 1902, the Presbyterian Council authorized *Chansuhngsi* as the official Presbyterian Hymnal.

On the other hand, the Methodist Church updated the 1892 version of *Chanmiga* and put it into official use in 1895. Chi Ho Yoon was the first Korean to compile and publish *Chanmiga* independently. It is interesting to note that his *Chanmiga* contained the present national anthem of Korea Aegukga (Country-love-song) for which he wrote the lyrics. It is a great misconception that the writer of lyrics for Aegukga remains unknown. Lyrics of Aegukga was written by Chi Ho Yoon.[166] This is one indication of the great patriotism the church had at that time. While different denominations used their own hymnals that differed from one another, people began to suggest that one common hymnal be used across all denominations. Thus, mission agencies in Korea at that time organized "Evangelical Mission Council in Korea" in 1905 and published

---

165 Young Jae Han, *Hanguk Suhngsuh Chansongga 100Yon* (100 Years of Korean Bibles and Hymnals) (Christian Publishing Co., 1987), 65.

166 A photograph of the verses 1 to 4 of the *Aegukga* in Yoon's handwriting with the note "Words by Chi Ho Yoon, 1907" is contained in *Jeongdongjeilgiohoeui Yeoksa, 1885-1990* (History of Jeongdong First Church, 1885-1990) (1992), 167.

Chansongga in 1908 as a joint publication between the Presbyterian and Methodist. This hymnal was commonly used by the two denominations until in the 1930's, when the Presbyterian church and the Methodist church published their own *Sinpyeonchansongga* and *Sinjeongchansongga* respectively.

Smaller denominations published and used their own hymnals. For instance, the Anglican church published *Suhonghoesongga* in 1903 and *Cheondochansa* in 1904. The Salvation Army published *Gusegunga* in 1908. Also, Oriental Mission, the predecessor of Holiness Church, published *Bogeumga* in 1911 and *Buheungsuhngga* in 1913. Churches also edited and published newspapers and magazines in addition to the Bibles and hymnals.[167] While such publication activities were carried out for Christian evangelization purposes, they contributed greatly to development of Korean literature. Among other things, missionaries showed their interest in the publication of newspapers first. The Presbyterian church and the Methodist church printed their first newspapers in 1897. Appenzeller published the first Methodist issue of *The Christian Advocate* in February, and Underwood published the first Presbyterian issue of *The Christian News* in April. While these weekly papers were designed to propag-ate the Christian truth, they were also intended to help develop the backward Korean economy through articles and information about global news, systems, civilization and customs of developed

---

167 For information on newspapers and magazines of the Korean Church, see Chun Byeong Yoon, *Hanggukkidokggiosinmun, Japji 100Yonsa* (100 Years of Christian Newspapers and Magazines in Korea) (Korea Christian Publishing, 1984).

countries, farming techniques for farmers, industrial technologies, and so on. Underwood's *The Christian News* was also delivered to royal palaces. When King Gojong read it, he declared that it would be good for many officials to read it. The Government subscribed to about 500 copies of *The Christian News* for officials to read it.[168]

The independent newspapers by the Presbyterian church and the Methodist church were merged and published as a unified newspaper *The Christian News* in July 1905 with formation of Mission Association Council. The Catholic church published *Gyeonghyangsinmun* and the Salvation Army published *Gusesinmun*.

Magazines were published as well. The first was an English magazine *The Korean Repository* published in 1892 by a Methodist missionary F. Ohlinger. This magazine carried many articles on Korea including her history and geography; it was an important tool for exposing the hidden treasures of Korea. This magazine was in print until 1898. Again in 1901, a Methodist missionary Hulbert published *The Korea Review* and, in the same year, a Presbyterian missionary C. C. Vinton published *The Korea Field*. In 1904, South Methodist Church and North Methodist Church jointly published *The Korea Methodist*. Then in the following year, the Presbyterian Church and the Methodist Church worked jointly to merge their *The Korea Field* and *The Korea Methodist* into *The Korea Mission Field*.[169] This magazine continued to be publi-

---

168 *The Annual Report, Presbyterian Church, North, for 1898*, 161.
169 Editorial, *The Korea Mission Field* (January 1907), 9.

shed until 1941, when the Japanese expelled missionaries out of Korea. Though it was in English, it carried a great deal of useful information such as the context of mission works in Korea and reports of missionaries and it presents a highly valuable tool for studying the initial stage of the history of the Church in Korea.

The first Korean magazine was *Theological Review* published by a Methodist missionary G. Jones in 1900.[170] This magazine also carried Christian news and introduction to theology as an excellent religious teaching material for believers. A Presbyterian missionary C. Vinton published *Yesugiosuhhoebo*(the Bulletin of the Christian Literature Society) in 1904 and Jeongdong Methodist Church published *Suhnggyeonggangronwolbo*(Lecture on the Bible) in 1906. In 1908, the Anglican Church published *Jonggyosuhnggi-ohoewolbo*(Bulletin of the Holy Church).

The first single volume books written in Hangeul(Korean) were *Yesusuhnggyomundap*(Questions and Answers on Christitnity) and *Yesusuhnggyoyoryeong*(Digest on the Christianity) which were published by Rev. Ross in Manchuria. First books printed within Korea include Underwood's *Sokjoejido*(Doctrine on the Redemtion) and Appenzeller's *Suhnggyochwaryo*(Digest on Christianity) in 1889. Christian Single volume titles were also published by Koreans, earlier ones including Jeong Hoo Hong's *Childeuk*(Seven Virtures) in 1895, Byeong Sun Noh's *Pahokjinsyeonron*(Overcoming Temptation and Encouriging the Goodness) in 1897, Sun Joo Kil's *Haetaron*

---

170 *Official Minutes of the Annual Meeting for Methodist Episcopal Church, North, 1901,* 24.

(On Idleness) in 1904, and Byeng Hun Choi's *Yesutyeonjuryanggi-obyeonron* (Comparing between the Roman Catholic Church and the Protestant Church) in 1909. At this time, there were few books written by Koreans because the Christian faith was still not widely preached across Korea, there were few men who could write books, and the Korean Church had not yet grown sufficiently enough to allow meaningful religious writings by Koreans.

4. Coming to Korea of Various Mission Boards

(1) Anglican Church

Following the arrival of missionaries from Northern Presbyterian Church and Northern Methodist Church of the United States of America, missionaries from many other mission organizations began to set foot in Korea. One of the first to do so was the Church of England, or Anglican Church.[171] Since the Britain-Korea trade agreement in 1884, the United Kingdom was highly interested in missions in Korea and was looking for the right moment. The year after the agreement, the Church Missionary Society, an Anglican mission organization in China, sent two Chinese missionaries to Busan. Bishop J. H. Wolfe, who had been in charge of Anglican churches in China and Japan, visited the Chinese missionaries in Korea, and then reported the urgency of missions in Korea to the Archbishop of Canterbury. The archbishop responded to this

---

171 Nak Jun Paik, *Hangukgaesingiosa* (History of the Protestant Church in Korea), 194-196.

by sending C. J. Corfe to Korea as her first Anglican bishop in 1889.[172] Thus the Anglican missions in Korea began as Bishop Corfe, M. N. Trollope, and a few others landed at Jemulpo in September 1890 with support from the Society for Propagation of the Gospel in Foreign Parts.

(2) Presbyterian Church of Victoria, Australia

After the arrival of the Anglican Church, the next organization to embark on missions in Korea was the Presbyterian Church of Victoria from the commonwealth Australia. Although small in size, this church was already actively involved in overseas missions. The Anglican bishop Wolfe's letter to England about the urgency of missions in Korea was also made known to Australia and thus this church burned with passion for Korea. Rev. J. H. Davies' church in Melbourne and affiliated churches in the region collaborated in sending him and his younger sister Mary as missionaries to Korea, and thus Davies arrived in Korea as the first Australian missionary in October 1889.[173]

Davies was born in Melbourne, Victoria in 1857, where he completed his undergraduate and graduate studies in literature major.

---

172 The Anglican Church in Korea was placed under the direct jurisdiction of Canterbury, England, until April 16, 1993, when the Archbishop of Canterbury Carey declared the independence of the Korean province and inaugurated Seong Soo Kim as the first Korean primate at the Grand Seoul Church. The Anglican Church in Korea now has about 100 churches and 200 priests and friars.

173 Nak Jun Paik, *Hangukgaesingiosa* (History of the Protestant Church in Korea), 196-197.

While continuing his education is law, he changed his mind and went to Edinburgh, England, to study theology. He then went to India to help out his missionary sister there but he had to return home due to deteriorating health. At home, he was running his own elementary school, when he read the letter calling for missionaries to Korea and he made his way there.

The Davies missionaries arrived in Korea in October 1889 and were received by American missionaries. Underwood once commented Davies as "······highly-gifted and holy man, one of the most invaluable missionaries who ever came to Korea······"[174] In order to search for areas to work in Korea, Davies decided to avoid Seoul and Northwestern regions where there were already many missionaries but instead focused on southern regions where there were hardly any missionaries yet. Even before recovering from the fatigue of voyage, he pushed himself to the limits of traveling along with a language teacher and a guide. His health deteriorated, he contracted smallpox, worsened by pneumonia. He eventually fell sick just before arriving his destination—Busan. He was hurried to the home of J. Gale, a missionary working in Busan, but he was already past the point of any treatment. On April 15, 1890, less than six months after his arrival, Davies passed away in this foreign land before getting involved in the kind of ministry he dreamed of. He became the first missionary to pass away in Korea.[175]

---

174 H. Underwood, *The Call of Korea*, 140.
175 Also in 1890, the Northern Presbyterian medical missionary Heron passed away by dysentery and his name is recorded in the list of martyrs. But J. Heron died in July 16, about 3 months after Davies' death.

Nevertheless, Davies's death was certainly not in vain. The Church of Victoria in Australia pressed on for mission in Korea all the more, sending four more missionaries just a year after Davies's death. Thus four missionaries including J. H. Mackay, B. Menzies, and J. Perry began working in the South Gyeongsang Province region. This is how the South Gyeongsang Province region came under the attention of the Presbyterian Church of Australia.

(3) Southern Methodist Church, United States of America

While the Northern Methodist Church of United States sent its first missionary Appenzeller to Korea as early as 1885, the Southern Methodist Church was actively engaged in missions in Korea beginning in 1896, about a decade later than its Northern counterpart. Chi Ho Yoon played a crucial role in the beginning of missions by Southern Methodist Church. At that time Southern Methodist Church was carrying out mission works in central China, and in February 1894 it sent Dr. F. C. Reid to Northern China in order to secure a base for mission works in that region. Then Reid learned that many mission boards have already been involved in missions in the region for a very long time.

Meanwhile, Chi Ho Yoon escaped to Shanghai during the Cou-pd'Etat of 1884 and enrolled himself in a two-year course at the Southern Methodist-run Anglo-Chinese College where he performed excellently. Just about that time, President of Emory University, United States, W. A. Candler visited the college, took notice of Yoon's great potential and made arrangements for him to further his studies at Emory. Chi Ho Yoon graduated Emory with outstanding grades and went on to Vandervilt University and picked up theology. While studying there, he traveled to various places for eloquence. He saved the money he earned by eloquence and donated to Southern Methodist Overseas Mission Board for use in missions in Korea.

After completing his studies, Yoon returned to the Anglo-Chinese-College in Shanghai. While teaching there, he was invited by the Korean Government to return to Korea and serve as a high-ranking official. As he made his way to Korea, he requested Southern Methodist Church to get involved in missions in Korea, and in response to the request Dr. Reid and Bishop E. A. Hendrix came to Korea in October 1895 to study the feasibility of missions there. Yoon arranged them to have an audience with the king, where they were impressed by the king's request for more missionaries. Yoon also made arrangements for them to buy a house before their departure.

Southern Methodist Overseas Mission Board's annual conference was held in May 1896. At this conference, major decisions on missions in Korea were made, and accordingly Dr. Reid was sent as a missionary to Korea in August 1896. Headquarters of Southern Methodist Church was in Songdo (Kyesuhng, Kyonggi Province) at that time. For some time Korea remained an integral part of the Chinese Annual Conference until 1907, when it became independent of the Chinese Annual Conference.[176]

---

176 Nak Jun Paik, *Hangukgaesingiosa* (History of the Protestant Church in Korea),

(4) Southern Presbyterian Church of United States of America

Southern Presbyterian Church of the United States[177] started her mission works in Korea in 1892, 7 years later than its Northern counterpart. Underwood was a vital person who made it possible for Southern Presbyterian to start mission works in Korea. A South ern Presbyterian missionary once spoke of Underwood as the "Dr. H. G. Underwood is the father of our(south) mission,"[178] When Underwood returned to the States for his furlough in 1891, he had a chance to speak about missions in Korea at McCormick Theological Seminary in Chicago. Here, a student at the seminary, L. B. Tate, was touched by Underwood's message and committed himself to serve as a missionary in Korea.

In October of the same year, the annual conference for United States Theological Seminary Association was held in Nashville, Tennessee, where Underwood spoke also. Present among the speakers at this conference was Chi Ho Yoon who was a student at Vandervilt University. Challenged by the call, C. Johnson and W. D. Reynolds, students from Union Theological Seminary in Virginia, and the afore mentioned Tate, a student from McCormick Theological Seminary, made up their minds to go to Korea as missionaries. Later W. M. Junkin would join them as well. These four people

---

208.

177 Presbyterian Church in the U.S.A. was originally one single entity but were divided into two during the Civil War in 1860. The Northern side, U.P.C.U.S.A., and the Southern side, P.C.U.S., came together as the Presbyterian Church (U.S.A.) in 1983 after 123 years of separation.

178 J. F. Preston, "Editorial," *The Korea Mission Field* (November 1921), 222.

requested Southern Presbyterian Overseas Mission Board to send them as missionaries to Korea. However, the mission board replied them that they did not have any plans to start missions in Korea at that time.[179]

Not giving up the hope, they traveled through many southern states in the U.S.A. along with Underwood, giving reports on missions in Korea and informing the urgency of the work. They also posted various Korea-related articles on Christian newspapers, arousing much interest among the believers. Their efforts reaped the first fruit within the Underwood family. Underwood's elder brother, John Underwood, donated 2,500 dollars[180] to Southern Presbyterian Church Overseas Mission Board with a specific request for the money to be used for missions in Korea. Much stimulated, the mission board finally made the decision to start missions in Korea. Thus in February 1892, it appointed seven missionaries: Tate and his sister Mattie S. Tate, Linnie Davis, the Reynolds, and the Junkins. Some of them arrived in Seoul in October of the same year, marking the beginning of Korean missions by Southern Presbyterian Church of the U.S.A.[181]

(5) Presbyterian Church of Canada – McKenzie's Martyrdom

---

179 W. C. Reynolds, "Genesis of the Southern Presbyterian Mission," *The Korea Mission Field* (January 1914), 17.

180 Nak Jun Paik, *Hangukgaesingiosa* (History of the Protestant Church in Korea), 199.

181 G. T. Brown, *Mission to Korea* (Board of Foreign Mission P.C.U.S., 1962), 23.

When considering the accounts of Korean missions by the Presbyterian Church of Canada, we must remember W. J. McKenzie who, as a Canadian, came to Korea and died a lonely death serving Christ faithfully.[182]

Born in Nova Scotia, Canada, McKenzie graduated from Halifax Theological Seminary in 1891. He decided to go to Korea as a missionary after reading an introductory book on Korea. He made known his intention to Presbyterian Church of Canada, but the church lacked any plans for missions in Korea at that time. He took to himself to travel from one church to the other, speaking of the needs in Korea and raising funds. When he gathered enough money for travels and missions that would last him a year, he left for Korea on his own in December 1893.

Determined to live among Koreans, learn the language and customs, and carry out personal level evangelization, he went to Sollae. He ministered in that rural village. He lived very much like a Korean along with the Korean residents there. He was also strong willed to get past his cravings for Western food to the extent that he did not even touch the cake sent from Underwood as a gift on Christmas. Instead, he gave it to the villagers. He was widely recognized and respected by the residents in the area. Even when followers of the Donghak(Eastern Learning) swept across the region, he was guaranteed of complete safety as the residents were in favor of him.

---

182 For information on McKenzie's life and death, see E. A. McCully, *A Corn of Wheat, The Life of Rev. W. J. McKenzie of Korea*, 2nd ed.

McKenzie lived as a sacrificial and unselfish saint among Koreans. But in the middle of a summer day, he had a sunstroke and suffered mental derangement in high fever. Unable to withstand the surge of great pain, he used his personal pistol to shoot his head and put an end to his own life. The Korean Church should never forget the dedication of McKenzie who went to the Lord in the quiet seaside village of Sollae, Hwanghae Province, after living alone among Koreans without the family or fellow missionaries.

While McKenzie was faithfully serving a rural village in Korea, Presbyterian Church in Canada was researching and evaluating the feasibility of missions in Korea. Then, they were informed of McKenzie's death. Believers at Sollae Church, where McKenzie pastored, also sent a petition to the mission board requesting for another missionary. McKenzie passed away with a will stating that his properties be used for Korean missions. His properties were valued at about 2,000 dollars then.[183] Soon there appeared a number of people who were willing to support the work financially. As mission funds accumulated, the General Assembly of Presbyterian Church in Canada appointed Mr. and Mrs. W. R. Foote, D. McRae, and Mr. and Mrs. R. Grierson, M.D. as missionaries to Korea. Arriving in September 1898, they intended to work at Sollae where McKenzie used to work. But realizing that it was just a small village, they started the work at Wonsan, South Hamgyeong Province, North-east part of Korea. This is how Presbyterian Church of Canada adopted Hamgyeong Province as their mission field.[184]

---

183 *Ibid.*, 252-253.

(6) Ella Thing Missions – Missions by Baptist Church

The first Baptist Church to start missions in Korea was the Clarendon Street Baptist Church in Boston, in America. S. B. Thing, a faithful and dedicated business man and a member of the church, founded "Ella Thing Missions" in memory of his only daughter Ella Thing. For the first assignment, this mission agency sent Rev. E. C. Pauling and his wife, and Miss Amanda Gardeline to Korea. Arriving in Busan in 1895, they moved to Gongju, Chungcheong Province, and started working there because Busan was already crowded with missionaries from many other mission agencies.[185]

Their work was quite successful and the number of Baptist believers increased there. However, support funds began to decrease substantially, and they were forced to return to the States in 1900. The believers had to be cared for by Korean leaders. The only external help was M. C. Fenwick, a missionary in Wonsan, who visited them occasionally.

(7) Independent Missionaries

While the majority of missionaries in Korea were sent from denominational mission boards, there were quite a number of missionaries who came on their own in the initial phase of missions

---

184 *The Report of the Foreign Mission Committee of the Presbyterian Church in Canada for 1898-1889*, 133.
185 D. L. Gifford, *Day Life in Korea*, 152-153.

in Korea. Let us look at some of such key persons in the aspect of their mission works in Korea.

First of all, James S. Gale was sent from YMCA of Toronto University, Canada, in 1889. Arriving in Korea in December of the same year, he spent a few months in Seoul. He attempted to secure a mission base in the North but in vain. After returning to Seoul, he went to Busan in the south and started working there. In the process, he changed his mind; he discontinued his relationship with Toronto University and instead joined Northern Presbyterian Church as their missionary. Later, he returned to Seoul, where he translated the Bible and ministered Yeondong Church.

When Gale was working in Busan, YMCA of Toronto University also sent R. A. Hardie, a medical doctor, to Korea. He worked with Gale in Busan, but when Gale left the city, Hardie also came to Seoul, where he worked at Jejungwon with O. R. Avison who was his teacher. Hardie also discontinued his relationship with Toronto University in 1898 and joined Southern Methodist Church of U.S.A. Thus Toronto University's support for Korean missions was put to an end.

Another independent missionary worth noting is M. C. Fenwick. Fenwick was a Baptist from Canada. Void of neither formal education nor theological training, after listening to a speech advocating foreign missions, he made up his mind and he came to Korea at the end of 1889. He spent some time in Seoul learning the language but he felt he was not progressing fast enough. As a result, he went to Sollae, where he lived among Koreans and learned the daily use of the language. He bought a Korean traditional house and a plot of land where he farmed his own vegetables, wore 'hanbok'(Korean clothes) and ate Korean food. He was convicted that missionaries must be fully absorbed into the local culture and live like the local people. He wrote,

> ......Corea has done more, very much more, for the peace and happiness of the race as a whole, than the civilization of the West.......It is, in my opinion, very far from desirable that the East should have the civilization of the West.[186]

His words were spoken directly against the cultural imperialists who believed that Western civilization was the best.

After returning to the States in 1893, Fenwick founded "The Corean Itinerant Mission" and organized a support group with his friends. In 1896, he returned to Korea as the head of the organization. While working in Wonsan, Hamgyeong Province, he wrote "he gospel can best be taught to foreign peoples by picked native converts."[187] Strongly convicted that local believers were more effective than foreign missionaries in preaching the Gospel, Fenwick reconfirmed the renowned mission theorist Rufus Anderson's teaching that "missions must be carried out by trained indigenous people."

---

186 M. C. Fenwick, *Church of Christ in Corea* (New York: Hodder & Stoughton, 1911), 49-51.
187 *Ibid.*, v.

Chapter 4

Mission Policies of Mission Boards

1. Adoption of the Nevius Principles

While most of the early missionaries came to Korea straight out of theological schools and armed with nothing but passion, they soon realized that there was more to missions than they thought.

Underwood was probably the first to seriously think about this problem. He wrote to his overseas mission board in the U.S.A. several times requesting for a chance to learn the practical methods from an experienced missionary and receive guidance of missions.[188] In response to this, the mission board made arrangements for John Nevius, who had been working as a missionary in China for a long time and was writing a series of papers on mission methodology, to go to Korea. Thus Nevius took his wife and came to Korea in June 1890. During his two-week-long stay in Korea, he taught

---

188 Lillias Underwood, *Underwood of Korea*, 99.

the missionaries mission strategies and methodology, which are now summed up as the "Nevius Principles." The Nevius Principles played a crucial role in helping the Korean Church take great strides. These principles are considered as one of the most important elements for the existence of the Korean Church as we know it today. Then, what exactly are the Nevius Principles?[189]

Let us examine some of the crucial points below:

1. Missionary personal evangelism with wide itineration.
2. The Bible central in every part of the work.
3. Self-propagation: every believer a teacher of someone, and a learner from someone elsebetter fitted; every Individual and group seeking by the "layering method" to extend the work.
4. Self-government: every group under its chosen unpaid Leaders; circuits under their own paid Helpers, who will yield to Pastors; circuit meetings training the people for later district, provincial and national leadership.
5. Self-support: with all chapels provided by the believers each group, as soon as founded, beginning to pay toward the circuit Helper's salary; even schools to receive but partial subsidy, and that only when being founded; no pastors of single churches provided by foreign funds.
6. Systematic Bible study for every believer under his group Leaders and circuit Helper; and of every Leader and Helper in the Bible Classes.

---

189 For more information on the Nevius Principles, see A. D. Clark, *The Korean Church and the Nevius Methods* (New York: Fleming H. Revell, 1930).

7. Strict discipline enforced by Bible penalties.
8. Co-operation and union with other bodies, or at least territorial division.
9. Non-interference in lawsuits or any such matters.
10. General helpfulness where possible in the economic life problems of the people.[190]

The Nevius Principles are often shorted as the 'Three-Self Principles.' They refer to 'self-government,' 'self-support' and 'self-propagation.' In other words, external forces must not manage the church the church should not be funded by external sources and the church should undertake evangelization on its own.

Given the circumstances of the time, these principles would take effect only if all the mission boards and agencies in Korea came to an agreement together. In other words, these principles were not to be observed by just few select mission boards, but cooperation between all mission boards was required. One thing worth noting is that a collaborative organization for all mission boards was established just a year prior to Nevius's visit to Korea. The "United Council of Presbyterian Missions"was founded in 1889 as a collaborative organization between the Mission Board of the Northern Presbyterian Church in U.S.A. and the Mission Board of the Church of Victoria in Australia. However, as mentioned earlier, this council was dismissed when Rev. J. H. Davies from Australia suddenly passed away. Then, following the arrival of the Southern Presbyterian Church in U.S.A. in 1892, the Northern

---

190 *Ibid.*, 33-34.

Presbyterian and the Southern Presbyterian resurrected the United Council in January 1893. Later joined by the Australian Presbyterian and the Canadian Presbyterian, the purpose of the council was to "organize a church in Korea that stands on the reformed church faith and takes on the Presbyterian system."[191] Although this organization was no more than a representative committee in the beginning, it was the only organization overseeing matters of the Presbyterian Church in Korea until the representatives of the Korean Church joined in 1901 and a Presbytery was formed in 1907. This council played an important role of dividing mission fields in Korea and also formulating mission principles for the Korean context based on the Nevius Principles.

'Comiity Arrangement' was first carried out between various Presbyterian mission agencies in Korea. Agreeing that it would be undesirable for same Presbyterian churches to duplicate works in the same region, the mission agencies adopted a plan that would allow them to divide Korea into several zones and be accountable for mission works in each zone. According to this plan, the Northern Presbyterian Churches were to be responsible for Pyeongan, Hwanghae, Gyeonggi, and North Gyeongsang Province; the Southern Presbyterian Church was to be responsible for Chungcheong Province and Jeolla Province; the Presbyterian Church in Australia for South Gyeongsang Province; and the Presbyterian Church in Canada for Hamgyeong Province.

---

191 H. A. Rhodes, ed. *History of the Korea Mission Presbyterian Church U.S.A.* 1884-1934, vol. I (Chosen Missions, Presbyterian Church, U.S.A., 1934), 385.

This comity arrangement policy was also carried out between the Northern Methodist Church and the Northern Presbyterian Church in June 1892. The arrangement stipulated that the two mission boards would be allowed to work in parallel to one another in large cities, but only the existing mission board would be allowed to work in towns with a population of less than 5,000 unless there were no missionary presence there yet. They agreed that it was wasteful and undesirable for many mission agencies to compete against each other in small towns. They also agreed that areas not yet evangelized should be reserved for new mission agencies. While this proposal never became official because Bishop R. S. Foster of the Northern Methodist Church did not approve, both mission boards essentially observed this spirit in their works.[192]

Another important role of the United Council was the drafting of the Nevius Principles to accommodate the context in Korea. Since these principles were directly connected to the revival of the Korean Church in years to come, let us look at them closely here:

1. It is better to aim at the conversion of the working classes than at that or the higher classes.
2. The conversion of women and the training up of Christian girls should be an especial aim, since mothers exercise so important an influence over future generations.

---

192 C. A. Clark, *The Nevius Method and the Korean Church*, 90.

3. Much could be affected in Christian education by maintaining elementary schools in countrytowns; therefore, we should aim to qualify young men in our boy's school and to send them out as teachers.

4. Our hope for an educated native ministry lies in the same quarter and should be constantly held in view.

5. The Word of God converts where man is without resources; therefore, it is most important that we make every effort to place a clear translation of the Bible before the people as soon as possible.

6. In all literary work, a pure Korean, free from cynicism, should be our aim.

7. An aggressive church must be a self-supporting church, and we must aim to diminish the proportion of dependents among our membership and to increase that of self-supporting, and therefore, contributing individuals.

8. Their own fellow countrymen must lead the mass of Koreans to Christ; therefore, we shall do well to thoroughly train a few as evangelists rather than to preach to a multitude ourselves.

9. The services of our physicians can be turned to best account when it is possible to keep the same patient long under treatment either in a hospital ward or in the patient's home, thus giving opportunity for instruction and example to sink deeply into the mind. Dispensary work is of comparatively little profit.

10. Patients from the country who have undergone a season of treatment ought to be followed up by visitation in their native villages, since their experience of compassionate

dealing is likely to open a wide door for the evangelist.[193]

The mission policies listed above are very important and crucial to the Presbyterian Church in Korea. Evangelism of the working class and women was definitely an excellent method of penetrating the Korean society, and distribution of all-Korean literature and Bibles was a much-needed step toward the rapid growth of the Korean Church.

On the other hand, there was also much criticism against the Nevius Principles. For instance, the Nevius Principles were accused of emphasizing self-government and self-support too much to the extent of down playing the importance of cooperation and focusing on the well being of individual churches. As the Korean Church today becomes more and more segregated and united church movements are dying out, many critics tend to blame the Nevius Principles.

However, it must be noted that the problems of the Korean Church today are direct results of inappropriate execution of the Nevius Principles, not because the principles were wrong in themselves. It must be remembered that Nevius strongly emphasized unity and cooperation more than anyone ever did.

2. Education of Ministers

The first and most critical problem faced by the foreign missio-

---

193 C. C. Vinton, "Presbyterian Mission Work in Korea," *The Missionary Review of the World XI-9* (September 1893), 671.

naries in Korea was the language. Although the curiosity toward white-faced Westerners was often helpful in evangelization, it was simply not easy to carry out effective evangelization activities to those who wanted to satisfy their superficial curiosity. Training local Koreans to evangelize their fellow citizens was more urgent than any other work. In addition, an effective plan had to be devised for preparing the quantity and quality of Christian ministers who would lead the ever-increasing number of churches.

As seen earlier, Underwood opened a theological class from the very beginning of his orphanage with an ambition of building a theological seminary. But his dream was rather short-lived. As mission works expanded continuously, there was an ever-increasing need for local Christian leaders. And even as the role of evangelists was emphasized by the Nevius Principles, the necessity of training local Christian leaders became ever more prominent. The question was about how Christian leaders should be trained.

W. D. Reynolds, a Southern Presbyterian missionary, answered this question with a practical proposal. In 1896, he proposed the following important points for training Korean Christian leaders:

➔ Don'ts
1. Don't let him know for a long time that you have any idea of training him for ministry.
2. Don't employ him as a preacher or evangelist on foreign pay, if you can help it.
3. Don't send him to America to be educated, at any rate in the early stages of Mission Work

→ **Dos**

1. Seek to lift him to a high plane of spiritual experience. Let him strive above all else to a "Holy Ghost man."

2. Ground him thoroughly in the Word and in the cardinal facts and truths of Christianity

3. Train the young pastor-to-be to "endure hardness as a good soldier of Jesus Christ."

4. As Korean Christians advance in culture and modern civilization, raise the standard of education of the native ministry. Seek to keep his education sufficiently in advance of the average education of his people to secure respect and prestige but nor enough ahead to excite envy or a feeling of separation.[194]

Reynolds concluded this proposal by saying, "Our goal must be to see the Korean Church being by Korean leaders. They must not be spineless, Westernized or have corrupted leaders ruling over groups of boneless and naïve believers. We must produce leaders with dedication, confidence, and self-esteem who would lead self-sustaining, self-governing and self-propagating churches."[195]

In his Hangukgaesingiosa (The History of the Protestant Church in Korea), Dr. Nak Joon Paik criticizes Reynolds for setting the educational requirement standards of Korean Christian ministers only slightly higher than those of the general population.[196] Many

---

194 W. D. Reynolds, "The Native Ministry," *The Korean Repository* (1896), 199.
195 *Ibid.*, 202.
196 Nak Jun Paik, *Hangukgaesingiosa* (History of the Protestant Church in Korea), 227.

Christian historians share this critical view. However, it must be noted that Reynolds wrote the proposal in 1896. In that period of time, there was no theological training facility in Korea. The Christians had a low level of theological knowledge, and there were inadequate supplies of study materials, lecturers and venues for theological training. It must also be remembered that the standards above were not meant to be perpetual standards; Reynolds simply proposed what seemed the best for his time. The quality and quantity of available theological education change over time. We must keep in mind that Reynolds simply proposed a standard appropriate for his time. Complete theological education in the Presbyterian Church became available a number of years later in 1901, and the first batch of official graduates emerged only about 10 years after that.

The theological training in the beginning was designed for producing evangelists rather than fully qualified pastors. Due to various inadequacies, theological training at that time was limited to just simple teachings of the Bible and basic doctrines that were sufficient enough to produce trained evangelists.

In evaluation of the Nevius Principles, it is true some criticize that the requirements were too low for theological training of local ministers and that missionaries tried to keep everything under their control. But it seems that most of these criticisms are based on much misunderstanding, and it is evident that the critics are simply trying to condemn the missionaries. Of course, no human system or principle is perfect. Furthermore, new systems are bound to undergo errors as they are put to practice. Despite various negative views of the Nevius Principles, they must be fully recognized and accredited for the massive growth of the Korean Church.

Chapter 5

Persecution of the Early Christianity and Activities of the Church

1. Paths of Introduction for the Christian Faith

(1) Conversion of Commoners

When Catholicism was first introduced to Korea, mainly scholars received the religion with curiosity and interest over the Western civilization, and then it was passed on to the ordinary class. But the Protestant faith in Korea emerged in a totally different way. In other words, if Catholic missions could be seen as an "top-bottom" approach, Protestant missions showed a "bottom-top" approach.

From the very beginning of his missionary career, Underwood focused on the lower class for evangelism. He did so because he determined that it would be more difficult for government officials and the yangban (nobility) class to embrace the faith due to many structural restrictions. This was especially true, as government officials were required to attend national religious festivals and participate in ancestral worship ceremonies. In addition, upper class men at that time customarily lived with several concubines in addition to their wives. It was not easy for the church to confront and abolish this practice, and thus efforts for evangelizing the yangban class ware deemed much too draining.[197] On the other hand, the common people continued to live in poverty and oppression. They were more than ready to receive the new faith as long as it would help them in some way and any way. This gives us a clear picture of why the missionaries focused on evangelizing the commoners instead of reaching the yangban class.

Regarding Underwood's missionary strategy, Gilmore, a teacher at Yugyounggongwon (National Public School), wrote a letter to the New York Headquarters in 1886, "In my opinion, Underwood has completely misunderstood the peculiarity of this place. Koreans must be reached (through missions) from the top to the bottom."[198] But the importance of reaching the peasants and laborers would be proven later in history. Also, schools and hospitals were extremely crucial for these people. The church was in the best position to offer them help and provide education, and thus be easily received by them.

Some criticized this strategy as much as missionaries adopted it. Many argue that Koreans accepted the Christian faith not entirely because they understood and appreciated the vital Christian truth,

---

197 Lillias Underwood, *Underwood of Korea*, 203.
198 G. W. Gilmore to F. F. Ellinwood, December 24, 1886, PHS.

but because they were blinded by the practical help they were receiving. It is true to some extent that the people were in a better place to receive material help when they were closer to Western missionaries. As statistics show, masses of people came to churches whenever there were nationwide problems, diseases, famines and so on. Some commoners were seen as seeking refuge under the foreigners' protection against the oppression of corrupted government officials. This view is supported by the fact that the number of Christians leaped greatly during the times of the Sino-Japanese War in 1895, the 1905 Protectorate Treaty, the dismantling of the Korean Army in 1907 and the Japan-Korea Annexation Treaty in 1910.[199]

(2) Conversion of the Learned

By no means did commoners and low class citizens monopolize the Christian faith. While it was rather difficult for yangbans to adopt the faith due to social constraints, there were significant evangelism efforts towards yangbans and the intellectuals. The intellectuals joined the faith for almost the same reasons as the commoners. While they were in direct need for the missionaries' help, material benefits or their protection, they certainly were looking for two practical elements. Firstly, they wanted to achieve an independence of the state by using Christianity, and secondly, they

---

199 See various statistics in Roy E. Shearer, *Wildfire: Church Growth in Korea*, tr. by Seong Ik Lee, *Hangukgiohoesungjangsa* (Seoul: Christian Literature Society of Korea, 1972).

wanted to utilize the Christian faith to raise the spirit of nationalism and establish a constitutional and democratic monarchy.

The Independence Club serves as an excellent window for examining the conversion of the learned and their Christian activities at the time. The Independence Club was founded by Jae Pil Suh (Philip Jaisohn), one of the core persons during the Coup d'état of 1884, Chi Ho Yoon, an interpreter for the U.S. Legation in Korea, and Sang Jae Lee, the first secretary for the Korean Legation in the U.S. The Club was established when Suh and Yoon returned after their exile of 10 years since the Kapsinjungbyon(Coup d'état of 1884). In April 1896, Jaepil Suh launched *The Independent*, the first Hangeul(Korean native letters) newspaper. Then in November, he reconstructed Mohwagwan(building for welcoming of the Chinese delegates) next to Yeongeunmun(Gate for welcoming of the Chinese degegates), which was used for receiving envoys from China, and later tore down Yeongeunmun and built the Independence Gate there. The Independence Club was established in July 1896 with the purposes of the educating the public and the developing democracy.[200]

Core leaders Suh and Yoon returned to Korea after having become Christians, and other key figures became to be quite familiar with the Christian spirit even though they were yet to be converted. Given the fact that Christian leaders such as Chang Ho Ahn and Sun Joo Kil took a central role in setting up the Independence

---

200 Woo Keun Han, *Hanguk Tongsa* (Entire History of Korea) (Seoul: Eulyumunhwasa, 1983), 499-500.

Club branch in Pyongyang, this association was surely headed by influential Christian leaders.[201] Objectives for this association were to set up a self-governed independent state by expelling foreign forces, to reform the corrupted government officials and politics and to secure franchise for the people. Although it started off as a moderate body, extreme opinions began to surface among its members. With the attempt to hold the 'All People's Congress,' adopt national reformation policies, introduce constitutional monarchy and open channels of political participation for the commoners, the government eventually dismissed the Independence Club, and its leaders were arrested and jailed in November 1898 when the government was steered by conspiracies.

Jailed at this time were Syungman Rhee, Sang Jae Lee, Heung Woo Shin and Jeong Sik Kim. Various missionaries including Underwood, Gale and Hulbert frequently visited them in prison and gave them Bibles and Christian books. The prisoners, who would later become important leaders for the Korean people and the Korean church, came to believe in Jesus through the books during this period.

After repenting of his sins and putting his faith in Jesus in prison, Syungman Rhee prayed, "O, God, save my country and save my soul."[202] This prayer shows that Rhee more was concerned for Korea than his own soul. This is one fine example that

---

201 In Suh Kim, *Kim In Suh Jeojak Jeonjip* (Colletion of Kim In Suh's Writings), vol. 5, 55.
202 F. A. McKenzie, *Korea's Fight for Freedom* (New York: Fleming H. Revell, 1920), 75.

shows the reasons why the intellectuals at that time joined the Christian faith. This not only shows the passionate fire in national leaders for the salvation of Korea rather than their own souls, but it also indicates the possibility of them coming to believe in Jesus as a means to secure national safety and independence instead of receiving Jesus as their Savoir based on personal and complete repentance of sins.

At this point, it becomes more sensible for us to suppose that the commoners joined the faith for selfish reasons and the yangban intellectuals received the faith as a means for their patriotic independence movement. Nevertheless, we must not deny God's divine plan of allowing the Gospel to be planted in the Korean soil. Regardless of motives, the Christian faith was widely accepted in Korea, and the church began to grow under God's guidance.

2. Persecution of the Early Church

(1) Counterattack by Traditionalists and Conservatives

It would certainly be unusual for Christianity to face no conflict s at all while taking root within the traditional Korean culture; it definitely involved a clash of cultures. Conservative and dominant groups were naturally uncomfortable with and hostile to missionaries.

The Baby Riots in 1888 is one typical example of misunderstanding Christian missionaries. Missionary works were much dampened when rumors spread saying that missionaries were kidnapping children to use their eyes as medicines and to cook them as meals.[203]

On the other hand, in 1894, Pyongyang Governor Byeong Suhk Min arrested a number of Christians for the sole purpose of oppressing the growing Christian influence in the Pyongyang region. Just if his actions for the safeguarding of Confucius traditions and preventing the disturbance of peace from Western missionaries, Min almost killed the Christians by beating and forcing them to abandon the faith. To this, Presbyterian missionary S. A. Moffett and Methodist missionary W. J. Hall, who were residing in Pyongyang, immediately contacted the U.S. and U.K. Legations in Seoul and used diplomatic channels to reach the King so that he could issue a royal order to release the arrested Christians.[204]

Then in 1899, a missionary was directly persecuted in Hwangju, Hwanghae Province. When Presbyterian missionary Graham Lee was passing through Hwangju, the residents "destroyed the church, beat the church members, burned the pastor's books, and stole 56 dollars in cash."[205] After learning this, U.S. Chargé d'Affaires Allen immediately sent a note of protest to the Korean government, strongly demanding punishment of the offenders.

At one time, a nationwide persecution was staged against Christians simply because of a few personal grudges. When the tram construc-

---

203 L. Underwood, *Fifteen Years among the Top-knots*, 14-16.
204 Association of Christian History in Korea, *Chosun Yesugio Jangnohoesagi* (History of the Presbyterian Church in Korea) (1968), vol. 2, 136-139.
205 *Guhanguk Oegyomunsuh* (Diplomatic Documents of the Korean Empire), vol. 11, U.S. Documents II, 502-503.

tion was well in progress in Seoul in 1899, Superintendent General Young Joon Kim and Royal Treasurer Young Ik Lee presented a memorial to the King, as they feared for the depletion of national resources if the general public would to use trams on a daily basis. When the tram construction was complete, they even staged a campaign against riding trams. But as foreigners began to voice their complaints to the King, Kim and Lee presented the King with a memorial containing every detail of the influence exercised by Protestantism in Korea. In fact, they were also planning to send secret letters ordering simultaneous eradication of all Christian missionaries and believers in the country on December 1, 1900.[206]

Underwood, who was on his missionary journey, first learned this conspiracy. Realizing the gravity of the situation, he urgently sent a telegram to O. Avison in Latin so that the Koreans could not read it. Underwood requested Avison to inform Allen so that necessary actions could be taken to protect the churches and believers. To this, Allen immediately had an audience with the King and reported the details. Thus, King Gojong sent a telegram to every province in the country and ordered for immediate termination of the conspiracy. So the conspiracy of Young Joon Kim and his accomplices was exposed and the church was spared from its imminent threat of eradication.[207]

---

206 Jae Myeong Cha, *Chosun Yesukiojangnogiohoe Sagi* (History of the Presbyterian Church in Korea), vol. 1 (ChosunKidoggio Changmunsa, 1928), 80.
207 *Guhanguk Oegyomunsuh* (Diplomatic Documents of the Korean Empire), III, 14, vol. 20, Legal Documents II, 84.

(2) Persecution by Catholics

Although Catholics and Protestants essentially believe in the same God, believe in the same Jesus, read the same Scriptures, are rooted in the same background and embrace each other as brothers in Christ in the light of ecumenical spirit these days, the two branches of the Christian faith had tremendous conflicts with one another during the early phase of missions in Korea. Granted that such conflicts were not ordered by denominational policies but existed between individual persons and local churches, the fact remains that the Catholics oppressed and persecuted the early Protestants in Korea.

The very first persecution of this sort took place in Jaeryeong, Hwanghae Province. When Jaeryeong Wonnae-dong Church members were building their church building, some 100 Catholics stormed the site, demanded shared usage of the church building and beat the Protestants. Also in 1902 at Sinhwanpo, Hwanghae Province, the Catholics demanded for the Protestants to make financial contributions toward their building of a Catholic Church. When the Protestants refused, the Catholics detained them and beat them.[208] In order to resolve this matter, the Hwanghae Provincial Governor sent police to arrest the offenders, but the Catholics even beat the police. This incident was reported to Seoul and foreigners were made aware of it. One interesting thing to note is that the Catholics were able to take on such evil actions because J. Wilhelm, a difficult

---

208 *The Korea Review* (1903), 25-26.

priest near Anak, was backing them. At that time, foreigners were enjoying extraterritorial rights and even government officials were not able to deal with them freely. In particular, Catholic priests were receiving absolute protection by the French Legation, and thus Wilhelm's tyranny was not easy to be suppressed. The Provincial Governor's account of Father Wilhelm's evil deeds clearly shows the seriousness of the situation.

The governor replied: "······is it right that you should arrest and beat Koreans?······You, a private citizen, arresting and beating Koreans and doing wrong, and your written orders to your people, have caused them to break the laws in eight different ways. They resist the authority of the government, beat the underlings, and refuse to pay their taxes.······Still further, without order, in companies they rush into the presence of magistrates to terrify him. Still again, of their own accord they arrest, beat and imprison the people. Again, calling it money for the building of churches, they extort contributions by force from the people.[209]

This incident eventually concluded when King Gojong ordered the prime movers to be arrested, transported to Seoul, judged and given grave punishments. In short, it was the indiscreet people who largely caused conflicts between the Protestants and Catholics.

---

209 Lillias Underwood, *Fifteen Years among the Top-knots or Life in Korea* (New York: American Tract Society, 1904), 264-265.

(3) Persecution by Donghak(Eastern Learning) Followers

Founded by Je Woo Choi, a man from Gyeogju, Gyeongsang Province, during the times of confusion at the end of the Chosun Dynasty, 'Donghak' (the Eastern Learning) incorporated doctrines of Feng Shui, Confucianism, Buddhism and Taoism and stood against the influence of the Western Learning (Christianity) by advocating that God's divinity dwells in man and that the new world is not to be experienced after death but is to be realized in this life. Donghak quickly gained popularity among the commoners who were oppressed by yangbans and government officials.[210]

Just as the name Donghak signifies its opposition against Suhhak (the Western Learning-Christianity), it was more than natural for Donghak followers to exhibit hostility against Christians. They particularly revolted at the foreigners' propagation of their own religion among the yangbans and stuck posters on missionaries' houses demanding the missionaries to leave the country. Nevertheless, Donghak followers hardly directed their attacks on Christian missionaries of believers, nor did they damage church buildings. On the contrary, later they began to join the Christian front in protesting the Japanese. While the Donghak followers actively sought to boycott the Japanese and the Western in the beginning, they were found to reject only the Japanese around the time of the Sino-Japanese War.[211]   Although the church was somewhat disturbed

---

210 Woo Keun Han, *Hanguk Tongsa* (Entire History of Korea), 391-394.
211 Kyoung Bae Min, *Hanguk Gidokgiohoesa* (History of Christian Church in Korea), New Revised Edition, 184-188.

by Donghak, the damage was not as grave as from other sources.

3. Patriotic Activities of the Church

(1) Assassination of Queen Min and Missionaries

After the victory of the Sino-Japanese War in 1895, the Japanese carefully undertook their conspiracy to colonize Korea. Queen Min was regarded by the Japanese to be the single biggest obstacle against their conquest, and thus they made plans to eliminate her. Ultimately, the Japanese assassinated Queen Min in her bedroom. This is called the Eulmi Incident because it took place in the year of Eulmi(1895).

Underwood's wife Lillias frequently met with Queen Min at the Palace and faithfully recorded her accounts:

> Slightly pale and quite thin, with somewhat sharp features and brilliant piercing eyes, she did not strike me at first sight as being beautiful, but no one could help reading force, intellect and strength of character in that face, and she became engaged in conversation, vivacity, naïveté, wit, all brightened her countenance, and gave it a wonderful charm, far greater than mere physical beauty·····although like all Asiatics, her learning consisted chiefly in the Chinese classics,·····she was, moreover, a sovereign of broad and progressive policy, patriotic, and devoted to the best interests of her country

and sought the good of the people······[212]

They undertook ruthless acts just to get rid of the Queen. The Palace was heavily occupied by Japanese government officials, the Korean soldiers were trained by Japanese drill sergeants and the Korean armed forces were under the direct command of the Japanese. Japan appointed Lieutenant General Miura Goro of the Japanese Army as the Japanese Consul to Korea and commissioned him to eliminate Queen Min. Miura was a man burning with such patriotism that he would not hesitate to do anything for Japan. Finally on October 8, 1895, a band of Japanese assassins commanded by Goro took advantage of Daewongun to infiltrate the palace, murder Queen Min and drag her body into the woods within the palace, where they poured oil on the body and burned it.[213] Fortunately, the entire crime was seen by General W. M. Dye, a U.S. military adviser, and Sabbatin, a Russian engineer, and was made known to the outside world.

On the day of Queen Min's assassination, missionary J. Gale was requested by a Methodist missionary G. H. Jones to come to the palace as an interpreter. This is his account of King Gojong:

The plight into which His Majesty had fallen was pitiful to be hold. He wept for his Queen; the Japanese he said had murdered her. Could no one help him in this time of need! He would cut off his hair and weave shoes of

---

212 L. Underwood, *Fifteen Years among the Top-knots*, 24.
213 *Ibid.*, 149-150.

it for those who would avenge her death.[214]

On the next day following the queen's death, King Gojong's second prince Prince Uihwa sent a man to Underwood to ask whether it was possible for him to stay at his place. Underwood immediately accepted the request, and thus Prince Uihwa fled to Underwood's house. In addition to Prince Uihwa, a number of high-ranking government officials were also staying in Underwood's guest room and spies watched Underwood's house day and night.[215]

Those who killed the queen detained King Gojong. The entire palace was overwhelmed with fear this caused the King have an extreme mental breakdown. It became more and more difficult for him to stay sane from the fear of him becoming the next victim. Diplomats from Russia, the U.K., France, the U.S. and many other countries came and comforted the King on a daily basis. At this point, Underwood was also helping out as an interpreter for the U.S. diplomats and even for the Russian and the U.K. counterparts from time to time.[216] Instilled with much distrust against others after the death of the queen, King Gojong was disturbed to the point that he could not eat freely. Held captive by his own fear that people could use his food to poison him, the King refused to eat any meal prepared in the royal kitchen. He was only able to eat from canned food that he opened himself

---

214 J. S. Gale, *Korean Sketches* (Edinburgh: Olimphant Anderson and Ferrior, 1898), 206.
215 L. Underwood, *Underwood of Korea*, 157.
216 *Ibid.*, 147.

and other simple food such as sweetened milk and eggs.

In an effort to help the King eat proper food, Underwood's wife prepared some special food for him, put it in a galvanized iron safe and locked it with a Yale lock. King Gojong would then eat the food in it using the key Underwood passed to him. [217] King Gojong's diet was also assisted by the Russian legation. This led to the spreading of the news that "missionaries saved the King's life."

One day, Underwood met with Daewongun in the palace. Dae-wongun asked Underwood, "Why are you giving such good food to the King? He won't need such good food. I am old and toothless. You'd better give me the food to me." But Underwood records Daewongun as having his teeth in excellent condition.[218]

Missionaries criticized the violation committed by the Japanese. Not only did they send reports to their mission boards, but also did everything within their power to inform the world of this incident. Such dedication shown by the missionaries toward the King was widely known even to the government officials and the general public. As the missionaries were regarded as the protectors of the King and the nation, Christianity, too, was perceived as a religion of patriotism. Here, it must be noted that the Roman Catholic Church was originally perceived as a religion denying the kingship and parentage and was received with heavy persecution. On the contrary, Protestantism was perceived as a religion of patriotism;

---

217 L. Underwood, *Fifteen Years among the Top-knots*, 156. *Underwood of Korea*, 147-148.
218 L. Underwood, *Fifteen Years among the Top-knots*, 156.

the number of Protestants surged greatly right after the assassination of Queen Min.[219]

(2) The Chunsaeng-Mun(Gate) Incident

The Chunsaengmun Incident refers to the plan devised by some Westerners and the King's aides to guide King Gojong out of the palace through Chunsaengmun, the Northeastern gate of the palace, and into safety. Since the murder of Queen Min, King Gojong had been detained within the palace by the pro-Japanese forces. However, this plan ended in failure with the betrayal of renegades. Underwood learned of this when he visited Avison's place on his way home from the palace. There he learned that General Ung Ryeol Yoon and his company were planning to rescue King Gojong on that very night. A staff member from the U.S. legation was present at this meeting. He expressed his concerns to a U.S. diplomat and requested Underwood to enter the palace and ensure the safety of the King. The legation staff gave him the diplomat's name card and told him to use it as a pass. Underwood informed Hulbert, a teacher at Yugyounggonwon, and Avison, a doctor at Jejungwon, of the plan and went into the palace with them.

---

219 For instance, the Presbyterian members totaled no more than 1,000 in 1895, the year of Queen Min's assassination, but the number grew to over 10,000 in 1905 in just ten years. Roy E. Shearer, *Wildfire: Church Growth in Korea*, tr. by Seong Ik Lee, *Hangukgiohoesungjangsa* (Seoul: Christian Literature Society of Korea, 1972), 56.

However, when the men arrived at the main gate of the palace, the gate was tightly shut and the gatekeeper insisted that no one was to enter the palace. Then, Underwood showed him the name card of the U.S. diplomat, entered the palace and ran straight to where King Gojong was. He immediately had an audience with him and explained that he was concerned for the King's safety over the night. In response, the King ordered him to wait in the U.S. military advisor General Dye's room. The general's room was within a close distance from the King's court. It was a good place for Underwood to monitor the situation and respond immediately.[220]

At about midnight, a gunshot was heard. Immediately Underwood got up and ran to the King's court. He overcame the soldiers' resistance and kept running toward the King. A few army officers standing with swords attempted to stop him, but Underwood took out his personal pistol and pressed on to the King's court. At that very moment, King Gojong cried out, "Where are the foreigners (missionaries)? Where are the foreigners?" Underwood and the two other missionaries immediately appeared before King Gojong and replied, "Here we are, Your Majesty." Holding their hands, King Gojong asked them to stay with him. Thus, the missionaries spent the entire length of the night with the King, comforting and protecting him.[221]

Thus, the so-called Chungsaengmun Incident became a failure

---

220 Gwang Lin Lee, *Chodae Underwood Suhngyosaui Saengae* (Life of Missionary Underwood) (Seoul: Yonsei University Press, 1991), 157.
221 L. Underwood, *Underwood of Korea*, 150.

because of renegades. On the following day, General Ung Ryeol Yoon, one of the masterminds behind the plan, fled to Underwood's house; he was an old friend of Underwood's. Having determined it was no longer safe for him to remain in the country, he changed into a set of clothes prepared by Underwood, sneaked out of the city and fled to Shanghai via Jemulpo.

However, this Chungsaengmun Incident backfired "was hatched in Underwood's establishment" F. H. Harrington concluded that this incident was "devised in Underwood's house."[222]

The incident was reported all over the papers and immediately became a national issue. In his report to the Minister of Foreign Affairs in Japan, the Japanese diplomat in Seoul, Uchida, wrote of this incident, "In regards to this incident, various foreigners namely, Underwood, Avison, Hulbert, and General Dye, are suspected of involvement."[223] In addition, the Japanese-published *The Hansu-hng Sinbo* featured an article stating that Allen supported the missionaries for this incident.

On the other hand, F. McKenzie said, "There is absolutely no conne-ction,"[224] completely denying the accusation that missionaries took to their own hands to devise the plan. Nevertheless, for the Japanese who had always been uneasy with the pro-king missionaries, it is quite evident that they had to exaggerate the facts and

---

222 F. H. Harrington, *God, Mammon, and the Japanese*, translated by Gwang Lin Lee, *The Korea-US Relation during the Enlightenment Period with a focus on activities of Dr. Allen* (Seoul: Iljogak, 1991), 107.
223 *Japanese Diplomatic Documents*, vol. 28, Book 1, 593.
224 F. A. McKenzie, *Korea's Fight for Freedom*, 87.

make false reports that the missionaries were primarily interested in the involve-ment of politics rather than in mission works. It must be noted that the missionaries certainly had no intention of getting involved in politics. Isn't it the right thing to protect and care for the king of a nation, especially if he has bestowed the best of treatment? Isn't it only human to show sympathy and compassion to a man in grave danger? It certainly shouldn't be labeled as political invo-lvement.

Concerned with political involvement of missionaries, the State Department of the U.S.A. instructed J. H. Sill, the U.S. diplomat in Korea, to calm down the missionaries and to remind them that they should "strictly confine themselves to the missionary work, whether it be teaching in schools, preaching the gospel, or attending to the sick"[225] in order to stay within the protection of their legations. Thus, missionaries were discouraged from voicing anti-Japanese comments. Sill stated that,

> Anti Japanese opinion should not be announced, and Sill should stop, if possible, the habit which has steadily increased since the arrival of American citizens in Korea, of irresponsible persons advising and attempting to control, through irregular channels, the Government of the country.[226]

This is a clear example of the stance taken by the U.S. government.

---

225 F. H. Harrington, *God, Mammon, and the Japanese*, 107.
226 *Ibid.*

This, on one hand, shows that the U.S.A. was in favor of total separation of politics and the church. Missionaries were expected to concentrate on their mission works rather than getting involved in different aspects of the politics in the receiving country. On the other hand, this is often interpreted as the U.S. taking a shrewd diplomatic approach whereby it was deciding to forge a closer relationship with Japan than with Korea for much more far-ranging diplomatic policies in Asia. In any case, although missionaries were incidentally involved in the Chunsaengmun Incident, the general Korean public had now become aware that the missionaries were truly patriotic individuals willing to put their lives at stake for the safety of their King.

(3) King Gojong's Birthday Celebration

One of the most important milestones marking patriotic acts of missionaries was their holding of a celebration worship service on King Gojong's birthday. King Gojong's birthday was September 2 (25th day of the 7th lunar month), and Underwood planned to hold a celebration worship service for the King's birthday in 1896.[227] Underwood took this opportunity to make a public proclamation of Christianity as a religion of patriotism as well as to evangelize people. Despite the shortness of time for preparation, he worked within the best of his ability for this event.

While searching for a large gathering place, he found there was

---

227 L. Underwood, *Underwood of Korea*, 163-167.

no building of such capacity within the city limit. So he obtained permission to use a government office building, which could hold up to about 1,000 people, near the Independence Gate just outside the West Gate. He set up a platform, hung flags and mobilized students to publicize that a prayer meeting will be held to celebrate the King's birthday. Underwood worked throughout the night to print invitation fliers. He also published booklets introducing Christianity, prepared hymnals and circulated them across Seoul. His fliers and publications were in such a great demand to the extent that even on the actual day of the event people came to grab them away from one another. The hymnal also featured a song for the King. Written to sing to the tune of the hymn "God is Our Refuge Strong," this song read:

Through thy Almighty power,
Our king enthroned.
Thy Holy Spirit might keep our country;
May the king live long by Thy holding.
We sing to Thou,
Who is maker of heaven and earth.
When we praise Thee,
Under Thy laugh;
Our country will be happy, strong and free.[228]

---

228 The entire lyrics for this hymn are featured in *Saemunangyohoe 70 Yonsa* (70 Years of Saemunan Church) (1958), 334.

Key figures of all fields and ranks, as well as the cabinet ministers, were invited to the event, and honorable guests prepared speeches. Missionaries of all mission boards in Korea also attended the event.[229] The entire building was full with invited guests and members of the general public. The service commenced quietly with a prayer. There were speeches, followed by hymns. Then the service was concluded with the Lord's Prayer. Underwood's wife later accounted, It was thrilling to hear those words repeated with such a volume of sound.[230] Underwood wrote of this event in one of the magazines.

> Methodist and Presbyterian missionaries and converts were there on the platform with several members of the cabinet and high officials, and one of them addressed the audience. The singing was grand, and hundreds of voices joined reverently in the Lord's Prayer. It was thrilling to us who have watched this work from the beginning.[231]

The service celebrating the King's birthday served as a great opportunity to inform the public that Christianity was a patriotic religion praying for the King and country. It not only allowed the public to think positively of Christianity, but also become more receptive to further evangelism works. In this light, Underwood

---

229 L. Underwood, *Underwood of Korea*, 163.
230 *Ibid.*, 165.
231 *The Missionary Review of the World*, XX-1 (January 1897), 80. L. Underwood, *Fifteen Years among the Top-knots*, 179-181. G. H. Jones, "Korea for Christ," *The Missionary Review of the World*, XX-9 (September 1897), 694.

definitely had an ability to look to the future.

One of the immediate results of the King's birthday celebration service was the founding of Eunyul Church in Hwanghae Province. A wealthy yangban was visiting Seoul to look for a position in the government and attended this service by accident. When he read the evangelistic flier, he was deeply touched and decided to believe in Jesus. He also used his money to buy numerous fliers and books, which he brought back to his hometown and evangelized many other people. As the number of Christian grew, Eunyul Church was established there. Later, he requested Underwood to come and baptized those who confess the faith at Eunyul. Thus, Underwood went to Eunyul and baptized them.[232]

This was definitely a serious lesson of history for the church, teaching the church that she should not become directly involved in matters of politics. Of course, it is a good thing for Christian individuals to be involved in politics or become politicians themselves. However, it must be remembered that organized political actions or assertion of political pressure is clearly against the mission of the church. In this light, we can imagine that the missionaries were getting involved in matters of political nature as they became closer to the King, not primarily as a foreign influence over the King but merely as a close friend helping another in need. It would have been only natural for them to repay the King for the help he had bestowed earlier. Therefore, it would be inappropriate to view the deeds of Underwood and other missionaries over Queen

---

232 Lillias Underwood, *Underwood of Korea*, 166.

Min's assassination and the Chunsaengmun Incident as political involvement of the church.

4. Anti-Japanese Activities of the Church

(1) The Church and the Issue of Anti-Japanese Movement

Was there ever an inevitable reason why the Protestant Church in Korea had to be anti-Japanese? Even for an ordinary person, unless he or she is truly a national traitor, it is only natural for him or her to be angry to see his or her own country becoming another country's colony and their people exploited. At this point, it must be noted that even though the anger and resentment may be of one kind, Christians and non-Christians are bound to show differences in the way they exhibit this anger and undertake their actions against the colonizers. For instance, non-Christians would have acted against the Japanese simply based on the spirit of patriotism as a citizen of the country. It would have been also natural for them to use all available methods and undertake all possible actions in order to regain the independent state of the country.

However, Christians cared for the country in a much different way, and the methods they used to oppose the Japanese were very different as well. In other words, they were not relying on patriotism alone but advocated the justice taught by the Christian faith. They were longing for the fulfillment of God's justice against the powerful nations that exploited the weak. Christians in this country were holding fast to the Word of God that taught them to help the weak and look after the poor. And this principle was at work in the heart of each Christian to resist the evils of the Japanese in Korea. In addition, the Christians exhibited absolutely non-violent resistance against the Japanese, contrary to the indiscreet and unconditional resistance shown by others.

A prime example of non-violent Christian resistance took place in 1907. During this year, the Japanese dethroned King Gojong and passed the throne to King Sunjong, the last king of the Chosun Dynasty, on the grounds that Jun Lee and other secret envoys were sent to the Hague Peace Convention. The whole nation was immediately caught up in protests. So-called civilian 'Euibyong' (righteous armies) staged anti-Japanese guerrilla attacks at every corner of the country, infiltrating Japanese camps and terrorizing the Japanese. In Pyongyang, this righteous army movement also sprang up quickly, but it was immediately self-contained. The inside account of this is found in the Presbyterian mission record of 1908:

> The wise church leader, Elder Kil(Sun Joo), determined that this was without hope. He persuaded the people neither to run away nor to resist the forces⋯⋯ Thus he was able to contain the unrest in the North and saved the entire country from the imminent bloodshed.[233]

---

233 *The Annual Report, Presbyterian Church, North, for 1907*, 251, for 1908, 269.

Such deeds of Elder Sun Joo Kil, i.e. his advice for the righteous army to stop its armed protest, could be seen as unpatriotic opposition against the anti-Japanese spirit of the people. However, in fact, Sun Joo Kil knew very well that Korea was being trampled by the Japanese at her weakest and that it would only result in the shedding of innocent blood if the unarmed people were to take up their farming equipment and fight against the heavily armed Japanese soldiers. Therefore, he encouraged people to accumulate their energy through education and commercial development instead of continuing violent resistance so that they could regain the national power and fight against the Japanese when the time was right. In this way, the Korean Church engaged itself in non-violent resistance against the Japanese. This was the message preached by Jesus's Sermon on the Mount and also the teachings of Christ advocated by L. Tolstoy, M. Gandhi and M. L. King. In 1910, the North Presbyterian missionary W. Blair stated, "If the Korean Church were to officially declare its anti-Japanese stance, she woul d have become the second Roman Catholic Church in Korea."[234]

This was how the Korean Church began her anti-Japanese movement. However, this Christian principle of resistance was not equally applied to all Christians in the country. In fact, during the half-century Japanese Occupation, the Church undertook different forms and methods of resistance. While it is a separate topic by itself to evaluate reasonability all the different forms of resistance undertaken

---

234 William Blair & Bruce Hunter, *Korean Pentecost and the Sufferings which Followed* (Carlisle, Penn: The Banner of Truth Trust, 1977), 63.

by the Church, we are left with no option but to discuss the history of the Church in light of her anti-Japanese movement. This constitutes an important part of the church history.

(2) Anti-Japanese Movement through Faith — Prayers for Nation

Unlike the Catholic Church, which was misunderstood as a religion denying the kingship and parentage and was persecuted accordingly, the Protestant Church was received as a religion respecting the king and the people. Patriotism of the Protestant Church was first displayed through the hoisting of the national flag since the very beginning of her establishment. In his report after the tour of Korea in 1895, R. E. Speer, the General Secretary of the Overseas Mission Board of the North Presbyterian Church of the U.S.A., wrote of the patriotism shown by Koreans:

> One of the most interesting and striking features of the Korean church is its patriotism. Our belated coasting vessel deposited us in North Korea on a Sunday morning, and along the Tatong River our attention was called to villages in which on bamboo poles, small Korea flags were flying. Those flags marked the residences of Christians or were flying over churches. It is a practice which has grown up among the Christians without missionary pressure, to run up the national colors over their homes and churches on

Sunday. They do it to proclaim the character of the day and to mark their own respect it. [235]

Hoisting of the national flag was not a common practice of the time. A majority of the people did not even know there was a national flag.[236]   Hoisting of the national flag was naturally a rarity on its own. Nevertheless, Christians expressed their spirit of patriotism by hoisting the flag at their homes and churches on Sundays even though no one told them to do so. Photographs of early churches clearly show that it was quite a common sight to hoist the national flag at churches whenever there was some event going on. This is just one of the many evidences that show patriotism of the Korean Church.

Whenever in national crisis, the church also cared for the country and took initiatives by holding prayer meetings. As Japan forced Korea to sign the 1905 Protectorate Treaty, the people were thrown into times of great suffering. Even during this great difficulty, the church stood up with prayers. At the Presbyterian General Council in September 1905, Elder Sun Joo Kil proposed holding prayer meetings for the country. The plan was accepted at the council, and one whole week was set aside as a week of prayer

---

235 R. E. Speer, *Missions and Politics in Asia*, 253.
236 Taegeukgi, the national flag of Korea, was originally designed in 1882 by Young Hyo Park, the Korean ambassador sent to Japan after signing the Treaty of Ganghwa-do with Japan, aboard the Meijimaru on his voyage to Japan. It was first hoisted on the roof of Nishimuraya Honkan, Kobe, where he stayed. "Flags," *Donga Segye Daebaekgwasajeon* (Donga Encyclopedia of the World), vol. 4 (1985).

for Korea throughout the country.[237] In November of that year, when the Protectorate Treaty was signed, hundreds and thousands of people came to pray for nation everyday at prayer meetings led by Rev. Duk Kee Chun and Sun Man Chung at Sangdong Methodist Church.

Even as the Korean Army was dismantled and King Gojong was dethroned in 1907, the Korean Church continued to pray for the nation and asked the churches worldwide to pray for Korea, effectively establishing a global prayer network.[238] The Church in Korea continued to harness the national power through prayers and was able to devise her anti-Japanese movement through prayer meetings. To this, the Japanese classified church-going Christians, who became anti-Japanese movement leaders, as impure elements and became hostile toward the Church. The Japanese government ordered, "The Internal Affairs Ministry is to instruct all thirteen provinces to investigate all who go to prayer meetings and report their addresses and names."[239] Praying Christians were labeled as anti-Japanese rebels and treated as suspicious people.

(3) Anti-Japanese Movement through Protests and Violence

Among the Korean Christians, some were not content with holding anti-Japanese prayer meetings and ventured into collective protests

---

237 An Ryeon Kwak, *Jangnogiohoesajeonhwijip* (Compilation of the Presbyterian History), vol. 1 (Chosun Yesugiosuhhoe, 1917), 248.
238 "Mangukgido," *Daehanmaeilsinbo* (The Korea Daily News), August 22, 1907.
239 *Ibid.*, October 5, 1907.

and even violent forms of resistance. Here, let us not get into the controversial debate of whether or not it was acceptable for Christians to undertake such violent resistance against the Japanese. Instead, let us briefly examine some of their important achievements.

When the Protectorate Treaty of 1905 was announced, furious Christians began to stand up in resistance. First of all, Duk Kee Chun and Sun Man Chung recruited a number of strong men in Pyeongan Province to carry out their plan of assassinating the five signatories of the treaty.[240] About the same time, a few Pyongyang Christians went to Seoul, where they circulated their manifesto that the treaty should be called off and that the five signatories be punished. Also, another group of Christians clashed with the Japanese police while circulating the "Message for the Twenty Million Compatriots" Unable to bear the anger of the King's dethroning, Tae Sun Hong in Yangju, Gyeonggi Province, killed himself at the Daehan Gate and Jae Hong Chung, an educator, also killed himself when he failed to carry out his plan to assassinate Ito Hirobumi, the Japanese Residency-General.[241]

Such anti-Japanese movement was equally active overseas. One of the key incidents was In Hwan Chang's shooting of D. W. Stevenson. In San Francisco on March 21, 1908, Chang used his pistol to shoot Stevenson who worked as a foreign affairs advisor for the Japanese administration in Korea and contributed to the expansion of the Japanese power in various ways. While in the

---

240 Gyo Chung, *Daehan Gyeyonsa* (History of Year of Ke of Korea) (The National Institute of Korean History, 1957), 191.
241 *Ibid.*, 255, 274.

States for vacation, Stevenson did not hesitate to speak in a press conference saying, "The Korean royal court and the government are corrupted and Koreans are ignorant; they do not deserve to be independent." The angered Korean organizations in America demanded him to withdraw his statement, but Stevenson refused. To this, In Hwan Chang took it to himself and killed Stevenson. This incident instantly made global headlines, and naturally, Chang's trials were at the center of media focus. Chang was sentenced to imprisonment of 25 years and was released in 1924 after a reduction in his sentence. This incident resulted in consolidation of various patriotic organizations within the U.S. and led to the founding of the Korean National Association, which later became an influential organization supporting the independence movement.[242]

One unforgettable event in the history of the Korean independence movement is definitely the assassination of Residency-General Ito by Jung Keun Ahn. On October 26, 1909 at Harbin Station, Jung Keun Ahn shot Ito, who was returning from Russia after informing Russia of the Japanese dominance in Korea and establishing a new relationship between the two countries. Born in Haeju, Hwanghae Province, Ahn was a Catholic who was baptized at the age of 18. The following text reveals his point of view on murders as a Catholic.

---

242 *Dongnibundongsa Jaryojip II Pyeon*(Resources on the Independence Movement Part II), *Uiyeol Tujaengsa Jaryojip*(Resources on the Heroic Struggle), 30-31.

Q According to the Roman Catholic Church, which you believe in, "Is murder is sin?"

A 'Yes'

Q "Then, you are committed against human rights?"

A "I know that the church teaches us that the killing of a man can only be done by the authorities. Also, the Bible says that murder is sin. But if anyone endeavors to seize someone's country and kill numerous people, and he or she watches this sin as an unconcerned spectator becomes a sinner, thus I was going to remove this sin." [243]

While recognizing the wrong of killing someone as a Christian, he stated that he carried out the rightful duty of eliminating the evils that infiltrate other countries and take people's lives. While it is beyond the scope of this book to discuss the validity of Ahn's assassination, it is important to note that Ahn stood out as a patriotic man, so much so because he was a Christian.

Talking of Jung Keun Ahn, there is another person worth mentioning. It is Yeon Joon Woo (original name was Deok Soon Woo). He was a sincere Protestant believer from Jecheon, North Chu-ngcheong Province. After the signing of the 1905 Protectorate Treaty, he fled to Vladivostok where he established Gyedong School and educated students as anti-Japanese righteous soldiers. Then in

---

243 "The 10th Interrogation of Defendant Eung Chil Ahn," *Hangukdongnibundongsa* (History of the Independence Movement in Korea), 6th Resource, 284.

1908, he met with Ahn and together they plotted the assassination of Ito. They carefully handpicked two locations for the assassination; Ahn was to be stationed at Harbin and Woo at Caijiagou. However, Ito's train passed through Caijiagou at 6.30 a.m. without stopping and arrived at Harbin at 9.00 a.m., and thus Ahn had to take Ito down. Woo was prevented from killing Ito simply because the train did not make its stop at Caijiagou.[244] In essence, this enormous task was carried out together by Jung Keun Ahn and Yeon Jun Woo, a Catholic and a Protestant. This is one fine example of the Catholic Church and the Protestant Church coming together for the welfare of the country.

Another important incident was Jae Myeong Lee's assault of Wan Yong Lee, chief of five traitors, on December 23, 1909. On that day, Wan Yong Lee was attending the memorial mass for the Belgian Emperor at Myeongdong Cathedral. Then, as Wan Yong Lee walked out of the cathedral, Jae Myeong Lee, who had disguised himself as a roasted-chestnut seller, stabbed him three times in the shoulder and the waist with a dagger. However, his plan failed as he was hindered by a policeman and a rickshaw man. Born in Suncheon, North Pyongan Province, Jae Myong Lee graduated from Pyongyang Ilsin School and fled to the U.S. After returning to Korea in 1907, he traveled back and forth to Vladivost ok, engaged himself in the independence movement and decided to eliminate national traitors. In June 1909 at the Pyongyang Taegeu

---

244 See "Woo Deok Soon's Recollections," *Ahn Jung Keun Suhnsaeng Gongpangi* (The Trial Record of Ahn Jung Keun), 1946.

k Bookstore, Chang Ho Ahn, Dong Hui Lee, Tae Gook Ahn and other Christians had a meeting and appointed Jae Myong Lee with the task of taking Wan Yong Lee down.[245] Soon afterwards, Woo Gyu Kang and Dong Hui Lee also carried out several terrorist attempts. As seen above, many Christians continued in their endeavor to eliminate various Japanese leaders and pro-Japanese traitors during the Japanese Occupation. However, the fact that many Christians were key leaders of the anti-Japanese movement should not be generalized to mean that only Christians monopolized the resistance.

(4) Economic Aspect of the Anti-Japanese Movement

Korean Christians also resisted the Japanese in economic aspects as well. Especially evident in the Northwestern region of the country, this economic resistance mainly appeared in the form of refusing to pay taxes. This region of the country was one of the first places to embrace the Christian faith. Also much neglected during the Chosun Dynasty, there were few government officials from this region. Naturally, many residents were directly involved in commerce and industry, and much taxes were required of them.

As the Japanese began to materialize their scheme of colonization, great numbers of Japanese traders arrived in Korea. They used all possible means to acquire important land at cheap prices wherever they went. As they aggressively expanded their commercial foothold

---

245 *Daehanmaeil Sinbo* (The Korea Daily News), December 23, 1909.

in the country, the Korean traders began to lose their marketability in serious degrees. They also acquired every plot of farmland across the country, essentially robbing the peasants of their livelihood with excuses of development and construction of railroads, etc. Seeing such mishaps of the Japanese, it would have only been natural for Koreans to rebel against them in economic ways.

The easiest and most effective method of economic resistance for the ordinary class was to boycott buying Japanese products and to refuse paying taxes. Most notable of them all were the Christian traders in Yongcheon, North Pyeongan Province, and in Suncheon, South Pyeongan Province, who refused to pay taxes. In April 1909, the Governor-General enacted the market tax and began collecting it from the public. The market tax was a new tax requirement promulgated as the 12th regulation in April 1909.[246] To this, the Christians put forth strong resistance. The first of the resistances surfaced in the marketplace of Yangsi, Yongcheon of North Pyeongan Province. Christian leaders played the central role in refusing to pay market taxes. This resistance movement quickly spread to neighboring regions, and the resistance was at its peak in Suncheon, South Pyeongan Province. In January 1910, Elder Bong Hwan Choi of Suncheon-eup Church organized the Traders' Association and staged a movement to refuse paying market taxes. Later this movement became violent, where several furious traders destroyed and burned down Japanese shops and

---

246 The National Institute of Korean History, *Daehandongnibundongsa*(History of the Independence Movement in Korea), vol. 1 (Seoul: Jeongeummunhwasa, 1983), 510.

even killed a number of Japanese people.[247]

Similar resistances to taxes were seen in many other parts of the Northwestern region. Japanese records have it that missionaries were promoting such resistance in some places. According to their records, for instance, in Gyeongsuhng-gun of Hamgyeong Province, Christians joined forces with missionaries there in their refusal to pay taxes for growing tobacco and selling liquor. They also assaulted tax collectors.[248] This was probably based on the strict Christian teachings against smoking and drinking. It is also recorded that in Suhngjin, Hamgyeong Province, missionaries A. R. Ross and R. Grierson ordered the people not to pay market taxes.[249] While it is difficult to rely on just one piece of government record to determine whether the missionaries actually made such an order, it certainly is a clear indication that the Japanese saw the missionaries as the primary force behind the resistance of Christians.

The Japanese also accused the missionaries by saying, "Americans are misleading this people to joyfully pay 160,000 won a year in donations (offerings) to church but to refuse market taxes of 1 or 2 jeon and create disturbances." [250] Another record by the Japanese Legation also states that Christians in Jinnampo, South

---

247 See Yongcheon Recording and Editing Committee, *Pyeongbuk Yongcheonji* (The Records of Yongcheon, North Pyeongan Province) (1968), 145. The National Institute of Korean History, *Daehandongnibundongsa* (History of the Independence Movement in Korea), vol. 1, 505-515.
248 The Records of the Japanese Legation, November 6, 1909.
249 *Ibid.*
250 Gukusanggyeom, *105 In Sageon Jaryojip* (Resources on the 105-men Incident), vol. 2, 323-334.

Pyeongan Province, staged a large-scale tax refusal campaign because they believed that complying with the demands of the Governor-General would result in the ultimate fall of the nation.

Yet another important milestone in Korea's economic resistance to the Japanese was the movement for repaying national debts. This movement started in Daegu, North Gyeongsang Province. Gwang Je Kim, president of the publishing company Gwangmunhoe, acted as the central figure to organize the National Debt Repayment Association. This movement was reported in newspapers, and soon afterward, the association's branches were set up across the country and became a nationwide movement. Korea owed much money to Japan at this time, and the total amount stood at 13 million won by the year 1906 and 1907.[251] Thus, Korean nationals believed that it was necessary for them to repay the debts in order to achieve independence from Japan. The plan involved 20 million Koreans abstaining from drinking and smoking for three months to save all they could.

This movement was perfectly in line with the stringent instructions of the church against drinking and smoking, and thus the church was actively involved in the movement as well. The headquarters for the National Debt Repayment Movement was established at YMCA Seoul, where fundraising events were held among Christians for Bible classes, seminars, debates and concerts. This movement became a great success as Christians nationwide were much stimulated by this and sent in donations. A number of Christian organiza-

---

251 *Daehanmaeil Sinbo* (The Korea Daily News), February 21, 1907.

tions were also founded at this time, including Seoul Women's Education Association, Jinmyeong Ladies' Association, Korean Ladies Association, Suncheon-Uisuhnghoe, Anak National Debt Repayment, Talhwanhoe(Ring Donation Association) and Samdori Ladies' Association in Jeju Island. King Gojong was also in favor of this movement; he quit smoking and made donations.[252]

Let us now examine the women-led Ring Donation Association more in depth. This movement involved taking the rings off the participants' fingers and offering them as donations to repay the national debts. Methods and motives behind this movement are clearly stated in its official statement:

> The place where are bodies are located is our country……If we lose our country, where should we bury the bodies of our parents and our child in the cradle will be whose servants?……our national debt of 13,000,000 yen in our minds? Our population is around 20 million, and 10 million are women, and over half of them might have rings. Each ring might be worth 2 yen, and with 10 million on our women's hands……thinking deeply, it can be affordable. Dedicating the rings, on the pay day of national debt will be a happy day and day of life.[253]

---

252 Suhn Ae Joo, *Jangnogio Yeosuhngsa* (History of Women in the Presbyterian Church) (National Woman's Association of Korean Presbyterian Church, 1979), 76.

253 *Daehanmaeil Sinbo* (The Korea Daily News), February 23, 1907.

The official statement of the 'Pemulpegihoe'(Jewelry Abandon
ment Association) also read:

......among the 20 million, 10 million are women. They
do not have enough money, but they do have gold or silver
ornaments worth of over 3 yen. The total amount of these
would be 30 million. 10 million would be for the national
debt, 10 million for the founding of the banks, and 10
million for the schools. This endeavor would be great for
our country......The ornaments are not used everyday, and
have no benefit lying in all the clothes chests. With this
great amount of national debt, decorative gold and silver
ornaments are like a medal on a naked body. The founding
members offered some ornaments and formed an association
to propagate this plan...... [254]

It was truly radical of Korean Christian women to put their
jewelry together for the sole purpose of repaying the national debts,
and establishing banks and schools. By May 1908, the donations
totaled at 2.31 million won.[255]
Nevertheless, the Japanese were not to sit quietly and watch
such a grand civil movement continue. Labeling it a National Rebel
Movement, they accused Gi Tak Yang, general secretary of the
Daehan Maeilsinbo, which was keeping a portion of the donations,

254 *Ibid.*
255 Edited by Jeong Sik Lee, *Hangukdongnibundongsa* (History of the Independence
    Movement in Korea), vol. 1 (Jeongeummunhwasa, 1983), 175-176.

of embezzling public funds and ordered him to court. Although the Japanese repression put a halt on the movement, this clearly was a significant milestone in the Church's anti-Japanese movement in both a lawful and evangelical manner.[256]

The Church steadfastly resisted the Japanese right from the beginning of the Japanese infiltration to the end of the 1930s when the Japanese forced the people to bow to idols at shrines. Despite a number of renegades and pro-Japanese activists, many patriots and martyrs held fast to their faith and belief, even to the point of death. Although different methods were used, sometimes in unbiblical and non-evangelical manners, they did not even for once abandoned their love for their country. They lived day after day, longing for the moment of national liberation, like watchmen waiting for the morning.

5. Social Reformation Efforts of the Church

Among many things, the primary concern for the Church in Korea was, of course, evangelism. Nevertheless, this evangelism effort was accompanied by much efforts of reforming the backward Korean society. Chosun, which had closely followed the Chinese civilization for a long time, shut its doors against Western civilizations and was later forced to open herself up and come in direct contact with foreign cultures. But it was certainly not easy for the largely Confucian Koreans to take off their old shell. Rapid

256 *Ibid.*

changes were taking place around them; it was simply inevitable to undergo changes themselves, and the Church played a crucial role in this. The Church was the primary vehicle that brought about medical and educational reformations. Since we discussed the topics of medicine and education in earlier sections, let us now consider the other aspects of social reformations.

(1) Establishment of the YMCA and YWCA

Before discussing the contributions made by the Christian Church in Korea toward social reformations, it is in order to mention the founding of the Young Men's Christian Association, or YMC A. When Underwood and Appenzeller requested the YMCA U.S. A. and the YMCA Canada for funds to start the YMCA in Korea, they replied that no financial support would be available until and unless there were a good number of members and leaders for the organization in the country. As a result, the two missionaries worked to recruit some 150 members, but their work was put to a halt because the King feared that this organization would take on a political nature.[257]

Then, later in 1901, the International Council in New York dispatched Philip Gillette as the General Secretary of the YMCA Korea. Gillette commenced the work with students from Baejaeha-kdang and Hanyeongsuhwon in Seoul. Finally in October 1903,

---

257 Geon Ho Song, "The YMCA Movement during the National Ordeals," *Hanguk YMCA Undongsa 1895-1985* (History of the YMCA Movement in Korea 1895-1985) (The Korea YMCA, 1986), 9.

the YMCA Korea was officially inaugurated and 28 key guests witnessed the event. J. Gale was elected as the first chairman and Chi Ho Yoon as the vice chairman. Chi Ho Yoon would later be elected as the first Korean general secretary. The YMCA functioned not only as a venue of socialization, fellowship and education for children of high ranking officials, but it also provided education to financially challenged children around the clock. The Department of Industry provided them vocational training for woodwork, painting, photography, metal work, weaving and so on.

The YMCA also introduced and promoted various sports, providing youths with many opportunities for fellowship and training. The YMCA had definitely made much contribution to the mass education of the public as well.[258]

The YWCA, on the other hand, was founded in 1922, and it became a member of the World Young Women's Christian Association two years later in 1924. Among the many things Christianity has achieved in Korea, it is never too much to emphasize the importance of contributions made by the YWCA in terms of improving the human rights and social status of Korean women.

(2) Improvement in Women's Human Rights

The most chronic predicament of Korean society faced by the Church was the discrimination against women. While it was a

---

258 A. D. Clark, *A History of the Church in Korea*, fifth ed. (Seoul: The Christian Literature Society, 1991), 360-366.

natural practice of the Confucian culture to treat males and females differently, this was not in agreement with the Christian doctrine and the Church made tremendous efforts to remove this evil. The Presbyterian Council declared the following five points regarding human rights for women: "First, boys and girls should not be forced to marriage before they fully mature. Second, widows should not be prohibited from getting married for the second time. Third, believers should not marry unbelievers. Fourth, no money should be paid before officiating the wedding. Fifth, girls and women should never be abused."[259]

One of the most representative forms of discrimination against women in Korea was the keeping of concubines by yangban and government officials. In direct conflict with the Christian doctrine, which strongly advocates monogamy, the Church strictly forbade this practice. Any man who still kept a concubine could not be baptized.

Having decided that educating women was the first step to improving the human rights of women, missionaries concentrated in setting up educational institutes for women. The establishment of Ewhahakdang by the Methodist Church was mentioned earlier. As the statement of the *Daehan Geuriseudoin Hoebo*, "Betterment of families, prosperity of the nation, and power of the people truly depend on education of all women nationwide."[260] the newspaper emphasizes the enormous importance education of women has

---

259 *Geuriseudo Sinmun* (The Christian News), October 3, 1901.
260 "Education of Women has the Highest Priority," *Daehan Geuriseudoin Hoebo* (The Korean Christian Advocate), February 15, 1899.

on the future of the Church and the nation. It is recorded that Gambawi Church in Pyeongsan, Hwanghae Province, "decided that husbands and wives should respect one another in language and eat at one table."[261] The Church's decision of prohibiting men from mistreating their wives and encouraging them to use formal language to one another was certainly a radical move at that time.

The following record also shows us the tremendous success achieved by the Church's education of girls.

At Yondong Girl's School, there are 20 students. This school educated students not only in the sciences, but also in morality, physical education, cooking, sewing, Korean characters, writing, reciting the Bible, music, mathematics, geology, history, Chinese characters, Chinese character writing, chemistry, gymnastics... thus being well educated and knowing not only geography and history, but also arithmetic and geography. Also, these students know about 2,000 Chinese characters, which brings great thankfulness to God, and is profitable for the church and country. If any church member would like to send his or her daughter to this school, they will need to pay 500 yang per year. The school will provide the room and board. Please send a letter to Miss Dotty at Yondong Girl's School.[262]

---

261 *Geuriseudo Sinmun*(The Christian News), June 20, 1901.
262 *Ibid.*, April 10, 1902.

The previously mentioned Nevius Methods, which encouraged Christians to focus their evangelism efforts on girls and women, effectively recognized the importance of women even in missionary works. Eradication of discrimination between males and females was based on the Word of God, which taught that God's creation of a man and a woman was so they could be united together in care, respect and love for one another. Restoration of women's human rights and eradication of gender discrimination were invaluable achievements of the early Christian Church in Korea.

(3) Overthrowing the Social Ranks

In accordance to the Confucius tradition, clear social ranks and classes existed in the Korean society. There were four main classes: aristocrats, farmers, artisans and tradesmen. Scholars were highly respected, while skilled workers and commercial workforce were neglected and oppressed. It is needless to mention that members of the lowest class—slaves and baekjeong (butchers)—were treated at the equal level to stock animals. The Church emphasized the Christian teaching that God created all men and women equal with no ranks or classes to separate them. The Korean Church has definitely made a breakthrough in her attempt to reform the society, especially by promoting equality of all men and women. The spirit of love and care for the neglected was translated into active and continuous relief campaigns for the orphans, the sick, the handicapped and the aged.

While the law had prohibited the slave and butcher systems since the Gabo Reformation(Reformation in the year of Gabo) in 1894, many people continued to keep their former practices. Thus, the Church took the lead in eradicating all forms of social discrimination through her evangelism efforts, and many neglected members of society were attracted to the Church.

The Christian News once reported of a man who realized the importance of human equality and freed her own slaves after believing in Jesus:

Our Christians became free from the servant of the Devil and became God's children and also realized that it is not right to have slaves who are God's children. As written before, Mrs. Park, In See liberated her maid-servant and adopted her daughter. Mrs. Lee who live at Chang Village in Pyongyang bought a maid-servant with 1,000 yang after she became a Christian, knowing that she had become a daughter of God and redeemed through Jesus Christ by the grace of God. She talked to the her servant, "I was anxious when I prayed to God and while reading my Bible, because I use you as a servant. I can not sell you as an animal, and thus I made up my mind to let you become free from servanthood." She burnt the slave paper of the servant and treated her as her own daughter. It can not be compared with non-Christians who use their servants, she thought deeply and moved in her love. This mind set comes from fearing the God and believing in Jesus Christ and loving mankind. This holy decision is a symbol of 20 million people of this country being saved from the Devil and their sins. Thus, let us reform our minds from formal lip-service and reform.[263]

This is just one of the many aspects the Christian faith has on removing and reforming wrong social practices and traditions of the past.

(4) Sacredness of Labor

Koreans were accustomed to disregarding any form of manual labor. The Confucian tradition had taught people that labor was a job for the lowest class and that it was a noble thing for yanghans to read books and write poetry. To this, Christianity pointed out the wrongs of the tradition and advocated the sacredness of labor. There was a question-and-answer newspaper article designed to promote the sacredness of labor.

Labor Questions:

Q Is it good or bad in the Korean custom to labor?
A It is not good.

---

263 *Ibid.*, May 24, 1906.

Q How do you know?

A When one meets another, they ask, 'What do you do?' Then the other person says, 'I do not do any work.' It is a common phenomenon as a gentleman, but in the Western custom, this is not good and they are regarded as an hopeless fellow.

Q Is there another area of labor that is considered not good?

A Yes, any lower level men called a 'Ilgun'(hired servant: coolie) do this type of work.

Q Whom should we teach how to work?

A From princes to a coolie's sons.264

(5) The Issue of Ancestral Worship

As discussed in the earlier chapter on Roman Catholicism, the issue of ancestral worship was one of the age-long traditions deeply rooted in Korean society, and many believers had to lose their lives because of it. In the same way, the Protestant Church not only strongly advocated the doctrinal truth prohibiting any form of ancestral worship, but also began to promote social reformations regarding the issue. The Church worked hard to eradicate this practice, not as a means to deny the importance of respecting parents and ancestors, but to eliminate all elements of idol worship

---

264 *Ibid.*, July 14, 1901.

and all ill effects of it. *The Christian News* described the social ill with the following words:

Ancestor worship is vain and abused in various ways. It is time utilized, which disturbs work, spent energy, spent money……If someone does not have a son, he takes a concubine to get a son, which is the root of ruin in a home and causes great disturbance……If all the money that was spent on ancestor worship was spent for the country it could be much more advanced. They do not think about education and are dedicated to superstitious worship. It is a great sin to God, because they think of their ancestors as gods and glorify them. This is against God's ordinances and blasphemous.[265]

In addition to the ill effects of ancestral worship, the newspaper continued on to point out the problem of Koreans engaging in filthy talks.

……The first thing what our people need to reform is their filthy talk. Despite being high or low status people, where people gather they speak words of obscenity. When they make a vow, you hardly hear filthy words……When the lower class people talk a common word, two or three filthy words follow……if a women passes by, people talk

---

265 *Ibid.*, February 18, 1913.

foolish things to her and even the policeman does not get involved in such things. It is shame to other foreign people from a country of etiquette……if this custom changes, then people shall behave well and the status of the country will become high.[266]

The above-mentioned practices and customs of Korean society presented the biggest issues requiring social reformations. Although such ill practices could not be removed overnight, the Church patiently worked on eradicating them and was able to see much success in these areas.

(6) Inclusive Use of Hangeul (Korean Native Letters)

Perhaps no other achievements of the early Church in Korea carried so much significance than her exclusive use of Hangeul. In 1972, the famous author on nationalism, L. L. Snyder, made a statement regarding the linguistic and ethnic identity:

National vocabulary, syntax, word formations, and word rhythms accurately reflect the intellectual and emotional qualities of a people. Moreover, it is through language that the accumulated historical traditions and memories of a people are transmitted from generation to generation to help maintain the unity of culture that partly distinguishes

---

266 *Ibid.*, April 11, 1901.

one nation from another.[267]

In this light, exclusive use of Hangeul was crucial for maintaining the identity and homogeneity of the Korean culture. In 1893, Presbyterian missionaries in Seoul made two crucial decisions regarding literal mission works in Korea: first, the Bible was to be translated as soon as possible; and second, all documents were to be published in "pure Korean(hangeul)."[268] The "second-best alphabet in the world,"[269] as labeled by linguists, had been looked down on and neglected for a long time, but missionaries recognized its true value and decided to fully utilize it so that even girls and women could learn to read it. *The Christian News* records the following in regards to the exclusive use of Hangeul:

> ......some Korean scholars are arrogant and thus neglect the uneducated people. They do not want to educate the uneducated people and do not teach special skills even to their own children, because they are afraid that these skills will be known to others. Because of not knowing the Truth, they act like this. Also, they respect the Chinese characters, but neglect the Korean characters, which is their own language. A particular company (The Bible Society) publishes

267 L. L. Snyder, *The Meaning of Nationalism* (Westport, Conn.: Greenwood, 1972), 21.
268 C. C. Vinton, "Presbyterian Mission in Korea," *The Missionary Review of the World* (September 1893), 671.
269 H. G. Underwood, *The Call of Korea*, 71.

their books in Korean characters, and the uneducated people have begun to read gradually, and carpenters and shepherds, women, and children have begun to understand the Korean language. Thus, Korean characters, which have been hidden for 400 years have appeared as this time, it is with great thankfulness to God.[270]

Thanks to the missionaries' nationwide efforts of promoting Hangeul, even women in the countryside could master the writing and read the Bible and other Christian publications. Thus, Hangeul was able to function as the locomotive of evangelism and public education.

Missionaries also concentrated their efforts on publishing dictionaries, which were absolute necessities in learning and studying Hangeul. Remembering his initial difficulty of having to learn Korean without a dictionary, Underwood spent five years to publish *A Concise Dictionary of the Korean Language* in 1890 in Yokohama. Comprising of two parts, this volume was compiled in a way that Korean-English and English-Korean sections could be viewed in parallel to each other. The greatest challenge for this work was that there were no unified spelling rules for Hangeul at that time.

Hangeul was much neglected in Korean society, but missionaries discovered its true value and widely promoted its use. This not only allowed Koreans to take pride in their culture, but also possess a much stronger sense of ethnic identity.

---

270 *Geuriseudo Sinmun* (The Christian News), February 14, 1901.

Chapter 6

Formation of the Korean Church and the Japanese Oppression

At the dawn of the twentieth century, powerless Korea was faced with a series of tragic events as superpowers ruled over her. On July 27, 1905, the so-called "Taft-Katsura Agreement" was secretly signed between William Howard Taft, United States Secretary of War, and Katsura Taro, Prime Minister of Japan. This agreement was intended for the U.S. to approve the Japanese rule in Korea and to confirm that Japan had no plans to invade the Philippines.[271] This agreement also became the basis for the unequal signing of the Protectorate Treaty in November of that year, which led to the establishment of the Residency-General in Seoul for the full-scale preparation of colonizing Korea. The Japanese rendered Korea powerless by effectively dismantling the Korean Army in 1907 and by deposing King Gojong. By 1910,

---

271 Tyler Dennet, "President Roosevelt's Secret Pact with Japan," *The Current History Magazine* (1921), 15-21.

the signing of the Korea-Japan Annexation Treaty was concluded, putting an end to the 500-year-old Chosun Dynasty. The history of the Japanese pillage of Korea continued on with extreme persecution and exploitation until the Japanese forces withdrew after their defeat in the Second World War in 1945.

Despite the harsh conditions, however, the Church continued to grow; the Independent Presbytery was founded in 1907, the General Assembly of the Presbyterian Church in 1912, and the Methodist Annual Conference were organized for a more systematic approach in missions and education.

1. The Great Revival of 1907

(1) Origins and Process

The Great Revival of 1907 opened a new era for the Korean Church. Although many Christians had received the faith on the grounds of selfish or patriotic reasons, this revival movement allowed them to come in direct contact with the core of the Christian truth and provided them the experience of being born again. In this sense, the revival movement is recognized as having contributed tremendously in establishing the indigenous church in Korea.

This revival movement has an indirect cause and a direct cause. The indirect cause dates back to 1903. Methodist missionaries in the Wonsan area of South Hamgyeong Province began to hold a prayer meeting when M. C. White, a missionary in China, came to Korea. Soon several Korean Christians as well as Presbyterian and Baptist missionaries attended this prayer meeting, and the meeting was held nightly for a week at Changjeon Church. Also attending was R. A. Hardie, a South Methodist missionary who worked a number of years in Gangwon Province but with no real results. Here, Hardie recognized his powerlessness and prayed a prayer of total surrender to God, which acted as a spark for the revival movement.

Originally a YMCA-based medical missionary from the University of Toronto, Hardie joined the South Methodist Church in 1898, a few years after his arrival in Korea, and carried out mission works in Gangwon Province. He was essentially involved in pioneering missions, but there were no significant results. He wrote, "For three years I had worked, and laboured hard in the prefecture of Kangwon (Province), and the failure of the work there had done more than anything else to break me down and bring to the end of myself.[272] This shows that his work was not a simple task. He openly confessed his failure and its reasons before the other missionaries. And as he prayed, he felt the Holy Spirit fall on him. This is his account of the experience:

With confidence of the Holy Spirit fully in my mind,
I confessed my arrogance, wickedness, and lack of faith
with a shameful and awed face. The congregation began
to realize their strong guilty feelings of repentance through

---

272 *The Annual Report, Methodist Episcopal Church, South, for 1905,* 39-44

experiencing their Christian belief. I confessed to them that
I received the Holy Spirit through believing in God's promise.[273]

Witnessing Hardie's frank confession of his sins and his experience of the Holy Spirit's downpour, those present at the prayer
meeting also joined in the special experience of the Holy Spirit
and the fire of revival began to burn stronger.

Such meetings took place again in Wonsan in the following
year of 1904, and many more were baptized in the Holy Spirit.
However, such movement of the Holy Spirit was limited locally
in the Wonsan area. Then in the summer of 1906, the missionaries
in Pyongyang, already aware of the revival in Wonsan, invited
Hardie for a weeklong combined prayer meeting for Presbyterian
and Methodist missionaries. Following this prayer meeting was
the Annual Conference of the North Presbyterian Church in Seoul,
where Rev. H. A. Johnson from New York came to share the
news on the revival in India and Wales.

Also speaking to a Korean congregation at Pyongyang Jangdaehyeon Church, Rev. Johnson spoke about revivals in foreign countries and asked, "Who in Korea wants to be filled with the Holy
Spirit? Raise your hands and stand on your feet if you want the
Holy Spirit." But nobody responded. At that moment, Elder Sun
Joo Kil raised his hand and stood up, deeply touched. Seeing
this, Rev. Johnson prophesied the revival of Korea.[274] God was

---

273 *Ibid.*
274 In Suh Kim, "A Short Biography of Kil Sun Joo," *Kim In Suh Jeojak Jeonjip*
(Collection of Kim In Suh's Writings), vol. 5 (Gyomunsa, 1976), 57.

setting aside Elder Sun Joo Kil for the Korean Church. The missionaries continued holding various Christian meetings in order to give spiritual comfort and the heavenly hope to the destitute people deprived of their own nation.

On the other hand, the direct cause of the Revival of 1907 was the outpouring of the Holy Spirit at the South Pyeongan Province Men's Meeting in January 1907. Held for ten days from January 6, this meeting featured Bible Study during the day and evangelistic meetings in the evening. The revival started off mainly because the church was preparing for the meeting with many days of early morning prayer.

Elder Sun Joo Kil had been leading the early morning prayer meeting, which began in the Fall the previous year. Concerned with the difficult situation Korea was faced with, Sun Joo Kil went to church early every morning to pray along with Elder Chi Rok Park. Soon many other church members joined the early morning prayer meeting and the number quickly grew to 300 and then to 500. Thinking that it was not good for hundreds of church members to gather in church to pray without official permission, Kil obtained an official permit from the church session and officially began the Early Morning Prayer Meetings. So this is how early morning prayer meetings in Korea started at Pyongyang Jangdaehyeon Church in the Fall of 1906.

As many prayers have gone into the early morning prayer meeting s in preparation of the weeklong men's Bible Study meeting, the revival broke out in just a few days on the evening of January

14. The fire fell when the North Presbyterian missionary W. N. Blair read 1 Corinthians 12:27 and preached, "We are the body of Christ, and each one of us is a part of it." The people clearly felt the overflowing of an unusual power within the church, and they had first-hand experience of the Holy Spirit moving within them. Let us take a look at a news article featured in *The Times*, a prestigious English newspaper. This is a first-hand account as witnessed by Sir William Cecil of England.

This fire of revival spread out like wildfire. At this point, it is important to recognize Elder Sun Joo Kil as the core figure behind the revival movement.

> When he began to pray with "My Father," a mysterious power then came externally and it seemed that the whole congregation was seized by it. The Westerners wrote that this phenomenon was panic. Then most of them fell into mourning. Each person felt strongly to confess one's sins. One stood up and tried to confess his sins; one touched his head on the ground with his fists; and one fought with some power, which forced him to confess his sins. Some missionaries were frightened with the Korean Christians' sins and some missionaries shed tears due to the spiritual power, which made them confess their sins. Even though the meeting was through the night, many people did not return to their homes, and prayed or struggled with their terrible sins in their mind through the whole night. The

next day, the missionaries tried to comfort them and make a normal setting, but the same phenomenon continued for many days.[275]

(2) Rev. Sun Joo Kil

Often reputed as the "father of Christianity in Korea"[276] and "one of her (Korean Protestant church) brightest ornaments and greatest men."[277] Rev. Sun Joo Kil was born as Bong Soon Kil's second son in Anju, North Pyeongan Province, on March 15, 1869. Having born to parents in their old age, Sun Joo Kil was given much love and care. Although not a wealthy family, they were not hard-pressed for survival and the parents were able to provide Sun Joo Kil with adequate education. At the age of 11, in accordance to the customs of his time, Kil married Suhn Haeng Shin, the only daughter of Hyeop Shin in Anju. They had three sons and a daughter and maintained a happy family until their passing away in good old age.[278]

Kil was once contracted with a disease. Determined to cure himself and also to train his mind, he went to Mt. Yongak to

275 *The Annual Report, Methodist Episcopal Church, North*, for 1907, 419, Mrs. W. M. Baird (Annie A.). "The Spirit among Pyeng Yang Students," *The Korea Mission Field* (May 1907), 65-67.
276 Jin Kyong Kil, *Yeonggye Kil, Sun Joo* (Seoul: Jongno Publishing, 1975), 129.
277 C. W. Bernheisel, "Rev. Kil, Sunju," *The Korea Mission Field* XXXII-2 (February 1936), 29.
278 In Suh Kim, "A Short Biography of Kil Sun Joo," *Kim In Suh Jeojak Jeonjip* (Collection of Kim In Suh's Writings), vol. 5, 44.

meditate alone. There he was engrossed with Gwansuhnggyo(a branch of Budhism), a shamanistic religion worshiping Guanwoo,[279] and read their scriptures ten thousand times. But he soon realized that there was no real spiritual satisfaction in Gwansuhnggyo. Thus he abandoned Gwangsuhnggyo and began to train himself in Suhndo (Mysticism) at the age of 21.[280]

Despite the diverse religious experiences, Kil was not able to settle for anything that could satisfy him spiritually. In fact, he was becoming more and more desperate. Then in 1893, the American North Presbyterian missionary Samuel A. Moffett first arrived in Pyongyang and engaged in mission works. Suhk Jin Han, who would later become the first seminary graduate along with Kil, assisted Moffett.[281] As Kil's close friend Jong Seop Kim became acquainted with Moffett, he gave Kil some Christian books and encouraged him to explore the Christian faith. Being a man of great academic curiosity, Kil began to read the books and learn about the Christian truth. Among them, it was J. Bunyan's *The Pilgrim's Progress* that provided the turning point for Kil to accept Christ.

Kil was also able to surrender his life to Jesus when he had the experience of hearing the voice of God while praying. Encouraged by Jong Seop Kim, Kil was able to have the decisive experience while he was concentrating in meditation and prayers in pursuit of knowledge of the Christian God. Kil's son, Jin Kyeong Kil,

---

279 Jin Kyong Kil, *Yeonggye Kil Sun Joo*, 26.
280 *Ibid.*, 30.
281 *Ibid.*, 42.

writes of Kil's experience:

Before he finished his prayer, "Let me know whether Jesus is the real Savior of the world," he was surprised with sound of drums and of gun shots. Suddenly, he heard his name being called three times, 'Kil Sun Joo,' 'Kil Sun Joo,' and 'Kil Sun Joo.' He was fearful of his name being called and kneeled down and prayed, "My beloved Father, please forgive my sins and save me." Then he could call Him Father with a clear mind. He realized that he was a great sinner and cried bitterly······his prayer continued without ceasing······with full joy, he shed tears continually······ When he prayed, "Let me know whether Jesus is my Savior," and called God as Father, he became a captive of Christ.[282]

Having become a follower of Gwansuhnggyo at the age of 19 and remained a Suhndo disciple until the age of 29, Kil was finally able to obtain his spiritual satisfaction from the Christian faith, "like Saint Augustine of Africa."[283] On July 12, 1897, Kil was baptized by missionary Graham Lee and became a Christian at the age of 29.[284] In reference to Kil's confession of the Christian faith, Rev. In Suh Kim wrote,

---

282 Ibid., 72.
283 Gil Seop Song, Hanguk Sinhak Sasangsa (History of Theological Thoughts in Korea) (Seoul: Korea Christian Publishing, 1987), 93.
284 C. F. Bernheisel, "Rev. Kil Sunju," The Korea Mission Field (February 1936), 29.

Congratulations! The day you confessed your faith of Christ was the day that a foundation stone was laid for the Church in Chosun, and the day you began reading the Word and praying was the day that the construction work commenced for the Church in Korea. The Lord called you and appointed you to the early Church for He stretched out His hands of blessing on the land of Chosun.[285]

The story of Kil's conversion was featured in the *International Sunday School Lessons of the U.S.A.* At one point, a Sunday school in Germany was touched by the story and sent an offering.[286]

In the same year he was born again, Kil was appointed as a youngsoo (deacon) at Pyongyang Jangdaehyeon Church, and then he was elected as an elder at the age of 33. In 1902, missionary Moffett appointed Kil as a pastor's helper for Pyongyang Jangdaehyeon Church and various churches in Hwanghae Province. Although the pay was significantly low, he gladly accepted the offer and dedicated himself to the cause. In 1903, Kil enrolled at the Pyongyang Presbyterian Seminary, which was founded by Moffett. He graduated as one of the first batches of graduates in 1907. He was then ordained by the Independent Presbytery, which was founded in the same year. He began pasturing Pyongyang Jangdae-hyeon Church, where he would minister for 20 years until the church experienced internal conflicts. He then founded and pastored

---

285 In Suh Kim, "A Short Biography of kil Sun Joo," *Kim In Suh Jeojak Jeonjip* (Collection of Kim In Suh's Writings), vol. 5, 48.
286 *Ibid.*

Ihyangri Church, and led revival meetings across the country.

Sun Joo Kil passed away in the morning of November 26, 1936, just a day after he fainted on the pulpit after his last sermon during a bible study meeting for the Pyeongsuh Presbytery. He was indeed one of the greatest leaders the Korean Church ever had.

(3) Expansion of the Revival

The fire of the revival was further fueled by Sun Joo Kil's great passion as his sermons began to captivate many people. Elder Ik No Chung, who listened to Kil's sermon, wrote of his experience:

> From the beginning it was not Kil's face······Kil was once stone-blind, was partially blind still, but here his face was full of great majesty and power, a face on fire with purity and holiness. It was the power of Jesus and it was not Kil. He spoke of John the Baptist, and how he called on men to repent and confess······There was no escape······God was calling. An awful fear of sin, not experienced before settled over us. How to deal with this reality of sin and escape was the question······"O God what shall I do?······" ······Kil, in this moment of inspiration, was John the Baptist to the crowd······ Confess was the word that he was compelled to say, and confess was the act that they were compelled to do.[287]

---

287 J. Gale, *Korea in Transition* (New York: Laymen's Missionary Movement, 1909), 205-206.

Such fire of the Holy Spirit burned in the hearts of everyone present at the meetings, and the fire continued to spread out across the country. The revival fire that started in Pyongyang in January began to spread in schools as they opened for a new school year in February. The revival quickly spread to a total of 2,500 students at Sungsil College, Sungsil Middle School, Sungdeok Middle School, Gwangsuhng Middle School and Sungui Middle School.[288] Even elementary school children were a part of the revival. The students called off their classes and attended church meetings instead. In March, women's meetings for the Presbyterian Church were held for 12 days. Every participant of these meetings also experienced the miraculous movement of the Holy Spirit. Then in May, students of the Presbyterian Seminary gathered in Pyongyang for the new semester that was to open in three months. When the classes began, the missionaries held a special meeting for these students. A strong wind of the Holy Spirit wept through the meeting as well. Many students shed tears of repentance and were challenged to stand firm as ministers in training. One of the missionaries stated, "These men, who are to be the pastors of Korean churches, experienced the fire of the Holy Spirit burning sin out of their lives."[289]

The revival that started off in Pyongyang spread out to every other part of the country. R. Hardie, J. Gerdine, Kil and others traveled across the country and held meetings at every church

---

288 "The Spirit Among Pyeng Yang Students," *The Korea Mission Field* (June 1907), 65-67.

289 G. S. McCune, "Opening Days at the Theological Seminary," *The Korea Mission Field* (June 1907), 89.

they could find. The Holy Spirit greatly moved everywhere. G. Lee went to Suncheon, W. B. Hunt went to Daegu and W. L. Swallen went to Gwangju to hold meetings where the Holy Spirit moved in the same great manner.

Dr. J. R. Mott-General Secretary of the World YMCA, Chairman of the World Student Christian Federation and a leader of the world ecumenical movement-said of the following after seeing the churches in Korea in 1907:

> During my recent tour in the Far East I formed the deep conviction that if the present work on the part of the cooperating missions in Korea is adequately sustained and enlarged in the immediate future Korea will be the first nation in the non Christian world to become a Christian nation. I know of no mission field where larger or more substantial results have been secured, in proportion to the expenditure, than in Korea.[290]

Seeing the geometrically increasing number of Christians and the active evangelism involvement of all Christians as the great revival overtook the whole of Korea, Mott realized that evangelization of Korea was at hand, and he forecasted that Korea would become the first mission field to be truly Christian. The situation at that time was certainly more than enough for him to think and believe this way.

---

290 J. R. Mott, *Annual Report of the Board of Mission Methodist Episcopal Church, South, 1908, 10. The Korea Mission Field* (May 1908), 67.

This wave of revival reached as far as China. Chinese pastors in the Manchuria region came to Pyongyang to attend revival meetings so that they could return to their own country and spread this fire of revival. The Chinese revival spread through Shenyang, Liaoyang, Manchuria and Beijing. Considering the fact that Koreans had always learned things from China, it was such a great grace of God that Koreans were now able to share the Word of God with the Chinese and teach them the ways of the Lord.

(4) Impacts of the Revival

The Great Revival greatly impacted the theology and formation of the Korean Church.

First, this revival allowed Koreans to understand the true meaning behind the Christian doctrine, and it served as an excellent opportunity to cultivate the Christian truth in the hearts of Korean Christians. Koreans had received the Christian faith for a variety of reasons and only a few understood the true meaning of Christianity. But the revival gave them the experience of the typical Christian life, i.e. true repentance, inspiration of the Holy Spirit, and dedication as a new creation. Such consolidation of the Korean Church signified that she truly now was able to stand as a national church. Just as the World Missionary Conference at Edinburgh in 1910 spoke of the Great Revival in Korea as "an independent work of the Holy Spirit has begun in the infant Korean Church,"[291] the revival

---

291 The World Missionary Conference at Edinburgh, 1910, *The Report of*

can be interpreted as the beginning of God's work in the independ ent Korean Church.

Second, the Korean Church underwent rapid growth. Being a common feature of any typical revival movement, the 1907 revival of Korea was accompanied by revival of churches throughout the country. Underwood presented the following statistics in regards to church growth: between 1906 and 1907, the Presbyterian Church had a 29% increase in the number of baptized members from 12,506 to 15,097 and a 34% increase in the number of new members from 44,587 to 59,787 with an increase of 15,200 persons. In short, the total membership increased by 34% from 54,987 to 73,8 44 between 1906 and 1907. The growth in the Methodist Church was also significant, with a 118% increase from 18,107 to 39,613 between 1906 and 1907.[292]

The revival also impacted the expansion of Christian schools. While there were 208 schools in June 1906, there were 344 of them by the same time the following year. Following the establi- shment of over 130 schools, the number of students also increased from 3,456 in 1906 to 7,504 in 1907.[293] The increasing number of students in Christian schools signified that there were more students being educated with Christian principles. This is also con- firmed by the fact that there were a great number of anti-Japanese

Commission, I, 77.

292 H. G. Underwood, "The Growth of the Korean Church," *The Missionary Review of the World* (February 1908), 100. H. A. Rhodes, ed., *History of Korea Mission*, 285.

293 H. A. Rhodes, *ibid.*

movement leaders in the years to come. It is no coincidence that the March First Movement broke out about the time these students reached their full adult age.

Third, the revival produced the indigenous and unique characteristics of the Korean Church. As mentioned earlier, this revival started off with the uniquely Korean "early morning prayer meeting" led by Elder Sun Joo Kil. Early morning prayer meetings are unique to Korean churches, and they are found in no other churches in the world. The early morning prayer meetings provided the pastors and laymen the venue and time to tap into God's power, repent their sins and say their petitions to God. As the early morning prayer meetings continue on in today's Korean Church, they provide the fuel for growth and spiritual life of the Korean Church in very much the same way a hundred years ago.

Another intriguing characteristic is that Tongsuhng (unanimous) prayers-two or more persons praying aloud simultaneously-first started during the revival. Several eye witnesses noted the beginning of Tongsuhng prayers:

> After a short sermon, Mr. [Graham] Lee took charge of the meeting and called for prayers. So many began praying the Mr. Lee said, "If you want to pray like that, all pray," and the whole audience began to pray out loud, all together. The effect was indescribable-not confusion, but a vast harmony of sound and spirit, a mingling together of souls moved by irresistible impulse of prayer. The prayer sounded me

like the falling of many waters, an ocean of prayer beating against God's throne.[294]

The revival of 1907 created the uniquely Korean prayer methods of Tongsuhng prayer, as well as early morning prayers. These two prayer methods are very much alive in today's Korean Church and act as important vehicles of Korean spirituality. Another form of prayer that started at this time was "Chulja" (vigil) prayers." As meetings went on until late in the night, those living far away did not go back home but stayed awake praying throughout the night until the early morning prayer meeting for the following day was held. Such unique characteristics of the Korean Church made "No longer could Christianity be described as a Western religion."[295]

Fourth, the revival gave birth to the ecumenical spirit in Korea. In other words, conflicts between the Korean Church leaders and missionaries were lifted through the revival and their bond became stronger. Before the revival, missionaries were in the position of preaching the Gospel to the Korean Church and guiding the people in the Christian walk. Many missionaries naturally had a sense of superiority over the Korean church leaders and they assumed the position of teaching them from above. At the same time, Koreans also thought it right for learners to be in the lower position. In

---

294 W. N. Blair, *The Korean Pentecost*, 403.
295 K. M. Wells, *New God, New Nation, Protestants and Self-Reconstruction Nationalism in Korea, 1896-1937* (Honolulu: University of Hawaii, 1990), 37.

such relationships, the two groups of people were bound to have conflicts that nobody was talking about. However, as the revival began to take hold of the Church, missionaries themselves realized that they were sinners as well and that it was not possible for them to remain as holy teachers at all times. One of the missionaries confessed:

> Until this year I was more or less bound by that contemptible notion that the East is East and the West, West, and that there can be no real affinity or common meeting ground between them······though there may be a thousand things, on the surface, that are the direct opposite of the West, the Korean is at heart, and in all fundamental things, at one with his brother of the West.[296]

Now missionaries became humble enough to accept Korean believers as true brothers of equal status, Korean church leaders and lay people no longer had to treat missionaries as noble teachers and both Korean believers and foreign missionaries could enjoy the intimate and borderless fellowship. This was one of the great fruits of the revival. In addition, the Presbyterian Theological Seminary in Pyongyang saw seven of its first graduates in 1907. The Koreans were now able to serve as fully qualified pastors alongside foreign missionaries. This also meant that lay missionaries and

---

296 J. Z. Moore, "The Great Revival Year," *The Korea Mission Field* (August 1907), 118.

missionary family members had to recognize Korean pastors as their teachers. This way, the revival confirmed, "there is neither Jew nor Greek, slave nor free, male nor female, for you are all one in Christ Jesus (Galatians 3:28)."

The ecumenical spirit of this revival appeared as being interdenominational. The Presbyterians and the Methodists held the revival meetings jointly. The two denominations actively shared their resources. Rev. Sun Joo Kil conducted meetings in many Methodist churches, and Methodist pastors led meetings in Presbyterian churches. Therefore, the revival movement also brought about elimination of the visible differences and invisible gaps between denominations.

So far we have looked at a number of positive results of the revival movement. Nevertheless, there are some criticisms of the revival movement. Most of the criticisms were based on the speculation that the revival movement rendered the Korean Church insensitive to politics and the history.[297] It is argued that, as the Japanese colonized Korea after signing the 1905 Protectorate Treaty and as angry ordinary citizens and Christians alike became essentially anti-Japanese in their attitude, the missionaries tried to divert

---

297 This view is supported by Sun Kyong Park, "The Korean Race and the Problem of Christian Missions," *Minjoktongilgwa Gidokio* (The Unification of Race and Christianity) (Hangilsa, 1986); Kyoung Bae Min, *Hangukminjokgy ohoe Hyeonsuhngsaron* (A Study of the Development of the Korean National Church) (1974); Jeong Min Suh, "Understanding the Great Revival of the Early Korean Church," *Hangukgidokgiowa Minjokundong* (Christianity in Korea and the National Movement), co-written by Man Yeol Lee and six others (Bosuhng, 1986); and Dae Joon Noh, "Characteristics of the Great Revival of 1907," *Hangukgidokgiosayeongu* (A Study of the History of Christianity in Korea), vol. 15, 16 (August 1987).

the people's attention from political involvement to only things spiritual, i.e. believing in Jesus and going to heaven. The critics claim that missionaries led the revival movement so that Christians would not remain interested in secular things, especially politics, and in the due course, the anti-Japanese spirit became much weaker in the Korean Church after the revival. It is believed that Christians focused on spirituality and nothing else.

However, it must be noted that this view is not in agreement with the actual cause of the revival meeting. Any revival movement, or Holy Spirit movement, can never be intentionally induced by a handful of missionaries just by want. In the same way, the issue of the Church becoming non-political should never be raised if one correctly understands the age-long question of "church and state" and the history of the bloody struggle the Christian Church carried out in order to ensure complete separation of the Church from the State. For instance, it should be noted that the 1789 Constitution of the United States of America clearly states the separation of the state and the church.

In short, "The church must be non-political." The church is not a group that can become political or non-political. The church is never meant to be a group of people that carries out collective political actions or undertakes an independent movement. On the other hand, the church should not completely ignore social ills, structural evils and reality of the world and just read the Bible, pray and sing songs. The correct stance for the church should be that it must be able to demand corrections when the government carries out certain acts in conflict with the Gospel and that it must take every possible action to remove social irregularities. However, the moment the church manipulates its entire organization to respond to political issues, the church is no longer a church but a political party. Individual Christian can definitely take part in political parties or become politicians. However, it must be noted that the church is never meant to become political.

The claim that the revival movements made the Korean Church disregard the Korean history and Korean nationality is hardly convincing. Despite the apparent absence of violent resistance, true Christians can never remain indifferent or ignorant of any national trials or the colonization of their nation. If a Christian were to take such an attitude toward his or her country, there is no other reason than the person incorrectly understanding the Christian truth. We must not forget the fact that it was almost always Christians who stood at the forefront in national struggles. The importance of Christian patriots will be discussed further in the section on the March First Movement. In this light, if anyone claims that the revival movement made the Church non-political and ignorant of the nation and thus a large number of national leaders left the Church, he or she has simply failed to get the whole picture. If the Church became non-political and any national leaders left the Church because of it, then it should be interpreted that such leaders misunderstood the "true nature of the church."

The Great Revival of 1907 was undoubtedly the movement of the Holy Spirit, specifically planned by God to save the Koreans.

This revival movement allowed the Korean Church to lay the foundation as a truly indigenous church and provided the spiritual power with which the Church could negotiate the thorns of suffering awaiting her.

2. The Million Souls for Christ Movement

A couple of years after the Great Revival of 1907, the fire of revival began to cool down among Christians. At the same time, the Japanese sped up their colonization of Korea and by August 1910, they forced annexation on Korea and completely made her their colony. Seeing such social tension and despair of the people, the Church undertook yet another revival movement with the objective to preach the Gospel to the general public. This was the "Million Souls for Christ" movement.

In 1909 in Gaesuhng, Kyonggi Province three Methodist missionaries, M. B. Stokes, F. K. Gamble and W. T. Reid, decided to hold a series of revival meetings and prayer meetings for a week in order to ignite the fire of revival in the Korean Church once again. Thus they held prayer meetings on a mountaintop and a number of Korean Christians attended them. The missionaries who participated in these prayer meetings later attended the Annual Conference of the Southern Methodist Church in September 1909, where they requested for the adoption of the slogan "200 Thousand Souls for Christ" and the requested slogan was adopted.[298] Then,

---

298 The Annual Report, *Methodist Episcopal Church, South, for 1909*, 87. G. T.

immediately after the closing of the Annual Conference, the General Council of the Evangelical Missions was held in Seoul. Again, the three missionaries attended the Council and suggested the Council adopt a goal for evangelism, a "Million Souls for Christ." This is how the "Million Souls for Christ" movement officially began.

Considering that Christians numbered a few tens of thousands at that time,[299] one million was definitely an unrealistic number to achieve. Nevertheless, they adopted the goal with a mind to evangelize the entire nation. Missionary J. Gale wrote of this movement:

> The great movement calls for special effort in Korea, the watch-word of "A Million Souls" rings out at a time of supreme national hopelessness. Wretched and humiliated through her own failures, incapable of self-defense or self-government, she had fallen to a place of contempt among all nations. Authority no longer rests with her, finances are out of her control, the world of graft and fraud in which she lived has been spirited away... This is the supreme moment. Now is the moment, and it is here: the wide open door, the humbled people, the waiting heart. The missionaries

---

B. Davis, *Korea for Christ*, 6, 7.

299 Dr. Nak Jun Paik wrote that the Christian population at that time numbered no more than 8,000. *Hangukgaesingiosa*(History of Protestantism in Korea), 403, but this is incorrect. On p. 407 of his book, he recorded the number of Presbyterian believers to be 70,000 at the time the Independent Presbytery for the Presbyterian Church in Korea was established.

are convinced the NOW is the hour of crisis for Korea.[300]

At this time, the renowned revivalists W. Chapman and C. M. Alexander visited Korea during their world tour. They immediately decided to participate in the "Million Souls for Christ" movement and held evangelistic meetings for the missionaries for five days. Although the revivalists left Korea at the end of the meetings, G. T. B. Davis, a member of the traveling team, remained in Korea and conducted evangelistic meetings across the country. Now that the Japanese had taken away everything from the Koreans, many identified with a government official in Gyeongsang Province who said, "We are left with no other options than to believe the Christian God."

The Fourth Independent Presbytery of the Presbyterian Church that met at Suncheon, North Pyongan Province in 1910 also decided to actively participate in the Million Souls for Christ movement and instructed the seven representative councils to appoint special committee members to spearhead the movement. This was exactly 20 days after the annexation of Korea to Japan. This was a nationwide movement that "men and women of all ages, believers and students, laymen and ministers dedicated their lives to realize the slogan"[301] for the evangelization of Korea.

One intriguing phenomenon during this movement was the practice of "day offering," which was observed by financially burdened

---

300 *The Missionary* (May 1910), 213.
301 Nak Jun Paik, *Hangukgaesingiosa* (History of Protestantism in Korea), 404.

Christians who did not have money to give to the cause of the movement but instead offered their time. Those who could not give financially chose to tithe one day every week or every ten days and spend the time in direct evangelism works. In areas where paid evangelists could not be sent to, they set aside a certain portion of their time to circulate evangelism tracts and Christian documents and evangelize people. This movement became highly popular among the believers; nearly a thousand Christians in Pyongyang offered 22,000 days a year and those in Jaeryeong, Hwanghae Province, offered 10,000 days in total. A report indicates that the number of days offered during this period was more than 100,000 days. *The Korea Mission Field*, a monthly magazine published by missionaries, featured the following article on day offering:

> Poor and hard working Koreans were inspired to give at least 100,000 days of work in all, for 76,000 days of earnest personal work was done last winter, and this fall several hundreds of native workers gave a whole month to special service going from house to house, as well as dealing with men personally in great meetings. Many millions of tracts and 700,000 gospels of Mark were purchased by native Christians and given to unbelievers with prayer and earnest persuasions; nearly every home in Korea has been visited, and daily prayer has been offered for this by thousands of Korean.[302]

---

302 "The Million Movement and Its Results," *The Korea Mission Field* (January

This record shows us that Korean Christians sacrificed a great amount of time, money and labor for this cause. However, the end-of-year evaluation of the movement showed that the results were not quite satisfactory. Of course, reaching a million souls for Christ would have been quite a difficult feat; the results were not within the range of their expectation. Nevertheless, Northern Presbyterian missionary W. Baird in Pyongyang said,

> All churches participated in the movement with such an unprecedented intensity of faith and enthusiasm. The Gospel has never been preached nationwide like this······By the time everything is made known, I believe that more than a million souls would have become interested in Christianity during this period of the Million Souls for Christ movement.[303]

As Baird stated, there might not have been a million converts, but a million souls could have heard the Good News. In this case, they had every reason to pray and evangelize, hoping that the Gospel will make its way through everyone's heart.

Some critics underestimate the importance of the movement as a scheme of missionaries to maintain social order for the Korean Church and the general public in regards to the Korea-Japan annexation. They claim that the Million Souls for Christ movement dampened the anti-Japanese spirit and made the Church ignorant of

---

1911), 5.

303 W. M. Baird, "An Address to the Presbyterian Mission on the Million Movement," *The Korea Mission Field* (November 1911), 310.

national matters. But these incorrect evaluations are purely based on misunderstanding the true power of the Gospel. Even though believers of the true Gospel did not appear to resist the Japanese through violent acts of the Euibyong (righteous army), they were full of passion to save their own country in resistance against injustice and great misery, and they prayed to God for help. We must remember that prayers are more powerful than anything else.

3. Efforts for an Union Church

(1) Missionaries Collaborate to Establish an Union Church

The missionaries had great ambition for the Protestant Church in Korea to be established as one church with no distinction of denominations. It was not just ambition, for much practical effort was made. Underwood once wrote to Arthur Brown, the General Secretary of the Overseas Mission Board of Northern Presbyterian Church U.S., in regards to establishing a union church for Korea:

> ·····in regard to the Union Church for Korea, you can readily see how essential it is that all of the Presbyterians working in this land should unite in one Union Church, and we cannot expect that this one Union Church shall be connected with either one of the Churches whose representatives are sent here and it certainly cannot be connected with them all.[304]

Among the many things planned by the Korea Evangelical Fellowship, a joint organization for various mission agencies, was "······to have but one evangelical Church in Korea." In an attempt to form a union church, the Fellowship worked with the Presbyterian Church and the Methodist Church and was able to witness a significant breakthrough in 1904.

Decision:

It is the decision that the time has come to establish one protestant church in Korea. The name of this church is "Korea Jesus Church." The union of all denominations working together published one hymnal and church newspaper. In the fall, all protestant missionaries will meet together. After this, despite any result, the educational, medical, and evangelical work should be continued.[305]

This spirit of unity, referred to as the "leading of the Holy Spirit," was evidently shared by all participants of the prayer meeting for missionaries that was held at Rev. D. A. Bunker's home in Seoul in 1905. In August that year, another missionary prayer meeting in Seoul strongly expressed the demand for "One Union Church."

Underwood, who was the central figure steering this task in 1905, expressed his desire:

---

304 H. G. Underwood to A. J. Brown, February 18, 1904, PHS.
305 *Assembly Herald* (1905), 529. *Presbyterian Council Minutes, 1904*, 43.

⋯⋯an organized church with a competent, well-trained, thoroughly consecrated native ministry, a united non-sectarian Church of Christ, where there are neither Methodists, Presbyterians, Episcopalians, Jews nor Greeks, Barbarian, Scythian, bond, nor free, circumcised, nor uncircumcised, but CHRIST IS ALL IN ALL. I see this nation reaching out strong, glad arms of influence to China on the one hand and to Japan on the other, softening the prejudice and conservatism of the one, and steading the faith of the other; and thus, Korea with a hand in that of either sister, the three join the great circle of Christian nations who praise the Lamb for ever and ever, and hail Jesus King of kings and Lord of lords.[306]

That year Underwood also wrote:

They differ in the statement of their faith, in forms of worship, in methods, and in Church government, but their real aim and purpose in one, the Christianization of the Nation. One in faith and hope, with one Father, one Saviour, one Spirit. God grant that they may go forth unitedly in the work of winning this land, and that in His Divine Providence the time may soon come when they shall be able to demonstrate the unity of their faith by the

---

306 H. G. Underwood, "Twenty Years' Missionary Work in Korea," *The Missionary Review of the World XXVIII-5* (May 1905), 376.

establishment of one united Christian Church in Korea.[307]

Since the responsibilities of the Evangelical Fellowship covered fields of education, medicine, documents and publication, the missionaries worked in total collaboration. But these tasks were ultimately groundwork for the founding of a union church. Their minds were focused on establishing one church for Korea.

In 1905, they organized a special committee for establishing one church and appointed H. G. Underwood, S. A. Moffett, A. M. Sharrocks, J. E. Adams and R. H. Sidebotham as its members. In the same year, in response to the strong desire of establishing one church, the Presbyterian Church and the Methodist Church agreed that when the time comes for establishing one national church for Korea it would be named "The Church of Christ in Korea."[308]

The two denominations also made a commitment by saying, "Let us earnestly hope and pray that this union may be consummated, and that the young Church in Korea may thus lead Christendom in conforming to the Master's prayer for oneness."[309]

(2) The Union Church Fails

Despite the endeavor of the missionaries, establishment of a

---

307 H. G. Underwood, *The Call of Korea*, 188.
308 "Movement for Church Union in Korea," *The Missionary Review of the World* XXVIII-10 (October 1905), 796.
309 *Ibid.*

union church in Korea never materialized. A number of factors are thought to have been at work. One fundamental reason was that the home countries of the missionaries were not sufficiently cooperative. The Southern Presbyterian Church, which was more conservative than the Northern Presbyterian Church, learned about the plans for a union church for Korea and responded:

> The extent to which they propose to carry the idea of Church union strikes us as a something startling. What is to be the form of Government of the "Church of Christ in Korea?" What deliverance will the creed of this new Church contain, or will it contain any deliverance at all on those points concerning which the Methodist or Presbyterian Churches in this country hold different views?[310]

Thus, the Southern Presbyterian Church of the U.S.A. sent an official letter to the missionaries in Korea saying that the issue of a union church for Korea could be discussed later, but the time was not yet ripe for it at that time. The official letter read, "While it would be possible to collaborate with other churches to establish a free church at a later date, it is better to leave the issue for further discussion for now."[311]

---

310 S. H. Chester, "Church Union in Korea," *The Missionary* (March 1906), 207.

311 *English Council Meeting Minutes for 1904*, 31-33. Translated by Kwak Anryeon, *Koreajangnohoesa Jeonhwijip* (Collection of the History of the Korea Presbyterian Church) (Seoul: Northern Presbyterian Church Mission Board, 1935), 37.

Southern Presbyterian missionary G. T. Brown pointed out two reasons for the failure of this unity in 1962. The first reason was that the homeland churches (of missionaries) were uncooperative. Especially for the Methodist Church, unlike the Presbyterian, the Northern and the Southern Church each established their own churches, and it was difficult to strike any meaningful unity even within the boundaries of the Methodist Church.

The second reason was the lack of desire for unity among the Korean church leaders. Many Presbyterian mission boards lost the zeal for unity due to their establishment of the Independent Presbytery. The issue of a union church was discussed within the mission board of the Northern Presbyterian Church. The conclusion was that this issue should be considered, "Until after the organization of the independent Presbyterian Church in 1907."[312]

The plan for founding a union church for Korea was eventually aborted as the Presbyterian Church organized a General Assembly in 1912 and changed the name of the Fellowship from the "General Council" to the "Federal Council." Its constitution no longer seriously mentioned the issue of a union church. It is such a deep scar for the Korean church that the anxious endeavors of the missionaries did not materialize with the establishment of a union church, unlike the unparalleled successes in India and China.

---

312 G. T. Brown, *Missions to Korea* (The Presbyterian Church of Korea Department of Education, Seoul, Korea, 1962), 78.

4. Formation of Churches in Korea

(1) Presbyterian Church Establishes an Independent Presbytery

Since the Great Revival of 1907, the Korean Church began to expand in membership and experience rapid growth. Just about this period, the Presbyterian Church had the honor of producing the first graduates of the Presbyterian Theological Seminary in Pyongyang.

The Presbyterian Theological Seminary first began when missionary S. A. Moffett started teaching two Korean young men, Jong Seop Kim and Gi Chang Bang, in the guest room of his house. From there, the seminary kept growing; there were six students in 1902, nineteen in 1904 and then forty students in three classes in 1905. The five-year course included three months of classroom lectures and nine months of church ministry with assignments and self-study each year.

The first batch of students graduated on June 20, 1907. There were seven graduates in all: Sun Joo Kil, Gee Chang Bang, In Suh Song, Suhk Jin Han, Gee Pung Lee, Jeon Baek Yang and Gyeong Jo Suh.

Now that there were graduates from the seminary and they were to be ordained as pastors, a presbytery was required for their membership. As there was no presbytery in Korea yet, they had to be registered under presbyteries in the missionaries' countries or a new presbytery had to be created for Korea. In regards to this, mission boards of the Southern and Northern Presbyterian Church of the U.S., the Canadian Presbyterian Church and the Australian Presbyterian Church agreed to establish a presbytery for Korea. Each of them obtained permission from their home headquarters, and thus the work began for establishing the Presbytery of Korea.

Finally on September 17, 1907 at Pyongyang Jangdaehyeon Church, 78 people, including 38 missionaries and 40 Korean elders, came together for the inaugurating presbytery. Moffett was selected as the first moderator and Rev. Gi Chang Bang as the vice-moderator.[313] Suhk Jin Han was elected as the secretary, In Suh Song as the assistant secretary and Graham Lee as the treasurer. Thus, the Presbyterian Church in Korea now had an organization of seven pastors, 53 elders, 989 churches, 19,000 baptized members and 70,000 in total membership.

The presbytery also adopted a confession of faith that would outline the doctrines of the church. They decided to take after the Twelve Confessions of Faith that the Free Church of India adopted at their founding in 1904. This was largely because the missionaries wanted it as they hoped the Presbyterian Church of Korea would play a central role in networking Presbyterian Churches in various parts of Asia. But this had actually robbed the Koreans of a great opportunity. Even though a new presbytery could be established just 20 years after the initial contact by missionaries, the fact that the presbytery could not possess its own confession of faith that embodied the Korean sentiment and Korean spirit

---

313 *Chosun Yesugio Jangnohoe Sagi* (The Chronicle of the Korea Presbyterian Church), vol. 1 (The Korea Presbyterian Church General Assembly, 1928), 181-182.

left a shameful mark in the history of Christianity.

The Twelve Confessions of Faith strictly adhered to the Calvinistic theology with emphases on the sovereignty of God, divinity of Christ, the virgin birth, wages of sin, the gift of the Holy Spirit through the Father and the Son, predestination, irresistible spiritual gifts, faith in sacraments, resurrection of the body and the final judgment.[314] These confessions were basically acceptable as traditional Presbyterian confessions of faith, but they were too conservative and did not leave any room for new thoughts of theology. This had the potential pitfall of not allowing new schools of theology, and therefore the risk of factions in years to come. In other words, should new theologies that are not within the boundaries of acceptance for the traditional Presbyterian Church arise, it would be virtually impossible for the Church to be spared of serious conflicts and factions.

Decisions were made to inform the International Presbyterian Council of the establishment of the Presbytery of the Korean Presbyterian Church. Missionaries on furlough were delegated with this task. Arrangements were also made to write letters of appreciation to the Northern and Southern Presbyterian Church of the U.S., the Canadian Presbyterian Church and the Australian Presbyterian Church for having given permission for the establishment of the presbytery. It was also agreed to inform missionary Underwood, who was the first missionary in Korea on furlough in the States, of the presbytery's establishment.[315] Planted on the phrase, "a

---

314 Nak Jun Paik, *Hangukgaesingiosa* (History of Protestantism in Korea), 408.

church is not a church without a mission"[316] the newly established presbytery organized the Department of Evangelism and began various significant programs, which included dispatching Rev. Gee Pung Lee, one of the first seven Korean pastors, to Jeju Island for evangelism. Two years later, the presbytery sent Rev. Gwan Heul Choi to Vladivostok and Rev. Suhk Jin Han to Tokyo, Japan, to teach Korean students. The Association of Pyongyang Women's Evangelism also sent Gwan Suhn Lee to Jeju Island for a 5-year term evangelism mission. Then in parallel to the Million Souls for Christ movement in 1909, Rev. Young Je Kim was sent to Buggando (North Gando in Manchuria) and Rev. Jin Geun Kim was sent to Suhgando (West Gando) as evangelists. Rev. Hwa Jung Bang was also sent at this point to minister to Koreans living in California and Mexico.[317]

The presbytery established seven district councils for Hamgyeong, Pyeongbuk, Yeoungnam, Gyeonggi-Chungcheong, Hwanghae, Jeolla and Gyeongsang areas and delegated them the presbytery's responsibilities. Establishment of the presbytery now raised the issue of the missionaries' association. The presbytery made the following decision:

The missionaries who work with the Presbyterian Church

---

315 *Koreayesugiojangnohoe Sagi* (The Chronicle of the Korea Presbyterian Church), vol. 1, 183.

316 S. A. Moffett, *The Christians in Korea* (New York: Friendship Press, 1962), 346.

317 *Ibid.*, 185. *The Annual Report, Presbyterian Church, North, for 1910*, 61.

in Korea have membership in the presbyteries and the General Assembly. However, the disciplinary punishment or appointment belongs to the missionary sending church or the mission agency. When two-thirds of the missionaries support the renouncement of membership of the presbyteries or the General Assembly, the General Assembly, the supreme judicial institution, will decide the best way.[318]

By granting the missionaries the full rights to the Korean Presbytery while reserving the matters of the missionaries' reprimands and appointments to their home churches, the presbytery acknowle-dged extraterritoriality for missionaries and clarified that the missio-naries were not meant to be fully subjected to the Korean Church.

(2) Establishment of the Presbyterian General Assembly and Overseas Missions

Since the establishment of the Independent Presbytery in 1907, the Church continued to persevere despite the harsh conditions. The Korea-Japan Annexation in 1910, the 105-men Incident in 1911 and series of other devastating events took place both in and out of the country. Nevertheless, the Church held fast to her missions. All Presbyterian churches in the country were managed directly by one presbytery up until 1911, when seven Presbyteries were organized and preparations were made for the establishment

---

318 *The Annual Report, Presbyterian Church, North, for 1910*, 61.

of a General Assembly. Then at 9 a.m. on September 2, 1912, the historical inaugurating General Assembly was held at Presbyterian Theological Seminary in Pyongyang.

On September 2, 1912, at 9 am, the meeting was convened by the moderator William Reynolds. The moderator had Park, Yehyung read Micah 6:8 and deliver the sermon. After the worship service the moderator addressed the purpose of creating the General Assembly, and the secretary called the roll of the delegates from Kyong-Chung Presbytery, Cholla Presbytery, Kyungsang Presbytery, Hamkyung Presbytery, South Pyungan Presbytery, North Pyungan Presbytery, Hwanghae Presbytery·····96 ministers (44 missionaries, 52 Korean ministers) 125 elders, a total of 221 were gathered.[319]

Underwood was elected as the inaugurating Moderator, Rev. Sun Joo Kil, the central figure of the Great Revival of 1907, was elected as the vice-moderator.[320] The formation of the General Assembly served as confirmation that the Presbyterian Church in Korea was now officially a part of the Universal Church. Presbyterian churches from all over the world, including Shandong Presbytery of China, the Christian Church of Japan and the World Alliance of Reformed Churches, sent congratulatory messages. The newly

---

319 *Daehan Yesugio Jangnohoe Changnip Chonghoe Hoerok* (The Minutes of Inaugural Meeting of the General Assembly of the Korean Presbyterian Church).
320 Rev. Suhk Jin Han as the secretary, missionary W. N. Blair as the treasurer, and Rev. Suhk Chang Kim as the assistant treasurer.

established General Assembly also notified its establishment to the World Alliance of Reformed Churches and General Assemblies of Presbyterian churches worldwide. The Presbyterian Church in Korea had now officially become a part of the worldwide Presbyterian Church and universal church. Although the country had lost its governance over to the Japanese, the church was recognized as a fully independent entity, rubbing shoulders with churches worldwide. The church established a regulation stating that the number of missionaries should not be more than 40 among the 200 representatives in the General Assembly, ensuring full independence of the Korean Church. It finally became difficult for foreign missionaries to dictate matters of the Korean Church. With the absolute majority of Korean pastors and elders, the responsibilities were directly laid on the Korean church leaders.

One of the most important assignments of the General Assembly was overseas missions. Although Rev. Gee Pung Lee was sent to Jeju Island at the time of establishing the Independent Presbytery and many other missionaries to Manchuria, Tokyo, Siberia and the U.S.A., they were all intended to cater to Koreans living overseas, not other ethnic groups. In this sense, it was not a cross-cultural mission. Nevertheless, dispatching our own missionaries to foreign people groups at this time had great significance of confirming the strong presence of the Korean Church. There was probably no other means to forge identification for the Korean Church, especially during the period when Koreans were regarded as the same as Japanese.

Martin Marty, a professor at University of Chicago and famous American church historian, said in 1970, "The national identity and missions are intertwined."[321] This statement was perfectly applicable to the Korean Church's missions during the Japanese Occu-pation. The General Assembly selected Laiyang, Shandong, in China as its primary mission field and decided to send Rev. Young Hoon Kim, Byeong Soon Sa and Tae Ro Park as missionaries.[322]

Originally the birthplace of Confucius and Mencius, Shandong was one of the only places where the U.S. missionary forces have had much difficulty. The General Assembly of the Korean Presbyterian Church decided to work in this harsh area rather than send missionaries to already successful mission fields. Sun Joo Kil, the head of the Department of Evangelism, wrote the following in regards to the start of missionary works in China:

It is very difficult for the Korean church to send missionaries to China due to a variety of reasons. It is very meaningful matter that even though the country is under control by a foreign country, the church realizes its role as a sending missionary church as a member of the world's church community. It is one of the duties of the Korean church, and also sending missionaries is a reward of receiving

---

321 Quoted from W. S. Hudson, *Nationalism and Religion in America, Concept of American Identity and Mission* (New York: Harper and Row, 1970), 54.
322 *Daehan Yesugio Jangnohoe Chonghoe Je 2hoe (1913) Hoeuirok* (The 2nd Minutes of the General Assembly of the Presbyterian Church of Korea), 25.

missionaries and obeying Jesus' teaching of receiving freely and giving freely. We will do our best to accomplish this work.[323]

A. Brown, the general secretary of the Northern Presbyterian Church of the U.S., wrote the following in regards to the Korean missionary works in China:

> the historic relations of the two countries, and Chosen's indebtedness to China for its civilization and literature, combined to reinforce the missionary obligation which they held to be binding upon them as well as upon Western Christians. They realized that the Chinese had long regarded Koreans as a small and inferior people, but their consecration was illustrated by a prayer that a missionary happened to overhear in a church service: "O Lord, we are a despised people, the weakest nation on the earth. But thou art a God who choosest the despised things. Wilt thou use this nation to show forth Thy glory in Asia."[324]

Given the fact that all academic and bureaucratic influences had been received from China and Korea had been paying respect to China as a greater nation, it was definitely more than impressive

---

323 Jin Kyong Kil, *Yeonggye Kil Sun Joo*, 243.
324 A. J. Brown, *One Hundred Years, A Story of the Foreign Missionary Work of the Presbyterian Church in the U.S.A.* (New York: Fleming H. Revell, 1936), 428.

for the Koreans to be able to guide the Chinese in the Way of the Christ.

One important aspect of the reports released at the inaugurating General Assembly was that there were records that describe the strict handling of disciplines in the early Church. It was reported that the North Pyeongan Presbytery observed "the Word and the governance of the Presbyterian Church" to discipline 303 people "who violated the rules regarding marriage, and who committed all immoral, detestable and unlawful acts" and excommunicate 47 people who violated the laws of the church on various grounds.[325] Such relentless actions taken by the early church clearly reflects the intentions of our ancestors who were determined to lay a strong foundation for the church as a body of strict training and discipline. This is definitely something the Korean Church today must learn to put into practice.

Even though the Church was faced with the most tragic piece of Korean history, the leaders held fast to strict discipline for harnessing the spiritual power of the Church and making known the law-abiding nature of the Church to everyone.

Even before one full generation had passed since the arrival of the first missionary in 1884, the Korean Presbyterian Church now had a full-scale organization as an independent church.

---

325 *Yesugio Jangnohoe Changrip chonghoe Hoeuirok* (The First Minutes of the General Assembly of the Korea Presbyterian Church), 50.

(3) Formation of the Methodist Church

Although the Methodist Church started its mission works in Korea the same time as the Presbyterian Church, the Methodist Church in Korea was established in a somewhat different way due to notable differences in governance. Northern Methodist Church of U.S. began organizing its presence in Korea by establishing the Seoul Circuit in 1897. This circuit was originally a part of the Korea Mission until 1901, when it was divided into three different regions: the West District around Incheon, the North District around Pyongyang and the South District around Seoul. The establishmen t of the Korea Mission Conference in June 1905 further expanded separation of the districts. Shortly after the Great Revival of 1907, a complete Methodist organization of "The Korean Annual Conference" was established at Jeongdong Church in Seoul in March 1908.[326] This conference was presided over by M. C. Harris, who was a resident in Japan. Harris was appointed as the bishop over the Korean Church, and all American missionaries in Korea transferred their membership from the U.S. to the Methodist Church in Korea.

On the other hand, the Southern Methodist Church of the U.S. established its district in September 1897. This district was under the Annual Conference of China until December, when it became independent as the Korea Missions. The Annual Conference of

---

326 *Official Minutes of the Korea Mission Conference of the Methodist Episcopal Church*, 28.

China was formed in 1914, and the official inauguration of the "Korean Annual Conference" took place in Gaesuhng, Kyonggi Province in October 1918 with the arrival and arbitration of Bishop W. F. McMurry earlier that year.[327] These two Methodist Churches maintained their own organizations until December 1930, when the Northern Methodist and the Southern Methodist merged as a single "Christian Korea Methodist Church." Rev. Joo Sam Yang was appointed as the founding bishop.

(4) The Beginning of the Evangelical Holiness Church

Unlike the Presbyterian or the Methodist, the Evangelical Holiness Church of Korea was not an international Christian body. An organization called "The Oriental Missionary Society" was later renamed as "The Evangelical Holiness Church." In other words, the Oriental Missionary Society was the present Evangelical Holiness Church. The Oriental Missionary Society was a mission agency founded in 1901 by two missionaries, C. E. Cowman and E. A. Kilborne, who came to Tokyo, Japan, for missions in the East Asia. Originally an electrician from Ohio, Cowman studied at the Moody Bible Institute and was ordained as a Methodist minister. Without a regular church membership or sponsorship, he sold off his only possession-his wife's piano-to pay for his traveling expenses. With total reliance on God alone, he and his wife arrived in Tokyo,

---

327 Suhng Sam Lee, *Hangukgamrigiohoesa* (History of the Methodist Church in Korea) (Education Department of the Korea Methodist Church, 1978), 139-144.

got a room, hung a sign that read "The Oriental Missionary Society Gospel Hall" and began evangelizing people.

A year later in 1902, he urged his former colleague Kilborne to join him as a missionary, and thus Kilborne arrived in Tokyo as well. Cowman had evangelized Kilborne. He too studied theology and was ordained as a Methodist minister in 1902. Upon Kilborne's arrival in Tokyo, the two of them opened a Bible School, trained evangelists and concentrated their efforts on evangelizing the people there. Originally they did not have any intention to set up a separate denomination, and thus encouraged people to attend any church. But as the number of followers increased, they had to create an independent denomination called "The Evangelical Holiness Church of the Oriental Missionary Society" in October 1917.

The Oriental Missionary Society started in Korea when Sang Joon kim and Bin Chung, who graduated from the Bible School in Tokyo, returned to Korea, bought a tile-roofed house in Mugyo-dong, Seoul-the location of the current Evangelical Holiness Church headquarters-and posted the sign "Gospel Hall" in 1907. The church began to expand as the British pastor J. Thomas, who came to Korea as the bishop in 1910, returned home when his wife became ill and Kilborne came back to Korea in 1920 as the second bishop. Although they continued evangelizing without any distinction between denominations in Korea, they were forced to take on a church organization to cater for the increasing number of followers. Thus, the gospel hall was changed into a church system with the name "The Evangelical Holiness Church" in 1921.[328]

(5) The Salvation Army

The Salvation Army was a religious organization founded by a British Methodist pastor William Booth and his wife Catherine. Its original intent was to carry out charity and social welfare programs for the class of poor people that began to surface after the Industrial Revolution of the 19th century. Booth established the headquarters in London in 1865. He set up tents and focused on hevangelism. Initially called "The East London Christian Revival Association" or "The Christian Mission," it was renamed as "The Salvation Army" in 1878 taking after Booth's statement, "The mission of Christians is to be a Salvation Army."

They took on a military model for the organization and Booth himself became the General. The Salvation Army grew quickly, expanding its presence to the U.S.A and also reaching Japan in 1895. The Salvation Army began its work in Korea when Col. R. Hoggard and his company set up a division at Samunan in Seoul in October 1908.[329] They were well known for wearing military uniforms at all times and attracting people for evangelism on the streets by blowing trumpets and beating drums. Naturally, the Japanese persecuted them on a regular basis because of their military uniform. The Salvation Army largely became known as an organization that collects donations with their charity pots during the Christmas season and uses the money to feed the poor.

---

328 Cheon Young Lee, *Suhnggieolgiohoesa* (History of the Holiness Church) (Korea Evangelical Holiness Publishing, 1970), 18-29.
329 *The Korea Mission Field* (October 1908), 154.

In 1909, the Academy for Officer Training (seminary) was set up to train officers (pastors), and they persisted in their original mission of fighting off poverty and social evils by proclaiming the Gospel in order to bring salvation to the suffering Koreans.[330] The Salvation Army fought against various evils of the Japanese society, partly by running an orphanage for girls at Aeogae in Seoul.

(6) The Seventh-Day Adventist Church

The beginning of the Seventh-day Adventist Church dates back to the middle of the 19th century by William Miller, a godly Baptist farmer in America. By carefully reading and studying the Book of Daniel in the Old Testament and the Book of Revelation in the New Testament, Miller calculated the date of Jesus' second coming. He prophesied that Jesus would return in early 1843 and preached to everyone to prepare for the Lord's Return. Many gave in to the temptation, abandoned their daily life, put on white dresses and went up to a mountain to receive the returning Lord. But the Second Coming did not happen. Then Miller admitted that there was a problem with his initial calculation and prophesied that Jesus would come again in 1844. But this prophecy was incorrect as well, and many followers scattered away. After some time, several of those followers came together and established the Seventh-

---

330 For more information on the history of the Salvation Army, see Hyeong Il Chang, *Hanguk Gusegunsa* (History of the Salvation Army in Korea) (Salvation Army Korea Territory, 1975).

day Adventist Church. One of their striking arguments was that God's commandment of keeping the Sabbath must be observed; they prohibited worship services on Sundays.

Hong Jo Sohn, an immigrant to Hawaii, and Gee Ban Lim, an employee of the Hawaii Development Corporation introduced the Adventist Church to Korea in 1904 by. On his journey to Hawaii, Sohn spent some time in Japan. There, a Seventh-day Adventist priest named Kuniya baptized him in Kobe, and thus he became the first Korean Adventist. Due to inadequate documentation, Sohn and Lim were prevented from continuing their journey to Hawaii. Instead, they returned to Korea and began evangelizing in Yonggang, Pyeongan Province.

However, they soon experienced difficulties due to their lack of understanding of the doctrines, and thus the Japanese pastor Kuniya and the American missionary F. W. Field arrived in Korea to assist their efforts. Instead of spending time on teaching biblical doctrines, they argued that the most crucial thing was the keeping of the Sabbath. They proclaimed the importance of the Sabbath by explaining that Sunday was merely a holiday declared by Constantine the Great in 321. Taking their own doctrine rather than the Bible as the core value in evangelism, it was inevitable for the Adventists to experience conflicts with other evangelical chur-ches. [331]

---

[331] For more information on the history of the Adventist Church, see Young Lin Lee, *Hangukjaerimgiohoesa* (History of the Adventist Church in Korea) (Sijosa, 1965).

As seen above, various Christian denominations began to take shape in Korea around the early 1900's. The Great Revival allowed the churches to undergo substantial quantitative growths, and thus it became possible for churches to be established in Korea at a much rapid pace.

5. The Church under Persecution

(1) The Japanese Policy on Christianity

The Japanese policies on religions in Korea, especially those concerning Christianity, were consistently characterized by persecution and eradication. Although there were some degrees of differences from one Governor-General to another, the underlying principles remained the same. When the Japanese Residency General was set up in Seoul and Ito Hirobumi arrived as the inaugurating Resident-General following the promulgation of the 1905 Protectorate Treaty, Ito publicly praised the missionaries for their educational and medical projects in Korea. He appeared rather friendly to the Christian faith.

In the early years of Japan's reformation, the senior statesmen were opposed to religious toleration, especially because of distrust of Christianity. But I fought vehemently for freedom of belief and religious propaganda, and finally triumphed. My reasoning was this: Civilization depends on morality and highest morality upon religion. Therefore religion must be tolerated and encouraged.[332]

Given the facts, Ito certainly had an appeasing attitude towards Christianity. However, he was soon assassinated by Jung Keun Ahn and was succeeded by Terauchi, the first Governor-General, when Korea was annexed to Japan in 1910. Unlike Ito, Terauchi was fundamentally anti-Christianity, and his arrival marked the beginning of persecutions for the Korean Church. Although, while in Japan he once stated, "Freedom of religion will always be respected and I am ready to extend due protection and facilities to the propagation of all religious doctrines, provided they do not interfere with politics."[333] This was simply propaganda for American missionaries. The series of events that took place during his rule clearly testify that he was consistently hostile to Christianity.

The policies he carried out in regards to the Korean Church were fundamentally hostile and destructive. Among all things, he thought that Christian schools forged the spirit of nationalism among Koreans, and thus he began to demand that all students in these Christian schools were to bow to the photograph of the Emperor of Japan on national memorial days.[334] He used the central Christian doctrine of prohibiting idol worship to directly challenge Christians.

The Japanese saw the Million Souls for Christ Movement in

---

332 F. A. McKenzie, *Korea's Fight for Freedom*, 211.
333 H. Loomis, "The New Korean Governor and Missions," *The Missionary Review of the World* (December 1910), 952.
334 *Ibid.*

1909 as an outpost combat that the Church used to prepare itself for an organized resistance movement against the Japanese. Terauchi argued that this movement was purely political and used this as an excuse to put a brake on the religious activities of the Church. He believed that the Church was the strongest anti-Japanese organization in Korea. To him it seemed impossible to rule over Korea efficiently unless he dismantled this organization. Thus, he sought ways to oppress the leaders of the Korean Church. The first of his many schemes, he fabricated the so-called "105-men Incident."

(2) The 105-men Incident

Before we examine the 105-men Incident, it is necessary to understand the background as to why the Japanese had to fabricate such a senseless conspiracy. Having decided that Christianity was the single biggest obstacle to their colonial rule of Korea, the Japanese felt the need to oppress the Christian leaders in Hwanghae Province and Pyeongan Province where the growth of churches was most noticeable. There was a great number of Christians in this area because Christianity was introduced here earlier than other parts of the country. This area had many schools, as well as churches, with a heavy emphasis on education. The Presbyterian statistics alone shows that there were 405 schools in 1907, 561 in 1908 and 719 in 1909, with an average addition of about 150 schools each year.

In 1908 in Hwanghae Province, Goo Kim, Gwang Ok Choi,

In Gwon Do and other Christian leaders organized the Haesuhgio-yukchonghoe (the Hwanghae Provincial Education Assembly) with the determination to educate the people by opening a school in each county. However, such a movement was immediately regarded as a resistance threat against the Japanese, and the Japanese sought ways to eradicate the movement altogether. So, the Japanese police arrested Myeong Geun Ahn-the brother of Ito's assassinator Jung Keun Ahn-when he returned to Korea to raise funds for setting up a military academy in Suhgando. The Japanese indicted Myeong Geun Ahn for attempted rebellion, and they also arrested all the members of the Haesuhgioyukchonghoe and obtained false confessions by torturing them. Thus, Myeong Geun Ahn was given a life sentence, Goo Kim and six others were sentenced to fifteen years, other members were sentenced between ten to five years and another 40 were sent in exile to Uleung Island and Jeju Island. This is known as the "Anak Incident."[335] Thus, important Christian figures in Hwanghae Province were essentially wiped out. Now the Japanese shifted their focus to the Pyeongan Province area and began to fabricate another conspiracy against the Christian leaders there. This is the "105-men Incident."

As mentioned above, the "105-men Incident" was a conspiracy fabricated by the Japanese to eliminate all Christian leaders in Korea because they believed that Christians in Korea were the strongest anti-Japanese resistance force since the annexation of Korea to Japan.[336]   Terauchi, the first Governor-General in Korea,

---

335 Young Hun Lee, *Hangukgidokgiosa* (History of the Korean Church), 147-148.

was previously a Minister of the Army and equipped with an uncompromising military spirit of the Japanese imperialism. He ruled Korea through a systematic authoritarian structure complete with police and military. To further strengthen his rule over Korea, he delegated the command of the police and the military to Akashi Genjiro, a former Japanese military officer, and practically turned Korean into one big barrack under complete military rule.

The 105-men Incident was schemed by Akashi, the commander of the Japanese military and police superintendent in Korea. Having determined that Christianity had a strong presence in the Northwestern region and that many Christian leaders were residents there, he planned to stifle the Christian power by jailing all the Christian leaders in the Northwestern region. Pyongyang was the center of Korean Christianity with exceptional leadership and vast number of followers. It was difficult for the Japanese to simply ignore this highly anti-Japanese group of people. Here, Chang Ho Ahn, who had returned from the States in 1907, set up the secret Sinminhoe (New People's Association) whose objectives were: (1) to promote the sense of nationalism and the spirit of independence among the people; (2) to identify and unite with comrades for building the foundation for national movements; (3) to promote education of the young people by establishing educational institutes in various places; and (4) to strengthen the organization's finance and national power by setting up various commercial entities.

---

336 For more information on the 105-men Incident, see Gyeong Ro Yoon, "A Study of the 105-men Incident," *Hansuhng Sahak* (The Hansuhng Sahak), Opening Edition (1983), 47-54.

The central figures included Dongn Young Lee, Dong Hwui Lee, Seung Hoon Lee, Tae Gook Ahn and Gee Tak Yang. This movement was later joined by Chae Ho Shin and others. By 1910, the Sinminhoe grew into a stable organization with several hundred members.[337]

In line with the Sinminhoe's intent, a number of schools were set up to provide highly nationalistic education to Koreans. Chang Ho Ahn established Daesuhng School in Pyongyang, and Seung Hoon Lee established Osan School in Jeongju, North Pyeongan Province. These schools acted as the pivot of nationalistic education with a strong anti-Japanese spirit. Among many schools opened by missionaries, Sungsil School in Pyongyang and Sinsung School in Suncheon, North Pyeongan Province, had a particularly strong nationalistic spirit and, thus, were largely anti-Japanese. It is not difficult for us to imagine that such factors served as more than sufficient reasons for the Japanese to eradicate any Christian presence in the Pyeongan Province region.

The Japanese-fabricated 105-men Incident was based on the false testimony that Christian leaders conspired a "premeditated murder of Governor-General Terauchi." They claimed that this incident was steered by a few missionaries, such as W. L. Swallen, G. S. McCune and W. M. Biard.

This was their conspiracy. The Japanese claimed that Christians attempted to assassinate Governor-General Terauchi at Suncheon Station when his train made a quick stop while on his way to

---

337 "Sinminhoe," *Gidokgio Daebaekgwasajeon* (Encyclopedia of Christianity), vol. 10 (1986).

the opening ceremony of the Yalu River Railroad Bridge on December 27, 1910. The detailed account of the conspiracy was that Tae Gook Ahn and Seung Hoon Lee had coerced 60 influential men from Pyeongan Province, 20 followers of Hyeok Sunwoo, and another 20 people from Hwanghae Province to take five handguns they had hidden under the roof of a classroom in Sinsuhng School at Suncheon. The Japanese claimed that the assassinators planned to shoot the Governor-General from among the crowds of welcoming people when the train would make a quick stop at Suncheon Station at 1 p.m., but their plan failed because the train never made the stop at the station. The Japanese further fabri-cated the story that the Christians then planned to take the Governo-rGeneral down when he shook hands with missionary McCune at Suncheon Station on his way back the following day, but they failed to shoot a bullet because the security was too tight.[338]

The Japanese held fast to this pure fabrication and staged a massive roundup in Pyeongan Province and other parts of the country from the very beginning of the following year. According to the Japanese prosecutor records, the number of Christian leaders arrested during this roundup totaled as many as 500, including Seung Hoon Lee, Jeon Baek Yang, Chi Ho Yoon, Tae Kook An, Gwan Bin Ok, Gyu Chan Kang, Ik No Chung, six pastors, fifty elders, and eighty deacons in the Northwestern region.[339] While

---

338 *The Report of the Korea Mission, Presbyterian Church U.S.A. Report of Syen Chun Station* (1912), 66.
339 Yang Sun Kim, *Hanguk Gidokgiosa Yongu* (A Study of the History of the Korean Church), 105.

the number of those arrested is recorded as any number between 480 and 700, Gyeong Ro Yoon suggested that the actual number was 700.[340]

This was no more than a conspiracy fabricated by the Japanese and there was absolutely no evidence to prove that such a crime was ever planned. Naturally, the Japanese police had to torture the suspects to obtain their confessions. Hoon Suhnwoo, then a student at Suncheon Sinsuhng School, wrote about the kind of torture he experienced in his The National Ordeal.

> They tied my two fingers and inserted a small iron bar and hanged it up high on a gate post and pulled the string. My body was sore, and there was pain in every joint. My body was full of perspiration, out of breath, and toppled over continuously. My heart burned and nostrils blazed······ when the viper-like investigator pulled the string, my arms and legs crumble and the bones of my fingers were pulled out of joint······in the bitter winter, my body was freezing and stiffened. They began to scorch my legs with a fired iron bar and my face with a cigarette. The man pumped smoke into my throat. He beat me with a bat and kicked this way and that way. He pulled my hair and dragged me here and there and thrust my head on the ground. Lastly, he poured water into my nostril.[341]

---

340 Gyeong Ro Yoon, *Hanguk Hyundaesaui Gidokgiosajeok Eehae* (Understanding the Modern History of Korea in the Christian Perspective) (Yeokminsa, 1992), 178.

Nothing but such confessions was taken as the basis for prosecuting the case, and thus an open trial was held at the Gyeongsuhng (Seoul) District Court. However, the defendants' statements eventually revealed that the Japanese fabricated the entire incident. Dong Yeol Yoo, claimed to have been at Suncheon at the time of the attempted assassination, was in fact arrested earlier for a violation of the security law. He subsequently served a term at Suhdaemun (West Gate) Prison and was released on December 26. Seven other defendants also claimed to have been at Suncheon, including Gi Tak Yang, Seung Hoon Lee and Tae Kook Ahn, were having a meal together at Myeongwolgwan to celebrate Dong Yeol Yoo's release. A restaurant receipt issued to the name of Tae Kook Ahn proved this. A telegraph stating that Seung Hoon Lee would travel to Pyongyang the following day was also produced as evidence. In response to the prosecutor's claim that about 60 conspirators met together at Jeongju and went to Suncheon the day before the attempted murder, the court secretary checked with the Jeongju Station. It was found that only five tickets were issued to Suncheon and that the total number of tickets sold at the station that day was no more than eleven. However, the Japanese ignored such crucial pieces of evidence and valid alibis, and proceeded with the trials. The corrupted court eventually closed the case and issued the verdict in October 1912. Central figures such as Gee Tak Yang and Seung Hoon Lee were sentenced to ten years in prison, and others were either sentenced to as many as seven years in prison

---

341 Hoon Suhnwoo, *Minjokui Gonan* (The National Ordeal) (1946), 9-59.

or found not guilty.

The decision of this trial clearly contained elements of hostility towards Christianity.[342]

> This case was realized by the staffs of the Sinminhoe, but they are vips of the Korean church, thus, many teachers and students of the Christian schools were involved. There are many missionaries in Korea and they favored to the poor Koreans, thus, their missionary works were spreaded widely. It is needless to say that the Korean Christians try to depend to the strong power of the US through the missionaries.[343]

The number of people found guilty was 105, and thus this incident is referred to as the "105-men Incident." All of the 105 men appealed to the High Court. The fight continued on until a final decision was reached. Even the much-corrupted Japanese court was afraid of criticisms of the world and declared 99 people not guilty. Only the six central figures were sentenced to six years in prison. When these six were released under an amnesty for the Japanese emperor's coronation in February 1915, about 9,000 people came to receive them at Pyongyang Station, recognizing their suffering for the nation

---

342 "Transitions in the Korea Independence Movement," *Geukbimunsuh* (Top Secret Documents), Issued by the Governer-General in Korea, November 18, 1931, 14-15.

343 "Korea Doklip Undongeui Byunchun," (Change of the Independent Moveme nt in Korea), *Kukbi Munsuh* (Top Secret Documents) Published by the Governor General of Korea, Sowha 6, Nov. 18.

and their faith.

One thing that must not be overlooked from this incident was the role played by missionaries. The U.S. Missionaries residing in Pyongyang tediously documented all the details of this incident and sent the records to A. J. Brown, the secretary of the overseas mission board in the U.S. Brown initially showed a rather passive attitude towards this incident. However, this incident was made known to the rest of the world through another channel. P. L. Gillett, the general secretary of the Hwangsuhng(seoul) YMCA, wrote about this incident to his friend in China, and this Chinese friend sent it to *The Hong Kong Daily News*. This article was then subsequently published in *The New York Herald, The Sun, The Times* of Britain, *The Japan Chronicle* of Japan, *The Japan Gazette* and *The Japan Advertiser*, making international headlines.[344]

The initially passive U.S. mission board began to realize the seriousness of the incident as the trials progressed and the press exposed the cruelty of tortures as well as the irrationality of the conspiracy. Interpreting this as an active persecution of Christianity by the Japanese, the mission board began to contact the United States President, the Secretary of State and congress leaders to resolve the issue. Brown wrote a report titled "The Korean Conspiracy Case" and made it available for publication by various papers both in and out of the States. Such active participation of the mission board made the Japanese consider the importance of the

---

344 Yong Ha Shin, *Hanminjok Dongnibundongsa Yongu* (A Study of the Independence Movement of the Korean People) (Euryumunhwasa, 1985), 131-134.

responses from the international community and the relationship with the U.S., eventually concluding the second trial with much reduced penalties. The clumsy fabrication of the Japanese to eradicate the Christian presence in the Northwestern region eventually ended with no significant result. Instead, the evil schemes of the Japanese were made known all over the world. This incident proved that the Japanese thought it necessary to eradicate Christianity in order to successfully establish its colonial rule. The Church was once again seen as the strongest source of the anti-Japanese energy. Furthermore, the Church was able to stand firm against persecutions and ordeals, and keep the tradition of not giving in to any type of external pressure.

(3) Oppression of Christian Schools and the Revised Private School Regulations

The Japanese knew very well that any kind of direct persecution of Christianity would result in direct confrontations with missionaries, which would lead to complications in Japan's relations with the U.S. and other Western states. In order to bypass such tragic outcomes and at the same time efficiently oppress and eliminate the Christian power, they decided to oppress Christian private schools. At that time, there were about 40,000 schooling children from Korean Christian families. About 20,000 of them went to 1,000 schools belonging to Korean churches. This meant that many future leaders in Korea would be educated with Christian principles, and this became a heavy burden for the Japanese.

Determined to take control of the Christian students, the Japanese Governor-General promulgated the so-called "Revised Private School Regulations" in March 1915.[345] The regulations included some positive requirements, such as the necessity of schools to expand their facilities and to secure more qualified and further trained teachers. However, the regulations also required schools "to remove biblical education from regular class hours and to abolish religious rituals such as worship services." This was directly in conflict with the founding principles of Christian schools. It was clear that the Japanese wanted to get rid of Christian education in Christian schools.[346] While the ten-year period granted for expanding facilities seemed reasonable, the underlying intention to remove biblical education and services was more than just a problem to the Christian community in Korea.

The Government-General had a rather good reasoning. It told the missionaries to let the government take care of education and just concentrate on religious works. The Government-General advocated that education is an important task of building faithful people for the empire. Komatsu, the Minister of Foreign Affairs for the Government-General, wrote the following article in the *Gyeongsuhng(Seoul) Daily* to explain their position.

---

345 For more information on the regulations, see Kokiobokil, *Korea Kioyouksako* (Study on the History of the Education in Korea) (Seoul: Imperial Regional Administration Conference, 1927), 423-425.
346 C. A. Clark, *The Korean Church and the Nevius Method*, 197.

Our object of education is not only to develop the intellect and morality of our people, but also to foster in their minds such national spirit as will contribute to the existence and welfare of our Empire······I sincerely hope that you will appreciate this change of the time and understand that missions should leave all affairs relating entirely to education entirely in the hands of the Government, by transferring the money and labour they have hitherto been expending on education to their proper sphere of religious propagation······ Education must be decidedly nationalistic and must not be mixed up with religion that is universal.[347]

They reasoned that education and religion are separate. Their short sighted view was that religion was universal, but education was national. They were completely ignorant of the Christian principle that education enables people not only to be faithful to their country, but also to work and serve all the peoples of the world. They were deceived by their ignorance that the kind of education designed to produce men and women only faithful to their country will eventually result in the dangerous and blinded allegiance as seen in the total obedience to A. Hitler in the Nazi philosophy or the unconditional death for the emperor in the Kamikaze philosophy. They were yet to realize that close-minded nationalistic education would produce millions of chauvinists, who would bring about their own destruction. They did not understand that Christian

---

347 F. A. McKenzie, *Korea's Fight for Freedom*, 214.

education was indeed the perfect tool for producing the greatest patriots and philanthropists. They were just concerned that Christian education was promoting the independence movement and producing anti-Japanese leaders.[348]

The Private School Regulations brought much suffering to Christian schools, especially Presbyterian schools. There were several different reasons for this. The first was the strong demands by the students. Public schools had better facilities and better teachers. The students in public schools not only enjoyed better education, but were guaranteed of good career paths after graduation. In contrast, the Christian school students had to put up with inferior educational environments, and they had no guarantee of jobs after graduation. With so much dissatisfaction, the students went on strikes and demanded the schools to meet the requirements put forth by the government.[349]

Another important factor was disagreements between mission boards. History might have become quite different if the different mission boards and schools had stood together as one in resolving this issue with the Governor-General. Instead, the Methodists and the Presbyterians had many disagreements, eventually making things more difficult for the Presbyterian Church. The Methodist missionaries thought that it was better for them to follow the requirements of the government and keep schools open rather than to have the schools be forced to close. In this line, they decided to observe

348 A. J. Brown, *The Mastery of the Far East* (New York: Charles Scribner's, 1919), 353.

349 J. W. Hitch, *Minutes of the Korean Missions of the Methodist Episcopal Church, South, for 1926*, 57.

the governmental requirements in the shortest time possible. Therefore, Baejae, Ewha and Baewha in Seoul, Gwangsuhng and Jeong
ui in Pyongyang, Songdo and Hosudon in Gaesuhng, Louis in
Wonsan and many other schools requested for the Governer-General's
approval and renamed themselves to *Godeungbotonghakgyo*(General
High School).[350]

However, the Presbyterian Church took a different approach.
They saw the true purposes of Christian schools in teaching the
Bible and having services so that the students would be exposed
to the Christian truth and, ultimately, become Christians themselves.
Determined that there would be no purpose of schools if there
was no biblical education or services, the Presbyterians refused
to request for governmental approval until the very end. In addition,
they deemed it out of the question to even consider the requirement
of students to visit shrines on all school events. The Japanese
attempted to advocate that visiting shrines was not a religious
ritual, but a national ceremony. Such resistance of the Presbyterian
schools led to the Governer-General classifying all of them as
illegal schools. The only Presbyterian schools that complied with
the regulations were Osan School in Jeongju, which was set up
by Seung Hoon Lee, and Yeongsaeng Girls' School in Hamheung.
Unlike other Presbyterian schools, these two schools had no connection
with missionaries. With such strong oppression of the Japanese,
the number of Christian schools began to decrease; there were

---

350 Government-General in Korea, Department of Education, *List of All Schools
in Korea* (May 1927), 337-343.

only 318 schools in 1918 as compared to 494 schools in 1912. However, the strongest of the Japanese oppressions against Christian schools had to give in to the victorious triumph of Presbyterian schools when the Japanese were forced to allow biblical education and worship services in Christian schools under the so-called cultural politics, shortly after the end of the March First Movement in 1919.

Chapter 7.

The Korean Church
and the March First Movement

1. Origin of the March First Movement

For the first decade since the Japanese takeover in 1910 up until the March First Movement, the situation in Korea was at its worst. The policy exercised by the Japanese after the annexation of Korea can be summarized into the following points.

First, it was a policy of assimilation. The Education Regulation promulgated in 1911 was aimed at "making Koreans the faithful people of the Japanese Emperor."[351] In this line, the Japanese attempted to uproot the very historicity and authenticity of Koreans by burning all historical documents. Determined to vaporize any superior accounts of the Korean history, they also strictly prohibited presenting or teaching stories, songs or performances that tell of the heroic acts of those Korean ancestors who fought for the country.

---

351 Korea, *Its Land, People, Culture of All Ages* (Seoul: Hakwonsa, 1960), 92.

In addition to restricting history and language lessons in schools, they also identified and took away every single piece of literature that was deemed to arouse the spirit of nationalism among the people.

Second, the Japanese were engaged in economic exploitation. Although Korea had been under political control of the Chinese who worked to preserve Korea's right of self-government and refrained from exploiting the Korean economy,[352] the Japanese was quite different in this aspect. Of the economic differences, Prof. D. A. Swain wrote the following account:

In the land survey program, unregistered land became government domain and then were sold to the Oriental Land Company and other Japanese land companies, as well as to individual Japanese immigrants. Between 1909 and 1915, Japanese landowners increased ten times; and their holdings, four times. Moreover, in the 1911-1920 period, the land tax was doubled·····In the same period, purely Korean capital fell from 17 percent of the total to 12 percent; Japanese capital went from 32 percent to 80 percent of the total. These figures attest to the deliberate suppression of Korean enterprises.[353]

---

352 Sun Yat-sen, "The Principle of Nationalism," *Nationalism in Asia and Africa*, ed. Elie Kedulie (New York: Ward, 1970), 312.
353 David L. Swain, "The Church and Japan's Colonial Legacy," *The Japan Christian Quarterly* (Fall 1981), 208.

Such economic oppression of the Japanese forced the Koreans to be left without a land and place of dwelling. Many of them had to wander to Manchuria, Siberia, and Hawaii, looking for new homes.

Third, they introduced a decadent culture into Korea. They adopted licensed prostitution by migrating a large number of Japanese prostitutes to Korea for the purpose of corrupting Korean young men.[354] They also encouraged the planting and selling of opium, which was strictly forbidden in Japan. Their policy was precisely targeted at corrupting the minds and bodies of the Korean people.

Fourth, they began to oppress the church in a systematic manner. According to the 1915 "Propagation Regulation," it is stipulated that all religious workers must obtain licenses from the Government-General and that establishing or relocating churches and other places of worship must have valid approval. The police monitored every worship service and screened every sermon. Their supervision was not confined to regular worship services but included all other meetings, such as prayer meetings, Bible classes and revival meetings. They often prohibited pastors from speaking of David's victory over Goliath, Joshua and Caleb, or Gideon's 300 warriors on the grounds that such stories were suggestive of the weak Korea winning the strong Japan.[355] Above all, worship of the Emperor and shrine worship were the greatest factors that pushed the Korean Church

---

354 Eun Sik Park, *Hanguk Dongnibundong Jihyeolsa* (Bloody History of Independence Movement of Korea) (Seoul: Dankook University, 1920), 54.
355 Edmund F. Cook, "Japan's Imperialistic Program as seen in Korea," *The Methodist Quarterly Review* (July 1915), 483.

to directly and actively resist against Japan.

As for the persecution of Christian schools, the 1915 "Revised Private School Act" forbade Bible classes and worship services in schools. They even attempted to eradicate the Korean language by making schools use Japanese exclusively. They used all means to oppress Christian schools, which they thought were important vehicles of promoting nationalism.

However, such oppression of the Japanese could not dampen the rapid growth of Christianity. Cooperation among denominations was well on the way, and the churches were able to stick together during the harshest times of persecution. Presbyterians and Methodists jointly published *The Christian Messenger(Kidok Sinbo)* in 1915, and Presbyterian and Methodist leaders met in YMCA Seoul to inaugurate the "Korea Christian Presbyterian-Methodist Union" in 1918. Nevertheless, the Japanese oppression over Korea intensifie d each day. II. D. Grieswold wrote of the oppression in 1920:

······an extreme militant policy, de-nationalization, complete objection of political participation of the Koreans, discrimination of the Koreans, forbidden liberty of mass communication, publishing, trust, restricted freedom of religions, forbidden study of the Korean language, restricted travel to foreign countries, requisition of the royal land, de-moralization of the people through public prostitution and use of opium, forcing of immigration to Manchuria, and favor to the Japanese at the industrial and commercial areas.[356]

The harsher the oppression by the Japanese, the deeper the grudges of Koreans who were determined to stand up in resistance. Koreans could only wait for the right moment as they did not possess any power or maturity for meaningful retaliation. While anti-Japanese movements existed at individual and regional levels, there were virtually no national-level or organized resistance movements. But when the right moment came, a truly national movement erupted like a volcano. H. Hulbert once foretold of this back in 1908 much like a prophet:

> The time will come when the civilizing influences of Christianity must come into clash with the cupidity and oppression of the Japanese······The Japanese regime there makes for corruption in every grade of Society······Christianity stands for justice, cleanliness, kindness, public spirit, patriotis m, helpfulness, education.[357]

After a long period of perseverance and patience, the Koreans and churches stood up against the Japanese in what is known as the March First Movement.

The March First Movement was directly motivated by the notion of "self-determination" declared by the U.S. President Woodrow

---

356 H. D. Griswold, "The Korean Crisis," *Woman's Work for Woman* (February 1920), 26-27. A similar account was given in The Korean Situation, which was a special report written on the March First Movement by the Committee on Oriental Issues, Christian Association, U.S.A.

357 H. B. Hulbert, "Japanese and Missionaries in Korea," *The Missionary Review of the World* (March 1908), 208-209.

Wilson in 1917, just a year before the end of the WW I. The self-determination principle, which states that weaker nations should be set free from the control of stronger nations and that each nation should be able to make decisions by itself, was applicable to colonies of the states that lost in the First World War. Nevertheless, the declaration was a ray of hope to Koreans who were living under the oppression of the Japanese.

2. Progress

Following the declaration of self-determination, Korean leaders acted quickly, having decided that the principle was applicable for Korea as well. They began to look for ways to send a delegation to the Peace Convention in Paris in April 1918 in order to present a petition for the independence of Korea, and in the summer of that year, Woon Hyeong Yeo, Deok Soo Chang and Hyeok Suhnwoo established the New Korea Youth League in Shanghai, China. Woon Hyeong Yeo, the leader of the League, arrived in Korea in September 1918 in order to talk about an independence movement with various national leaders at the presbytery at Suncheon, North Pyongan. He met with many leaders including Seung Hoon Lee and Sang Jae Lee informing them of the activities overseas and the issues to be addressed within Korea.

Then Yeo met C. R. Crain, a U.S. presidential envoy who was visiting China for matters pertaining to the conclusion of WWI. While asking for help in sending a Korean delegation to the Peace

Convention in Paris, Yeo also requested that a petition for the independence of Korea be forwarded to the Chairman of the Convention and the U.S. President. This was promptly followed through and Gyu Sik Kim was sent to the Peace Convention early the following year.[358]

On the other hand, the Korean National Association in the U.S. A. held a general meeting in December 1918 where it was decided that a delegation be sent to the Peace Convention as well. Thus a delegation of several members led by Syungman Rhee was organized for the task of presenting the petition for independence. In the same month, they also attended the annual general meeting of the League of Small Nations in New York, agreeing and declaring the independence of small nations in accordance to the principle of self-determination. When *The Japan Advertiser*, an English newspaper published in Japan, reported such activities in the States,[359] Korean students in Japan began to discuss the matter of Korean independence in a more systematic manner. At their end-of-the-year dinner, the students decided that they would stage an independence movement. They met again in January the following year at YMCA, Tokyo, where they drafted a declaration of independence that would be sent to the Japanese government, the Japanese diet and diplomatic offices of various nations. As a means to encourage their work, Deok Soo Chang and others came from Shanghai and Beijing to help them, and Kwang Soo Lee came from Beijing and wrote

---

358 Woo Keun Han, *Hanguk Tongsa* (Entire History of Korea), 542.
359 *The Japan Advertiser*, December 15, 1918.

the draft of the declaration of independence.[360]

Then on February 8, the so-called February Eighth Tokyo Students Independence Declaration, which was a crucial stepping-stone tow ard the March First Movement, was solemnly conducted at YMCA Tokyo with about 400 students and Korean residents. As was planned, they undertook the noble task of declaring the independence of Korea to Japan and to the world by sending the declaration to the Japanese government, foreign diplomatic offices and the press. This incident gave great motivation to independence workers and Christian leaders in Korea. As a whole, a path was being paved for a greater independence movement.

Within Korea itself, independence movements were mainly conceived by religious organizations. First of all, Chondoists(Those who followed the religion of Chondo) planned to stage an independence movement near towards the conclusion of WW I. In January 1919, Dong Jin Kwon, Se Chang Oh, Lin Choi and other Chondoist leaders reported their plan for an independence movement to the Leader Byeong Hee Sohn and obtained his permission. They also agreed on three principles: first, the independence movement must involve everyone; second, the independence movement must be olcnt.[361] While the decision of not using violence against the heavily armed Japanese military was definitely a futile attempt, almost like beating one's head against a wall, it was a decision influenced

---

360 Suhng Sik Kim, *Iljeha Hangukhaksaeng Dongnibundongsa* (Independence
    Movement of Students under the Japanese Rule) (Jeongeumsa, 1981), 49.
361 Hyeon Jong Lee, ed., *Hanguk Dongnibundongsa* (History of Korean
    Independence Movement), vol. 2, 115.

by the non-violent and non-resistant movement by M. Gandhi in India.

On the Christian side, Hyeok Sunwoo came to Pyongyang to meet leaders like Seung Hoon Lee, Jeon Baek Yang and Sun Joo Kil to confirm that the Christian presence in the Northwestern region should stage an independence movement jointly as one body.[362] In Seoul, Hee Do Park, a staff worker at the YMCA, Gap Suhng Lee, a pharmacist in Severance Hospital, and Won Byeok Kim, a student at Yonhee University, were organizing a student-led independence movement. When the Chondoist Nam Sun Choi suggested that Chondoism and Christianity join forces in the independence movement, Seung Hoon Lee came to Seoul to discuss the issue. After learning that the students were already planning a movement, Lee decided that Christian efforts should be joined with the Chondoists for the work.

Among the Buddhists, on the other hand, Yong Un Han and Yong Suhng Baek were also involved in the movement. Unlike the Chondists or Christians, the Buddhists at this stage were not carrying out an interreligious work. The two leaders joined in the movement purely based on their personal contacts with the Chondoists. Although a few Christian leaders opted out of the movement because they did not agree with the coalition with Chondoists, this independence movement now became an inter-religious

---

362 Yang Sun Kim, "3.1 Undonggwa Gidokgiogae (The March First Movement and the Christian Circle)," *3.1 Undong 50 Junyeon Ginyeomnonjip* (Fiftieth Anniversary Commemoration Compilation of The March First Movement) (The Donga Daily, 1969), 235-270.

movement involving Koreans from all walks of life.

Sixteen Christians, fifteen Chondoists and two Buddhists, 33 in all, were appointed as national leaders. It is worth noting that the Christian population numbered less than one tenth of the Chondoist population at that time but there were more Christian leaders for the independence movement. The leaders began to discuss practical issues such as determining the date and venue of the event, drafting and printing the declaration, presenting the declara-tion to the Japanese government and foreign diplomatic offices, and sending a delegation to the Peace Convention in Paris.[363]

They decided that the event would take place on March 1. The date was chosen because on March 3, Monday, Emperor Gojong's funeral was planned to take place and crowds of people were expected to arrive in Seoul from all parts of the country. So it seemed ideal to stage the protest the day before, but Christians objected to the notion of protesting on a Sunday. Thus, March 1, Saturday, was selected for the date of the protest.

The Pagoda Park in Jongno in Seoul, which was the most heavily congested place in the city, was chosen as the venue. But this venue had to be changed to Myeongwolgwan (Restaurant) in Insadong, Seoul just a day before the actual event. This was because A. L. Backer, Gap Suhng Lee's professor at Severance, advised Gap Suhng Lee that a declaration protest in the Pagoda Park would result in a bloody clash between the students and the police, and

---

363 Yong Ha Shin, *3.1 Dongnibundong* (March First Independence Movement), 61-62.

thus the independence declaration should be proclaimed at a less crowded place without having the potential problem of public interference.[364]

Finally on March 1, 29 out of the 33 national leaders came together.[365] After the declaration ceremony, the leaders had lunch together and then contacted the Jongno Police Station. All of them were arrested on the spot. On that day, Rev. Sun Joo Kil was leading a Bible Study meeting at Jangyeon Church in Hwanghae Province. Having heard of the news of the declaration of independence, he immediately rushed to Seoul. When he visited the national leaders at the Jongno Police Station, he was arrested as well.

On the other hand, a multitude of people was waiting for the national leaders at the Pagoda Park. When the leaders did not turn up, Jae yong Chung, a Gyeongsin School graduate and a Sunday school teacher, walked up to the platform and began reading a copy of the Declaration of Independence he had in his possession. After reading the declaration, he shouted, "Long Live the Independent Korea!" The crowd joined him in shouting, "Long Live the Independent Korea!" at the top of their lungs, a cry which they were not allowed to say for over a decade. Then the crowd began to spill into Jongno Street for a peaceful demonstration. Leaders

---

364 Gwang Soo Kim, *Hanguk Gidokgio Sunansa*(Suffering History of Korean Christianity), 71.

365 Among the 33, absent for the historic moment of the declaration of independence were Rev. Yeo Dae Yoo who had to lead a demonstration in Uiju, Rev. Sun Joo Kil and Rev. Chun Soo Chung who had to lead revival meetings outside Seoul and Rev. Byeong Jo Kim who had to travel to Shanghai for an urgent matter.

of the movement appealed to the crowd for strict non-violence:

> Oh, our dear colleagues and fellow countrymen! Under whatever circumstances do not humiliate, throw stones, strike with your fists, the Japanese. These manners are of the barbarians who we are not, and such acts only hurt our noble cause. Be attentive not to violate![366]

People of all ranks and backgrounds joined the movement. It was literally a national cry of independence by people of all faiths. The report has it that close to half a million people participated in the protest for the entire day, but not a single count of violence was seen.[367]

The declaration of independence movement was also carried out not only in Seoul, but simultaneously in other places including Pyongyang, Jinnampo, Anju, Suncheon, Uiju and Wonsan. In Pyongyang, Rev. Sun Doo Kim, the moderator of the Presbyterian General Assembly, Rev. Gyu Chan Kang and Rev. Il Yong Lee took leadership of joining six churches in Pyongyang to hold a memorial service for Emperor Gojong in Sungdeok School with about 3,000 believers. After the service, Rev. Suhn Doo Kim asked the people to stay back and he began to read the Declaration of

---

366 "The Struggle for Liberty in Korea," *The Missionary Review of the World* (June 1919), 161-162.

367 Hyeon Jong Lee, ed., *Hanguk Dongnibundongsa* (History of Korean Independence Movement), vol. 2, 178.

Independence. After reading the declaration, they began a peaceful protest by shouting Long Live the Independent Korea! Missionary Moffett, the Principal of the Pyongyang Presbyterian Seminary at that time, wrote, "I testify that among all the Koreans I have encountered and the protesters in and out of the city that I have seen during these five days (March 1-5) there was not a single person acting violently."[368] Rev. Sun Doo Kim was arrested for his partaking and was not able to attend the Presbyterian General Assembly in the autumn of that year. Vice-moderator Rev. Moffett led the meeting in proxy.

In Jinnampo, some 120 Methodist students gathered at a chapel to stage a movement. And in Suncheon, Sinsuhng School teachers and students led a protest. By the time they reached the police station, the crowd increased to several thousands. Feeling threatened, the Japanese police fired at the protesters and more than a dozen lives were lost. In Suhngjin, North Hamgyeong Province, students of Bosin School, a Christian school, also marched in protest toward a Japanese settlement. Student-led demonstrations took place in many other cities as well: Rev. Man Jip Lee led Gaesuhng School and Sinmyeong School students in Daegu, North Gyeongsang Province, Ilsin Girls' School students staged a protest in Busan and Sinheung School students in Jeonju, North Jeolla Province staged a movement. Wherever there was a Christian school, it became the pivot for

---

368 Mah, Samnak, "Suhyangsarami Bon Hangukui Dongnibundong (The Korean Independence Movement as Seen by a Foreigner)," *Aseawa Sungio* (Asia and Missions) (Institute of Missiological Issues, Presbyterian Theological Seminary and College, 1976), 62.

studentled protests in the area.

Although the protests were strictly peaceful in the beginning, the Japanese police and military continued to oppress the protesters brutally, and thus the crowds began to take on an aggressive position in self-defense. In some areas, the protesters raged and destroyed military posts, police stations and government offices, as well as using violence in resisting the police and military.[369]

At that time, religious organizations were just about the only bodies with national networks; it was common for these religious organizations, i.e. Christians, Chondoists and Buddhists, to plan and stage protests either jointly or independently.[370] The March First Movement continued on for about six months involving millions of people in various forms and styles, which are too many to be described here. One outstanding aspect of the March First Movement was that it was a direct result of the grudge of the Korean people under oppression and the Christian faith that stood against all forms of injustice. Nevertheless, the prolonged movement brought much damage in every way.

---

369 Hyeon Jong Lee, ed., *Hanguk Dongnibundongsa* (History of Korean Independence Movement), vol. 2, 213, 358-359.

370 Among the 300 demonstrations for which the leaders had been identified, 78 demonstrations were led by Christians, 66 were led by Chondoists, and 42 were jointly led by Christians and Chondoists, indicating that about two thirds of the demonstrations were led by religious leaders. Gyeong Sik Park, *Korea Samildongnibundong* (The March First Independence Movement of Korea) (1976), 186-188.

3. Damage to the Church

As Christians played central roles in most of the protests across the country for about six months, circulating the declaration of independence and producing and distributing Korean flags, it is obvious that Christians were being more devastated than any other organization or religion.[371] Korea was home to one Japanese army division, more than ten thousand military police and numerous military police assistants and civil policemen. Their retaliation to churches and Christians were more than brutal. The wife of a missionary resident in Pyongyang at that time wrote the following account:

> So many Japanese officials came and smashed the bells
> in the towers of the church buildings, and all the windows,
> the Bibles, hymnals, and rolls of Sunday School. They arrested
> the church staff and stripped them of their clothes and
> beat them on the church ground.[372]

Having perceived that the movement was planned and led by

---

371 The number of arrests by religion and denomination shows the extent of damage suffered by the church. The Japanese were targeting to arrest Christians, more than any other group. Chondoism and Sicheongyo: 2,200(1 1.8%); Buddhism: 220(1.1%); Confucianism: 346(1.6%); Methodist: 560; Presbyterian: 2,486; Other Protestant: 320; Catholicism: 55; Total Christiani ty: 17.6%; Other religions: 21(0.1%), Non-religious: 9,304(47.7%); Religion not identified: 3,907(20%); Total: 19,525. Chung Sik Lee, *The Politics of Korean Nationalism* (Berkely, 1963), 115.

372 Letter from W. L. Swallen to Olivette Swallen dated April 23, 1919.

churches, the Japanese staged a nationwide roundup of Christians and severely tortured them. The following is a statement of a female Christian who was tortured:

······I was arrested by the police in Pyongyang on March 2nd. In prison, there were many women and men. The police meticulously asked us whether we were Christians······ There were twelve Methodist women, two Presbyterian women and one Chondoist women. Three of the Methodist women were evangelists. The police whipped us, stripped us and made us stand naked before many men. The police could not find any charge against me, other than having cheered, "Long Live Korea" on the street. They indiscriminately beat me as they turned my body around and I was sweating all over.,,, Both my hands were tied tightly behind my back. They kept beating my naked body. They threw cold water on me whenever there was too much sweat on my body. When I told them I felt cold, they seared my skin with their cigarette butts······One woman was beaten so badly that she passed out······And another evangelist not only had her hands tightly bound, but her feet as well and was hung on a pillar for a long time. All our Bibles were taken away. We were prohibited from talking to one another, let alone pray. We suffered the worst humiliation and ridicule that a person could ever withstand.[373]

---

373 "Samil Undong Bisa" (Secret History of the March First Movement), *Gidokgio*

Human language cannot possibly fully describe the pain suffered by the individuals and churches. Some major incidents suffered by the Church include the massacre in Gangsuh, South Pyeongan Province, the arson massacre in Cheongju, the crucifixion massacre in Seoul, the chapel arson in Uiju, North Pyongan Province and the massacre in Byeongcheon, Chuhnan. But the most tragic was the massacre at Jeamri Methodist Church in Suwon, Kyonggi Province.

Around 2 P.M., April 15, when protests were still going on steadily, the Japanese Lieutenant Arida and his troops raged the Jaeamri village. They gathered the church members(about 30 of them), tied their hands and forced them into the church building. After locking them in, they set the church on fire and shot everyone who attempted to run out of the building, whether women or children. This formidable brutality was carried out "in the broad daylight as the villagers watched."[374]

Statistically speaking, 7,509 were killed, 15,961 were injured, 46,948 were arrested, 47 church buildings were destroyed, 2 school buildings were destroyed and 715 houses were destroyed between March 1 and May 30, 1919. Statistics between March 1, 1919 and March 1, 1920 show that a total of 7,645 people were killed, 45,562 were injured, 49,818 were arrested, 724 houses were burned down, 59 church buildings were burned down and 3 school buildings

---

Sasang (The Christian Thoughts) (March 1966), 88-89.

[374] Hyeon Jong Lee, ed., *Hanguk Dongnibundongsa* (History of Korean Independence Movement), vol. 3, 214. "First Account of Massacres and Burning of Villages," *The Korean Situation*, 68-72.

were burned down. [375]

The Japanese concentrated on arresting Christians only; they would ask any passers-by if they were a Christian, arresting or releasing them depending on their response. The Presbyterian Church suffered the greatest loss. According to the data reported to the General Assembly, not counting for the possible omissions, those arrested numbered 3,804, among who were 134 pastors and elders, 202 leaders, 2,125 male members and 531 female members. Those beaten and then released numbered 2,162, 41 were killed, 6 were beaten to death and 12 church buildings were destroyed. While only 1% of the 20 million Koreans were Christians, as many as 17.6% of those arrested were Christians. This is a clear indication of the great loss suffered by the Korean Church.

4. Involvement of Missionaries

It is a matter of great interest to discuss the roles played and attitudes adopted by the missionaries during the March First Movement. It was mentioned earlier that missionaries are supposed to maintain neutrality concerning political issues in their mission fields. It is true that missionaries did not wish for the believers to become deeply involved in politics, which could lead them to become engrossed with matters other than faith itself, and thus abandoning the Christian life or walking in ways that are not conducive for the Christian way of life. As far as the Koreans'anti-Japanese move-

---

375 *Ibid.*, vol. 2, 215.

ment was concerned, the missionaries could not render any direct support other than moral support. In this line, the missionaries could resort to only one position during the March First Movement. In short, they could offer nothing but moral support. In other words, they had to maintain neutrality.

They could have been completely unaware of this movement as they claimed to have been(considering the fact that the Japanese police or military were completely unaware of it as well). Or, they might have known all about it. Either way, it is obvious that they were in a position where it was not possible to encourage or discourage the Koreans. In this aspect, the missionaries were neutral.

Nevertheless, the missionaries could not remain neutral as the Japanese began to exercise brutality over the peaceful protesters and as the churches and Christians began to suffer great losses. A missionary best expressed this by stated, "We were not neutral in regards to brutality."[376] One of the key figures who informed the world of the Japanese brutality was the Canadian missionary at Severance Hospital, F. W. Scofield. He took pictures of the barbaric acts performed by Japanese troops at Jeamri and sent them overseas. He also wrote a booklet titled *The Unquenchable Fire* in order to report the Japanese brutality to the world. As the press worldwide was reporting his report and pictures, the world began to pay attention to the March First Movement.

---

376 Mah, Samak, "Suhyangsaramibon Hangugui Dongnibundong" (Korean Independence Movement as Seen by a Foreigner), *Aseawa Suhngio* (Asia and Missions), 80.

Churches in the United States gave tremendous support in this aspect. Heung Woo Shin, the principal of Baejaehakdang and a Methodist lay leader, traveled to the States in order to attend the 100th anniversary conference of the Northern Methodist Church in the U.S.A. in May 1919. As Shin was personally acquainted with F. M. North, the chairman of the conference, Shin informed him of the protest movement in Korea and the brutality exercised by the Japanese. This was made known to the executive committee of the Federal Council of the Churches of Christ in America(FCC CA), and the executive committee decided to investigate the facts further for report.[377] This led to the committee's publishing of 5,000 copies of a booklet entitled *The Korean Situation* in April that year.

The Oriental Relations Committee of the Christian Association in the U.S.A. submitted this publication to the Congress and sent a telegraphic message to the Japanese government for immediate halt of the persecution and administrative reformation in Korea. The U.S. government also demanded a full explanation and action from the Japanese Minister to the U.S.A. Thus the March First Movement was now in the center of the world's attention. Overcome by the power of the world press, Japan was forced to change its attitude. In May that year, the General Assembly of the Northern Presbyterian Church of the U.S.A. also expressed sympathy towards the Korean Church and resolved to give "moral support until

---

377 *Annual Reports of the Federal Council of the Churches of Christian in America, for the Year 1919*, 129-130.

Christians in Korea find practical and continuous improvement to their conditions."[378]

A number of missionaries were also oppressed at the individual level. Prof. E. M. Mowry of Pyongyang Sungsil College was sentenced to six months in prison for hiding the students who produced copies of the declaration of independence and Korean flags in his house and for translating the declaration of independence into English and sending it to the mission board. Principal G. S. McCune of Suncheon Sinsuhng School was deported under the charge of conspiring to organize the movement with the church leaders in the area, and Rev. S. Moffett was detained for some time for having spoken in favor of supporting the independence of Korea at the World Missionary Conference. Rev. Thomas of the Oriental Missionary Society was beaten by the military police in Ganggyeong, Chungcheong Province, for assisting in the movement, and the Methodist missionaries W. A. Noble and B. W. Billings in Seoul were persecuted for actively participating in the movement as well.

Although none of the foreign mission boards systematically helped in the preparation of the movement, many missionaries were urged to support the work personally and secretly as they saw the churches suffering. Therefore, it would be accurate to say that missionaries and mission agencies, both personally and collectively, did all that they were allowed to oppose the brutal acts of the Japanese even though missionaries were not officially involved in the movement.

---

378 *The Minutes of the General Assembly of P.C.U.S.A.*(1920), 94, 98.

5. Outcome

So, what is the outcome of the March First Movement? It is difficult to pinpoint the exact outcome of the March First Movement. However, although the movement was not able to successfully secure the political independence of Korea, the movement itself can be seen as successful in many aspects. By and large, the movement was a clear exhibition of the strong desire for independence to the Japanese and to the world. In spite of its political failure, the movement brought about a number of positive results. The major outcomes are as follows.

First, this movement united Koreans together as one. It was by far a radical fact that the Korean people, who were divided into many groups with conflicts due to various reasons, came together in one spirit and one heart for the movement. This is comparable to the American War of Revolution against the British when the residents of the 13 colonial states-who were divided due to their diverse ethnic, linguistic, and cultural backgrounds-fought united under one flag and secured their own victory.

Second, this movement resulted in the establishment of the Provisional Government of the Republic of Korea. The Provisional Government was established in Shanghai in the winter of 1919 with Syungman Rhee as the inaugurating president. There is great significance in the fact that a government, though a government in exile, existed for the Republic of Korea. It is also remarkable to note that among the eight key persons of the Provisional Government, seven were Christians.[379] The government took on the democratic republic system, and thus "the March First Movement signified that Korea was reborn as a member of the international community."[380]

Third, this movement forced the Japanese to switch its regime over Korea from a militaristic rule to a so-called cultural politics. Suppressed by the demands of the world press, Governor-General Yoshimichi Hasegawa was replaced by Makoto Saito. Adopting cultural politics, Saito played soft by allowing restricted freedom to Koreans and loosening religious regulations. After the appointment in September, he restructured the government, replacing the military police with civil police. He claimed that he would prohibit the carrying of swords by government officials, change the appointment and payment regulations for Korean government officials, allow the publication of Korean newspapers, at which, *Dongailbo*(The Donga Daily) and *Chosunilbo*(The Chosun Daily) were founded, and abolish all forms of discrimination against Koreans. However, these claims were hardly supported by any concrete action. In fact, the Japanese ever more tightened their grip on the colonial rule.

In regards to Christianity, the new Governor-General summoned missionaries in September to listen to their opinions. The missiona-

---

379 "Korea Ready to become Christian," *The Missionary Review of the World* (July 1919), 551.
380 Il Chul Shin, "National Views of March 1 Independence Movement," *Nationalism in Korea*, Chong Shik Chung, ed. (Seoul: Research Center for Peace and Unification, 1979), 252.

ries submitted *The Report on Joint Religious Meeting* to the Governer-General. They argued that while "the Japanese Constitution guaranteed freedom of religion" such freedom was not granted under the laws and regulations in force. And thus they demanded the following points:

- Fewer restrictions be placed upon the Church and upon missionaries.
- Discrimination against Christians and Christianity by officials be not allowed.
- We be allowed to include the teaching of the Bible and religious exercises in the curricula of Church schools.
- Restrictions on the use of Korean language be removed.
- Koreans be allowed the opportunities for education as are provided for Japanese, and greater freedom be granted in the selection of the textbooks and the restrictions on the study of the Korean and universal history be removed.
- Graduates of private schools holding Government permits be eligible for all privileges accorded to graduates of Government schools.
- The censorship of Christian books be abolished.
- We be not restricted in our Church newspaper, magazine and other publications.
- Facilities for the incorporation of the Korean Church and of the Missions so that property can be held and registered in their names.
- Christian men who are convicted for political offences only

be not forced for Sunday labour or other forms of work.
- The law requiring special permits for soliciting contributions
for hospitals, schools and benevolent work to be too stringent.[381]

Saito Speaks about His Policy, *The Seoul Press*, 14th January
1920. Accepting the suggestions of the missionaries, Saito amended
the "propagation regulations," modifying and relaxing the existing
policy. Part of these changes is reflected in his instructions.

⋯⋯As far as Christianity and Buddhism were concerned,
the Department of Religions was installed within the Office
of Culture and Education, for all religious matters. Installation
of the Department of Religions was well received by religious
leaders because they were given the assurance that the
Government values the importance of religious matters and
that the Government is keen at supporting religious propagation
in the society. In terms of our relationship with Christians,
it was of urgent necessity that we approach them to resolve
all their misunderstandings and explain to them the agenda
of the new political paradigm. In this respect, the Governor-
General had a comprehensive view of the matters and appeased
them. The most vital element in our relationship with Christians
was supervision and improvement of mission schools. However,
we amended regulations concerning private schools, set out
our directives clear, and exercised strict supervision. We

---

381 Jeonbogogiol, *Chosun Tonghicsa Nongo* (Theisis on History of Ruling of
Korea) (Seoul: Sungjin Moonhwasa, 1972), 180-181.

also simplified the regulations for propagation of religions and recognized religious organizations as legal entities, granting full freedom in spreading of religions in the society.[382]

Regaining the approval for Bible classes and worship services in schools as well as the attempt for reconciliation by changing the existing policy concerning Christianity were the invaluable fruits of the March First Movement. Nevertheless, this was nothing close to a complete freedom of Christianity. They continued to "control and restrict participation of worship services in churches and schools. They arrested students under various charges, screened all publications, and often objected to articles written in church bulletins."[383]

Fourth, this movement taught the Korean people that Christianity was no longer a foreign religion but the most patriotic religion that loved Koreans. Ever since its introduction to Korea, Christianity has been actively involved in nationwide movements as this, even more than Chondoism. This is clearly seen by the number of leaders directly involved in the protests, the number of those arrested and even the human and material losses in terms of damage to church buildings, school buildings and other offices. Some view Christianity as having played the role of "a vehicle rather than a subject"

---

382 Society of Regional Administration by Imperialists, ed., *Chosun Tongchibiwha* (Unknown Episodes of the Reign in Chosun) (1937), 290-291.

383 Wee Jo Kang, *Iljetongchiha Hangukui Jonggiowa Jeongchi* (Religions and Politics of Korea under the Japanese Rule) (Korea Christian Literature Society, 1977), 45.

for the March First Movement, but many factors indicate that Christians provided the central energy for the movement.

In conclusion, despite the failure to secure political independence, the March First Movement proved to be a vital chance of displaying Koreans' united passion and desire for independence to the world. The Church could fully actualize the patriotic spirit that it has been teaching for a long time. For Christianity, the March First Movement was a crucial opportunity of identifying with Koreans as a national religion.

Chapter 8

The Church in the 1920s and 1930s

At least superficially, the Church seemed to enjoy greater freedom after the March First Movement. However, persistent oppression of the Church by the Japanese continued on in ways that were not obvious. When many were still in the despair of failing to gain independence and in the sorrow of having lost families and friends, the Church allowed them to have hope in heaven. This led to waves of Christian prayer and revival meetings for spiritual awakening and revival of Koreans across the country. Key leaders of the prayer and revival movement included Rev. Sun Joo Kil-who was the flag-bearer of the Great Revival in 1907-and Rev. Ik Doo Kim for the Presbyterian Church and the mystic evangelist Yong Do Lee for the Methodist Church.

1. Bible Study Meetings by Rev. Sun Joo Kil

Rev. Sun Joo Kil was jailed as one of the 33 national leaders for the March First Movement. However, he was greatly misunderstood by the people when the Japanese decided he was innocent after only two years of imprisonment. In Suh Kim explained that the Japanese released Rev. Kil for two reasons: to show that they gave preferential treatment to religious workers, and to ostracize him by making him appear as a national traitor.[384] During his two years in jail, he nearly memorized the entire Book of Revelation. Backed with thorough studies, he wrote a Revelations expository titled *The Malsehak* (The Eschatology), traveled across the country with it, and led Bible studies in eschatology.

By teaching eschatology and the second coming of Christ, Rev. Kil gave the new hope of new heaven and new earth to the people who were lost in the dark reality hard pressed by socialist and communist ideologies in the 1920s. Generally speaking, a large number of people have criticized Rev. Kil and his eschatology lectures for inducing the Korean Church to concentrate on the world beyond and ignore the realities. However, it is safe to say that such critics misunderstood his doctrine of eschatology. While speaking on eschatology, Rev. Kil never mentioned that this world will rot away and amount to nothing, and therefore our minds must be on the things of the eternal world instead of this temporal world. On the contrary, he had a peculiar school of eschatological thought that the paradise would be established on this earth.

---

384 In Suh Kim, "The March First Movement and Kil Sun Joo," *Kim In Suh Jeojakjeonjip* (Collection of Kim In Suh's Writings), vol. 2, 388-391.

This earth that Jesus walked on will become a new earth that will last forever. The earth which once contained the Garden of Eden will not cease to exist. Instead, the heavily guarded Garden of Eden will be revealed to us again and the earth will be an everlasting home of rest.[385]

In Suh Kim referred to this peculiar theology of Rev. Kil's as "Korea Theology." [386] Rev. Kil was in fact guiding the oppressed people to the light of liberation by proclaiming that this earth would not pass away but remains as their inheritance. He was encouraging them to keep the unique qualities of being Korean.

······We cannot be another race. We should not even wear clothes of other people. We must not forget that we are Korean people and we ourselves are the cultural embodiment of the Korean race. Let us not forsake our own. We can grow and exist forever only as we cherish our heritage and respond to the changes of time.[387]

This man of foresight persisted in teaching people to love things Korean and safeguard the Korean culture until the last moment he collapsed on the pulpit while proclaiming the Gospel. He was

---

385 Sun Joo Kil, "Malsehak," (The Eschatology), *Yeonggye Kil Sun Joo Moksa Jeojakjip* (Writings of Rev. Yeonggye Kil Sun Joo), vol. 1 (Korea Christian Literature Society, 1968), 139.

386 In Suh Kim, *Kim In Suh Jeojakjeonjip* (Collection of Kim In Suh's Writings), vol. 5, 70.

387 Jin Kyoung Kil, *Yeonggye Kil Sun Joo*, 250.

indeed a man of the Word, a man of prayer, and a giant of evangelism who stood at the forefront of the evangelization of Koreans.

Rev. Sun Joo Kil was assaulted and threatened to leave by some delinquent young people who had been influenced by socialistic ideals at Pyongyang Jangdaehyeon Church, the mother church of Suhbuk (North-West) Presbyterian Church which he pastored for the entire length of his lifetime. Thus he had to resign from the church he had been pastoring for over 20 years and assumed the position of honorary pastor.[388] Although his expulsion from his beloved church would have been a regretful incident, In Suh Kim interpreted this as how God destined him not to be tied down to one specific church but rather travel around the country and evangelize the people freely.[389]

2. Miracle Crusades by Rev. Ik Doo Kim

Born in Anak, Hwanghae Province, Ik Doo Kim grew up to be a merchant. But when his business failed, he became a libertine. Ik Doo Kim's dissipation and misconduct were extremely horrifying; it is told that those going to the market prayed at shrines, asking gods to prevent them from meeting him. Then one day, he met a female missionary in the market, received a tract, went to church, repented his sins, and confessed his faith in Jesus. He was a man of great passion. He read the New Testament as many as a hundred

---

388 In Suh Kim, *Kim In Suh Jeojakjeonjip* (Collection of Kim In Suh's Writings), vol. 5, 73.
389 *Ibid.*

times before his first Holy Communion and he never stopped praying. He became an evangelist for Jaeryeong Church in Hwanghae Province at the age of 29, and he enrolled in the Pyongyang Presbyterian Theological Seminary in 1906. In one incident, he saw a crippled man on his way back from visitations. He shouted, "Get up and walk in the name of Jesus," but the man could not get up. Kim believed this to be because he lacked prayer, so he persevered to pray more and achieve a deeper Christian walk, and God eventually gave him the gift of healing. In Suh Kim writes, "miracles were performed at his early revival meetings, reproducing the signs and wonders of Acts in the 20th century."[390]

Rev. Ik Doo Kim's gift of healing was most explicitly displayed during a Bible Study Meeting at Hyonpung Church in Dalsuhng, North Gyeongsang Province, in December 1919. There was a man with a dislocated lower jaw that made it impossible for him to close his mouth. He was living such a miserable life because he could not talk or chew food; he could only take fluids and water lying down. But this man was a believer and he came to the church. When he showed up at the Bible Study Meeting, Rev. Kim had pity on him and prayed for him many days but in vain. Then Rev. Kim fasted and prayed. Soon, the man's loose jaw moved up to its original position and he started saying, "Good, good!" This had occurred after ten years of living with the disability.

Since then, miracle crusades by Rev. Kim began drawing many crowds. Miracles took place on a consistent basis and people with

---

390 *Ibid.*, 107.

all sorts of illnesses were healed in the name of Jesus.[391] At Gyeongsan-eup Church, several dozens of people were healed at the same time; people were healed of paralysis and dacryohemorrhea. At another meeting in Daegu, numerous people gathered and hundreds were healed. A crippled man walked at a Busan meeting, a woman with dacryohemorrhea was healed after 23 years of suffering at Jinyeong-ri, Gimhae-gun, and a mute woman started talking after 11 years when Rev. Kim prayed for her in Pyongyang.

As miracles continued on, some people began criticizing Rev. Kim. In response to this, Rev. Taek Gwon Lim at Jaeryeong, Hwanghae Province founded the "Miracle Certifying Committee" in 1919. After three years of research, he published Rev. Kim's miracles as a single volume titled *The Chosen Yesugiohoe Eejuk Miongjeong*(Proofs of Miracles in the Church of Christ in Korea) in 1921. In addition, the Hwanghae presbytery proposed to the Presbyterian General Assembly in 1922 that it amend the Clause 1 of the Article 3 of the Presbyterian Constitution that stated, "The authority of performing miracles does not stand today." Although this was passed by the General Assembly and then passed down to all presbyteries, the end result was rejected.[392]

This came in direct opposition to the healing ministry of Rev. Kim. The ever increasing socialists and communists powers also could not allow Rev. Kim to exercise such great influence over Christians and non-Christians any longer. In other words, socialists

---

391 For details of Rev. Kim Ik Doo's miracles, see *ibid.*, 95-118.
392 *Chosun Jesugio Jangnohoechonghoe Je 12hoe (1923) Hoeirok* (The 12th Minutes of the General Assembly of Korea Presbyterian Church (1923), 35.

could not tolerate that more people were coming to healing services and that churches were increasing in number. When Rev. Kim was leading a meeting in Long Jing, Machuria, in 1926, a mob raided the place with steel rods, halting the service itself. Elite young people in Namdaemun(South Gate) Church in Seoul, which he had pastored previously, even reviled at Rev. Kim for turning Christianity into a shamanistic sect, curing the sick and fooling the unlearned.[393] This move was definitely anti-Christian in nature. It was evidence of the fact that liberalist theology was invading deep into the church in the form of renouncing the gift of healing through the Holy Spirit, which is clearly illustrated in the Scriptures.

For the entire Korean population under the bondage of Japanese oppression, Ik Doo Kim showed the hope of life to the Korean Church through the supernatural works of the Holy Spirit. Kim was a prophet of his time who gave courage and hope to the people who were in despair since the March First Movement. He was indeed a messenger sent by God for the Korean people when they needed him the most. For the entire length of his ministry, he led 776 revival meetings, preached 28,000 messages, planted 150 churches, inspired 200 people to became ministers and healed over 10,000 people through his ministry. Kim was essentially living for the Gospel itself. In the 1930s, he suffered greatly for having objected to the Japanese demand for shrine visits.

However, unfortunately, he was appeased and threatened by Yang Wook Kang after the independence to join the 'Korea Gidokgiodo-

---

393 *Donga Ilbo* (The Donga Daily), May 15, 1926.

Yonmaeng'(Federation of Christians in Korea) in North Korea and become its inaugurating moderator, thus tarnishing his exemplary reputation. On October 14, 1950, during the Korean War, the North Korean troops retreating from the U.N. forces killed Rev. Kim and six others who were stepping out of the church building after an early morning prayer meeting. His life ended in such a miserable way, after having been manipulated into helping the communists and then to be slaughtered by them.

3. Rev. Yong Do Lee and Mysticism

Yong Do Lee was born in April 1910 as the third son of Deok Hong Lee, a poor farmer in Suhcheon-myeon, Geumcheon-gun, Hwanghae Province. His father was a drunkard, but his faithful mother who was also an evangelist at Sibyeonri Church carefully nurtured him. He grew up as an unhealthy but affectionate child. When he was going to Hanyeongsuhwon(the antecedent of Songdo Middle School), he was imprisoned for 2 years for his active participation in the March First Movement. Later while he was studying at the Hyeopsuhng Theological Seminary(Methodist), he was found to be in the third stage of tuberculosis with hemoptysis. He then moved to his friend Hwan Shin Lee's home in Gangdong, South Pyeongan Province, for recuperation.

There he underwent an experience that would change his life around. When the people learned that a theological student was in town, they asked him to lead a revival meeting at a church.

When he stood on the pulpit, he could not stop shedding tears. As the people watched the young man weeping with no words, they began to weep together with him. Whether they sang hymns or prayed, the entire congregation was full of tears. The meeting on the next day was also flooded with tears. These meetings of tears were a real experience of Christ's love for both the congregation and for Yong Do Lee himself. The passionate love of Christ he experienced during these meetings was an experience of a lifetime that he would never forget. In this way, he was a classic mystic of his time who indulged in the passionate love of God. He wrote:

> Submit. Submit completely. Once you submit yourself completely to the Lord, He will deal with all your problems and He will even use your body according to His will.[394]

A life surrendered to the Lord, this was what Yong Do Lee's life looked like. After this mystic experience, he regained his health, returned to the seminary, and then graduated. He was assigned as a pastor to Tongcheon, Gangwon Province, and started his pastoral ministry there. But he found that his first love had gotten cold. So he prayed in the mountains and fasted, which provided him with yet another encounter of the Holy Spirit. He prayed, "Father, take away my soul, and fill me with a new soul that is crazy for Jesus. I need to be crazy about Jesus. Unless I am crazy about

---

[394] Jong Ho Byun, *Lee Yong Do Moksajeon* (Biography of the Rev. Lee Yong Do) (Seoul: Simuwon, 1958), 5.

Jesus, I am unable to obey you whole heartedly or win in the fight with the devil." His confession of needing to be crazy about Jesus signified his union with Christ. In one aspect, this included sexual love with Christ. This was the core of his mysticism.

> Oh, the principle of the (mystical) union in which I am swallowed by the love of the Lord, and the Lord swallowed by my love! Oh, my eyes, just lift up and look at the Lord with all my heart and soul. Do not turn away, oh my soul, even for a while from the sight of the Lord. The Lord caught up by my eyes will dwell and rest in the depth of my soul.[395]

His theology pursued the complete union with the Lord, which coincided with the mysticism of the Middle Age.

Yong Do Lee's revival meetings created a great sensation wherever he went. His revival meetings were not limited to Methodist churches. Even Presbyterian churches invited him to lead revival meetings. He also spoke for a large revival meeting at Jangdaehyeon Church, which was the home base of Presbyterian churches in Pyongyang. His influence was so great that all Christians in Pyongyang were challenged to join in a prayer movement after the revival meetings. However, his revival ministry was soon criticized by a number of people. As seen during the First Great Awakening

---

395 Jong Ho Byun, *Lee Yong Do Moksa Suhganjip* (Collection of Rev. Lee Yong Do's Letters) (Seoul: Simuwon, 1958), 189.

in the U.S., these criticisms were firstly due to the jealousy of other pastors. The second reason was that Lee himself provided the materials on which people could base their criticisms.

Interestingly, his ministry was restricted first in Hwanghae Province, which was his home. The Hwanghae Presbytery of Presbyterian Church issued a prohibition order under the charge that Yong Do Lee disturbed Jaeryeong Church, corresponded frequently with female believers, prayed with the lights off, offended other Christian workers, was a non-church movement advocate who promoted *The Sungsuh Chosun* and was a man causing disorder in churches.[396] At the end of a revival meeting he had led in Pyongyang, some deacons gathered together for a Bible Study Meeting. As they began meeting regularly, the meeting was named "Prayer Band" and at this point the Pyongyang Presbytery began to be very cautious of their activities.

Around this period, the Korean Church was in much confusion caused by Gook Joo Hwang's claiming of himself as Jesus Christ and Tae Yong Choi's non-church movement, and it was natural for the Christian community to be cautious about the prayer band. The Pyongyang Presbytery immediately organized an investigatory committee of five persons including Rev. Hyeok Namgung and Rev. Pil Geun Chae to obtain a detailed report on this issue. The presbytery in April 1932 decided that ① teachers or lecturers at worship services, prayer meetings, and revival meetings must be

---

396 Jong Ho Byun, *Lee Yong Do Moksajeon* (Biography of the Rev. Lee Yong Do), 113.

those approved by the Presbyterian Church, ② prayers must be said in a quiet manner, ③ unordained persons must not lay hands on the sick, and ④ all organizations not approved by the presbytery must not be tolerated. This decision was specifically targeted at stopping the activities of the prayer band and Yong Do Lee within the Presbyterian boundary. Hyeok Namgung, the moderator of the presbytery, warned all churches of Yong Do Lee and his followers by writing in his letter, "······this spiritual movement is a form of mysticism, placing heavy emphasis on personal experiences of religious faith······they are clearly promoting special revelations and new doctrines outside the Scriptures."[397]

Finally at the 22nd General Assembly in 1932, the Presbyterian Church named Yong Do Lee a "heretic" and excommunicated him from the Presbyterian Church. The Presbyterian Church judged Yong Do Lee, Nam Joo Baek, Joon Myeong Han, Ho Been Lee and Gook Joo Hwang as heretics.[398] The Methodist Church too formed an inquiry commission, investigated his activities and the Annual Conference suspended his ministerial position. This effectively put an end to Yong Do Lee and his revival ministry. This is a classic illustration of the Christian faith diverting to the extremes of being mystic.

Generally speaking, Yong Do Lee's revival movement started off in a rather unique way compared to the revival movements of the Presbyterian pastors Sun Joo Kil and Ik Doo Kim, and

---

397 *Gidok Sinbo* (The Christian Messenger), May 25, 1932.
398 *Chosun Jesugio Jangnohoe Je 22hoe(1932) Hoeirok* (Minutes of the 22nd General Assembly of Korea Presbyterian Church 1932), 71.

his ministry was eventually labeled heretic. While Rev. Sun Joo Kil's revival ministry was based on strict biblical training and Rev. Ik Doo Kim's revival ministry was based on miraculous signs of healing, Rev. Yong Do Lee's revival ministry was essentially a mysticism based on his own spiritual experience.

Due to his failing health, Yong Do Lee passed away at the young age of 33 in 1934, incidentally coinciding his age of death with that of Jesus whom he loved so ever passionately.

4. The Pseudo-theosophists

Perhaps it was only natural that Yong Do Lee's extreme mysticism roused great rejection by the existing churches, and thus he was labeled a heretic. His mysticism eventually went overboard to the extent of contradicting the fundamentals of Christianity, which effectively proved his theology wrong. This is clearly shown in the incident when he thought he heard God's voice from Myung Hwa Yoo, a spirit-possessed woman in Wonsan, bowed before her and cried, "O Lord." Yong Do Lee later explained the situation by saying, "Of course Myung Hwa herself is not the Lord. She is not a god. But the Word of the Lord revealed through her was the Lord. That was why I could not help but to bow before the Word."[399]

This incident of spirit possession dates back to 1927 when Myung Hwa Yoo, a woman at Wonsan Methodist Church, had a spiritual

---

399 *Gidok Sinbo* (The Christian Messenger), March 21, 1933.

experience. Claiming that Jesus came upon her, she put on a show as if she was Jesus himself and forced other women to join her act of spiritualism. Soon later, Myung Hwa Yoo was joined by other key players including Nam Joo Baek and Joon Myeong Han at Mr. Sinhak in Wonsan. They were indulged in mysticism after having been inspired by the Swedish mystic Emanuel Swedenborg's book. They prayed together at the home of a woman named Jang. Jang would prepare food on the table to pray as if having an ancestral worship service, and Myung Hwa Yoo would prophecy in a trance. Joon Myeong Han and Nam Joo Baek put on a whole show of spiritualism by saying that God came upon them this way. While vigorously leading the mystic show in Pyongyang in November 1932, Joon Myeong Han prophesied, "Joon Myeong Han will marry a woman on June 9 and 270 days later on March 4, 1934, give birth to a great son Gwangjin who would rule the day. Seung Chan Park will marry a woman and have a great son Jae Kwang who would rule the evening sun." [400]

By the time Nam Joo Baek, the chief of the Wonsan Sinhaksan, joined forced with Myung Hwa Yoo and coerced the former Methodist pastor Ho Been Lee and others into their cause for establishing the Church of Jesus, they were well over the borderline. Nam Joo Baek also cohabited with Jeong Il Kim, one of his female followers. When this became an issue, he explained that it was God's call for his life. He then established and founded Suhngju Church with Suhng Do Kim, a newly emerging religious leader

---

[400] *Sinang Saenghwal* (The Christian Life), (August 1933), 32.

at Cheolsan, North Pyongan Province.[401] Although Yong Do Lee strongly objected to Baek's founding of a new church with Lee listed as the leader, Baek eventually used Lee's name when submitting reports to authorities. Albeit manipulated, Lee could not evade his responsibility for having been associated with this cultic sect.

5. Gook Joo Hwang and Orgies

Heretics are bound to appear in times of chaos, seducing the people and leading them astray. While the spirit-possessed heretics were polluting the society, yet another group was bringing disorder into the Church and society. A young man named Gook Joo Hwang was one of them. Originally from Jangyeon, Hwanghae Province, he migrated to Jiandao, China, and attended Long Jin Central Church. Being a man of handsome features, his face resembled that of Jesus usually seen in paintings.

For a hundred days of prayer, he let his long hair down and did not shave his mustache. Having achieved Jesus-like appearance, he started making an absurd remark that, while praying, his head was lifted off from his body and then Jesus' head was attached to his body. He made a blunder stating that "his head was (the head of) Jesus, his blood of the blood of Jesus, and his heart was the heart of Jesus······everything was Jesus."[402] His outstanding eloquence captivated many people, overpowering them through

401 *Ibid.* (December 1937), 37
402 Kyoung Bae Min, *Hanguk Gidokgiohoesa* (History of the Christian Church in Korea) (Seoul: Yonsei University Press, 1993), 445.

sermons and prayers. The entire situation was by far beyond any sensible comprehension, taking into account the fact that even his father, Elder Hwang, knelt before his own son, Gukju, and called him "Lord."

Claiming that the Jesus in him was headed to the New Jerusalem, Gook Joo Hwang set out for Seoul. He was accompanied by a large crowd, which included his father, his sisters, and many other women. When the news spread that the New Jesus was passing by, people from all places came to see him and his followers. Dozens of virgin girls, married women and men formed a large crowd while following him. They took on a lifestyle of liberal eating, sleeping and traveling together. It was definitely impossible for this lifestyle to be free of any immorality. In fact, they were full of indecency. Seung Je Kim, the pastor of Samho Church in South Hamgyeong Province, saw the crowd on the journey and wrote the following account:

> I had come to the vicinity of Samho Church of South Hamkyung Province in July 1935, when I saw a group of 60-70 mixed men and women lying down under the shadow of trees near the church. Among them ten in a group were here and there spread out······their state of disorder made them look like lawless people.[403]

---

403 Seung Je Cho, "Naeui Mokhoesaenghwal 40yoneui Baeksuh," (White Paper on My 40 Years of Pastoral Ministry), Mokhoeyeohwa (Stories of Ministry) (Seoul: Hyangryeonsa, 1965), 109.

By the time Gook Joo Hwang and the crowd of over sixty married and virgin women arrived in Seoul, churches across the entire nation were in a commotion about them.

Hwang called himself Jesus; he bragged that it was impossible for him to sin because he was a perfect man. He built a prayer camp on Mt. Samgak, taught doctrines on so-called neck separation and blood sharing and engaged in orgies. He called this the exchange of spiritual bodies. When the Anju Presbytery in Pyeongan Province sent investigators and asked for explanation on the orgies, they boasted, "We have crossed the Jordan River and we are no longer bound by the sexual issues between male and female." [404] However, Gook Joo Hwang eventually "committed an irreversible act of sin with a kindergarten teacher at Unsan and ran away for good."[405]

In 1933, the Anju Presbytery named Gook Joo Hwang, Myung Hwa Yoo and other dangerous figures as heretics and prohibited churches from inviting them for their revival meetings. This was ratified by the General Assembly that met in the autumn that year. In any turbulent period, there are bound to be acts of chaos that make groups of immoral adulterers who are fooled by the devil to label sexual temptations as "God's revelations" or "bodily exchange of spirits." We must take a serious note of this because the same will be witnessed through Sun Myung Moon's Unification Church later in the Korean history.

---

404 *The Yeonggye* (Spiritual World) (November 1933), 3.

405 Suhn Hwan Kim, "Kuksan Jaerae Eedaneui Hoogeja" (Successors of Korean Indigenous Heretics), Gyeong Rae Kim, ed., *Sahoesakgwa Idanundong* (Social Evils and Heretic Movements), 165.

6. Gyo Sin Kim and the Non-church Movement

Gyo Sin Kim was born in Hamheung, South Hamgyeong Province, in 1901. After graduating from Hamheung Agricultural School, he studied at Masanori English School in Tokyo, Japan. Then in April 1920, he came upon the Oriental Missionary Society Bible School students evangelizing on the street, accepted Christ and soon became a baptized believer at an Evangelical Holiness Church. But when a conflict arose in his church and the scholastic pastor was expelled from the church, he began to take on a skeptical attitude toward the established churches.

He was much inspired by the famous non-church movement leader, Uchimura Kanzo, through his books *Guanrok*(Writing of Look for Safety), *Religion and Literature and Biblical Studies*. Perhaps Uchimura influenced his thoughts more than any other Christian leader. Gyo Sin Kim learned the true meaning of patriotism from Uchimura who loved Japan more than anyone. Kim was challenged to love his homeland, Korea, in the same way.

Upon his return in April 1927, he began teaching at Yeongsaeng Girls' High School in Hamheung. He also worked with Suhk Heon Ham, Doo Yong Song, and Suhk Dong Yoo, who were Uchimura's followers, to publish the biblical study magazine Sungsuh Chosun (the Bible Korea) in July that year. As explained by the title, this magazine addressed the two key subjects of *"Sungsuh"*(Scripture) and "Chosun"(Korea). But the editorial of the first issue indicated that they were against the established churches; they were intending to actualize the non-church movement in pursuit of the perfect church they had in mind. The editorial contained the following passage:

> *Seongseo Chosun!* Hurry to the house of Israel. Do not find rest in the hands of ordinary believers. Shake the dust off your feet at the house of the one who worships other gods other than Christ and cares for the church more than the Scripture. Seongseo Chosun! Go to Chosun people with the true heart of Chosun, instead of ordinary Christians. Go to the country. Go to the mountains. It is your duty to attend to even the smallest woodcutter in the mountains.
>
> – Kim Gyosin –[406]

Gyu Sin Kim's *Sungsuh Chosun* rejected doctrines, systems and sacraments of the established churches but instead advocated the forging of his independent Christian community. This led to them being referred to as being involved in the non-church movement. Since they did not belong to any church, they were never punished by any of the denominations. Nevertheless, *The Gidoksinbo*(Christian Messenger) accused them as the "Isabelle's mob" in the December 1932 editorial. However, Kim never intended to criticize or reject the established churches. Speaking himself of only as "a layman believing in Jesus Christ and doing his best in studying the Bible and its commentaries," [407] he sought the model of faith found

---

406 *Sungsuh Chosun* (The Bible and Korea), the First Issue (1927).

in the Scriptures. Nevertheless, he is still considered as an advocate of the non-church movement rejecting the established churches because his theology had the following characteristics.

First, he did not regard tangible and visible buildings as real churches but regarded any place of worship where believers met as churches. Second, he did not recognize any of the authorities within the church, including those bestowed by ordination(for example, by disrespecting the significance of baptisms and other sacraments performed by pastors). He also disregarded any lay ministerial positions such as elders and deacons. Third, he did not recognize the right to interpret Scriptures reserved by the Church. He advocated the concept of the Universal Priesthood of All Believers by saying that each believer was to meet God on his or her own by reading the Word individually as God revealed his truth in degrees appropriate for each person. From the viewpoint of established churches, such elements of faith were seen as aggressive rejection of the Church.

However, above all, he adhered to the concept of divine predestination. He regarded it as his highest mission to identify God's call for the Korean people and put it to practice. Naturally, he emphasized the spiritual and Christian mission of the Korean race. This led him to reject the denominational faith passed down by missionaries and instead advocate a national and indigenous form of faith that should be unique to Koreans. He also disapproved

---

407 Pyeong Goo Noh, ed., *Kim Gyo Sin Sinangjujakjip* (Collections of the Gyo Sin Kim's Christian Reflections), vol. 2 (Seoul: First Publications, 1965), 355, 357.

of any church organizations that relied on the finance of missionaries. He was left to emphasize independent and indigenous form of faith for Koreans.[408]

It did not take long for such an ethnocentric tone of *The Sungsuh Chosun* to be noticed by the Japanese. Over a number of occasions, the Japanese trumped up charges on the content of the magazine and reprimanded it in the form of deletion and suspension. *The Sungsuh Chosun* finally had to be discontinued in March 1942 when the opening article titled Jowa[409] became a problematic issue. In addition, Gyo Sin Kim was imprisoned for one year along with Suhk Heon Ham and Dal Young Yoo. Then in 1944, he started working for the welfare of laborers at Hamheung Nitrogen Company. He died of a disease in April 1945, just a few months before Korea's independence.

From the viewpoint of the established churches, Gyo Sin Kim was by no doubt a non-church movement advocate who criticized, rejected and divided the established churches. Whatever the reason, it was an act of intolerable nature to reject the established churches and church fathers-which were established by Christ and passed down through the Twelve Apostles-and to pursue a non-church movement. Nevertheless, much like the fact that Nestorius, Patriarch of Constantinople-who was labeled as a heretic and was expelled

---

408 See "Kim Gyo Sin," *Gidokgio Daebaekgwasajeon* (The Christian Encyclopedia), vol. 3 (1985).
409 "Jowa" means "condolence to frogs." When a few frogs were spotted alive in a pond after a cold winter, one rejoiced, "Oh, some of them survived!" This inferred to the remaining hope for Korea.

by the Council of Ephesus in 431 for having regarded Mother Mary as the "Mother of Christ (Christokos)"-was once referred to as "the most falsely charged man among those accused as being heretic," there would not be many who could throw the first stone of accusation at him, considering the great depth of his love for the people and the country. How many would there actually be who loved the Word of God and Korea as much as Gyo Sin Kim did? Nevertheless, it must be pointed out that all of his great works are no longer in their fullness of glory because he had renounced the established churches and pursued the non-church movement.

7. Tae Yong Choi and the Gospel Church

Born in Yeongheung, South Hamgyeong Province, Tae Yong Choi, like Gyo Sin Kim, was highly influenced by the Japanese non-church advocate Uchimura Kanzo. He returned from Japan in 1924 and started criticizing the established churches in Korea by publishing his personal magazine *The Chunraejisung* (Sound of Heaven). "The Lord commanded me……. I cannot but destroy all the artificial systems in the secularized and corrupted churches and proclaim the revival of life and faith."[410]

His accusing of the established churches as corrupted churches and claiming of the church systems as being artificial, seriously

---

410 Tae Yong Choi, "Neonun Nugoonia?" (Who Are You?), *Cheollaejisuhng* (The Sound of Heaven), 2nd Issue (July 1924).

hinted of his intension to set up his own church. As such renunciation of the established churches was in the same line with the non-church movement, it was only natural for the established churches to disregard him. He was in fact accused as "a heretic that can never be tolerated by the Presbyterian Church of Chosun."[411] Besides advocating the non-church movement, these organizations were labeled as heretics because they had elements of Gnosticism, which were heretic during the days of the early church and could not be tolerated by the Church at any level. When Hyeongn Yong Park pointed out in his "Genosis Christianity" that they claimed "……when the Logos reincarnated He abandoned the divine property. He became all flesh," he was talking of Nam Yong Baik, who was adopting the ideals taught by Tae Yong Choi. But above all, he was actually accusing Tae Yong Choi's ideals themselves. By 1936, Choi rejected the general revelation in the New Testament and claimed that God "was alive forever, working freely in men and women for continuously regenerating Christianity… He is working in me to lead a spirit-filled Christianity."[412] He was clearly opposing to the Christianity adopted by the established churches. He could not be seen as a part of the Christian Church in any way.

When he went to Japan again in 1929 and learned from Takakura,

---

411 *Sinhak Jinam* (The Sinhak Jinam) (September 1922), 18. *Gidok Sinbo* (The Christian Messenger), December 14, 1932.

412 Dong Sik Jee, "Choi Tae Yong's Si, Nonpiong, Sinhak" (Choi Taeyoung's Poetry, Comments, and Theology), *Hyeondaewa Sinhak* (Modern Time and Theology), vol. 6 (1970), 141.

an evangelical theologian at the Department of Theology of Meiji University, he began criticizing the non-church movement as well. Upon his return in 1930, he again tried to start a new religious movement in Korea through his publication *Younggwa Jilli*(The Spirit and Truth), which he had started publishing in Japan. As a community of believers began to form among the readers of *The Spirit and Truth* from 1930, he founded what was known as the "Gospel Church of Chosun." Upon its inauguration at Sogyeok-dong, Seoul, in December 1935, the church was introduced as taking on the following characteristics:

1. The faith must be evangelical and living
2. The faith must be sufficiently academic
3. The Church must be the Church of Koreans themselves[413]

It is interesting to note that the phrase "a church of Korea itself" in the third clause was implying that the existing churches in Korea, which were started by foreign missionaries and were still governed by missionaries, could not be churches of the Korea people. On the flip side of it, he had a highly anti-missionary intension of removing missionaries and eliminating their influences in order to establish churches that truly belong to the Korea people. The logic that a national church could be built by rejecting missionaries was definitely a result of misunderstanding the true fundamentals

---

413 Tae Yong Choi, "Urieui Pyo-o" (Our Slogan), *Yeonggwa Jilli* (The Spirit and Truth) (December 1935), 1.

of the Christian faith. Missionaries were no enemies of the Gospel or enemies of the national church. They were friends and partners who deserve mutual understanding and cooperation in Christ. In fact, Koreans were indebted to them for having received the Gospel of life through them. The Gospel Church was in a serious need of understanding the truth that the Gospel was never exclusive but inclusive.[414]

8. The Jukgook Sinangdan (Positive Faith Group)

In 1932, there appeared an interdenominational religious move ment group with a strong nationalistic tone under the leadership of Heung Woo Shin, then General Secretary of YMCA Seoul and a Methodist leader, and other leaders from Presbyterian Church and Methodist Church. Church leaders in the southern part of Korea were not pleased with the fact that the Christian presence was always stronger in the Northwestern part of the country rather than in Seoul, which was regarded as the center of Korea. It was obvious that they felt jealous or even threatened of the Christians in the Northwest. The steadily emerging concept of ethnocentricity, anti-missionary tendency, and the slowly brewing incorporation of liberalistic theology in the 1930s worked in tandem for the appearance of Heung Woo Shin's Positive Faith Group Movement which were largely characterized as being "anti-Northwest," "anti-

---

414 For Tae Yong Choi's life and thoughts, see Byeong Ho Chun's *Choi Tae Yongeui Saengaewa Sasang* (Choi Tae Yong's Life and Thoughts) (Christian Resource Publications, 1983).

missionary" and "anti-conservation."

Heung Woo Shin first attempted this movement as the General Secretary of YMCA in 1927 when he created a group named 'Gidokgio Yonguhoe'(Council for Christian Studies) that professed to be anti-missionary and anti-conversation with the objective of "establishing Korea Christianity and weakening the spirit of denominationalism."[415] He then represented Korea in the International Missionary Conference(IMC) in Jerusalem the following year. Having been deeply influenced by the "indigenization" theology, which was one of the themes of the conference, he began working on establishing "Koreanized" Christianity in Korea. As this movement progressed, the group named "Positive Faith Group" was inaugurated in June 1932 with the participation of Presbyterian leaders including Tae Young Ham, Pil Soon Chun, Geo Deok Choi, Suhk Joo Choi, Young Sik Kwon, Byeong Deok Hong and Young Suhp Kim and Methodist leaders including Heung Woo Shin, Chun Soo Chung, Eok Gyeom Yoo, Gong Sook Shin, In young Kim, Yeon Suh Park, Jae Hee Um, Geon Chun Lee, Ja Ok Goo and Suhng Chae Chung. The leaders adopted the following as the principles of the organization.

1. I believe in God who is revealed in Nature, History, Jesus and Experience.
2. I consider it my first principle of life: to be one with God,

---

415 Taek Boo Chun, *Ingan Shin Heung Woo* (The Man, Shin Heung Woo) (Seoul: Christian Literature Society, 1971), 223.

to be victorious in struggling with evils.

3. I believe there must be complete equality of human right, duty and action, man and woman, and complete freedom not to be infringed by others.

4. I believe there must be the substitution of the private desire for acquisition with the human desire for service in order to build up a new society.[416]

Their intentions were not entirely in the wrong. But it was obvious that such an organization would not get full support from the churches. Time was just not ripe for such an anti-conservation and anti-missionary Christian organization to surface for the relatively conservative Korean culture. Voices of condemnation were first heard from the Methodist Church, which Heung Woo Shin was serving as his denomination. This organization became very much a secret society by itself. Convinced that they were the only truly patriotic, progressive and idealistic Christian leaders and that existing churches and Christian organizations were hopeless, conservative and abnormal, they believed that the only means to save the Christian community was to infiltrate themselves into churches in Seoul, the Methodist Annual Meeting, YMCA, Christian publications, the Bible Society, *Kidoksinbo*(The Christian Messenger) and other Christian organizations. The most dangerous part of their activities was that all their meetings and events were carried out in total secrecy.

---

416 *Ibid.,* 255.

Their fall was accelerated when the 'Jaekyong Gidokgio Yoojihoe' (Council of Christian Supporters in Seoul) submitted to the Methodist Annual Conference and the Presbyterian General Assembly proposals for opposing this religious group. At its Combined East-West-Central Annual Meeting in April that year, the Methodist Church resolved that "the Group is not a committee approved by our constitution and so we reject it," and that "ministers must not join organizations not approved by the General Assembly."[417] This was in direct response to the Positive Faith Group.

The Presbyterian Church responded in a more intense manner. After receiving the proposal by the Council of Christian Supporters in Seoul through the Gyeongsuhng(Seoul) Presbytery, they openly accused the pastors involved with the organization by stating, "it is appropriate for our Presbyterian Church not to tolerate the principles of faith adopted by the Positive Faith Group."[418] But the key Christian leaders in Seoul stood in tight defense. Perhaps it was more than natural for these anti-Northwest leaders to exhibit rebellion against the decisions of the General Assembly that were represented by the leaders in the Northwestern part of the country. As the members of the Positive Faith Group strongly objected to the conservative attitude of the Gyeongsuhng Presbytery, they organized a separate Gyeongjung Presbytery, risking a complete break-up of the General Assembly. In order to resolve this issue, the General Assembly summoned a special committee and achieved

---

417 *Sinang Saenhwal* (The Christian Life), (May 1935), 37.
418 *Chosun Jesugio Jangnohoe Chonghoe Je 23hoe(1934) Hoeirok* (The 23rd Minutes of the General Assembly of Korea Presbyterian Church (1934), 18, 54.

reconciliation and re-merger of the two presbyteries in 1937. The entire issue was concluded when Tae Young Ham and other leaders apologized in the following year.

The Positive Faith Group was not able to achieve the objects it originally set out for, not only due to the pressure from the established churches, but most of all because Heung Woo Shin, one of the key figures of the group, resigned as the General Secretary of the YMCA. The YMCA itself was being divided into those in favor of Heung Woo Shin's activities and those against it since the early 1930s. But when Shin was involved in a scandal with In Deok Park, a divorced woman, he was forced to resign from his position. Shin's resignation in turn led to the dissolution of the Group, which was largely backed by the YMCA organization and its members.

The issue of the Positive Faith Group was an inevitable issue that the Korean Church would have to face sooner or later. We should find significance in that the entire issue of reshaping the Korean Church that was dominated by certain local powers, preparing the conservative Church for its inevitable clash with the ever progressing society, and repositioning the Church from the reliance and control of foreign missionaries was carefully brought up by the Positive Faith Group, but its timing was just not right. Although the Positive Faith Group did not produce good results and it had many problems, the fact that Presbyterians and Methodists worked hand-in-hand to address the chronic problems of the Korean Church for the better deserves a high praise. At the same time, the story of the Positive Faith Group teaches us that the hearts of the people can only be moved by the pure motivation of the Gospel. Anything with a political nature is not the best vehicle for professing and practicing all its good intentions.

Chapter 9

The Church Responses to Social Changes

1. Emersion of Communist Ideals

In 1917 in Russia, led by V. Lenin, Bolshevik executed the final emperor of the Romanovs Dynasty Nicholai II and successfully staged the Communist Revolution. This marked the beginning of the proliferation of communist ideals around the world. In particular, the communist ideology spread very quickly as it became appealing to the poorer laborers and peasants. When the Japanese started exercising cultural policy over Korea since the March First Movement, new ideologies and schools of thoughts were introduced to Korea, along with socialism and communism. This ideology was mostly injected into the country through the migrants and students in the North side of the country. For the Korean peoples who were in great despair after having been suppressed as a colony under Japanese rule for ten years and with the recent failure to secure independence during the March First Movement, the communist ideology was quite a seducing message, especially among those learned and thoughtful. And perhaps it was quite natural for those who thought the U.S.A. was being too passive in terms of its involvement in the independence movement of Korea, which was spearheaded by Christians, to turn to the newly rising power of communism and U.S.S.R. which seemed to be able to offer Koreans more than what Christianity could.

When socialism or communism was first introduced to Korea, none of its violent aspects was visible and rather it appeared to be a viable means of achieving independence that the people have longed for so much. The bottom line was that they could work with nationalists to achieve this goal. But as obvious as it could ever be, this was very much an atheist ideology, and the Church could not remain idle watching its aggressive proliferation among the people. Just as the Korean Church was being established as a national church, it was at the verge of a serious crisis. And this crisis was not an external one, but a crisis of ideology among the Korean themselves. Communism was in effect a serious rival to Christianity as it was gaining popularity among the general public and members of low classes, who were the main adherents of the faith. In other words, communism was infiltrating among the people who were the main target audience of Christian evangelization, turning them away from and making them hostile toward Christianity. Communism was not only a tangible obstacle to Christian expansion but a serious enemy of its existence.

As the socialist ideology gained ground among Koreans, one of the first persons to organize the movement was Gyu Sik Shin, who organized the Korean Socialist Party in Shanghai in 1917.[419] But Hee Yong Byun and Bong Am Cho, who came in proximity with the ideology while studying abroad in Japan, introduced socialism into Korea itself from Japan. They urged that the whole nation, whether rich or poor, had to stand united under the communist ideology in order to put an end to the Japanese capitalism and achieve the grand goal of independence. This led to the formation of the Seoul Communist Party at Asawon(Chinese Restaurant) in April 1925 under the leadership of Jae Bong Kim, Bong Am Cho, and Huhn Young Park. As the communist ideology was introduced to Korea, there were also those leaders who turned their backs on Christianity because they thought Christianity was not active enough in the pursuit of national independence. One such person was Dong Hwui Lee. Upon becoming a Christian in 1904, he said, "Christianity is definitely capable of saving this collapsing nation and people."[420] But he eventually abandoned the faith and set up the Korean Socialist Party in Khabarovsk, Russia, in June 1918, and then he set up the "Korea Communist Party" in Vladivostok in April the following year.[421]

Nevertheless, communists were willing to cooperate with Christians

419 Young Hun Lee, *Hangukgidokgiosa* (History of Christianity in Korea), 170.
420 Sang Pyo Hong, *Gando Dongnibundong Sosa* (A Brief History of the Independence Movement in Jiandao) (Pyeongtaek: Hangwang Middle and High School, 1966), 11.
421 "Lee Dong Hwui," *Gidokgio Daebaekgwasajeon* (Christian Encyclopedia) vol. 12, (1986).

in the early stages. For instance, communists were seen as working with Christians when Gyu Sik Kim, an elder at Saemunan Church, and Woon Hyeong Yeo, who studied at the Pyongyang Presbyterian Theological Seminary and also at the English Department of Jinling Institute of Technology in Nanjing, China, used the name "Federation of Christians" when participating in the "First Congress of the Toilers of the Far East" held in Moscow in 1922.[422] This was probably either because Christian leaders were not fully aware of the communist ideology or because communism was deliberately infiltrating Christians by wearing a mask.

2. Communists Damage the Churches – The Beginning of Ideological Tragedy

After some time since the introduction of communist ideology to Korea, communism began to exhibit its fundamental differences to Christianity. "……Young people call themselves socialists and go to the extremes of even denying the existence of God. They say God is dead."[423] Ideological differences were bound to result in harsh clashes. While none of the clashes in the country were big because of the common enemy of Japan, clashes between Christians and communists began to take on serious appearance in the Northern part of the country, where the Russian influence was greater. Though we call them clashes, they were really one-sided

---

422 D. S. Suh, *Documents of Korean Communism*, 1918-1948, 18.
423 F. Y. Kim, "Glimpse of Korea After Ten Years' Absence," *The Korea Mission Field* (January 1932), 3-4.

devastation of churches.

The first ever-recorded persecution of Christians by communists was the persecution of Donga Christian Church(Baptist Church) in 1925. Four of the missionaries sent by this church to Jilin in China, including Hag Young Yoon and Ee Joo Kim, were accused by communists as Japanese spies and murdered in the foreign land in September 1925. They were the first recorded martyr skilled by communists. This was really the beginning of deathful tragedies to come. Following this incident were countless other accounts of persecution, including the Yeosu-Soonchun Uprising in 1948 and the tremendous suffering of churches by communists during the Korean War in 1950. The Bible verse saying, "If every one of them were written down, I suppose that even the whole world would not have room for the books that would be written (John 21:25)," is quite apt here.

The second batch of victims also came from Donga Christian Church: Rev. Young Jin Kim and Elder Young Gook Kim who were also brothers.[424] Originally from Jongsuhng, North Hamgyeong Province, they were involved in pastoral ministry in Yanji, Jiandao. This village was largely populated by immigrants from Jongsuhng, North Hamgyeong Province, and was thus also called Jongsuhng-dong. Some 30 communists raided this village in October 1932. They forced all the villagers into a church building and threatened to either kill them if they would continue following Jesus or release

---

424 Chun Bae Kim, *Hanguk Gidokgio Sunansahwa* (A Story of the Tragic History of Christianity in Korea) (Suhngmunhaksa, 1979), 86.

them to freedom if they would join the communists. When no one responded, the communists demanded of the Kim brothers why the people were not responding to their threats. To this Rev. Kim replied, "I believe in Jesus," and the communists committed the unimaginable foul by "skinned him to death which was a cruel and immoral act."[425]

Chang Hee Suh, a Presbyterian pastor who was also present at the scene, wrote the following letter to The Christian Messenger in reporting the incident:

> Who would ever have imagined the unthinkable calamities of bloodshed and casualties inflicted upon the men and women of our country, scattered here and there day after day! Who would ever have known beside God that they were tormented and shed blood, and ran away, weeping and sighing in grief unknown to others! The number of casualties in this vicinity of our church is enormous and serious, so I am reporting to you, not being able to stand any more, as much as I know about the calamities.[426]

According to Rev. Suh's letter, Yanji Waryong-dong Church was burned down and its members scattered away, Jin Suhng Noh, a leader of Jeogam-dong Church, was killed by communist guerrillas and the church members had to flee away, and Rotougue Church

---

425 Daehan Gidokgio Chimnyegiohoesa (History of Korean Baptist Church), 43-44.
426 Gidok Sinbo (The Christian Messenger), November 9, 1932.

was attacked twice by communist guerilla with financial loss amounting at thousands of won(yen). He concluded his letter by saying, "Please pray for this Dongman(East Manchuria) Presbytery."

Young Hak Kim, a Methodist pastor, was dispatched by the Annual Conference of the Methodist Church as a missionary to Vladivostok, Siberia, immediately after his ordination in 1922. During his missionary ministry at Sinhanchon in Siberia, communists there harassed him in various ways. He was eventually arrested by the Soviet police in February 1930, was charged for being a reactionary element, and was sentenced to 10 years of heavy labor. While working in the coldest temperatures below negative 50 degrees and a thousand miles away in the deepest of Siberia, ice broke and ten people drowned in the freezing water. Rev. Kim was one of the victims.[427] When the Methodist Church had sensed that the situation was worsening by the day, they advised him to return home, but he resisted, "I will remain here as long as there is one Christian I need to minister to." He eventually had to pay for this passion with his own life. This is indeed an example of a faithful shepherd.

In the Presbyterian Church, Rev. Kyong Hee Han is remembered for being slaughtered by communists. After his ordination, he evangelized and planted many churches in Southern Manchuria. He would then pastor a church in Changsuhng, North Pyeongan Province, for a while, but he was sent back to Northern Manchuria

---

427 Chun Bae Kim, *Hanguk Gidokgio Sunansahwa* (A Story of the Tragic History of Christianity in Korea), 76-79.

by the General Assembly. His friends urged him not to go because the area was infested with communist guerilla. But he disregarded their plea by saying, "My ambition is missions in Manchuria." In 1933, he set out for the banks of the Ussuri River in Northern Manchuria. Then in January 1935, Rev. Han traveled to Hulin in Northern Manchuria for church visitations and evangelism. But he was encountered by communist guerilla when he was passing by the Ussuri riverbanks in sleighs with four other Christians including the leader Chang Geun Kim. The guerilla had initially threatened to steal their money, but when they found out that they were Christians, they shot Rev. Han down on the spot. The others fled for their lives and one of the survivors relayed this tragic news.[428]

When the General Assembly of the Presbyterian Church heard this news, it dispatched Rev. Chang Keun Song to investigate the situation. Rev. Song submitted a report after his on-site investigation, and Rev. In Suh Kim incorporated the report in The Christian Life, a periodical that he was publishing:

> The Korean churches in Northern Manchuria are the churches which have been piled up with the blood of martyrs. When we think of the martyrs in the region, we only know the case of Rev. Han, but there are countless others we could not trace. The martyrs who were killed, stricken by clubs, who were killed by a nail at a crown of the head, those who were slain with unspeakable cruelty: It is said

---

428 *Ibid.*, 80.

that these victims reached hundreds. Even if they were not martyred, there were those, like the case of Rev. Kim Hyun Jum, whose skin was torn limb from limb······So the homes of certain ministers were just dugouts difficult to live in, and for the wives of the ministers there were no clothes worthy of their character, and also their children were not dressed to cover up themselves from the cold wind······How could we be heedless to those in misery and ravaged![429]

We are only left speechless by the knowledge that these hungry wanderers in the far away and bitter cold land were brutally victimized by their fellow countrymen simply because they had differing ideologies. With such historical facts behind us, how could we possibly say that it was possible for Christians to work alongside communists for the good of the nation?

3. The Church and the Rural Problems

While communism and socialism were causing ideological conflicts within the Korean society and undermining the Christian influence in the country, the church began to take countermeasures against problems faced by the poor people, laborers and peasants.

In the 1920s, peasants made up 80% of the total population,

---

429 In Suh Kim, "Bukmanjoo Giohoee Natanan Hananimeui Supri" (God's Divine Provision Revealed in the Churches in the Northern Manchuria), *Sinang Saenghwal* (The Christian Life) (April 1936), 3.

and 75% of all churches in Korea were in rural areas. This implied that rural problems were actually problems for the church and that all church problems were closely related to rural problems. Thus, the biggest problem faced by the church at that time was to devise workable measures for the peasants.

Peasants are the most victimized single social class ever since the beginning of the Japanese occupation of Korea. The Japanese loaned farming funds to poor farmers by holding their farming lands as securities. Whenever the farmers failed to repay the loans on time, the Japanese took possession of the farming lands. Large Japanese corporations intentionally bought over farming lands at dirt-cheap prices. Large areas of land were taken over for the supposedly purpose of constructing railroads, and unregistered far ming lands and forest lands were nationalized, which were later handed over to Japanese immigrants at unreasonably cheap rates or for free. So, for instance, 75% of all farming lands in the Honam (Jeolla Province) region came under the Japanese possession.

Deprived of farming lands, the peasants were forced into tenant farming. They had to pay a high rent and many of them were put into absolute poverty. This led to the migration of many farmers to Manchuria and Northern Jiandao, where they heard were plenty of fertile land. Missionaries, on the other hand, realized that an absolute majority of Koreans were farmers and began to seriously pay attention to the rural problems.[430]

---

430 For instance, in his newspaper *The Christian Time*, Underwood introduced various methods of advanced farming and rural profit-making activities under the title "Nongmin Pyeonsuhl" (Farmers Column). A series of articles

When the rural problems reached their peak, D. N. Luts, an expert in the field, came to Korea in 1920 as a missionary. Seeing that the Korean farmers were relying on conventional farming methods, he taught them crop improvement, soil improvement and crop rotation. He also started a farmers' school program for shortterm leadership training, investing his time into the development of agricultural leaders. He later spearheaded the establishment of the Department of Agriculture for Soongsil College as a means to lengthen and organize his training program. He was also one of the key publishers for Nongmin Saenghwal(The Farmers' Life), a magazine for farmers.

The YMCA was probably the most engaged organization in the field of rural issues. Heung Woo Shin, the general secretary of the YMCA Korea, went to the U.S.A. to meet Dr. J. R. Mott, the general secretary of the YMCA International. They agreed on the following points in regards to the rural areas of Korea:

1. America dispatches the professional specialists to the selected region in Korea
2. specialists will be sent each year for 5 years.
3. they must be agricultural specialists and apt to the spirit and purpose to the YMCA.

---

useful to farmers were featured, covering topics of plowing fields, maximizing yields, keeping poultry, building stables, planting green onions, processing sunflower seeds, informing the usefulness of straws of different colors, making hens lay eggs better, relaying important messages for farmers, preventing diseases of fruit trees and useful animals, and so on.

4. YMCA of Korea will select 10 Korean staffs who will work with these specialists.

5. each reign is supposed to provide the place to educate and a certain land where to show agricultural improvement and model.[431]

In accordance with this agreement, a number of agricultural experts were sent from the USA. G. W. Avison and F. T. Shipp came in 1925 to oversee rural education and rice issues, H. C. Bunce came in 1928 to oversee livestock and fruit trees, and F. O. Clark and B. P. Barnhart came in 1929 to oversee rural economy and rural development projects, respectively. They worked closely with the Korean YMCA staff, such as Byeong Suhn Hong, Byeong Ho Kye, Young Gyun Choi and Sun Gee Lee, to deal with various rural issues.

In addition, Mott collaborated with the International Missionary Council in sending E. B. Brunner, a sociology professor from the Michigan University, to Korea for two months in 1927. Brunner surveyed the rural situation in Korea and directed Gyeong Duk Ha to write a report titled *Rurality of Korea.*

In April 1926, the YMCA proposed the following as its directions for rural campaigns to come:

---

431 "The Rural Program of the YMCAs in Korea," The National Council of the Korean YMCAs, September 1932. Taek Boo Chun, *Hanguk Gidokgio Cheongnyeon Undongsa* (History of the Christian Youth Movement in Korea) (Suhngeumsa, 1978), 334-337.

Primary objectives of the rural program are to achieve intellectual, cultural and economic improvements. Above all, it is of the highest importance to facilitate the farmers to live in right relationship with God and their neighbors, and to enable them to recognize the spiritual values through their daily life. Therefore, it is necessary to eradicate illiteracy by teaching them to read and write, as well as to improve their economic status by cultivating agricultural improvements and the spirit of collaboration.[432]

In summary, the YMCA aimed to eradicate illiteracy, improve farming practices, and cultivate the spirit of collaboration. Among the Christian denominations, Presbyterians were the most actively engaged in rural programs. When the Methodist Church was approaching the rural issues through various organizations such as the YMCA, the Presbyterian Church was relatively withdrawn in terms of participating in such organizations. Nevertheless, the Presbyterian General Assembly was vigorously interested in the rural issues; it began to handle rural issues in full-scale by installing the Department of Rural Issues within the General Assembly in 1928. Rev. In Gwa Chung, who was the only Presbyterian representative at the International Missionary Conference in Jerusalem in 1928, was elected as the general secretary of the Department of Rural Issues.

The first thing Rev. Chung undertook to do was publishing.

---

432 Taek Boo Chun, *ibid.*, 187.

The Farmer's Life, a magazine for farmers. The first issue was published in June 1929 and became highly popular with over 5,000 copies sold each month. This magazine was not only the vehicle of vital information for farmers but also an important component of the rural enlightenment drive. In addition, the General Assembly decided in 1930 that every Presbyterian should keep the Rural Sunday as a symbol of collaboration in rural mission works.[433]

The General Assembly was also concerned with the training of rural leaders. In 1931, it set up the "Advanced Farming School" was established within the Department of Agriculture at Soongsil College with a two-month-long rural leader-training program. But in 1935, Rev. In Gwa Chung resigned as the general secretary of the department as a result of the so-called Chung Hymnal Incident and Rev. Min Soo Bae was elected as the new chief. Rev. Bae was particularly interested in establishing a farmers' collaborative association, but then the key leaders including Jae Kee Yoo and Hak Jeon Park were arrested due to the 'Nonguhoe Incident'(Society of the farmers' Friend)[434] and Bae's work had to be left unaccomplished. Recognizing that churches were actively facilitating enlightenment campaigns, farming improvement campaigns and farmers'

---

433 *Chosun Jesugio Jangnohoe Chonghoe Je 20hoe(1931) Hoeirok* (The 20th Minutes of the General Assembly of Korea Presbyterian Church (1931), 40.

434 The Incident in 1938 Nonguhoe was a cooperative association set up for rural movement in Uisuhng, North Gyeongsang Province. The Japanese police recognized it as a rebellious organization and arrested the key leader Rev. Jae Kee Yoo. This was the Nonguhoe Incident. Like the 'Suyangdonguhoe Incident' and the 'Heungeop Club Incident,' the 'Nonguhoe Incident' was a conspiracy by the Japanese to eradicate the groups of people involved in independence movement in the 1930s.

leadership training programs, the Japanese regarded churches as cultivating anti-Japanese attitudes among the farmers, and thus they began to thwart all such efforts. As political oppressions by the Japanese came upon the churches, it became difficult for the churches to actively promote various campaigns for the farmers and eventually all activities for peasants had to come to a halt.

4. Social Enlightenment Movement-Self-Control Movement

When Christianity was first introduced to Korea, the missionaries undertook various educational, medicinal and social enlightenment movements in order to facilitate development of the backward Korean civilization. Such efforts were targeted at transforming the senses and modernizing the lifestyle of Koreans. Then, in the 20s and the 30s, instead of missionaries, Korean church leaders vigorously led social enlightenment movements. While the enlightenment movements during this period were rooted in the Christian spirit, they embodied greater importance in patriotism and nationalism. The following examples illustrate the details of those movements.

Although the Japanese practiced the so-called cultural politics and granted a certain degree of freedom to Koreans since the March First Movement, this was only a deceitful measure. They were constantly working to eliminate the Korean people and culture. One of the methods the Japanese used was to pollute Koreans from within, such as by exposing the young people to the corrupt cultures of alcohol, tobacco, opium, and prostitution. This was a highly calculated strategy of corrupting Koreans mentally and culturally, in line with their existing political and economic aggres sion against Korea.

The church was most sensitive towards this issue. While political or economic corruption may be recovered later, the church realized that this mental corruption would leave long lasting effects in the form of a disease that would take away the spirit of the people. Deeply concerned with such mental corruption of the people, the church leaders staged a self-control movement in May 1923, when Miss C. L. Tinling of the World Congress of Christian Women's Self-Control visited Korea. During her six months in Korea, she traveled to different parts of the country and spoke on the self-control movement.[435]

In conjunction with this, female missionaries in Korea set up an Association for Women's Self-control. Korean women also set up their own self-control association, primarily headed by Jeong Gyu Son, a teacher at Ewhahakdang. Thus the "Association of Korea Women's Christian Self-Control" was founded in August 1924 with Gak Kyung Yoo, who was also the general secretary of the YWCA, as the chairperson and Jeong Gyu Son as the general secretary. Jeong Gyu Son sacrificially worked for this cause and played a crucial role in securing 52 branches and over 3,000 members by 1928. The association was primarily focused on promoting abstinence from alcohol.

---

435 "Miss Tinling's Work in Korea," *The Korea Mission Field* (January 1924), 12-13.

......While alcohol is like a gun without any ammo, it deceives people in that it gives courage. After so many years of study, we found out this secret. Therefore we must abstain from alcohol in order to ensure the survival of Chosun. The temperance movement in Chosun is the greatest movement of all. This movement is for the well-being of the body and the soul; this is for the well-being of the dying Chosun.[436]

As it is noted here, the temperance movement was more than a movement within the church. It was truly a patriotic movement for the well being of the nation. The movement was closely followed as lectures on temperance were given at women's Christian meetings, and booklets on temperance were given out whenever the Gospel was preached on the street. During a Sunday school conference in Hwangju, Hwanghae Province in November 1927, a "Conquest against the Devil of Alcohol" parade took place and the people joined the temperance movement.

The Salvation Army was particularly active in this temperance movement. Just as the original founding spirit of the Salvation Army was to eliminate all social evils, the church actively engaged itself in the movement. They even published and distributed a special temperance edition of their magazine *The War Cry* and they took part in the enlightenment movement by utilizing their bands.

---

436 Jeong Gyu Son, "Chosuneui Gumju Undong" (The Anti-Alcohol Movement in Korea), *Gidok Sinbo* (The Christian Messenger), April 30, 1930.

One of the most fundamental achievements of the temperance movement by the church was that a law was finally drafted to prohibit the sale of alcohol and tobacco to young people. In December 1932, Christian leaders across all denominations, joined with other leaders of society, filed a petition to the Governer-General for a prohibition law against drinking and smoking by young people. This led to the promulgation of the "Youth Protection Act" in April 1938, which included clauses prohibiting drinking and smoking by the underage.

The temperance movement by the church exercised so much influence to the extent that when the *Sinjeong* Hymnal was published in 1931, it included the *Temperance Song* by Bae Se Lim. This highly popular song of that time read:

My friends in this land, keep alcohol away from your mouth;

It will fail your body and soul, ruining you beyond repair.

You who borrow to buy the wine that will destroy your home;

You resist spending a penny for the education of your children.

If we were to spend all the wine money for building schools;

Our children will be well-taught and be the light of civilization.

Your talents from God and riches from your parents;
Don't lose them to alcohol, but work for the country.

Chorus:

Oh, don't you drink that cup! Oh, don't you even give it a look!

*The well-being of the Korea society depends on your te mpe-ranc*e.[437]

Hyo Deok Lee published a magazine titled *Jeoljehae*(The Self-Control) and undertook an anti-alcohol and anti-tobacco movement, which was also characterized by wearing colored clothes. Koreans had traditionally worn white clothes, but white clothes were prone to get dirty and required frequent washing. Lee's movement was aimed at wearing colored clothes instead to save the resources, time and energy of washing frequently.

The church also did its best in removing prostitution. Prostitution was an evil Japanese social system designed to corrupt the minds of young people and kill the national spirit of Koreans, and the church could not afford to remain silent about it. Commissioned by the Methodist Annual Conference of America, the Committee for Abolishing Prostitution was formed in November 1923, and thus an anti-prostitution movement took off. Geung Sun Oh at Severance Hospital also organized the Association for Abolishing Prostitution, contributing greatly to the furtherance of the move-ment.[438] This movement was later approved for support by the General Assembly as well. The 1926 General Assembly minute records that Oh's speech was "welcomed with applause and the General Assembly decided to support his work."[439]

---

437 *Sinjeong Chansongga* (The Sinjeong Hymnal) (Korea Christian Literature Society, 1931), hymn, no. 230.
438 *Gidok Sinbo* (The Christian Messenger), March 19, 1923.

Going beyond the self-control movements, the church actively engaged itself in social welfare works. Works of the Salvation Army is most noteworthy. Not only giving away relief goods to the poor, but the charity works of the Salvation Army also involved providing jobs and homes to the people. For instance in 1918, Kobayashi, a Japanese member of the Salvation Army, contributed to gather the street boys to teach certain vocational skills in order for them to fit into society. The Salvation Army also steadily worked on providing vocational training schools for women, lodges for beggars and food for the poor. During the winter of 1927 alone, they provided 15,000 meals to over 6,000 people.[440]

In addition, the churches lived out the Christian love of selfless service and charity by building hospitals for tuberculosis patients, hospitals for leprous patients, schools for the blind, and providing other forms of help to those neglected in society. When socialists and communists acted as if they were the only people caring for the poor, the churches clearly displayed the true philanthropic spirit through their works.

5. Theological Disagreements – Signs of Division in the Church

Missionaries came and taught Christian doctrines to the Korean church. Naturally, the Korean church accepted all the lessons from

439 *Chosun Jesugio Jangnohoe Chonghoe Je 17hoe(1928) Hoeirok* (The 17th Minutes of the General Assembly of Korea Presbyterian Church (1928), 48.
440 "Temporary Relief Work," *The Korea Mission Field* (February 1939), 30-31.

the missionaries as the absolute truth of the Christian faith. But as Koreans one by one began to study overseas, people realized that there was more to Christian theology than what they had previously known. This led to the emergence of conflicts between two groups of people: one wanting to introduce new theological thoughts and facilitate the Korean church to embrace various theological perspectives and stances, and the other wanting the Korean church to keep the things of the past.

Such theological disagreements went beyond the context of the church; they were deeply rooted in the elements of localism that were so prevalent in the society. Complicated by political factors, these disagreements were difficult to resolve. The differing theological stances and elements of localism eventually resulted in splitting the Presbyterian Church twice in the 1950s.

The background for the differences of theological stances and localism was this. In the Northwestern region, where the Christian presence was the strongest in the entire country, Christians maintained an extremely conservative stance, especially in the Pyeongan Province. On the other hand, in the southern region where the Christian presence was weaker, Christians there were theologically more progressive. As far as theology and politics were concerned, it seemed that the conservative and strong North was pressing down on the liberal south. However, such disagreements led the church to the awful tragedy of division in the early 1930s. This occurred in the year of Jubilee, thus 50 years since the arrival of missionaries in Korea, when the Korean church accordingly needed to rejoice of God's blessing upon her and continue to strengthen the bond of unity within, especially as she would have to soon bear the cross of the aggressive oppression of the Japanese in the form of forced shrine visits.

The Presbyterian Church in Korea began to keep strict watch against other channels of theology since the early age. Concerning those graduates of other theological seminaries wishing to minister as Presbyterian pastors, the General Assembly laid out a set of strict requirements. The General Assembly decided in 1917 "in order for a graduate of another theological seminary to minister in the Presbyterian Church, he must first come under administration and management of the Presbyterian Church, enroll in the theological seminary of the church (Pyongyang Presbyterian Theological Seminary), and study the creed, politics, and regulations prior to the ministerial recruitment."[441] They were clearly determined to keep other theologies at bay. They were particularly cautious over those who studied theology in Japan. This was because theology in Japan was greatly influenced by the modernistic theology from Germany. While they reckoned diversity in theology as a great threat for division of the church, they failed to understand that exclusive theology could very well act as a snare for the church.

The first visible outcome of those theological conflicts was the resignation of Rev. Chang Keun Song as the pastor of Sanjeonghyeon Church, Pyongyang. Dr. Chang Keun Song, Rev. Kyu Chan

---

441 *Chosun Yesugio Jangnohoesagi* (History of Korea Presbyterian Church) vol. 2, 23.

Kang's successor after his resignation, was accused of holding theology that was far too progressive. Man Sik Cho and other conservative elders of the church forced him out of the church, and thus he had to move to Busan. He confirmed that the gap between the conservative and the progressive in Korea was already significantly wide when he said,

> It is lamentable to hear the mutual accusations that there is one party and another, glaring at and distrusting one another with enmity, and made the conflict between the Northerners and Southerners their business, whereas they are one nation and one people. Is it a jubilee of 50 years or sadness of 50 years?[442]

The conflict between the conservative and the progressive reached its peak when Hyeong Yong Park of Pyongyang Presbyterian Theological Seminary and Jae Jun Kim of Sungin Commercial School clashed against one another. Park was regarded as the Inquisition judge of the Korean conservative theology while Kim was reputed as the pioneer of liberalistic theology for the Korean church. The conflict between these two men eventually split the entire Presbyterian Church in Korea over theological issues.

Having returned from the States in 1928, Park attended Sanjeonghyeon Church and worked as a professor at Pyongyang Presbyteri-

---

442 Chang Keun Song, "Saesanghwaleui Chunje" (Premises for a New Life), *Sinhak Jinam* (The Sinhak Jinam) (January 1935), 12.

an Theological Seminary. Jae Jun Kim also had studied in the States and was teaching Bible at Sungin Commercial School, which was managed by his church. Jae Jun Kim attempted to get in touch with Pyongyang Theological Seminary with the help of Hyeok Namgung who was a professor there. But he found himself unwelcomed by the seminary as he was constantly criticizing the conservative theology. Then Jae Jun Kim denounced the dogma of the Verbal Inspiration of the Bible, which was the core Dogma of the theological conservatism in Korean Presbyterian Church, in his essay contributed to the *Sinhakjinam*, the journal of the Pyongyang Presbyterian Theological Seminary and attacked the missionaries for their obstructing the sense of sovereignty of Korean Church, deploring deeply the absence of the subjective history of the Korean Church which had to be delineated by the Korean Christians themselves.

Hyeong Yong Park, on the other hand, was deeply influenced by his professor at Princeton Theological Seminary in the U.S.A., G. Machen, who accused Princeton of having been polluted by liberal theology and founded Westminster Theological Seminary upholding conservative theology. Park was very much bound by Machen's conservatism and did not have any room for other schools of thoughts. He was fully convinced himself that theology would never change, regardless of time. He believed in upholding the apostolic, authentic and orthodox theology from the times of the Apostles. As a result, he believed in the infallibility of the Scriptures to the extent that there are no errors whatsoever. Standing on the side of fundamentalist theology, he adopted the dogma of the Verbal Inspiration of the Bible and claimed the Bible to be written by the inspiration of the Holy Spirit and containing no human errors. He thus safeguarded the Korean church from deviating to liberal theology.

Such theological differences were by no means a personal issue between Hyeong Yong Park and Jae Jun Kim. It affected all those supporting the two and it eventually led to the division of the church. Park recognized Kim's theological stance as dangerous liberalism and down played him by boycotting his contribution to the *Sinhakkjinam*. There was an attempt by Dr. Hyeok Namgung, the first Korean professor ever to be nominated at the Pyongyang Theological Seminary after earning his doctorate degree, to reconcile the two. When Hyeok Namgung was the editor of the Sinhakjinam, he featured one of Jae Jun Kim's essays and ever since then Hyeok Namgung was very much disliked by Hyeong Yong Park.

Another major problem within the Presbyterian Church was raised in the 23rd General Assembly in 1934: the problem of denouncing Moses' authorship of Genesis and the conflict over the understanding of women's rights. The authorship of Genesis was a problem of the biblical Theology, and the women's rights problem was the problem of interpretation of the Bible which is one of the toughest problems that even the church today has not seen to a permanent solution. Rev. Young Joo Kim of Namdaemun Church in Seoul denied the authorship of Moses for Genesis around 1934, and Rev. Byeong Joo Kang identified this as a serious problem. Hyeong

Yong Park added, "Anyone denying the Moses' authorship of Genesis is not fit to be a Presbyterian minister."[443] On the other hand, the women's rights issue was raised at the General Assembly because *The Christian Messenger* carried an article written by Rev. Chun Bae Kim of Suhngjin Central Church in North Hamgyeong Province. The article stated, "When women were told to be quiet and refrain from teaching, it was just a lesson and customs limited to one local church two thousand years ago. It was not meant to be anything permanent."

In response to this, the General Assembly formed a Research Committee. Headed by a number of professors at Pyongyang Theological Seminary, including Dr. S. Roberts and Dr. Hyeong Yong Park, the committee was ordered to research the matters at hand and give a report at the following General Assembly. The committee facilitated in passing the original bill, which stated that any pastor denying Moses' authorship of Genesis effectively "violates Clause I of the Creed and must be prohibited from being a minister of the Presbyterian Church." It also stated, "Despite the fact that women's ministerial role is never supported in the Scriptures, if any minister freely interprets the Scriptures to compromise with the contemporary context of women's civil rights, he must be reprimanded in accordance to Clauses 42 and 43, Chapter 6 of Disciplinary Regulations."[444] The problems were resolved when

---

443 *Chosun Jesugio Jangnohoe Chonghoe Je 24hoe(1935) Hoeirok* (The 24th Minutes of the General Assembly of Korea Presbyterian Church (1935), Appendix, 89.
444 *Ibid.*

Young Joo Kim and Chun Bae Kim, who were the central figures of these problems, eventually issued apologies and withdrew their original positions. At this point it seemed that progressivism was suppressed by the overpowering conservatism, but it was really a temporal appearance of things to come.

Another problem was the question of authenticity of the *Abingdon Exegesis* published by the publishing company Sinsaengsa. The *Abingdon Exegesis* was translated and published under the supervision of Rev. Hyeong Gee Yoo to commemorate the fiftieth anniversary of the Methodist Church in Korea. It became a problem because those involved in the translation included Presbyterian ministers such as Chang Geun Song, Pil Geun Chae and Kyung Jik Han. Rev. Sun Joo Kil raised this issue. Noting that the majority of the translators were liberal theologians and their influence over the Presbyterian Church must be prevented, he stressed, "It is a great pity that Presbyterian ministers were members of the translation team. We must strictly hold them responsible for their work and monitor their activities."[445] Thus, the General Assembly in 1935 accepted Rev. Kil's suggestion and promulgated that

the *Abingdon Exegesis* is not to be subscribed by the Presbyterian Communion because it has many points incompatible with the doctrines of the Presbyterian Church, and the Presbyterian pastors involved in compilation of this comm-

---

445 Yang Sun Kim, *Hanguk Gidokgio Haehang 10Yonsa* (Ten Year History of Korean Christianity after Liberation) (Missionary Education Department, Korea Presbyterian Church General Assembly, 1956), 177.

entary must be investigated by their respective supervising churches and details of their involvement must be made publicly known in the Presbyterian Journal.[446]

Rev. Pil Geun Chae immediately acceded to the counsel of the General Assembly and apologized for his involvement in the compilation. However, Rev. Chang Keun Song and other pastors claimed that the last thing they would do would be to apologize on the grounds of violating the Presbyterian doctrines. They were unwilling to submit to the dogmatism of the General Assembly as far as their theological freedom was concerned. Rev. Yang Sun Kim wrote that this was "the first challenge of liberal theology against conservative theology in the Korean church."[447]

Instead of wisely responding to the challenge of the liberal theology, the Korean church showed off her stubbornness by saying "never possible." Her failure to embrace theological diversity caged her within the boundary of conservative traditions, and this ultimately resulted in the division of the denomination some time later. The conservatives fell short in exercising flexibility of safeguarding the orthodox Presbyterian doctrines while embracing various theologies, and the liberal theologians went too far in introducing doctrines that people were not ready to embrace. Both parties will be held liable before the judgment of time and history.

---

446 *Ibid.*
447 *Ibid.*

Chapter 10

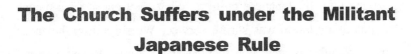

The Church Suffers under the Militant Japanese Rule

Since the Korea-Japan Annexation in 1910, the Japanese regard
ed the Korean Church as the primary obstacle against their colonization and persecuted it in everyway they could. Then finally in
the 1930s, they tested the Korean Church with shrine service.
Marching under the banner of Pacific War and dreaming of conquering Asia and beyond, the Japanese placed the snare of shrine
service right before the eyes of the Korean Church in order to
Japanize her completely. The Church, unfortunately, fell into the
trap by acceding that shrine service was nothing more but a national
ceremony, and thus this was how Korean Christians bowed to
foreign gods and forsook their faith. But even then, some fifty
Christian leaders including Kee Cheol Joo and Bong Suhk Choi
(nick name-Gwonneung:power) stood firm against compromise and
were martyred. Their precious blood washed away the dreadful
sins of their fellow Christians who had bowed down to idols.

1. Japan's Policy of Assimilation

Having recognized Korea as their indispensable training camp for the conquering of the entire Asia, Japan decided to assimilate Koreans into the Japanese culture. What they chose as a means to such assimilation was shrine service. Worshiping at Japanese shrines signified participation in worship of former Japanese emperors and warriors. It was an effective tool of forging uniformity among all people by forcing everyone to express their allegiance to the nation and the emperor. This policy was designed to completely wipe out any remaining Korean spirit. Shrine service then led to other policies of assimilation, such as 'Dongbangyobae' (bowing to the East where Japan's Emperor lived), reciting the 'Hwangguk Sinmin Suhsa'(the Oath of the Citizen of the Empire), abolishing Korean names and enforcing the mandatory use of the Japanese language. Although the policy of assimilation was not particularly aimed at the church, the church was probably the most victimized group of all simply because shrine service and Dongbang Yobae were against the central Christian doctrine of "thou shall not worship idols."

The Japanese introduced their shrines to Korea in 1918. They built a palace for their gods on Mt. Nam(South) in Seoul in 1925 and continued to build many other shrines and palaces at different locations ever since. But in the beginning, Koreans were not forced to worship at the shrines; only the Japanese. Then in the 1930s, Japan conquered Manchuria. As they aimed at defeating the entire

China, they emphasized the importance of unity among Koreans and Japanese and forced Koreans to participate in shrine service. The importance of unity they advocated was that "the Korean race has the same fate as the Japanese race and Koreans belong to the Japanese; Koreans are not the object of national liberation but subject of removing Western imperialism and setting Asians free along with the Japanese."[448] The Governor-General Minami Jiro even stated,

> Korean and Japanese must become one in image, heart, blood, and flesh. True unity is not in simple harmony or the shaking of hands; we must unite together in body and mind. The purpose of this unity is to eventually achieve equality inside and outside without any discrimination at all.[449]

Going a step further, they claimed a baseless theory that Koreans and Japanese shared the same ancestry and root in an attempt to convince the Koreans that they were indeed Japanese.

The Japanese first began attacking the schools with shrine service because schools were the easiest to control. Their oppression soon stretched onto religious groups. Their strategy was to tackle small groups first and then move onto the largest denomination, the

---

448 Jin Cheol Kang, Kang, Man Gil, and Kim, Jin Bae, *Segiesae Bichun Hangukeui Yoksa* (Korean History Reflected on the World History), 218.

449 Banso Irang, Han, Suk Hee, *Ilje Tongchiwa Ilbon Gidokgio* (Reign of the Imperial Japanese and Christianity in Japan) (Seoul: Somangsa, 1989), 255.

Presbyterian Church.

2. Oppression over Christian Schools

Having successfully predicting that Christians would not confirm to the requirements of shrine service because of their doctrine, the Japanese decided it would benefit neither party if there were to be a religious clash. Instead, they claimed that this was an issue of national ceremony. In other words, they explained that shrine service was not a religious ceremony but a non-religious national ceremony that was to be observed by every citizen of the country. The following statements show their claims regarding shrine service:

1. Shrine service is not a religion, but a national liturgy and not a worshipping activity, but respect to the ancestors.

2. The purpose of education is not only the rearing of the intellectual, but also to become a citizen of the Japanese king. Therefore, altogether, teachers and students must show their respect to the king. However, common citizens are not required by compulsion, but voluntarily.[450]

Japanese forced shrine service on all schools for no other reason

---

450 *International Review of the Mission* (April 1940), 18-83.

but to oppress Christian schools. Their intension was clear: to plant seeds of disunity between Korean church leaders and missionaries, and to bring schools under their full control in order to use them as institutes of colonial education.

In 1932, the Japanese embarked on their strategy against Christian schools with *Choongge Hwangriongje*(worshipping the dead national spirits in the spring) on Mt. Suhgi in Pyongyang. When they mandated Christian schools in Pyongyang to visit shrines, missionaries and teachers united to respond that no one was to participate in practices of idol worship. To this, the Japanese compromised their initial position by saying that students could go to shrines and participate in the national ceremonies, but they would be allowed to not participate in the religious ceremonies. Thus Soongsil College, Soongsil Middle School and Sungui Girls' Middle School participated in the ceremonies. The Japanese used this to force shrine service on other schools as well.

This issue naturally emerged as a significant problem for the church. In 1933, the Presbyterian General Assembly received inquiries regarding shrine service from various presbyteries.[451] In order to resolve the issue, the General Assembly attempted to send negotiators to government authorities, but the Japanese avoided any direct confrontation. Instead, they stated that if there were any problems of shrine service by schools, students opposing it

---

451 There were questions about Shrine service by the moderator of North Jeolla Presbytery in 1933 and the moderator of Hwanghae Presbytery in 1934. Also the minister of the Jasan Church in South Pyongan Province raised the question about the collections for the building for shrine service.

should file petitions individually. The issue of visiting shrines by schools, then really became a problem between the schools and Japanese authorities with no room left for negotiations for the General Assembly. However, this was nothing more than a deceptive strategy to exercise dominance over schools and, then, to oppress churches without having any direct confrontation with the churches.

Having decided to press hard on the issue, the governor of South Pyeongan Province called for a meeting of all public and private school headmasters within the province in November 1935 and ordered them to participate in visits to Pyongyang shrines. G. S. McCune, principal for Soongsil Middle School, V. L. Snook, principal for Sungui Girls' Middle School and H. M. Lee, principal for Later Day Saints' Sunan Uimyeong School, refused the order because complying with it would make them compromise their religious stance. In response, the government allowed them to think the matter over for two months and threatened to remove them from office if they did not abide by the government's requirement. Lee eventually conformed to shrine service, but McCune and Snook reported the matter to their missions board and, after discussing with the pastors in Pyongyang, the mission board decided to go completely against shrine service. As a result, the two principal were removed from office and were replaced. But even the new principal refused to visit shrines, and thus the two schools had to file for closure in 1937.[452] Soongsil College was haded over to Jong Man Lee and renamed Daedong Industrial College, and

---

452 A. D. Clark, *A History of the Church in Korea*, 222-224.

Sungui Girls' Middle School was taken over by the government and turned into the Third Public Middle School.

The closing of schools did not end with Presbyterian schools. Severance Medical College and Jeongsin School in Seoul, Gyesuhng and Shinmyeong Schools in Daegu, Shinsuhng and Bosuhng Schools in Suncheon, Myeongsin School in Jaeryeong, and Youngsil School in Ganggye closed as well. On the other hand, Yonhee College in Seoul was taken over by the Government-General in 1941.[453]

The Southern Presbyterian Church took this problem more seriously than the Northern Presbyterian Church. When the new semester started in September 1937, the Japanese government ordered all schools to pray to 'Amaderas Omigami'(goddess of the Sun: the spirit of opening Japan) for victory of the Japanese army fighting in China. The Southern Presbyterian Missions Board adhered to the decrees of the headquarters in the United States and decisions of the resident missionaries in Korea by sending students back home and closing the schools. Sungil Middle School and Sophia Girls' Middle School in Gwangju, Yeongheung School and Jeong myeong Girls' Middle School in Mokpo, Maesan School in Suncheon, and Shinhcung School and Gijeon Girls' Middle School in Jeonju were voluntarily closed, and about a dozen other schools, including Youngmyeong School in Gunsan, were forced to close by the government.[454] The Australian missions board also decided that they "could not participate in shrine service or teach people to

453 Young Hun Lee, *Hanguk Gidokgiohoesa* (History of the Christian Church of Korea), 201.
454 *Ibid.*

participate in it" and voluntarily closed all schools under their care in February 1936. On the other hand, the Methodist schools and the Canadian mission schools embraced shrine service and they underwent no significant difficulties.

Having played the central role of national enlightenment and development, these missionary schools were now fading away into history as a result of the colonial policy of Japan. It was certainly a heart-breaking moment for missionaries, teachers and students alike. Nevertheless, God's mercy for Korea and her people lasted much longer than the colonial rule. All the Presbyterian schools reopened and carried their torch of enlightenment as soon as liberty was bestowed on them after a long period of time. Only history can testify to who were of the right: pro-Japanese schools that embraced shrine service or anti-Japanese schools that rejected shrine service even at the cost of temporary closure.

3. Church Leaders Give In

After staging the 'Nogoo-bridge Incident' in July 1937, the Japanese started the Sino-Japanese War and used it as an excuse to expand the shrine service requirement to churches. They built shrines all across the country and promulgated laws requiring all citizens to participate in shrine service. Their policy was to set up one shrine per each village. At the same time, they installed Gamidana, a simplified shrine with Singungdaema(a piece of cotton of the shrine) in government offices, schools, police stations, etc., and forced private families to buy Gamidana and say prayers to it every morning. They designated the sixth day of each month as a patriotic day, forcing people to hoist the national flag, sing the national anthem, read royal edicts, Dongbangyobae and pray at shrines. Japanese established and proposed Hwangguksinminsuhsa in October 1938, and they distributed pictures of the emperor to all schools and demanded students to worship it in December. In February 1938, the Special Army Volunteer Program was set up, and in March they established the 'Korea law of Education' to change the names of schools and educational curricula to match those used in Japan. Any use of Korean language was prohibited as well. The 'Law of National Dedication' was applied to Korea in May and the 'Kugmin Jungsin Chongdonwon Korea Yonyaeng' (Korean Alliance of General Mobilization of Natioanl Spirit) was organized in July. In 1939, 'changsi gaemyong(creating of new surname) commenced and forced arrests were legalized as per the 'Gukmin jingyongriong'(Law of national drafting).[455]

With such social changes in place, the Japanese began to attack the churches, the last of their hurdles. Saying,

Nearly 500,000 Christians across Korea have a very cold attitude toward the state of affairs. They are not willing to accommodate national ceremonies like shrine service because of the disagreement with Christian doctrines. They even claim Jesus as the King of kings, and thus they should

---

455 Banso Irang, Han Suk Hee, *Ilje Tongchiwa Ilbon Gidokgio* (Reign of Imperial Japan and Christianity of Japan), 254-255.

be punished properly for their contempt,[456]

the Japanese began to tighten their grip on the churches.

The Korean Church was at a dead end. After so many years of persecutions, she now had to decide whether she was capable of pulling through this one more test. Shrine service was definitely an act of idolatry that all Christians ought to reject. If the church were to accede to shrine service, it would mean nothing less than her complete defeat before foreign gods. The church needed to fight against this at all costs; but she failed. History once again shows us that there will always bound to be those who seek to find the easy way out.

The first to embrace shrine service was the Roman Catholic Church. Even though Roman Catholics joined with Protestants in protesting against the idolatry of shrine service and refusing shrine visits in numerous occasions, their attitude suddenly changed when Germany, Italy and Japan joined forces in WW II. Pope Pius XII stated in his papal circular letter, "We permit shrine service as it is not a religious ceremony but a national one."[457] The same year, the Seventh Day Adventists accepted shrine service, followed by the Evangelical Holiness, the Salvation Army, and the Anglican Church. Even the Methodist Church decided to participate in shrine service after Rev. Joo Sam Yang, the then archbishop, was invited

---

456 Giungmugug Boangwha (Department of Police, Security Desk) Samhoil, "Sabyonhaeue Gidokgio" (Christianity under Turmoil), *Chosun* (Nov. 1938), 65. *Ibid.,* 255.
457 *Daehan Mailsinmun* (The Korea Daily), Korean Edition, August 2, 1936.

to a discussion by the Governer-General in June 1936. When the Methodist Church members began protesting against shrine service, the church issued the following statement in September 1938 to explain her position concerning shrine service.

As the Department of Education of the Government-General circulated printed information on the shrine service last year, we trust that you recognize the shrine service not as a religious ceremony, but as a national ceremony that ought to be observed by all nationals. Therefore, it is clear to us that there is absolutely no ground for the shrine service going against religious doctrines, no matter what religion one supports.[458]

What a pity! This fight was not meant for just one church, but after so many years of joy and pain the Methodist Church decided to kneel before foreign gods and the Presbyterian Church was the only one left to withstand the harsh winds. Seeing this, the Japanese adopted even harsher means to bring the Presbyterian Church under their oppression.

Prior to this in April 1938, the Japanese gathered Hyeong Gee Yoo, Suhk Mo Choi, Eung Jo Kim, Jeong Sim Chang, Yeon Suh Park, Yoo Soon Kim, Jong Woo Kim and other Christian leaders at Suhdaemun(West) Police Station and forced them to adopt a

---

458 Yang Sun Kim, *Hanguk Gidokgiosa Yongu* (A Study of the History of Korean Church), 189-190 footnote #32.

declaration that stated that the church should embrace shrine service and adhere to the 'Whangdojungsin'(imperial spirit) in accordance to Japanese Christianity.[459] In May 1938, the 'Chosun Gidokgio Yonhaphoe'(council of Korean churches) was inaugurated at the Bumingwan(Citizen Hall) Main Hall with the purpose of founding Japanese Christianity. In June, Chosun YMCA was removed from the World YMCA and placed under Japan YMCA; the YWCA went through the same fate.

In May 1938, claiming that the inner front must unite in Christianity, the Japanese used pro-Japanese Mun Hwan Oh to entice Seung Gil Lee, Eung Soon Kim and Un Gyeong Chang, who were adamantly against shrine service, and sent them to Japan. It is said that they "collected many types of significant resources on the issue of shrine service and were impressed by the warm hospitality of the Japanese government officials."[460] In June, Rev. Domita, the chairman of Japan Christian Association, was invited to Pyongyang. With all the major Christian leaders within the Pyeongan Province present, he held lectures and discussion sessions, emphasizing that shrine service was not a religious but a national ceremony. However, Rev. Kee Cheol Joo and evangelist Yang Won Son strongly objected to him.

---

459 Jong Kook Im, *Chinil Munhakron* (Treatise on Literature of pro-Japan) (Seoul: Piongwha Press, 1986), 351.
460 Banso Irang, Han Suk Hee, *Ilje Tongchiwa Ilbon Gidokgio* (Reign of Imperial Japan and Christianity of Japan), 257.

4. Distorted Images of the Church – The Presbyterian Church Gives In

By the time the Presbyterian Church met for its General Assembly in September 1938, the Japanese set out to exercise their plan to make the church participate in shrine service by any means. First of all, they devised to have each presbytery accede to shrine service before they came together for the General Assembly. They threatened presbyteries in any way they could. As a result, North Pyeongan Presbytery, the strongest of all presbyteries in Korea, was the first to give dedication to shrine service in February 1938,[461] and this led to the surrendering of 17 presbyteries(there were 23 in Korea at that time), as well as the General Assembly itself in September. The local police demanded all the presbytery delegates to accept shrine service or keep silent, or else they would be removed from office. Moreover, when the delegates went to attend the General Assembly, two policemen in civilian clothes accompanied each delegate.[462]

The 27th General Assembly of Presbyterian Church of Korea met at 8 P.M. on September 9, 1938, in a chapel of the Seomunpak

---

461 Chosun Chongdokbu Kyongmugug (Department of Police, Government of General Governer in Korea), *Chaegune Chosunei Chian Sangwhang* (Present Situation of Korean Public Peace), Sowha 13 (1938), 392.

462 Yang Sun Kim, *Hanguk Gidokgiosa Yongu* (A Study of the History of Korean Church), 188. At the time the total delegates are 193; 86 ministers, 85 elders, and 22 missionaries. *Chosun Jesugio Jangnohoe Chonghoe Je27hoe(1938) Hoeirok* (Minute of 27th General Assembly of Presbyterian Church of Korea) (1938), 1.

(West Gate) Church. On the first day of the Assembly was an election for executive officers. History tells us that even at this point some of the delegates took the stump to be moderator.[463] How silly this is! Could they have not known that matters concerning shrine service were to be decided at the Assembly and they would be standing on the wrong side of justice? Those elected were Taek Gee Hong as moderator, Gil Chang Kim as vice-moderator, Jin Geun Kwak as secretary, and Han Gyu Goh as treasurer.

The following day, when matters concerning shrine service were to be decided, Pyongyang policemen surrounded the chapel and prohibited the entry of any audience. Inside the chapel itself, dozens of police officers armed with long swords, including the chief of the South Pyeongan Province Police Department, were stationed across the altar. Also seated alongside presbytery delegates were policemen in civilian clothes and armed policemen lined up on the left and the right of the sanctuary.[464] Prior to the opening of the General Assembly, the Japanese police had already put Kee Cheol Joo, Jeong Min Chae, Gi Suhn Lee and Sun Doo Kim, who were against shrine service in jail. Missionaries and presbytery delegates were also told to remain silent if shrine service becomes approved, but the missionaries refused. On the other hand, pro-Japanese Rev. Seung Gil Lee and Il Sun Kim,[465] the moderator

---

463 Banso Irang, Han Suk Hee, *Ilje Tongchiwa Ilbon Gidokgio* (the Reign of Imperial Japan and Christianity of Japan), 260.
464 In Suh Kim, *Kim In Suh Jeojak Jeonjib* (Collection of Kim In Suh's Writings), vol. 5, 149.
465 Il Sun Kim was a (police) detective, but later he became a minister and positive pro-Japanese person. After liberation, the church members

of the North Pyeongan presbytery, set the mood of the gathering for approval of shrine service.

As the meeting resumed shortly after the morning devotion, Pyongyang, West Pyeongan, and Anju presbyteries jointly announced their statement on shrine service according to the plan devised by the Japanese side. Rev. Eung Yul Park, the moderator for the Pyongyang presbytery and also the pastor of Junghwa-eup Church, was designated by the South Pyeongan police department to announce, "Since the government declares that the shrine service is not a religious ceremony but a national ceremony, we at the General Assembly also find it rightful to participate in shrine service." To this, Im Hyeon Park of the West Pyeongan presbytery agreed and In Suhp Kil, a delegate of the Anju presbytery, seconded. When moderator Taek Gee Hong, trembling in fear of the hundreds of policemen, asked for an agreement, few of them[466] replied, "Yes," and it was indeed a "Yes" from the devil.[467] Records show that the moderator asked for no opposing comments, and the mode rator announced that it was passed unanimously. It was definitely an unlawful procedure. When B. F. Hunt, a missionary under Bongcheon presbytery, cried out, "Moderator, this is unlawful,"

---

objected strongly to him. So one day he brought a can of gasoline and burnt the church building and became a staff of the communist government of Pyungbuk. In Suh Kim, *Kim In Suh Jeojak Jeonjib* (Complete Collection of Kim In Suh's Writings), vol. 5, 55.

466 Rev. Yang Sun Kim wrote that it was less 10 in his book, *Hanguk Gidokgio Haeband 10Yonsa* (10 Years of the Liberation of the Christianity in Korea) at 188.

467 In Suh Kim, *Kim In Suh Jeojak Jeonjib* (Collection of Kim In Suh's Writings), vol. 5, 149.

Japanese policemen crowded around him and forced him out of the chapel. This is how the Presbyterian Church of Korea left an inerasable mark in history. The Secretary of the General Assembly followed by reading out this declaration:

> We understand the original meaning of the Shinto shrine service, which is not religious and does not collide by any means with the Christian doctrine, and we also are aware that the Shinto shrine service is a patriotic national ceremony. Thereby we pledge ourselves with uttermost devotion as following imperial subjects, to endeavor to be the first in attending the Shinto shrine service and, in addition, participate in the general mobilization of all nations under the national emergency.
>
> Sowha(1938) 13th year September 10
> Moderator of the Chosun Jesus Presbyterian Church
> Hong Taek Gi[468]

In the midst of this, Ik Hyeon Im, a member of the Pyongyang Christian Fellowship, proposed immediate exercise of shrine service by all General Assembly members and the proposal was accepted. Thus at noon the same day, the General Assembly, headed by the Vice-Moderator Gil Chang Kim along with all the moderators of each presbytery, visited the Pyongyang Shrine. It was a tragic

---

468 *Chosun Jesugio Jangnohoe Chonghoe Je 27hoe(1938) Hoeirok* (Minute of 27th General Assembly of Presbyterian Church of Korea (1938), 9.

moment when the Presbyterian Church officially bowed to idols. The distortion of the Presbyterian Church started this way when the people were willing to bow to foreign gods due to their fear of imprisonment. The General Assembly also "decided to relay their decision on shrine service by telegram to the Governor-General, Vice-Governor-General, Chief of State Affairs, Chief of Educational Affairs, Commander of Chosun Forces, General Secretary of Prime Minister and Minister of Internal Affairs."[469] This shows how the church was truly powerless.

The missionaries had a separate meeting of their own at 1 P.M. and decided to submit a letter of petition to the General Assembly. On the 12th of the same month, Chan Young Kwon and 24 others submitted a petition to the General Assembly that stated,

> Not only does the decision of the General Assembly violate decrees of our God and the constitution of the Presbyterian Church of Chosun, but the inappropriate proceeding of the meeting without sufficient hearing from the floor was clearly against the spirit of freedom of religion granted under the Japanese constitution.[470]

But this petition had to be called off due to the demands of the Japanese police. However, the fact that such a petition was submitted at all, despite the small number of people with a clear

---

469 *Ibid.*, 10.
470 Yang Sun Kim, *Hanguk Gidokgio Haebang 10 Yonsa* (10 Years of the Liberation of the Christianity in Korea), 189.

conscience, shows that even in the darkest times, the fire of a clear conscience can never be completely put out.

In October of the same year, the Presbyterian Church held the "Presbyterian Conference for State of Affairs" where the Governor-General attended. He gave the same address he gave at the Methodist Annual Conference a month ago, saying that he would not tolerate the existence of any religion that goes against the fundamental spirit of the imperial citizen. Nearly 3,000 participants recited the 'Oath of the Citizen of the Empire' and paraded across the city with Japanese flags raised high. After worshipping at the Chosun Shinto Palace, they held a Shinto gathering at Namdaemun Elementary School, bow to Tokyo(residence of Japanese king) sang the national anthem, prayed the brilliant victory of soldiers, heard a history lecture by general Okamodo and then dispersed.[471]

To strengthen its participation in shrine service, the Korean church sent Taek Gi Hong and Gil Chang Kim from the Presbyterian Church, Joo Sam Yang and Jong Woo Kim from the Methodist Church, and Myeong Gik Lee from the Evangelical Holiness Church to Japan in December and they worshipped at the Ise Shinto Palace and Kasihara Shinto Palace. Rev. Byeong Sun Hong said, "It is in order to respect the origin of our nation and participate in the shrine worship as a imperial citizen."[472] Yet another person said, "I must say that anyone claiming shrine service to be idol worship

---

[471] "Chegunui Chosun Chian Sangwhang," *Hanguk Dokrip Undongsa* (History of Independent Movement of Korea), 408-409.

[472] "Gidokgiodowa Sikug" (Christians and Present Situation), *The Chongyon* (the Youth) (July 1938), 7.

is in contempt of the law."[473] Indeed, the Korean Church went too far in participating in shrine service and bowing to foreign gods.

5. Refusing Shrine Worship

Despite the devious appeasement and threats of the Japanese, there were several brave souls who safeguarded their faith and went directly against the evil forces of idols. Because of those martyrs and resistors who remained steadfast, the Korean Church was able to keep a spring of life flowing within her.

Foreign missionaries, who had provided much help, care, prayer and support for the well being of the nation, were all deported in the early 1940s, and a majority of Christian workers compromised to Japan. Nevertheless, as many as 2,000 Christians resisted the evil schemes of the Japanese about 50 were martyred in jail and over 200 church buildings were closed down.

(1) Protests by Pyongyang Presbyterian Theological Seminary

Protests against shrine service were carried out both individually and collectively. Full-scale protests were seen after the Japanese forced all presbyteries to participate in shrine service in early 1938. When the news spread that North Pyeongan Presbytery, which comprised of the strongest Christian leaders at that time, accepted

---

473 *Ibid.*, 8.

shrine service for the first time in February under the leadership of the presbytery Rev. Il Sun Kim, students and lecturers of the Pyongyang Presbyterian Theological Seminary responded strongly against this. Hong Nyeon Chang, a student belonging to the North Pyeongan Presbytery, burned in rage and axed a tree planted by the Moderator Il Sun Kim on the seminary grounds.[474] As students belonging to various presbyteries were planning a movement to protest shrine service, the police learned about it and arrested many students. Professors Hyeong Yong Park and In Joon Kim were indicted without detention.[475]

Since a few missionaries and lecturers of the seminary, including the Chairman of the Board of Trustees W. Blair and President S. Roberts, maintained a strong position against shrine service, the seminary was left with no option but to close itself. Having trained quality Presbyterian leaders for over four decades since 1901, the seminary now had to declare a suspension for an indefinite period. Students already enrolled in the seminary were able to complete their studies through correspondence courses.

(2) Missionaries Refuse Shrine Service

Missionaries resident in Korea had differing views of shrine service depending on their denominations and theological back-

---

474 Il Suhn Kim had planted a tree to commemorate his entrance into the seminary.
475 *Jangrohoe Sinhakdaehak 70 Yonsa* (History of 70 Years of Presbyterian Theological Seminary, 1971), 94-95.

grounds. Methodist missionaries generally remained quiet about the issue, and Presbyterian missionaries generally opposed to it. But there were also a few individuals supporting shrine service. For instance, when the decision regarding shrine service was accepted, H. H. Underwood, then president of Yonhee College, shook hands with Chief of South Pyeongan Police Department and congratulated him. At a periodic operations report meeting, he also said, "I strongly regret that some of us have consistently refused to participate in the shrine service and that my college had to be closed. Shrine service has nothing to disturb my religious principles. It is definitely a right thing for the General Assembly to pass shrine service today."[476] But even with strong supporters of shrine service like Underwood, majority of missionaries undertook massive protest movement against it.

On the other hand, just after accepting of shrine service by the Presbyterian General Assembly, Southern Presbyterian missionaries met in Gwangju to reaffirm their stance against shrine service. They notified all mission boards to terminate their membership to their respective presbyteries and urged them to continue evangelizing non-Christians. But mission boards decided that they would cooperate with individual churches for evangelistic projects upon request even though they were officially out of presbyteries. In other words, they sought to maintain relationship with certain pastors and churches that were against shrine service. In fact, the mission

---

476 Cf. Rev. Yang Sun Kim, *Hanguk Gidokgio Haebang 10Yonsa* (Ten-Year History of the Korea Christianity of the Liberation), 190-191 footnote 34.

boards were planning to join hands with pastors and churches standing against shrine service and organize a whole new presbytery or a general assembly in order to continue on the history and tradition of Presbyterian Church. However, in October, McGill, the chairman of the Canadian mission board, met with Higher Section Chief of South Hamgyeong Province Police Department and told him that they would recognize shrine service as a national ceremony and that they would continue to operate educational institutes which were previously under their care. This obviously caused a conflict between Presbyterian mission boards. Nevertheless, the missionaries opposing shrine service maintained their stance by terminating their membership to presbyteries and continued to support the numerous pastors who refused shrine service.

(3) Rev. Kee Cheol Joo

Rev. Kee Cheol Joo was one of the most significant leaders in the fight against shrine service. He was also one of the most glorious martyrs in the history of Protestantism in Korea. Joo was born in November 1897 in Ungcheon-eup, Changwon-gun in South Gyeongsang Province as the fourth son among seven children born to Elder Hyeon Suhng Joo. The family was relatively well to do, and Joo graduated from the Osan middle school in Jeongju in North Pyengan Province as a high scorer at age of 20 after having finished Gaetong Elementary School in Ungcheon-eup. Osan School, founded by Elder Seung Hoon Lee, was a school built on a strong nationalistic spirit and was one of the most resistant to Japanese colonialism. Joo was brought up in strong nationalism and anti-Japanese perspectives, which would later enable him to stand up tall as a spiritual leader in the struggle against shrine service.

After graduating from Osan School, He enrolled in Department of Commerce at Yonhee College, but his eye disease worsened and thus he had to stop his studies and instead began serving as a deacon at his home church in Ungcheon. Around the same time, he attended a revival meeting by Rev. Ik Doo Kim, was challenged to receive the Holy Spirit and he experienced his second birth in repentance. Rev. Kim mentored Joo all his life. While reading the Word and praying, he was inspired to enroll in a theological seminary.

While studying at Presbyterian Theological Seminary in Pyongyang in 1921, he learned that dormitories in the seminary were built and maintained by four different Presbyterian sects according to their regions. He decided that it was not good for unity of the church and after discussing with other students he suggested to the president that the regional dormitory system be abolished. "Rev. Joo(being a man from Gyeongsang Province(south) married a woman from Pyengan Province(North), pastured in Pyongyang and was buried in Pyongyang. He was indeed a symbol of North-South unity."[477]

After graduating from the seminary at age of 30 in 1926, he

---

[477] In Suh Kim, *Kim In Suh Kim Jeojak Jeonjip* (Collection of Kim In Suh's Writings), vol. 5, 135.

started his pastoral ministry in Choryang Church in Busan. Rev. Joo's ministry was so successful that the church quickly grew and its members numbered several hundreds. While pasturing the church, he also taught Gyeongnam Bible School. It is certainly no coincidence that one of his students was Rev. Yang Won Son, who was imprisoned for opposing shrine service and was eventually martyred during the Korean War.

After pasturing Choryang Church for six years, Rev. Joo moved onto Munchang Church in Masan. Munchang Church also flourished thanks to Rev. Joo's capable pastoral leadership. Now a well-known speaker throughout the country, Rev. Joo led revival meetings in Japan and he also held meetings at Pyongyang Presbyterian Theological Seminary, which are characterized for the deep inspiration he instilled. But Rev. Joo had to withstand the pain of losing his wife here, and some time later he married Jeong Mo Oh, a teacher at Uisin Girls' School in Masan. Jeong Mo Oh was indeed the person who shaped Rev. Joo as the martyr as he is known today. Oh is one of the brightest wives of pastors the Korean Church is proud of.

When his six years of pastoral ministry in Masan was nearly over, Elder Man Sik Cho, former principal of Osan School, came to invite Rev. Joo as the pastor of Sanjeonghyeon Church in Pyongyang when Rev. Chang Keun Song had to leave the church due to his difference theological thinking. Firmly believing that this was God's calling in his life, Rev. Joo moved to Pyongyang, but this was in 1936, the year Japanese began to strangle the Korean

Church with the yoke of shrine service. At the welcome dinner for Rev. Joo, Dr. Suhng Hwi Lee of Pyongyang Presbyterian Theological Seminary said, "We are not only welcoming Rev. Joo into Sanjeonghyeon Church, but we are indeed welcoming the chief pastor of churches in Pyongyang and the chief pastor of all Korea." Rev. In Suh Kim records that "it was an exaggeration then but a fulfilled prophecy now."[478] Perhaps it is also no coincidence that Rev. Kee Cheol Joo came to Pyongyang just the following year after the death of Rev. Sun Joo Kil, who was a primary figure for Pyongyang and the Korean Church.

After his appointment over Sanjeonghyeon Church, Rev. Joo soon built a new sanctuary, but the Japanese arrested him in February 1938, just before dedication of the sanctuary. Church members had to carry out the dedication service without their pastor. When the 27th General Assembly accepted the shrine service in 1938, Japanese temporarily released Rev. Joo. But when Rev. Jae Gi Yoo was arrested in Uisuhng Police Station in July 1939 due to the Nonguhoe (The Society of the Farmer's Friends) Incident, they assumed that Rev. Joo was also involved in the incident and arrested him. After inflicting much pain on him for seven months they released him because they could not find any charges against him. Upon his return to Pyongyang, he gave a sermon entitled "Five Kinds of My Prayers,"[479] which was really like his last words. After this

---

478 *Ibid.*, 143.
479 My five desire were; 1) to overcome the power of death, 2) to overcome long time suffering, 3) entrusting my old mother and family and church to the Lord, 4) to live and die righteously 5) entrusting my soul to the

sermon, Japanese threatened Rev. Joo to resign from the pastoral ministry within three months. Rev. Joo was placed at a crossroad of having to choose whether to resign and live peacefully or to die a painful death fighting to the end. The decision was not an easy one as Japanese assured him that they would not demand him to partake in shrine service if he would resign from the pastoral position. But Rev. Joo chose to die a painful death fighting to the end rather than to give up on his faith and live an easy life. This decision was indeed a decision of life and death so dear not only to his life but to the fate of the Korean Church.

In 1940, Japanese ordered Rev. Joo not to preach any more. But Rev. Joo replied, "God gave me this permission to preach. I will stop only if God tells me to. Even if the police tells me to stop, I cannot, because his permission to preach was not granted by the police."[480] To this the police said, "If you continue to preach despite our prohibition, we will arrest you." Rev. Joo responded, "Preaching is my duty, and arresting me is your duty. I will just do my duty." The Japanese police arrested Rev. Joo a few days later. Rev. Joo requested to the police that he be granted to say good-bye to his 80-year-old mother. In front of his mother, he prayed to God, "God! This undutiful son departs before completing his duty of keeping his mother. Lord, I trust my mother into your hand. I believe that your caring hand is better than this undutiful son, and I trust her into your hand. This body of mine will

---

Lord. The contents of this sermon are in In Suh Kim, *Kim In Suh Jeojak Jeonjib* (Collection of Kim In Suh's Writings), vol. 5, 154-162.
480 *Ibid.,* 163.

follow your footstep." After saying the prayer, he parted with his mother. It was the last moment of seeing his mother. In a way he was promising her to meet again in heaven after tasting the glory of martyrdom.

While in prison, Japanese tortured Rev. Joo to give up his pastoral position but in vain. And so they forced the Pyongyang Presbytery to obtain a resignation letter from Rev. Joo. Rev. Ji Hwa Choi, the moderator, Pyongyang Presbytery, visited Rev. Joo in the Pyongyang Prison a several times and demanded his resignation letter. But Rev. Joo strongly objected by saying, "This ordination in pastoral ministry was given by God. I cannot resign unless and until God tells me to." The Pyongyang Presbytery had no choice but to remove Rev. Joo from its membership. In accordance to this decision, Pyongyang Police Station nailed planks across the entrance of Sanjeonghyeon Church and closed the church down.

When the next Pyongyang Presbytery met at Changdong Church, the Pyongyang Seminary[481] requested to use the parsonage Sanjeonghyeon Church as a residence for a professor of the seminary and the presbytery approved the request. Three pastors, including the moderator of the Pyongyang presbytery, met with Elder Gye Jun Yoo of Sanjeonghyeon Church and told him to vacate the residence, but he refused. At last, Pyongyang Police Station had to force Rev. Joo's family and belongings out of the residence and shut the building down.

---

481 Pyongyang Seminary began after the General Assembly passed the Shrine Worship. The president of the seminary was Rev. Pil Keun Chae.

After suffering all sorts of ordeals for six years in prison, Rev. Joo's eyes, lungs and heart deteriorated beyond repair. He was relocated to a clinical facility within the prison in April 1944, but his day of martyrdom was drawing near. One day in the same month, Jeong Mo Oh, his wife, was initially turned down by prison guards and then was eventually allowed to meet Rev. Joo. A prison guard helped him out by letting him meet his wife for the very last time. While still with his wife, he fell down powerlessly. His last words were:

1. Please take a good care of my mother instead of me.
2. I want to drink a warm rice soup.
3. I will pray for churches in Chosun before God's throne. Please tell this to churches.
4. Do not take me to Ungcheon[hometown] but bury me on Mt. Dolbak in Pyongyang.[482]

After saying these words, he passed away in his cell at 9 p.m. on April 21, 1944. It is said that at the last moment he shouted, "God of my soul, take hold of me," which echoed in the cell and startled all those around him. At the young and vigorous age of 47, he went to be with the Lord in heaven where there was no demands of shrine service or detestable pro-Japanese people. Indeed "when all his labors and trials were over, I was safe on that beautiful shore." Rev. Joo, a great martyr of the Korean Church,

---

482 In Suh Kim, *Kim In Suh Jeojak Jeonjib* (Complete Collection of Kim In Suh's Writings), vol. 5, 169.

was the Daniel of our church as an ever-conquering glory, beacon of faith and ever-flaming torch. Martyred with national independence only a year and a few months ahead, Rev. Kee Cheol Joo is a model of our faith for all generations.

In addition to Rev. Kee Cheol Joo, some 50 ministers were martyred in prison. Among them were: Rev. Young Han Lee of Methodist Church who was martyred in Haeju Prison, Rev. Bong Jin Park of Evangelical Holiness Church who was released after much torturing in Cheolwon Prison but was martyred soon after, and Rev. Bong Suhk Choi, also known as Rev. Choi Gwonneung (power), who was released from the prison but was martyred in Gihol Hospital in Pyongyang. Rev. Taek Gyu Jeon was martyred in Hamheung Prison, and Rev. Tae Hyeon Choi of the Seventh Day Adventist Church was martyred as well. Although the Korean Church sinned against God by bowing to foreign gods, the blood of the martyrs washed the sin away, and these martyrs are still shining upon us today as a beam of hope among Jezebel's crowd.

(4) Elder Gwan Joon Park

Born and raised in Yeongbyeon, North Pyeongan Province, Elder Gwan Joon Park submitted petitions to the Governor-General and other government officials stating that forcing shrine service on Christians was inappropriate. He attempted to meet the Governor-General over 13 times but failed. Having decided to resolve the issue in Japan proper, he traveled to Tokyo along with Miss Ee

Sook An, then a teacher at Bosuhng Girls' School. With the help of his son, Youngchang who studied a seminary in Japan he met key government officials and began to persuade them.

At last, he sat in the audience when the Japanese Imperial Assembly was discussing religious laws. There he distributed fliers that read, "Jehovah is the only true God."[483] The whole assembly was immediately caught up in a commotion and Park was arrested on the spot. After suffering all sorts of tortures in prison for six years, he was martyred. Ee Sook Ahn, on the other hand, was released after the independence. She published her autobiography *If I perish, I perish* in which she described the records fine details of her life in prison.

(5) Others Who Rejected Shrine Service

Perhaps a huge majority at the General Assembly did not really want to accept the shrine service. Nevertheless it is true that they made a compromise with reality and participated in shrine service. However, there were quite a number of ministers who argued unlawfulness of this practice and protested against shrine service in an organized manner. Some key leaders include Rev. Gi Sun Lee in North Pyeongan Province, Rev. Jeong Min Chae and evangelist Joo Won Lee in Pyongyang, and Rev. Sang Dong Han in South Gyeongsang Province. When the matter on the shrine service was passed by the General Assembly, Rev. Gi Sun Lee resigned

---

483 Ee Sook Ahn, *Jukuimyon Jukuirira* (If I perish, I perish), 94.

from Bukhadong Church in Uiju, which he had pastured for nine years, and traveled across the country with Rev. Jeong Min Chae to search for those who would stand with him against shrine service. And thus he met Hyeong Nak Kim, Ui Heum Park, Suhng Soo Kye, Suhng Sim Kim, Yeon Geun Oh and other supporters, who collectively arrived at two resolutions. The resolutions were: first, to stage an anti-shrine service movement in order to weaken or dismantle existing churches, and second, to unite Christians opposing the shrine service and organize house churches, which would later replace the existing churches altogether.[484]

In line with this, Rev. Sang Dong Han in South Gyeongsang Province planned the following as means to fight against the shrine service in his region:

1 dismantling the existing presbyteries,
2 refusing baptism and holy communion conducted by pastors who participate in the shrine service,
3 organizing new presbyteries with those opposing shrine service,
4 mutual aid among those opposing the shrine service, and
5 group worship services and active recruiting the supporters.[485]

In fact, Rev. Sang Dong Han planned to expand his anti-shrine service movement all across the country by joining hands with Rev. Nam Sun Joo, Rev. Sang Nim Choi, evagelisht Deok Ji Choi

---

484 Sung Joon Kim, *Hanguk Gidokgiohoesa* (History of Christian Church in Korea) (Hanguk Giohoe Gioyuk Yonguwon, 1980), 159.
485 *Ibid.*, 160

and Soo Ok Joo, and others. Fortunately, F. E. Hamilton and D. R. Masbery, missionaries in Pyongyang, were able to provide significant financial support toward this, and there were a great number of other pastors who contributed without actually participating in the movement directly.

Seizing the opportunity of Rev. Kee Cheol Joo's temporary release in April 1940, Rev. Sang Dong Han went to Pyongyang, where he met other supporters from Manchuria and held a combined meeting for those opposing the shrine service at Rev. Jeong Min Chae's home. There, they decided to organize a national anti-shrine service presbytery. But Japanese did not fail to interrupt this movement as well. By July that year, they managed to arrest and imprison all those involved in the national anti-shrine service movement, including Rev. Kee Cheol Joo. Only after five years on May 18, 1945, did Japanese charge the pastors with internal security violation, contempt of government and other charges. Although Rev. Joo and about 50 others were martyred in prison, it is such an unfortunate thing that details of struggle and fight endured by many of the martyrs are still unknown to us.[486]

6. Final Apostasy of the Church

1) Church Becomes Pro-Japanese

Having forced the church to accept the shrine service, Japanese

---

486 *Ibid.*

promulgated the Religious Organization Act in 1939 to oppress the church even more. Only one church was allowed to exist in each city; all others were closed down. Christians were forced to participate in the Shinto shrine installation, the national ceremony, the palace service, and the shrine service. They were also forced to give defense donations, patriotic donations, donations for airplanes (fighter), and even give away church bells and metal doors and gates. Other forms of physical labor and services were also demanded.

When Japan started the Pacific War against the U.S.A. and got actively involved in the WW II in 1941, the church began to show more of its pro-Japanese attitude. Around this period, the term "Japanized" became highly popular. The church was no exception, and the church actually took as its goal to establish "Japanized Christianity."

After approving the shrine service, in its General Assembly in April 1939, the Presbyterian Church set up "The Presbyterian Federation for National Spirit Mobilization" as a means to actively cooperate in affairs of the state. In order to facilitate efficient operation of this association, "Intermediate Operations Committee" was installed, for which Rev. In Gwa Chung was appointed as the General Secretary. The committee ordered churches to partake in shrine service, palace service and recite The Oath of the Citizen of the Empire. The committee also removed all nationalistic elements from the church constitution, doctrine and liturgies. Virtually everything was made Japanese, to the extent that the hymnal and all Christian literature were revised to accommodate the colonial policy.

Similarly in the Methodist Church, in an October 1940 meeting, supervising directors resolved on rejection of nationalism and liberalism, instillation of Japanese spirit, cooperation with the Japanese Methodist Church, and proclamation of the Japanized Gospel. They even stipulated that individual churches should engage in stronger patriotic activities to the extent that "many church members should sign up as voluntary soldiers."[487] Their resolution stated:

1. Guidance of the Thought
   - A thorough recognition of the principles of the Daitoa Kyoei-ken(Greater East Asia Co-Prosperity Sphere) and Naisen It tai(Japan and Korea One on Inside).
2. Education Reformation
   - The national principle must be taught in the theological seminary, colleges, high and middle schools.
   - The military drill also taught in those educational institutes.
   - Theological Education: The Gospel of Christ is to be the basis of its education. The history, the heathen thoughts and the customs of the Jewish people introduced by the process of the westernization must be eliminated. The Gospel is to be interpreted in accordance with the tradition of the philosophy and sages of the East.
3. (omitted)
4. Supporting the Armed Forces
   - The Christians are, as much as possible, to volunteer for military service.
   - The Church must be taught the significance of the military

---

487 *Maeil Sinbo* (Daily Newspaper), October 4, 1940.

service.
- The Church must be in the lead for anti-espionage.
5. The Program for Unifying the Structures
    - The Korean Methodist Church must realize a scheme of unification with the Japanese Methodist Church.
    - The foreigners are to be deposed from all positions of influence and power.[488]

This reform plan shows how much Methodist Church became pro-Japanese at that time. In addition to the Presbyterian and the Methodist Churches, smaller denominations took similar paths. The Salvation Army renamed itself in November 1940 as "Chosun Salvation Band" and declared to organize a structure through which they would support Japanese principles. In December that year, Anglican Church resolved to have a new start according to the Japanese spirit, and thus they hold a conference for church leaders in 1942. Heung Woo Shin vented out the following pro-Japanese statements:

> Our Great Savior Jesus taught us to love that country first······Our nation is the Japanese Empire. We may be religious and we may be Chosun people. But we must never forget that we are ultimately Japanese. People, as faithful servants of the Emperor, love Japan! This is God's command for us Christians in Chosun. This is what I firmly believe.[489]

---

488 *Ibid.*
489 Heung Woo Shin, "Chosun Gidokgioui Kukgajeok Samyong" (Commission

Here we can witness how confused the Korean Church was. The meeting minutes for the 31st General Assembly of the Presbyterian Church in October 1942 at Suhmunbak Church in Pyongyang shows us a clearer picture of confusion the church was in:

- 9 a.m., 17th. All members visit Pyongyang Shrine.
- 10:30 a.m., 17th. Members gather at the meeting hall, conduct national ceremony and then worship service, followed by a lecture on national affairs by Sinjung, Section Chief of High Police for South Pyeongan Province.
- 3:30 p.m., 18th. Changmoo, the chief of the Public Relations of Chosun Army, gives a special lecture entitled "Soldiers of Japanese."
- 7:30 p.m., 18th. Service held for victory in the war, followed by national ceremony. Chonan gives a lecture entitled "The Pacific War and Our Attitude." A offering for national defense forces collected.
- Ji Hwa Choi, Chief Director, and In Gwa Chung, General Secretary, of National Mobilization Federation of Presbyterian General Assembly give the following report:

1. During February 1943, lecturers are to be sent out by the headquarters to hold regional national affairs lectures in order to spur accomplishing of the objectives of the Pacific War and to encourage service by Christians(omitted).

---

of the State of the Christian Church in Korea), *The Dongyanggikwang* (The Light of Orient), (February 1939), 8

2. Regarding offering of a patriotic airplane, one patriotic airplane to Army-Navy, and seven ground-to-ground machine guns, worth 150,317 won and 50 jeon.
3. Three vehicle for transporting injured Army soldiers, worth 23,221 won and 28 jeon.
4. 2,165 brass items of contributed for war.
5. 1,540 church bells donated.
6. Efforts made to use Japanese as lingua franca, and Japanese Bible Study materials published.
7. Army recruit programs to be followed up strictly.
8. Existing Christian leaders to accept Japanized Christian spirit and align Christian theological thoughts to the Hwangdo(Royal Doctrines) spirit in strict integration(all seminaries later became training centers for the Hwangdo spirit).[490]

Even though it was during the time of a war and the church was under a great oppression of Japanese, this is definitely not how meeting minutes for a General Assembly should look like! In midst of this, the number of Presbyterian churches decreased by 750 in 1942 compared to the previous year, and the number of church members dropped by 76,747, which is not surprising at all.

In September that year, a month before the General Assembly, the money collected from all Presbyterian churches across the country as defense donation was used to buy one airplane and two guns,

---

490 *Chosun Jesugio Jangnohoe Chonghoe Je 31hoe*(1942) *Hoeirok*, (The 31st Minutes of the General Assembly of Korea Presbyterian Church (1942), 8, 26, 49-51.

which were dedicated on Mt. Nam. The only pro-Japanese Christian newspaper at that time, *Gidokgio Sinmun* (The Christian Newspaper) reported:

> To express our gratitude to our Army, Navy, and Air Force who fight in the North and South, in the West and East, we Presbyterian Christians, 370,000 in all, dedicate one navy airplane and two guns to our mighty Navy······ in naming of this new patriotic fighter······receiving the Navy chief General Wonpan, 80 Presbyterian representatives······ including Rev. Kimgok Ilchung from Sakju, Rev. Sinlim Ilwoong from Haeju, Rev. Kim Nagyeong from Jaeryeong, Rev. Andong Uibong from Wonsan, Rev. Lee Changgyu from Gunsan, Rev. Kim Jong Dae from Namwon, Rev. Tae Young Ham, Rev. Jeon Pil Sun, Rev. Cha Gwang Suhk, and Rev. Paik Nak Jun from Gyeongsuhng······we name the patriotic fighter "Korea Presbyterian."[491]

Toward the end of the article, the newspaper reported that a certificate of appreciation, a certificate of receipt, and pictures of the airplane and guns were kept in the General Assembly office.

The newspaper also wrote in the September 25, 1943 editorial the following statements under the heading "Let Us Collect More Metal."

The enemies continue to resist us······We remember it was

---

491 *Gidokgio Sinmun* (The Christian Newspaper), September 23, 1941.

not too long ago that Christianity in the peninsula got rid itself of the American and British dependency, gave away church bells and that Christianity was reformed as Japanized Christianity······A special collection of metal parts will be carried out across the nation in September······Let us collect more metal. Our soldiers in battlefields are crying for more weaponry.[492]

Church bells were supposed to be used for announcing the time of godly worship services, but these writers working under Japanese influence stated the church bells should be given away as bullets of shooting down Americans and British. The Korean Church was definitely getting it wrong.

Also in the Methodist Church, the National Mobilized Chosun Methodist Federation organized a grand conference in March 1941, where they resolved to practice reformative principles and build a highly defended nation. In October the same year, after the dismissal of the third Annual Conference, new denominational regulations were set out according to the denominational regulations of the Japan Methodist Church, and thus "The Chosun Methodist Group" was organized. About 50 pastors and laymen in the Gyeongsuhng parish participated in physical labor of the Shinto palace in Buyeo, South Chungcheong. When they returned, the Board of Directors for the National Mobilized Methodist Federation declared the following five religious practices.

---

492 *Ibid.*, September 25, 1941.

1. The first wartime Christian minister training conference is to be held for four days from October 28. The second conference is to cater for 100 more people, and the third conference is to accommodate the female ministers.

2. A representative from each parish should help in construction of Buyeo Shrine Palace.

3. All church premises should be dedicated to each village, eup, myeon, and jeong, whereby the premises should be used as venues for meetings, evacuation and special work space in emergencies, and church members should voluntarily help and cooperate for this cause.

4. All metal gates and doors in possession of churches should be donated to the government.

5. All regions must hold wartime lectures or panel meetings around the time of the winter Bible study course. Regional government officials must be in touch for preparation of these meetings. Speakers and meeting contents must be communicated to and approved by the denominational headquarters in advance.[493]

In February 1942, Rev. Chun Soo Chung, then the Archbishop of the Methodist Church, sent an official letter entitled "Regarding visits to the Imperial Army and donating metal items" to all parish bishops. In it, he urged churches to donate metal gates, metal doors and church bells in order to complete the holy war.[494]

In March 1944, a denominational executive committee meeting

---

493 *Chosun Gamlihoebo* (The Methodist Newspaper of Korea), September 25, 1941.

494 *Ibid.*, November 1941, 1.

was held and the following decisions were announced regarding "donations for patriotic airplanes."

Resolutions

1. Regarding Donations for Patriotic Airplanes

   As the battle fronts require even one more airplanes, this denomination decides to donate patriotic airplanes as stated below.

   1) Three patriotic airplanes (The Methodist)
   2) 210,000 *won* to cover the costs for patriotic airplanes
   3) This amount includes all of the donations made by Methodist church members and some of the proceeds from liquidation of surplus land resulting from merges of Methodist churches.[495]

In September 1944, the Methodist Church also put up the sign "The Royal Doctrines Cultural Center" at Sangdong Chapel and appointed Rev. Hong Gi Gal as its manager. Denominational pastors were forced to gather at the center, where they learned Japanese spirit and culture.[496] Then the pastors followed a Shinto priest to the Han river, where they partook in the Misogi Barai (clean ceremony), a Shinto ceremony, wore hoods with Japanese flags on it, and ran to Mt. Nam in order to worship at the Shrine Palace.

Japanese continued to place restrictions on signing of the hymns; they banned some hymns altogether, and there were some hymns that they blotted certain verses out.[497] Even in the Apostles' Creed,

---

495 *Gidokgio Sinmun* (The Christian Newspaper), April, 1, 1943.
496 It is one of ceremony of Shinto. The participants should wash or sprinkle water to clean their bodies before they attend the ceremony.

"I believe in God the Father Almighty, maker of heaven and earth" was seen to be against the Shinto creation story and "he shall come to judge the quick and the dead" was seen to violate the reincarnation cycle of the emperor and thus these lines were removed. Paying of respect to the emperor's picture or to the direct of the East was carried out five minutes before all worship services, followed by a moment of silence for the soldiers killed in war, prayer for victory of the armed forces, and reciting of the Hwangguksinm insuhsa(Oath of the Citizen of the Empire). Since 1943, all church meetings, other than Sunday morning services, were banned, and churches were forced to conduct Japanese language classes and carry out manual labor within the sanctuaries. Those churches seized by the government were turned into weaponry factories. Hwangguk-sinminsuhsa and Hwangdo Silchon(practice of the Royal Doctrine) were posted in church buildings as well.

Other denominations such as the Roman Catholic, the Anglican, the Salvation Army, and the Seventh Day Adventist were no exception in being pro-Japanese. When the army recruitment program was launched in Korea in 1942, Evangelical Holiness Church, Salvation Army and other denominations were quick to hold 'Congratulatory Seminars for Army Recruitment Program' or 'Seminars in Appreciation of Army Recruitment Program,' and put in action anything that they could use to earn approval of Japanese, such as by adopting pro-Japanese declarations and resolutions. But such

---

497 For Instance, 'A Mighty Fortress is our God,' 'Onward, Christian Soldiers,' 'Stand up Stand up for Jesus,' 'Alas, and did my Saviour bleed?' etc.

actions were in absolute futility as Japanese dismantled the smaller denominations not too long after this in order to destroy Christianity altogether. In May 1943, the Evangelical Holiness Church was dismantled because they were seen to emphasize the second coming of the Christ. About 200 of the ministers and elders, along with some 100 laymen, were arrested.[498] The Baptist Church and the Seventh Day Adventist were also dismissed for the same reason.

(2) Churches Merging and Integration Together

Japanese determine that it was to their benefit to fuse all the Christian denominations in Korea into one. They brought the chairman of the Japan Christian Association to Korea and urged colonial union and denominational integration of the Korean Church under the project name of "The New System of Christianity." In response to this, Korean Church leaders set up a denominational cooperation committee in January 1942. Those involved in this task met together at Saemunan Church and formed 'The Preparation Committee for Chosun Christian Cooperation.' And in the same place, around July and August, it was decided to establish a new denomination. But this was met with some disturbances as the Methodist Church submitted a proposal of 12 principles of reformation. This reformation proposal mentioned that "church doctrine must be declared based on the New Testament and a new interpretation rules for

---

498 Chun Young Lee, *Suhnggiul Giohoesa* (History of the Holiness Church), 90.

the Old Testament must be established in order to eliminate all Jewish thoughts in the Old Testament."[499] In other words, they were proposing to do away with the Old Testament. When it was suggested that the proposal by the Methodist Church should be amended, the Methodist Church opted out of the entire project and the cooperation plan was never actualized.

When the first attempt failed, the Methodist Church took the leadership in cooperating with the Gyeonggi Presbytery of the Presbyterian Church and setup a reformed denomination with the Presbyterian pastor Pil Soon Chun as its Premier.[500] While the theological foundation for this denomination remains unclear, we know that they attempted to remove Christianity in the Old Testament, by removing the most of the Old Testament including Pentateuch and Daniel as well as the Revelations. But the Gyeonggi Presbytery soon had an internal conflict, which caused Pil Soon Chun to be impeached. The presbytery was absorbed by the General Assembly, and the reformed denomination had to be absorbed by the Methodist Church.[501]

Japanese were also bold enough to integrate several churches in a region into one. In line with this, the Methodist Church released

---

499 *Maeil Sinbo* (The Daily Newspaper), March 21, 1943.
500 Staffs of the Renovation Denomination were the following: moderator Pil Soon Chun, administrator Young Sup Kim, General Secretary Dong Wook Lee, Director of Evangelization Yon Suh Park, Director of Education In Koo Yoon, Director of Treasure Suk Joo Choi, and Director of Training Soo Cheol Kim.
501 Hiang Lok Cho, "Moksa Bansegi," (Half century of Minister), *Christian Sinmum* (The Christian Newspaper), March 6, 1971

the following statements regarding merges of Methodist churches.

1. According to Paragraph 6 of the denominational activities, neighboring churches are to be merged together so that weaker churches will be strengthened and abandoned church premises will be liquidated in order to provide for donations for patriotic airplanes and operational funds for the denomination.
2. Church mergers are to be planned out by each parish; all mergers must be completed by April.
3. Mergers are to take place in Pyongyang, Haeju, Gyeonsuh, Incheon, Jinnampo, Wonsan, Ganggyeong, Gangneung and other places. If there are two or more churches in a given city, they are to be merged into one.[502]

According to this plan, churches merged were: six in Pyongyang, three in Haeju, Gaesuhng, Wonsan and Incheon respectively, two in Jinnampo, and one in Gangneung and Ganggyeong respectively, and 13 in Seoul. Abandoned church buildings and other annex buildings were sold to provide for national defense.

Finally in August 1945, Japanese integrated all Protestant denominations under one name "Japan Christian Chosun Denomination." Twenty seven Presbyterian representatives, twenty-one Methodist representatives, six Salvation Army representatives and one representative each from five smaller denominations declared establishment of this denomination in Jangdaehyeon Church in Pyongyang. At least officially all denominations were dismissed and the Korean

---

502 *Gidokgio Sinmun* (The Christian Newspaper) April 1, 1944.

Church was taken over by the Japanese Church.[503] Inaugurating denominational leaders-Gwan Sik Kim as the premier, Eung Tae Kim as the vice premier, and Chang Keun Song as the general secretary-were appointed by the Governor-General Abe. This was just two weeks before liberation. History had its own way with absolutely no hint on the future.

Those resisting such unlawful and irreligious demands of the government were either arrested or forced to resign from ministerial positions. Gag orders and standstill orders were placed on them to limit any activities. Only those submitting to the Japanese demands were allowed to function as church leaders.[504] Many of those on the opposing side went underground and thus Protestant believers, even though they numbered about 700,000 at one time, significantly decreased in number as much as by half. This was the most suppressed time for the Church.

(3) Pro-Japanese Practices of Christian Leaders

As Japanese became more oppressive, churches, presbyteries and general assemblies became pro-Japanese at organizational levels. But there were also individual Christian leaders who stood on the pro-Japanese side whether voluntarily or involuntarily. Although it is reasonable for us to trust that a huge majority of them became pro-Japanese because they were threatened and forced to, it has

---

503 Yang Sun Kim, *Hanguk Gidokgio Haebang 10 Yonsa* (Ten-Year History of the Korea Christianity of the Liberation), 44.
504 *Ibid.*, 43.

to be proven that simple sympathy is not sufficient to justify their deeds. Their deeds went far beyond their personal issues; they had serious influence over the church and the society at large. A number of church members abandoned their faith because they felt disgusted of the church. Even a large number of non-Christian nationalists detested their pro-Japanese practices.

When the Governor-General held lectures on national affairs throughout the country in September 1937, it was mobilizing many famous Christian leaders, including Heung Woo Shin, Hyeong Gi Yoo, Chi Ho Yoon, Hee Do Park and Jae Myeong Cha.[505] In addition, Chun Soo Chung, Jong Woo Kim, Woo Hyeon Kim, Jae Myeong Cha, Myeong Gik Lee, Joo Sam Yang and Dong Wook Lee were participating in the Chosun Christian Association, which was a puppet organization supporting and advocating Japanese policy.

Hee Do Park, one of the 33 national representatives during the March First Movement, published a pro-Japanese magazine named *Dongyangjigwang*(Light of the East). In it he carried many pro-Japanese editorials, some of which were:

- Nak Jun Paik: Civil Administration and Colonial Policy of the USA and the UK
- Heung Woo Shin: Characteristics of the British People
- Pil Soon Chun: Characteristics of the American People
- Yong Suhl Lee: Characteristics of the American People

---

505 Institute of study of national politic-economical-culture, *Chinilpa Gunsang* (gang of pro-Japan), 1948.

- Chun Soo Chung: Religious Policy of the USA and the UK
- In Gwa Chung: Religious Policy of the USA and the UK
- Joo Sam Yang: Why is the USA fighting?
- Hee Do Park: Why is Japan fighting?
- In Deok Park: An American Lady's Perspective on War

When the army recruitment program kicked off in 1942, Tae Yong Choi of Bogeum(Gopel) Church flattered Japan by writing an article titled "A New Start for Christians" in *Dongyangjigwang*.

> It was God who handed Chosun over to Japan. Therefore I think that we should serve Japan just as we serve God. Today, the only country for our people is none other but Japan. All our national duties and devotions must be rendered to the state of Japan. In fact, God is commanding us to surrender everything precious to Japan. The army recruitment program is just that.[506]

If a Korean pastor did not hesitate to say that the army recruitment program was God's command, what else would pastors have said? What would have been left of nationalistic spirit or patriotic spirit in any Christian? People of all walks, even female leaders, praised the army recruitment program. In her article entitled 'Jamado Damasi' (Japanese spirit) that mothers should acquire," Gak Gyeong Yoo of the YWCA wrote: "I think the time has come for us to take

---

506 Jong Kuk Lim, *Chinil Nonsul Sunjip* (Collection of the Pro-Japanese Articles), 346.

after the mothers in the mainland······What a great joy!······I believe that mothers themselves should realize the calamity upon Korea."[507] Maria Park and Helen Kim encouraged young Koreans to volunteer themselves into the Japanese Army as each of them wrote articles entitled "Reward of having a son, and duty of being a mother" and "The recruitment program and the determination of the women in the peninsula." Even if these did not write the articles voluntarily, their pro-Japanese deeds should never be accepted as justified.

There were other forms of pro-Japanese services performed by Christian leaders of all denominations. Perhaps there is no greater pain and shame than this in our history. Thinking of the pastors and laymen suffering ordeals of death in prison, these people objected themselves to Japanese threads in order to spare themselves a false freedom out of prisons. While we can humanely imagine and understand that they were left with no other realistic options, their deeds must be condemned and criticized sternly by history.

(4) Establishment of (latter) Pyongyang Presbyterian Theological Seminary and Chosun Theological Seminary

In May 1938, just a few months before the 27th Presbyterian General Assembly unjustly legalized shrine service, Pyongyang Presbyterian Theological Seminary went into an indefinite suspension.

---

507 In Soo Kim, "Ilje Malgiui Gidokgio Tanapgwa Giohoeui Euyonge Daehan Yonku" (a Study on Imperial Japan's Persecution against Korean Church and Church's Patronizing) *Giohoewa Sinhak* (Church and Theology), vol. 19 (1987), 243 footnote #59.

Although those already enrolled completed their degrees through correspondence courses, the only pastoral training institute of the denomination eventually ceased to exist. Having decided that training of pastors must not be stopped, the General Assembly began to explore the possibilities of reopening a seminary. Many claimed that "the seminary has not reopened for one whole year and it is delaying its reopening again. The General Assembly should see to it that the seminary reopens as soon as possible."[508]

All of the conservative missionaries, who opposed to the shrine service, were no longer in touch with the seminary, Dr. Hyeong Yong Park, the most conservative leaders of the Korean Church, was out of the country to avoid the threats of the shrine service. Most of other conservative pastors were in prisons. Thus it is quite reasonable for us to deduct that reopening of the seminary must have been based on liberal theology and pro-Japanese thoughts. The first one to propose this was Rev. Pil Geun Chae. Rev. Young Joo Kim and Rev. Jae Myeong Cha in Seoul supported this idea, and as Elder Dae Hyeon Kim pledged to give financial support, "the Action Committee for Establishing Korea Theological Seminary" was set up in March 1939.

The proposal for rebuilding the seminary was approved by the 28th General Assembly that year, but at the same time the rebuilding movement for the Pyongyang Theological Seminary began. This was rapidly undertaken; Rev. Pil Geun Chae organized an action

---

508 *Chosun Jesugio Jangnohoe Chonghoe Je 30hoe*(1941) *Hoeirok* (The 30th Minutes of the General Assembly of Korea Presbyterian Church 1941), 85.

committee and obtained approval for the seminary from the Government-General in February 1940. In due course of matters, Rev. Chae, who was a core leader for establishment of Chosun Theological Seminary, went to be the president of the Pyongyang Theological Seminary.

On the other hand, those working to see establishment of the Chosun Theological Seminary failed to obtain approval from the Government-General and so they opened the seminary in Seungdong Church in Seoul with a training institute approval from the Govern or of Gyeonggi Province in April 1940. Elder Dae Hyeon Kim was appointed as the president with Young Joo Kim, Tae Young Ham, Hee Ryeom Cho, Kyung Jik Han, In Gu Yoon, Gwan Sik Kim, and Geon Young Oh as Board of Directors and Rev. Jae Jun Kim as the lecturer. However, this seminary had its foundation in liberal theology as Rev. Jae Jun Kim claimed that the foreign missionaries passed on the theology in the Korean Church and that it had nothing Korean in it. This was a strong indication from the beginning that the Korean Church will walk a very different route than the one pursued by the conservative Christian leaders.

Even though we understand that the seminary was established in a harsh time and that they had to accommodate a certain degree of threats from Japanese, the fact that the establishing objectives of the seminar were "to study Christian theology based on evangelical faith and to train Christian ministers faithful and dedicated to Hwangguk (royal empire)" clearly shows the true intension of the seminary.[509] Their limitation was further proven when they "condemned missionaries and accused them for having robed of the Korean Church her very identity and appointed Japanese as the director of the Board of Trustees of the newly opened Korea Theological Seminary" in 1941.[510]

It is told that Rev. Pil Geun Chae, then the president of Pyongyang Theological Seminary, said, "we have unknowingly allowed ourselves to be infected with thoughts, ethics and customs of Americans and British; we deeply regret this and we want to repent of our sin committed against the state."[511] We can only hope that this statement was not his sincere words.

The Methodist Theological Seminary, which participated in the shrine service without much resistance from the beginning, was not spared of interruptions to its operation either. When anti-government documents were discovered within the school premises in June 1940, Japanese took it as an excuse to indefinitely suspend the seminary. Japanese then allowed the seminary to reopen the following year, but the seminary gate had to be posted with banners reading, "Ready to Fight in War" and "Religion Supports the State."[512] When the seminary was renamed as "Hwangdo Spirit Training Institute" in 1944, it became difficult to tell whether it was a seminary training godly ministers or an institute producing faithful

---

509 *Chosun Jesugio Jangnohoe Chonghoe Je 29hoe*(1940) *Hoeirok* (Minutes of the 29th General Assembly of Korea Presbyterian Church (1940), 43.

510 Kyung Bae Min, *Daehan Yesugio Jangrohoe 100 Yonsa* (History of the Centennial year of Presbyterian Church of Korea), 530.

511 Quoted from *ibid.*, 518.

512 Sung Sam Lee, *Gamrigiowa Sinhakdaehakgio* (Methodist Church and Theological Seminary) (Hanguk Gioyukdosuh Chulpansa, 1977), 217, 228.

slaves of the Japanese Empire. It was indeed a ship without a compass.

Japanese also had a plan to completely eradicate the church. The plan was to wipe out all Christian leaders who were against them on August 18, 1945.[513] But God of justice brought national emancipation to Korea just three days before this barbaric plan was executed. God's grace for the Korean Church was more than sufficient.

As time passed by, the Christian leaders and laymen who served and cooperated with Japanese were evaluated. Obviously, those imprisoned, martyred or released after serving their terms in the prisons for keeping their faith needed no more appraisals. They were on the right side and the winning side. They were like the beacon of the nation and the church, shining in the time of absolute darkness.

Of course, when appraising the pro-Japanese Christian leaders, it is pitiful to hear that they had no choice, they were forced to do so, and that at least they managed to keep the church and serve God in their own ways. But no matter what the excuse, their deeds were wrong, and they are in need of repentance. History always has to be judged between right and wrong; it should never be measured with double standards. We must remember that the Lord and the Church forgive those who repent, not those who give excuses. A right and just history is a history that can label wrongs as wrongs. The Church is said to have an external life

---

513 S. H. Moffett, *The Christians of Korea* (New York: Friendship, 1962), 36.

because it is organically designed to be reborn and restarted. It was right to oppose the shrine service; bowing to gods in the shrines was clearly a sin that needed serious repentance. Those who said that the Japanese emperor was higher than the Lord Jesus, even though they were forced to say so, should not be regarded as Christians until they repent of their sin.

PART III

Chapter 1

The Church in North Korea after Liberation

Liberation! August 15, 1945, the long awaited liberation was finally given to the Korean people. God of eternal love proved Himself by extending His hand of salvation to Korea. God had set the Koreans free after 35 years, just half of the 70 years of captivity the Israelites had to endure as slaves from the Babylonians.

> When the LORD brought back the captives to Zion, we were like men who dreamed. Our mouths were filled with laughter, our tongues with songs of joy. Then it was said among the nations, "The LORD has done great things for them." The LORD has done great things for us, and we are filled with joy. (Psalm 126:1-3)

Liberation! What a joyous word! For how many days and years did the forefathers of our faith endure the harsh ordeals and tortures of the Japanese, only longing for liberation? God heard all their prayers and He answered them in His due time. We could now freely praise the Lord without having to worry about being overheard. We could now read and preach any part of the entire Bible without having to worry about being censored. And we could now enjoy the full freedom from having to bow before heathen gods at Shinto shrines. Freedom eliminated the need for appeasing the Japanese and performing involuntary services in coercion. Now the task was given to the church to rebuild the altars that the Japanese tore down and to raise the foundation of the church that had long been polluted and distorted.

1. Rebuilding of the Church

While liberation was a true joy to all Koreans, it had a greater significance for Christians. Among the forefathers of faith who regarded shrine service an idolatry and fought for the truth in prisons, about 50 were martyred. Including Rev. Jeong Min Chae and Rev. Gee Sun Lee, about 20 leaders were released from Pyongyang prison. Countless other Christian leaders who had to go underground because of the pressure of shrine service now came back to the light of freedom. One of the most imminent issues for the church was to restore the names of those churches that had been replaced by Japanese names and to rebuild the church as it was meant to be. It was only natural for all the denominations, which the Japanese had forcefully dismissed, to come together and build themselves up again.

Those Christian leaders released from prison did not go back to their homes. Instead, they stayed together for about two months at Sanjeonghyeon Church where Rev. Kee Cheol Joo served as a pastor and discussed the matter of rebuilding the Korean church. After lengthy series of discussions, the following key principles for rebuilding the Korean church were released around the 20th of September.

1. The Church leaders (pastors and elders) should repent and purify themselves of the Shinto shrine service according to the Disciplinary Ordinances of the General Assembly.
2. The measure of disciplinary punishment is to be that of self-accusation and self-discipline; the pastors are requested to spend at least two months in contrition and repentance.
3. During the period of the suspension of the pastors and elders, either the deacons or laymen will lead the service.
4. The principle of the reconstruction of the Church is to be notified to all presbyteries and local churches so that they may be carried out altogether.
5. A Theological Seminary is to be reconstructed in order to train the church workers.[514]

Once the reconstruction principles were released, many churches and presbyteries confessed their sin of shrine service and applied the principles according to the guidelines.

Although the North Pyengan Presbytery was the quickest of

---

514 Yang Sun Kim, *Hanguk Gidokgio Haebang 10 Yonsa* (The Ten-Year History of Korean Christianity after Liberation) (Seoul: Education Department, General Assembly of the Korea Presbyterian Church, 1956), 45.

all others to legalize shrine service, it stood against the Japanese until the very end when all denominations in Chosun were forced to be integrated into one denomination. When liberation came and freedom was finally granted to the church, the six presbyteries in North Pyengan Province(East Pyengan, North Pyengan, Yongcheon, Uisan, Sanseo and Samsan) met for a week-long revival meeting to celebrate the liberation on November 14 of that year at Wolgok-dong Church in Suhncheon.[515] Speakers at the meeting were Rev. Gee Sun Lee, who had served his term in prison, and Dr. Hyeong Yong Park, who had fled to Manchuria to avoid shrine service and taught at Bongcheon Theological Seminary.

The retreat hosted by the six North Pyongan presbyteries aroused interest among many Christian ministers. About 200 ministers, including several from Hamgyeong Province, attended the retreat. Rev. Gee Sun Lee's testimony on his life in prison was more than enough to challenge and inspire the hearts of those at the retreat.

But when Dr. Hyeong Yong Park announced the principles for church reconstruction, the meeting quickly became tense. Pro-Japanese pastors, such as Taek Gee Hong, who had passed the matter of shrine service illegally at the 27th General Assembly, raised their voices in acute protest. He argued,

The load of hard work was the same for those suffering

---

515 The place where they got together was the home of Elder Sung Jun Kim (who later became a minister). Elder Kim's father was rich, and he invited the ministers and prepared a feast.

in prisons and those appeasing the Japanese in order to keep the church. In fact, the hard work of those working under Japanese oppression should be regarded as higher than the work done by those who avoided the Japanese oppression by going abroad or by retiring from ministerial positions.[516]

He continued that any repentance and punishment regarding shrine service were a matter to be resolved between each individual and God at the personal level. Those at the retreat could not believe what they were hearing; Rev. Hong's crooked conscience was in full display.

Although the retreat by the six North Pyongan presbyteries resul ted in a clash of interests among those who had suffered in prisons and those who had worked alongside the Japanese, they had to come to an agreement in order to rebuild the church. First, they decided to start in-depth discussions with the Pyongyang Presbytery and then with all the 16 presbyteries throughout the five provinces in the northern part of Korea. Thus, in early December that year, a combined meeting for the five Northern provinces was held at Jangdaehyeon Church in Pyongyang. A greater level of unity was required of the church now more than any other time, for the U.S.S.R. in North Korea was exercising more control over the church, reinforcing the security along the 38th parallel to restrict crossing of the border between the North and the South, and increa-

---

516 Yang Sun Kim, *Hanguk Gidokgio Haebang 10 Yonsa* (The Ten-Year History of Korean Christianity after Liberation), 46.

sing more stringent surveillance on church leaders and church care-takers.

As the five Provinces joined hands in forming one combined presbytery, they elected Rev. Jin Soo Kim as the chairman and appointed Rev. Cheol Hoon Kim and Rev. Yu Taek Lee as executive officers of the new presbytery. The combined presbytery also decided on the following resolutions:

1. The combined presbytery of the five Provinces in North Korea is to be the highest decision making body in place of the General Assembly until the North-South reunification is realized.
2. The constitution of the General Assembly is to be used as it was before the amendment, and no changes are to be made to it until the unified General Assembly is held.
3. All churches are to repent of the sin of shrine service; pastors are to spend two months in contrition and repentance.
4. The Theological Seminary is to be managed directly by the combined presbytery.
5. The Independence Memorial Evangelical Association is to be set up for the purpose of evangelizing and propagating the Christian faith throughout Korea.
6. A representative convoy is to be sent on behalf of the North Korean Church to express our gratitude to the commander of the allied forces.[517]

It was logical for the combined presbytery to disregard the consti-tution forced by the Japanese and go back to use the General

---

517 *Ibid.*, 47-48.

Assembly constitution before the amendment. It was also a reasonable decision to have a two-month-long period of repentance for the sin of shrine service. Restoring the Presbyterian Theological Seminary, which had to be closed in opposition against shrine service, was also an urgent matter. Their decision to send a representative convoy to the allied forces, on the other hand, was in fact a result of their intention to establish communication with the South Korean Church. It was their aim to meet with church leaders in South Korea to discuss the future of the church and to meet with Dr. Syungman Rhee, who had just returned from the United States, and Gu Kim, the sixth president of the provisional government of the Republic of Korea, to commend them for their hard work. But execution of their plans was somewhat disrupted by the political climate in North Korea.

2. Emergence of the Korea Christian Federation

With the joy of liberation still in its full parade, North Korea was put under the trusteeship of the U.S.S.R. forces in accordance to the treaty of the allied forces. The U.S.S.R. forces landed at Wonsan on August 20, and they entered Pyongyang on the 24th. Only two days after their entering of Pyongyang, the political commander A. A. Romanenko ordered the organization of South Pyengan Democratic People's Committee with equal ratio of nationalists and communists. Soon, the Five-Province Democratic Politics Committee was formed to commence the Soviet militant regime.

The U.S.S.R. leadership used Il Sung Kim, then a Soviet Army officer, as a puppet and rolled out its plan on turning North Korea into a territory of communist rule. Russians detained Elder Man Sik Cho, who was the chairman of the South Pyengan Province Reconstruction Preparatory Committee and a prominent leader for the right wing, in the Korea Hotel. Afterward, other right-wing leaders were detained or removed one by one until the Democratic People's Committee was eventually dominated by communists completely.

Communists devised a plan to completely eradicate Christians in North Korea as a means to lay a solid foundation for the communist regime. They declared that the elections for provincial, municipal and county level Democratic People's Committees were necessary components of the newly organized legislature on Sunday, November 3, 1946.

This was practically a declaration of war against the church. Telling Christians to vote on a Sunday, when they were supposed to worship God, was the same kind of trial that the Japanese had presented with shrine service.

Having realized that they were in need of a countermeasure for destroying the church, they set up a procommunist Christian organization named "Korea Christian Federation." This organization was formed under the leadership of Rev. Yang Uk Kang, a graduate of Pyongyang Theological Seminary. Rev. Kang was Il Sung Kim's maternal relative and was a communist himself. In October 1946, Kang coerced Rev. Hee Jeong Kwak, Rev. Ung Lee, Rev. Yeong

Cheol Shin and others to set up the Christian Federation. They appeased and threatened Rev. Ik Doo Kim, who was an honorary chairman and a renowned revivalist, Rev. Sang Soon Park, who was a missionary to Shandong, and Rev. Eung Soon Kim, who was an honorary chairman and a prominent leader at the Hwanghae Provincial Democratic People's Committee, to join the Federation. Rev. Sang Soon Park was appointed as the committee chairman.

Declaring that elections for the Democratic People's Committees were to be held on Sunday, November 3, 1946, Il Sung Kim released the following resolution using the name of the Korea Christian Federation.

1. We fully support the Kim Il Sung Administration.
2. We do not recognize the South Korean regime.
3. The Church pledges to be the leader of the people.
4. The Church resolves to participate in elections.

Such a declaration for elections on a Sunday was aimed at appeasing and threatening pastors in the combined presbytery to join the pro-communist faction. Those not participating in the elections or opposing the elections were to be eliminated.

When the Election Day was announced, the church once again began to split over this matter. At that time there were about 30 churches in Pyongyang. While most of the pastors had previously participated in shrine service, there were other pastors who had served their terms in prison or had hidden themselves underground. These pastors had an uncompromising perspective on the matter and they adopted the "Five Resolutions" as below.

1. Christians, who regard keeping of the Lord's Day as a sacred task, are not to participate in any event other than worship services on the Lord's Day.
2. Politics and religion must strictly be distinguished.
3. Maintaining the sacredness of church buildings is an absolute duty and a right. Church buildings are not to be used for any other purposes than worship services.
4. Should any Christian minister wish to become a politician, he/she has to resign from the ministerial position.
5. The church reserves the freedom of faith and assembly.[518]

Also, Rev. Yu Taek Lee of Sinhyeon Church, Rev. Cheol Hun Kim of Sanjeonghyeon Church, Rev. Gam Eun Choi of Sainjang Church, Rev. Yun Chan Kim of Yeonhwadong Church, and Rev. Gil Soo Kim of Sinam Church, who were primary leaders of the combined presbytery, had a series of meetings and using the official name of "Pyongyang Christian Fellowship," filed a petition to the government requesting that the election day be moved to a weekday. The government bluntly turned down their request, and the pastors pledged to stand fast by saying, "We will keep Pyongyang to our death. We pledge to commit our humble selves on the Lord's altar in order to keep our faith and to keep Pyongyang, the Jerusalem of Korea." They advised church members not to participate in elections and they themselves agreed not to take part in

---

518 Yang Sun Kim, *Hanguk Gidokgio Haebang 10 Yonsa* (The Ten-Year History of Korean Christianity after Liberation), 63.

elections by remaining within church buildings throughout the Election Sunday from the dawn prayer meeting until midnight. Many Christians followed the instructions and spent the whole day in churches instead of going to vote. However, communists arrested Christian ministers and laymen who did not participate in elections and forced all sorts of tortures on them at the Department of Political Security.

As Yang Uk Kang continued to strengthen the Korea Christian Federation, nationalist pastors and member pastors of the combined presbytery were arrested and tortured one by one. In such a situation, pastors were divided into "the pro-government faction, the opposition faction, and the realist faction." The Federation sent official letters to churches, ordering them to post Il Sung Kim's portraits on the front wall of church buildings in order to distinguish each church's ideological stance.[519] Since 1948, laymen were also forced to join the Federation. This was a clear indication of the conspiracy to make the Federation the official General Assembly of Christians in North Korea. Then in 1949, when church leaders of the five provinces were made to gather at Suhmunbak Church in Pyongyang, the formation the Christian Federation General Assembly as a puppet organization of the communist regime was completed; Rev. Ik Doo Kim was appointed as its chairman, Rev. Eung Soon Kim as vice-chairman, and Rev. Taek Soo Cho as secretary.[520]

---

519 Man Chun Hong, "Bukhan Jungkonchogieui Gidokgiowa Kang Yang Uk" (Christianity in the Early Stage of Northern Government and Kang Yang Uk), Hung Soo Kim, ed., *Haebanghoo Bukhan Giohoesa* (History of Church of the North Korea after Liberation)(Seoul: Dasan Gulbang, 1992), 370.

3. The Problem of the Presbyterian Theological Seminary

After liberation, it was decided that Pyongyang Theological Seminary(latter) should be operated under the direct management of the combined presbytery. Rev. In Joon Kim was appointed as its new president. Rev. Kim was a graduate of Pyongyang Theological Seminary himself. He studied at Union Theological Seminary at Richmond, Virginia, in the U.S.A. and taught at Pyongyang Women's Theological Seminary. But he refused to join the Korea Christian Federation and was taken to the Department of Political Security where he endured all sorts of ordeals and was eventually martyred. After Rev. Kim's death, Rev. Suhng Hwi Lee succeeded Rev. Kim in January 1947. Those teaching at the seminary at that time included Rev. Ji Hwa Choi, Rev. Tae Bok Kim, Rev. Hak Bong Lee, Rev. Gyeong Goo Park, Rev. Mun Goo Kang and Rev. Young Yun Kim.

The Christian Federation, on the other hand, could not afford to see the seminary flourish. At that time, Pyongyang was home to two theological seminaries: Pyongyang Theological Seminary and Suhnghwa Theological Seminary of the Methodist Church. The Federation undertook the work of rapidly merging the two into one, creating Christian Theological Seminary.[521] At that time, Presbyterian Theological Seminary had about 600 students and

---

520 Chang Joo Kye, "Bukhan Gidokgiodoyonmaengeui Jungche,"(Identity of the Korean Christian Federation in the North), *ibid.*, 70.

521 Jung Un Taek, "Haebangeehoo Bukhangiyokeui Gidokgio," (Christianity in the Northern Korea after Liberation), *ibid.*, 32.

Suhnghwa Theological Seminary about 200. Upon the order by Rev. Yang Uk Kang, the secretary of the Federation Rev. Taek Soo Cho posted portraits of Stalin and Il Sung Kim at the entrance of Pyongyang Theological Seminary and checked the ideological stance of each student. Using this as a guideline, 60 students were selected from each of the two seminaries and only about 120 students were allowed to continue their studies at the new seminary. All others were removed from any theological training.

In March 1950, the two seminaries were fully merged as one. Rev. Suhng Hwi Lee, the president of Pyongyang Theological Seminary, was taken to the Department of Political Security and Eung Soon Kim, the vice-chairman of the Federation, took Lee's place and began to brainwash the students according to the communist policy. Rev. Lee was eventually martyred during the Korean War when many right-wing figures were shot dead upon the recapturing of Pyongyang.

4. Dissolution of the Church

The damage done to the Korean people and the Korean land by the Korean War is beyond description. The extent of damage done to the church, in particular, is certainly beyond anyone's imagination, and the damage was greatest for the North Korean church. After the cease-fire, the North Korean church was completely dissolved by communists. Gwang Suhk Choi, a former professor of philosophy at Kim Il Sung University, witnessed:

Even during the three months when the communist army was invading South Korea, over 470 religious organizations were dismantled and 808 religious buildings were destroyed······ When North Korean communists worked on post-war restoration of religious buildings, they demolished those buildings that were severely damaged, and they altered the overall design of those buildings that were slightly damaged to the extent that they no longer looked anything like the previous ones. Crosses were taken down even from those church buildings that were not damaged at all; they were turned into kindergartens, communist offices, meeting halls and so on.[522]

The communists did not hesitate to shoot Christians dead within 30 minutes of the people's court. Many pastors and laymen had to escape to the south in fear of persecution, and those pastors and laymen remaining behind were massacred or deported by communists. As a result, official Christianity virtually became non-existent.

During the 1972 Red Cross talks between South and North Koreas, South Korean reporters met with Yang Uk Kang, who was the chairman of the Central Committee for the Unified Democratic Chosun, and asked him the following questions regarding the North Korean church:

---

522 Kwang Suk Choi, 'Bukhan Christians Sinansaengwhal) *The Kidokongbo* (Christian News), September 2, 1972.

Q **What is the situation of Christianity in North Korea?**

A "You would know even before I speak. Churches were completely destroyed during the three years of war inflicted upon us by the imperial Americans. The army chaplains who came with American troops coerced us into submitting to Americans by saying that opposing Americans was the same as opposing God. It was American missionaries who introduced the religion, but it was also American missionaries(chaplains) who destroyed the churches. If God really existed, how could they have done that? That is how the churches were removed. And many Christians gave up on their faith that way. While American missionaries passed on the faith, they also played a big part in abolishing it."

Q **How many Christians are there and how do they worship in North Korea?**

A "Many church buildings have been destroyed and there are just too many people giving up their faith, so it is hard to tell who the Christians are. Personally, I think there may be some individuals. Perhaps there might be some in rural areas."

...

Q **Rev. Kang, do you believe in God?**

A "I am a pastor. How can I not?"

Q **But we cannot see any church buildings on the street.**

A "Of course not. All of them were destroyed during the war."

Q **Don't you have plans to build a new one?**

A "I am not sure. If Christians wish to build one, we might do so. The 14th Article of the Constitution of the Republic guarantees the freedom of religion."

Q **Do Christians ever meet together?**

A "I suppose so. Maybe they do in rural areas."

Q **How well is the Bible distributed?**

A "Because so many Christians abandoned their faith, there are none left who need the Bible. God allowed the bombing of the country while Christians were having worship services ......"523

As seen from the conversation with Yang Uk Kang, we can only deduce that there were officially no churches or Christians in North Korea. A land that was so well evangelized, so full of Christians, and even "referred to as the Jerusalem of Asia with over a hundred Presbyterian churches within Pyongyang itself around the time of liberation," had become only a sad story with no trace of religious prosperity.

---

523 "Kang Yang Uk Hoegion," (Interview with Kang Yang Uk), *ibid*, September 9, 1972.

After his visit to Pyongyang as part of the Red Cross talks, Chang Yeol Kim, the head of the social department of the *Hankukilbo*, wrote this conclusion on the North Korean church: "Religion cannot exist in North Korea. If a religion ever exists, it would only be the communist ideology."[524] This statement is more than sufficient to describe the North Korean church.

---

524 *The Kidokongbo* (Christian News), September 16, 1972.

Chapter 2

Rebuilding of the Church in South Korea

1. Dissolution of the Southern Conference

The post-liberation church in South Korea was in a different footing than its northern counterpart. First of all, there were very few ex-prisoner Christians in South Korea, one of them being Rev. Yang Won Son. As such, South Korea had no substantial conflict between ex-prisoner Christians and those church leaders who participated in shrine service. Therefore, although those Presbyterian figures such as Rev. Gwan Sik Kim, who served as the general secretary of the Japanese Christian Chosun denomination just before liberation, Rev. Chang Geun Song and Rev. Young Joo Kim and those Methodist figures such as In Young Kim, Yeon Seo Park and Myeong Seop Sim by right needed to resign from their religious post and take time reflecting and regretting their deeds, few demanded them to do so. Even fewer were those capable of replacing them, and thus they remained in their post while the reconstruction of the church in South Korea commenced.[525]

While it is true that all the denominations in Korea were forced by the Japanese to be combined into one at the end of their occupation, the religious leaders felt that it was good for them to maintain the unified church structure. Definitely behind this was a fundamental reason that it is indeed God's will for the church to be united as one, but there was also a political reason that the key founding members of the new government, including Syngman Rhee, Gu Kim and Gyu Sik Kim, were Christians and that the new church needed to adopt the spirit of nation building.

Three weeks after liberation on September 8, a general assembly for the denomination was held at Saemunan Church under the name "Southern Conference (Nambu Daehoe)." Those present were denominational leaders, including Gwan Sik Kim, Young Joo Kim and Chang Geun Song from the Presbyterian side and Hong Gyu Byeong, Gyu Gap Lee and Yeon Suh Park from the Methodist side. The key matter of discussion was the preservation of the unified denomination, but Methodist representatives left the room, claiming that pre-Japanese denominational structure must be restored. As a result, the hard work of missionaries for actualizing one unified church in Korea never came true. Even though it all began under Japanese oppression, preservation of the Korean church as one might have been one of the best things for the history of the Korean church. Of course, it would not be fair to blame the

---

525 Yang Sun Kim, *Hanguk Gidokgio Haebang 10 Yonsa* (The Ten-Year History of Korean Christianity after Liberation), 50.

Methodists for the dissolution of the Southern Conference, since there were also a few Presbyterians who wanted an independent Presbyterian denomination. The post-liberation church in South Korea witnessed dissolution of the Southern Conference, separation of denominations and eventual confusion.

2. Reconstruction of the Presbyterian Church

Reconstruction of the Presbyterian Church was most actively undertaken by the South Gyeongsang Presbytery. This was naturally because the South Gyeongsang Presbytery had the most number of Christians against shrine service, key martyrs Rev. Kee Cheol Joo and Rev. Sang Nim Choi were both from this presbytery, and ex-prisoner Christians Yang Won Son, Nam Sun Joo and Sang Dong Han were all from South Gyeongsang Province who maintained a close link with the presbytery.

On September 2, 1945, churches in Busan came together for a combined worship service, where some twenty leaders including Rev. Jae Hwa Choi, Rev. Jin Hyeon Noh and Rev. Mun Tae Sim formed a preparatory committee for the Christian revival movement. At the service, they confessed and repented on all their past sins. They agreed to rebuild the church based on authentic theology and they proclaimed their intentions. In the same line, on the 15th of the same month, the Reconstructed South Gyeongsang Presbytery was established at Busanjin Church. On November 3 that year, the 17th Presbytery for South Gyeongsang Presbytery was held and the ex-prisoner Rev. Nam Sun Joo was appointed as the moderator. Following the lead of South Gyeongsang Presbytery, all other presbyteries were rebuilt. All presbyteries in South Korea were restored to their full operation by early 1946.

With all the presbyteries restored nationwide, the Southern Conference for Presbyterian churches was held at Seungdong Church in Seoul on June 12, 1946. Instead of calling it a General Assembly, they called this gathering a conference since it was a gathering of churches in South Korea only. Pastor Eun Hee Bae was appointed as the moderator and Rev. Tae Young Ham was appointed as the vice-moderator. Neither of them were direct participants of the denominational organization prior to liberation, so to some it appeared as if the authority was robbed from the previous denominational leadership, but the previous leadership was still very much intact since Rev. Bae and Rev. Ham were not involved in pastoral ministry. It was not surprising that the South Gyeongsang Presbytery complained of the situation. The following issues were decided at the Southern Conference:

1. The Constitution is to be used without any amendment until the South and the North are united.
2. The erroneous decision regarding shrine service made by the 27th General Assembly is to be revoked.
3. Chosun Theological Seminary is to be put under the direct command of the Southern Conference.
4. The decision of ordaining female elders is to be postponed until the united North-South General Assembly.[526]

We must note here that the Southern Conference ruled the decision regarding shrine service as illegitimate and repealed it but without any real spirit of repentance. We know this for sure because the decision on shrine service was repealed once again at the 34th General Assembly, when the Sunday, on which the decision on shrine service was made, was set as the day of mourning and repentance. Also at the 39th General Assembly in 1954, the exprisoner Rev. Won Young Lee was elected as the moderator and the shrine service decision was repealed for the third time.[527] Regarding such multiple counts to repeal the decision, Rev. Yang Sun Kim pointed out, "It proves nothing but that the General Assembly never got around to fully repenting the crime of shrine service. Certain denominational leaders were using it only to uphold their honor."[528]

In April 1947, the 2nd Southern Conference was held at Daegu Cheil Church. At this conference, it was decided that the 31st General Assembly of the Korea Presbyterian Church, which had been dismissed by the Japanese in 1942, would be reopened as the 33rd General Assembly.[529] This decision was based on the fact that security along the 38th parallel was becoming more strict, Il Sung Kim's communist regime in North Korea was gaining

---

526 *Ibid.*, 52.
527 *Daehan Yesugio Jangnohoe Chonghoe Je 39(1954)hoe Hoeuirok* (The 39th Minute of the General Assemble of the Korean Presbyterian Church), 263.
528 Yang Sun Kim, *Hanguk Gidokgio Haebang 10 Yonsa* (The Ten-Year History of Korean Christianity after Liberation), 53.
529 The 1st Nambudaehoe (Southern Conference) in 1946 was recognized as 32nd General Assembly.

more strength, the possibility of a unified Korea was fading away, many pastors were fleeing from the North to the South and the Syungman Rhee administration was being established as an indepe -ndent state in South Korea. It was becoming more and more clear that the church in South Korea could not indefinitely postpon e the General Assembly until unification of the two states.

Based on the recommendations made by three pastors in those presbyteries, the General Assembly facilitated the joining of three pastors who had escaped from North Korea to presbyteries in South Korea. Most of these pastors began pastoring new churches, thus greatly contributing to the revival of the churches.

3. Reconstruction of Denominations

(1) Methodist Church

Hong Gyu Byun, Gyu Gap Lee, Gwang Woo Kim and others, who expressed their intention of rebuilding the Methodist Church at the denominational conference at Saemunan Church after libera- tion, met together at Dongdaemun Church on the same day to organize the Committee for Reconstruction of Methodist Church. With Gyu Gap Lee appointed as the chairman of the committee, those present proclaimed the importance of rebuilding the Methodist Church.[530] Three Conferences were organized: East with Hong

---

530 Dong Sik Yoo, *Jungdong Cheil Giohoeui Yoksa* (History of the Jungdong First Church)(Committee of Edition of the Jungdong First Church, 1992), 380.

Gyu Byun as the bishop, West with Yun Yeong Lee, and Central with Gyu Gap Lee. They met at Dongdaemun Church once again in January 1946 to organize a Annual Conference and affirmed their decision to rebuild the Methodist Church. The same decision was made for establishing a theological seminary. The seminary opened in January that year with Hong Gyu Byun as the president.[531] As students enrolled in the new seminary, the reconstruction movement was gaining momentum. However, the churches numbered just around 70 and many of the major churches in Seoul were not involved in the reconstruction movement. This was because the leaders of the reconstruction movement were those outside the mainstream of the unified denomination that was set up toward the end of the Japanese occupation, thus previously popular leaders were structurally separated from the reconstruction movement.

As a result, the reconstruction faction released a statement stressing the importance of purity and conservatism as well as complete reconstruction of Methodist churches across the nation, "for the purpose of encouraging churches that were led by ministers who abused their authority in selling off their churches during the Japanese era." As such, the fate of the Methodist Church now rested on whether the reconstruction faction or the denominational faction dominates more. Unlike the Presbyterian Church, the Methodist Church was practicing a policy which bestowed more power to bishops. This meant that the amount of power reserved by each bishop had direct implications on the future of the church.

---

531 *Ibid.*

While the power battle was progressing among ministers, laymen came to the front in mediation. Mediation by capable laymen was quite successful and leaders of both factions came together in reconciliation and held a joint conference in 1949. Years of conflict within the Methodist Church came to a conclusion as Rev. Yu Sun Kim was appointed the sole bishop.

(2) Holiness Church

Along with the Adventist Church and East Asia Christian(Baptist) Church in Japan, the Holiness Church was dismissed because the concept of a Second Coming was thought to contradict with Japanese national policy. In May 1943, the government arrested all ministers. All worship services were banned in September, and the dismissal order was issued in December. Church buildings were converted into military supply factories and the like. Holi-ness believers, numbering about 50,000 at that time, had to continue their Christian faith under the umbrellas of Presbyterian Church or Methodist Church until the Holiness Church would be reconstructed after liberation.

Now that freedom came to Korea, the scattered ministers and laymen came together to work on rebuilding of the church. In November 1945, a General Assembly was held in Seoul. There, Rev. Hueon Myeong Park was appointed as the moderator. Gyeong-seong Theological Seminary, the denominational seminary, was renamed as Seoul Theological Seminary. Rev. Geon Lee was appointed as its president and Rev. Myeong Gik Lee as honorary president. Appointed as professors were Hueon Myeong Park, Yu

Yeon Kim, Eung Jo Kim and Seok Mo Choi. Thus, the seminary opened with some 70 students.[532] The denominational magazine *The Hwalcheon* was continued. The church administrative system, which had previously been separated into the board of directors and general assembly, was now about to be streamlined into a council system. Reconstruction gained speed and previously dismissed churches reestablished their original state. However, the Korean War in 1950 dampened the reconstruction effort as key Holiness leaders were either abducted or martyred. Nevertheless, their fervent passion for evangelism has made it possible for the Holiness Church to grow as the third largest Christian denomination after the Presbyterian and the Methodist.

(3) Baptist Church (East Asia Christian Church)

East Asia Christian Church, that is, the Baptist Church, was dismissed at the end of the Japanese occupation as well. In 1940, 34 pastors were imprisoned and Heungnam Court issued a decree for its dismissal in May 1944. The East Asia Christian Church embarked on its reconstruction right after liberation, led by Yong Hae Kim, Nam Jo Baek, Jae Cheon Noh and Seong Gyun Shin. At the dialog called by Rev. Jae Cheon Noh in September 1946, the church administrative system was changed to a general assembly system, and the pastoral administration was replaced by congregational administration. Various titles within the church were

---

532 Chun Young Lee, *Sunggiolgiohoesa* (History of the Holiness Church)(Korean Christ Holliness Church Press, 1970), 95-96.

renamed: ansa to moksa(pastor), gamno to jangno(elder), tongjang to gwonsa(deaconess), and chongjang and banjang to jipsa(deacon). It was also decided that the system for assigning ministers would be changed from dispatch to invitation.

At another dialog met at Yecheon in North Gyeongsang Province in September 1947, there was a suggestion to establish a working relationship with the Southern Baptist Church in the U.S.A. This suggestion was accepted and Rev. Tae Ho Woo took charge of facilitating communication. To this, the Southern Baptist decided to start missionary work in Korea instead of its Chinese missions that were already in place. On the other hand, at the General Assembly held at Ganggyeong, Chugnam Province in September 1949, the decision was made to change the denomination name from 'Dongagidokgio'(East Asia Christian Church) to 'Baptist Church,' marking a true starting point for the Baptist Church in Korea.[533]

(4) The Salvation Army

The Salvation Army, which was forced by the Japanese to take on the new name "Salvation Band" and then was forced to dismiss altogether, also began its reconstruction after liberation. In October of the year of liberation, officers that were scattered all across the country met together. An in-depth discussion was carried out whether to name themselves the "Salvation Church" or to continue using the old name "Salvation Army." It was decided to go with

---

[533] Jeong Soo Lee, ed., Hanguk Chimyegiohoesa (History of the Korean Baptist Church)(Baptist Church Press, 1990), 158.

the old name. Jong Yul Hwang was appointed as the secretarial commander, and the following year H. Lord came to Korea and was appointed as the territorial commander. Thus, the Salvation Army was restructured and all its regional commands were made operational again.

The officer training college(seminary) opened in 1947 to educate-cadets for ministry. But during the Korean War, an unfortunate event occurred when Commander H. Lord was abducted by communists. The Salvation Army was always actively involved in social welfare; the spirit of the founder W. Booth was very much alive in the running of orphanages, welfare schools, nursing homes and salvation clinics all across Korea. Above all, the Salvation Army became increasingly famous even among non-Christians as they staged brass bands and parades during Christmas seasons to raise funds to help the needy.

(5) Seventh Day Adventist Church

The Seventh Day Adventist Church also had to be dismissed in December 1943 due to their end-time theology. Although Samyu-kwon, Cheongyangni Hospital and the Publishing company Sijosa were all overtaken by the Japanese, they were reclaimed after liberation. A General Assembly was opened in October 1945 and the reconstruction work began immediately. Deported missionaries returned to Korea to expand the church's presence. Their hard work was paid off by the rapid growth of the church.

4. Establishment of Koryo Theological Seminary

The tragedy of separation in the Presbyterian Church in Korea was always closely related to seminaries. When liberation took place, in the North was the so-called post-Pyongyang Theological Seminary and in the South was Chosun Theological Seminary led by Rev. Jae Joon Kim in Seoul. As mentioned before, Pyongyang Theological Seminary in North Korea was dismissed by communists. On the other hand, Chosun Theological Seminary in Seoul were led by pro-Japanese figures and dominated by those with strong tendency for liberalistic theology. It just seemed more than inappropriate for this seminary to raise pastors, especially in the eyes of former prisoner Christians. It naturally became their priority to see a theological seminary set up in the same spirit as the Presbyterian Theological Seminary in Pyongyang, which previously stood strong against shrine service.

Rev. Sang Dong Han, who was pastoring Sanjeonghyeon Church, Pyongyang was visiting his mother in Busan. When he was trying to return to Pyongyang, military monitoring along the 38th parallel became too restrictive and he was forced to remain in Busan. Thinking that opening a new seminary is the only way to rescue the liberalistic Presbyterian Church in Korea, he met with Rev. Yoon Sun Park who had just returned from Manchuria and Park agreed to work on establishing the seminary. As they searched for a suitable building, they found Joo Suhn Kang who was pastoring a small church in a house previously owned by a Japanese in

Jinhae, South Kyeongsang Province. Kang gave them his approval to use the house for the new seminary.

On May 20, 1946, Sang Dong Han, Yoon Sun Park, Nam Sun Joo, Yang Won Son and others met in Jinhae to set up the committee for the seminary construction. When the first summer theological seminary was opened in June under the leadership of Dr. Yoon Sun Park, about 60 students enrolled. At the end of July, South Gyeongsang Presbytery had an interim meeting to discuss issues concerning the seminary. They were "given a detailed report by Rev. Sang Dong Han on organizing the Koryo Theological Seminary and the presbytery, in approval and in support of the seminary, granted the use of two annex buildings of Jinhae Church as lecture halls and dormitories for the seminary."[534]

In September that year, the seminary officially opened at Ilsin Girls' School in Jwacheon-dong, Busanjin, with the name "Korea Theological Seminary." Yoon Sun Park was appointed as the president, Sang Dong Han as the chairman of Board of Directors, and Yoon Sun Park, Sang Dong Han, Dong Myeong Han and so on as professors. At the end of the year, Missionary B. F. Hunt, who had been previously imprisoned in Manchuria, joined as a lecturer as well.

The seminary issue seemed to be progressing well, but at the 48th General Presbytery of South Gyeongsang Presbytery in December that year, the decision made at the previous presbytery was

---

534 Jonah Kim, *Chongsin 90 Yonsa* (History of Chongsin 90 Years) (Seoul: Yangmun, 1991), 314.

overturned. Reasoning behind it was that approval of a seminary was not a responsibility of the presbytery but the General Assembly. Thus, recommendations for all seminary students were called off. Rev. Sang Dong Han opposed to the such decision by the presbytery and declared that he would not remain in the presbytery any longer.

Rev. Han decided that it was necessary to invite Dr. Hyeong Yong Park of Bongcheon Theological Seminary in Manchuria as the president of Koryo Theological Seminary in order to strengthen the seminary. In May 1947, Rev. Han sent Rev. Sang Suk Song to Manchuria for this purpose. Upon arrival in Bongcheon, Rev. Song persuaded Hyeong Yong Park and they return to Seoul via Incheon on boat in September that year. When Park returned, many conservative figures claimed that it was necessary to set up a conservative seminary because Chosun Theological Seminary was a liberalistic one. Since Park was required to visit Koryo Theological Seminary, he decided to put forth some conditions to the seminary. Conditions were that the Koryo Theological Seminary must obtain full support of all churches within Korea and also that the seminary must collaborate not only with J. G. Machen missionaries but also with the mission boards of Southern and Northern Presbyterian Churches, the Canadian Presbyterian Church and the Australian Presbyterian Church. Sang Dong Han accepted these conditions and thus, Park went to Busan to be appointed as the president of Koryo Theological Seminary at Jungang Church in October 1947.

At around the same time, 51 students at Chosun Theological

Seminary in Seoul submitted a petition to the General Assembly and withdrew from the seminary on the grounds that Rev. Jae Joon Kim was teaching liberalistic theology. Their argument was based on two reasons. Firstly, theology must be based on conservatism and authenticity. Secondly, authority of the seminary must be strengthened to restore the traditions of Pyongyang Presbyteria n Theological Seminary.[535] The majority of these students rushed to Koryo Theological Seminary, where Dr. Hyeong Yong Park was teaching conservative theology. As a result, Koryo Theological Seminary had more students and gained more strength as an educational institute. In addition, in December that year, South Gyeongs ang Presbytery decided to accept an apology from the pastors who did not comply with the decision made at the 47th Presbytery regarding shrine worshippers. The Presbytery also decided to recognize Koryo Theological Seminary. With such a series of events, Rev. Sang Dong Han reversed his prior decision of withdrawal from the presbytery and returned to the presbytery.

But at the 34th General Assembly that met at Saemunan Church in Seoul in 1949, it was decided that recommendations would not be given to new students coming to Koryo Theological Seminary.[536] The General Assembly responded in such a negative manner because the seminary heavily depended on former prisoner ministers.

---

535 Hanguk Gidokgio 100 Yonsa Pionchanuiwonhoe, *Hanguk Gidokgio 100 Yonsa* (History of Centennial Year of Christianity of Korea)(Seoul: Hanguk Gidokgio Jangnohoe Press, 1992), 354.

536 *Daehan Yesugio Jangnohoe Chonghoe Je 34(1948)hoe Hoeuirok* (The 34th Minute of the General Assemble of the Korean Presbyterian Church), 23.

It was not only exclusive to other Christian groups, but it also went ahead to start its own operation without approval from the General Assembly. In response to this, South Gyeongsang Presbytery, at its 49th meeting at Hangsuh Church in Busan in September 1948, reversed its approval of Koryo Theological Seminary. This decision was reconfirmed at another presbytery meeting in December that year. The 35th General Assembly met in Seoul in April 1949 and gave the following statement in reply to questions from various presbyteries regarding Koryo Theological Seminary.

As the General Assembly announced last year, Koryo Theological Seminary has no relation with the General Assembly. Since it is against the decision of the General Assembly for the presbytery to have any relation with the seminary, this must not be so. All matters relating to the complications in South Gyeongsang Presbytery will be handled by the following five councilors plenipotentiary.[537]

Therefore, Koryo Theological Seminary became a seminary unrelated to the General Assembly.

5. Separation of South Gyeongsang Presbytery and Koryo Faction

Most of the presbyteries belonging to the Southern Conference

---

[537] Yang Sun Kim, *Hanguk Gidokgio Haebang 10 Yonsa* (The Ten-Year History of Korean Christianity after Liberation), 152.

were rebuilt without much difficulty mainly because these presbyteries contained few former prisoners and most of the pastors and elders were previously involved in shrine service. There were simply no reasons for any conflicts between the two groups. But South Gyeongsang Presbytery was in quite a different situation. Belonging to South Gyeongsang Presbytery were Rev. Sang Dong Han and Evangelist Duk Jee Choi,[538] former prisoner Christians. After being released from prison, they attended a ministers' retreat led by North Pyengan Presbytery where they announced the Five Principles on Church Reconstruction but only to be condemned by those pastors involved in shrine service. Much disappointed that pro-Japanese pastors were not regretful of their deeds, these former prisoner Christians came back to Busan and Jinju to consider rebuilding churches on their own. Former prisoners were, then, divided into two groups. While Rev. Sang Dong Han and others argued that the rebuilding of the Korean Church must be done within the framework of the existing churches, Evangelist Duk Jee Choi and others emphasized the need of gathering Christians from the outside. Choi stated that existing church buildings were "temples of the Devil and must be burned or torn down"[539] and new church buildings must be built next to them.

---

538 Duk Jee Choi was the chairperson of the Women's Association of the South Kyongsang Province and led the anti-Shrine Service movement. Later, she was imprisoned. Hoon Choi, *Hanguk Jaegeon Giohoesa* (History of the Korean Reconstruction Church) (Seoul: Seongkwang Moonhwasa, 1989), 120-121.
539 Jonah Kim, *Chongsin 90 Yonsa* (History of Chongsin 90 Years) (Seoul: Yangmun, 1991), 318.

When South Gyeongsang Presbytery first began rebuilding churches, Rev. Nam Sun Joo, a former prisoner, was recommended as the moderator of the presbytery and a high level of respect was shown to other former prisoner Christians. But when the presbytery met again, the pro-Japanese Rev. Gil Chang Kim was appointed as the presbytery moderator. Seeing shrine service participants take control of the presbytery, Rev. Sang Dong Han withdrew from the presbytery, declaring that it would be meaningless to remain in the presbytery. In response, a sizable number of people from churches belonging to the presbytery followed suit. As a result, Rev. Han organized a separate presbytery and undertook an aggressive church reconstruction campaign. This is how the so-called "Koryo Faction" came about.

The situation was that South Gyeongsang Presbytery in fact became two presbyteries, and there were two presbytery moderator for the region. At the 35th General Meeting held at Daegu Jeil Church in April 1950, there was a huge commotion regarding the moderator of the two divided presbyteries and the issue of Koryo Theological Seminary. One group of participants were trying to push the moderator standing at the podium away while the other was protecting him as the two groups went head-to-head in conflict. "The meeting hall turned into a battlefield. At the end, we had to bring police in and point guns at people in order to stop the fight. Pastors and elders were reprimanded by police and the General Assembly had to declare an emergency suspension."[540] This was "indeed the most shameful event in the 70 years of Korean Church history."[541] The General Assembly adjourned with the intention of meeting again in September that year at Cheongju, but within just two months, the Korean War broke out. To some, the war is seen as God's worst judgment on the people who caused disunity within the body of Christ.

Since the General Assembly that was to be held in autumn of 1950 could not meet due to the war, they had another meeting in Busan in May the following year. There, Rev. Gil Chang Kim of the existing presbytery was elected as the moderator of South Gyeongsang Presbytery and those supporting Korea Theological Seminary were cast out of the presbytery. Witnessing the disorderly state of the presbytery once again, Rev. Sang Dong Han decided to establish a new body of churches; he disassociated himself from Choryang Church, which was his first church of pastoral ministry, and founded Samil Church. Each of the churches within the presbytery suffered harsh conflicts and was split into two. Han and his supporters organized the Gyeongnambeoptongnohoe(Authentic Southern Gyeongsang Presbytery) and essentially declared to be unrelated to the established presbytery. This is the so-called "Presbyterian Church of Koryo Faction."

---

540 *Ibid.*
541 Yang Sun Kim, *Hanguk Gidokgio Haebang 10 Yonsa* (The Ten-Year History of Korean Christianity after Liberation), 152.

6. Founding of Presbyterian Theological Seminary and General Assembly Theological Seminary

Theological seminaries problems were becoming complicated issues within the General Assembly. During the time leading up to the split of the Presbyterian Church of Koryo Faction, there was an increasing demand for a conservative church in Seoul that would replace Chosun Theological Seminary and an endless plea that Hyeong Yong Park should not be trapped in Busan but come to Seoul. Even those students who came from Seoul requested Park to go to Seoul. While Koryo Theological Seminary was dominated by those who did not partake in shrine service, Park himself taught at Bongcheon Theological Seminary, which was involved in shrine service. Moreover, the seminary was not yet approved by the General Assembly. Thus, when the seminary urged Park to disassociate from established churches, his best choice was to leave Koryo theological Seminary and come to Seoul.[542] Naturally, those students originally from Seoul followed him to Seoul. Now in Seoul, Hyeong Yong Park decided to use the Christian Museum in Nam San(Mt.) as a temporary building and opened Presbyterian Theological Seminary in May 1948. When the new conservative seminary opened, those who detested liberalism taught at Chosun Theological Seminary and those who were studying at Pyongyang Presbyterian Theological Seminary rushed in. Those who played

---

542 Young Hun Lee, *Hanguk Gidokgiohoesa* (History of Christian Church of Korea) (Seoul: Concordia Press, 1978), 240.

central roles in setting up the seminary included Yeon Ho Kwon, Seon Doo Kim, Il Seung Kye and Hyeon Jung Kim. The seminary started its first term in June 1948 and it produced its first batch of graduates just one month later in July. This was because there were a large number of graduate candidates who had already completed three years of studies at Chosun Theological Seminary or Korea Theological Seminary.

As the seminary began to operate at its full capacity and produce graduates, many presbyteries throughout Korea, fearing that Chosun Theological Seminary would continue to train minister candidates in liberalistic theology, requested the Presbyterian Theological Seminary to be put under direct management of the General Assembly. As a result, despite disturbances from Chosun Theological Seminary, the General Assembly's direct management of Presbyterian Theological Seminary was decided at the meeting held at Saemunan Church in Seoul in April 1949.[543] The outcome was that there were now two seminaries that were under direct management of the General Assembly. Those supporting Presbyterian Theological Seminary intended to nullify the General Assembly's direct management of Chosun Theological Seminary. But this was not easy. The General Assembly was inevitably put in between the conflicts between Chosun Theological Seminary and Presbyterian Theological Seminary. Just then, Rev. Gyeong Gik Han of Youngnak Church proposed to set up a joint committee to explore means

---

543 *Daehan Yesugio Jangnohoe Chonghoe Je 35hoe(1949) Hoeuirok*, (The 35th Minutes of the General Assembly of Korea Presbyterian Church), 58.

of collaboration between the two seminaries. Responding positively to this, the General Assembly commissioned a collaborative committee with the intention of combining the two seminaries into one. Terms for collaboration put forth were: 1) the two seminaries must be combined unconditionally; major subjects should be taught by missionaries and other subjects by Korean lecturers, and 2) all employees and lecturers at both seminaries must be dismissed; the president and lecturers for the combined seminary would be appointed by the collaborative committee.

As mentioned earlier, the General Assembly, which was scheduled to meet in September 1950, could not be held due to the Korean War and was to be replaced by another meeting in May of the following year at Jungang Church in Busan. At this mid-war meeting, the agenda of greatest significance was the theological seminaries. Rev. Chang Gyu Lee of the Collaborative Seminary Committee reported that the collaborative efforts of the two institutes were unsuccessful. He proposed that the General Assembly's direct management of the two theologically distinctive seminaries be reverted and instead set up a whole new seminary. As a result, the General Assembly decided to call off direct management of the two seminaries and set up one seminary, the General Assembly Theological Seminary, under direct management of the General Assembly.[544]

Based on the decision of the General Assembly and with active support from Southern and Northern Presbyterian mission boards,

---

544 *Daehan Yesugio Jangnohoe Chonghoe Je 35hoe(1950) Hoeuirok* (The 35th Minute of the General Assemble of the Presbyterian Church of Korea), 124.

"General Assembly Theological Seminary" was given a new start in Daegu in September 1951. Appointed as the president was Archibald Campbell and lecturers were Hyeong Yong Park, Gyeong Gik Han, Se Yeol Kwon(F. Kingsler), Sin Hong Myeong, Chi Sun Kim and Il Seung Kye. When missionary Archibald Campbell returned to his home country for furlough, Hyeong Yong Park was appointed as the president in August 1953.

7. Separation of Chosun Theological Seminary and Korea Presbyterian Church

When the General Assembly reverted is direct management of Presbyterian Theological Seminary and Chosun Theological Seminary and ordered the two to be combined, Presbyterian Theological Seminary ceased its operation and became absorbed into General Assembly Theological Seminary; however, Chosun Thcological Seminary continued its operation. Those at Chosun Theological Seminary argued that it was illegitimate, disrespectful and illegal for the General Assembly to make such decisions without consulting the two seminaries. They made it clear that they would not abide by any decision made by the General Assembly. These reasons were superficial ones. Their essential position was that they thought it impossible to be on the same boat with successors of Pyongyang Presbyterian Theological Seminary, which cherished conservative theology. This is seen quite clearly in the history of the Christ Presbyterian Church of Korea, which came into being as the successor of Chosun Theological Seminary.

Chosun Theological Seminary opened in April 1940 at Seungdong Church. Chosun Theological Seminary, in its educational ideology, abided by theologies of the reformed church, and justly taught various theological ideas found in churches all around the world. Also, we secured freedom of academia for voluntary induction of knowledge, we applied historical and literal critique methods in biblical interpretation, and we supported the spirit of ecumenicalism. These were the areas that the Presbyterian Church of Korea(PCK) criticized us for and missionaries did not approve.[545]

We can see here that the theological characteristics of Chosun Theological Seminary cannot be merged with those of Pyongyang Presbyterian Theological Seminary.

In response, at the 38th General Assembly that met in April 1953 at Suhmun Church in Daegu, the General Assembly issued strict regulations concerning Jae Joon Kim and his Chosun Theological Seminary that maintained liberalistic views of theology and ignored decisions of the General Assembly.

1. No graduates of Chosun Theological Seminary will be approved as ministers.
2. Rev. Kim Jae Joon of Chosun Theological Seminary will be forfeited as a pastor. His presbytery, Gyeonggi Presbytery, will be ordered to take his name off the list and to announce this publicly.

---

545 Hanguk Gidokgio 100 Yonsa Pionchanuiwonhoe, *Hanguk Gidokgio 100 Yonsa* (History of the Centennial Year of Christianity of Korea), 356.

3. Rev. Scott, the Canadian lecturer at Chosun Theological Seminary who denounced divine inspiration of the Bible at the 36th General Assembly, will be investigated and necessary actions be taken against him by his presbytery.
4. Any members of each presbytery who advocate, support and promote ideologies of the two lecturers above will be punished by their respective presbyteries.[546]

Although this decision was a clear and necessary reaction by the General Assembly in regards to liberalistic theology, which was becoming popular at that time, this fueled a great deal of disunity within the church. The General Assembly's failure to embrace theologically different-minded leaders brought about the eve-ntual result of splitting the General Assembly.

Those supporting Chosun Theological Seminary decided they could not remain in the General Assembly any longer. On June 10, 1953, 47 representatives of nine presbyteries-North Jeolla, Gunsan, Gimje, South Chungcheong, West Gyeongsang, North Gye-ongsang, Mokpo, North Chungcheong and Jeju met together at the hall of Chosun Theological Seminary[547] in Dongja-dong, Seoul, for the 38th Authentic General Assembly. The new Genera l Assembly was held to call off all unlawful decisions made at the 36th and 37th General Assemblies. The new General Assembly

---

546 Jonah Kim, *Chongsin 90 Yonsa* (History of Chongsin 90 Years) (Seoul: Yangmun, 1991), 340.
547 In March 1951, the Government Department of Education of the Government permitted the name change of the seminary from Chosun Theological Seminary to Hanguk Theological Seminary.

declared not to "separate" but to "regenerate" in order to restore the fallen General Assembly with clear goals of freedom of the Gospel, freedom of conscience, eradication of slavish dependence menta-lity, and regeneration of the ecumenical world church.[548] With the two General Assemblies failing to reach an agreement, the new General Assembly met again in June 1954 at the hall of Chosun Theological Seminary (by then it was renamed as Han guk(Korea) Theological Seminary) and the name the Christ Presbyterian Church of Korea was given to the new denomination. The statement issued at its first General Assembly shows us the characteristics of this denomination.

On June 10, 1953, in Seoul, the General Assembly announced the process and purpose of the meeting and stated that we would contribute to new development as well as maintaining traditions of Presbyterian Churches in Korea. On June 10, 1954, we are meeting at the same place to make and confirm the following decisions:

1. Concerning the New Name: While it is a well-known fact that the General Assembly has played an important role of keeping peace in churches and spurring collaboration in regards to world evangeli-zation, the General Assembly resolves to temporarily use the new name "Christ Presbyterian

---

548 "Buptong 38 Chonghoe Sununmun,"(Declaration of the 38 Legal General Assembly) Daehan Yesugio Jangnohoe Hohunsa(History of the Constitution Keeping of the Korean Presbyterian Church), 191-194.

Church of Korea" in order to safeguard the mainstream movement of world Presbyterianism and to accomplish the ecumenical movement by minimizing all disputes and conflicts. It is theologically correct that one becomes a Christian when he/she believes in Jesus as the Christ, and this is where the churches all around the world stand. We believe that it is a good thing for us to use this name in harmony with the World Council of Churches.

2. Concerning the Statement of Faith and Constitution: The General Assembly adopts the Apostles' Creed as our statement of faith and abides by the common Presbyterian statement of faith.

3. The General Assembly follows World Presbyterian Churches in supporting the World Council of Churches and in actively promoting the ecumenical movement, specifically by actively supporting the operation of collaborative Christian organizations and other related activities.

June 10, 1954

Park Yong Hee, Moderator

General Assembly, Christ Presbyterian Church of Korea[549]

But the future of the PROK was not so bright. The majority of Korean Presbyterian laymen, who had been brought up conservative theology since the old days, found it difficult to keep pace

---

549 Yang Sun Kim, *Hanguk Gidokgio Haebang 10 Yonsa* (The Ten-Year History of Korean Christianity after Liberation), 288.

with those leaders at the General Assembly of the PROK. Later, Dr. Gyeong Yeon Juhn, one of the key leaders of the General Assembly, wrote Sinanggobeakui Giohoe(The Church of Confession of Faith), and North Jeolla Presbytery submitted a query concerning content of the book:

> ·····it sounds as though the Presbyterian Church in the Republic of Korea was set up to uphold a new doctrine. Arguing that the Westminster Confession of Faith must not be taken as it is, the 5-point statement of faith was announced. But when we look at some of it, as an example, it is clear that the biblical perspective has changed drastically. Specifically, matters concerning the virgin birth, final resurrection of believers and judgment are missing. ..... Is this really what we founded our church on? Is this the direction we are to take?[550]

Even within the Chstst Presbyterian Chuirch of Korea General Assembly, theological issues were not easily resolved. In fact, it could be seen that theological issues will pose a long-term problem haunting the church again and again.

As soon as the separate Christ Presbyterian Church of Korea General Assembly was set up, the Canadian mission board, one of the four Presbyterian mission boards—Southern and Northern

---

550 *Daehan Kidokgio Jangnohoe Chonghoe Je 47hoe Hoeuirok(1962)* (The 47th Minute of the General Assemble of the Christ Presbyterian Church of Korea), 182-183.

Presbyterian, Australian Presbyterian and Canadian Presbyterian that worked with Presbyterian churches in Korea since the beginning, joined hands with the Christ Presbyterian Church of Korea to advocate its liberalistic view of theology. At the time of separation of the General Assembly, the denomination boasted 568 churches, 291 pastors and 21,917 members.[551]

---

551 Yang Sun Kim, *Hanguk Gidokgio Haebang 10 Yonsa* (The Ten-Year History of Korean Christianity after Liberation), 288.

Chapter 3

The Korean War and Suffering of the Church

1. Background of the Korean War

Shortly after reveling in liberation from the 35-year-long bloody oppression, Koreans were dumb founded at the tragic reality of international politics. Liberation was not a prize won through nationalistic independence movement but more of a plunder of allied forces as they defeated Japan. Koreans helplessly realized how costly this liberty was by seeing Soviet troops landing at Wonsan Port, North Hamkyung Province.

The aggressive Soviet forces used the young officer, Il Sung Kim, as their puppet for establishing a communist regime. The church had already been hard-pressed to bloody oppression and martyrdom by communists since the 1930s. Now, the church found itself again at the dead-end of full-scale suffering.

Communists were planning a war to put South Korea under their regime. The Soviet forces, which came to Korea in 1945, completely withdrew from Korea by December 1948, after Il Sung Kim and his supporters successfully established a communist regime. After their strategic withdrawal, the U.S.S.R. demanded the U.S.A. to withdraw from South Korea as well. As a result, the U.S. forces facilitated founding of the government of the Republic of Korea under the auspices of the United Nations in 1948. The U.S. forces began withdrawing from Korea in December 1948 and their withdrawal was complete by June the following year. This was the first phase of the grand plan North Korea's communists had against South Korea. Dr. Syungman Rhee, a renowned anti-communist, habitually mentioned his ambition of creating a united Korea by absorbing North Korea. This caused the U.S.A. to be cautious about heavily arming South Korea in the fear of South Koreans attacking North Korea, which would inevitably lead to another international-scale war. Moreover, in January 1950, just half a year prior to the Korean War, Dearn Atison, the Secretary of State of the U.S.A. stated at the National Press Club that Korea and Taiwan were outside the defense front of the U.S.A. This effectively meant that Americans would not be responsible of defending Korea and this had direct implications to the fate of Korea.

Early Sunday morning of June 25, 1950, tank driven and heavily armed communist troops crossed over the 38th parallel and swept across South Korea. Void of any significant weaponry and lack of properly trained soldiers, South Korea had to suffer tremendous loss words cannot describe. When North Korean communists seized most of South Korea with the port of Busan remaining as the last target, God's sovereign hand caused the United Nations Forces to join the Korean War to save South Koreans. After three years of ideology driven genocide, the war came to a cease-fire in 1953 only to have a Demilitarized Zone, instead of a proper border, dividing the two nations.

2. Damages Suffered by the Church

The Korean War, being the only incident of genocide in the entire Korean history, left drastic results in all walks of Koreans. Among them all, the most devastated were churches. Those who reacted to the war most sensitively were North Korean church leaders who fled to South Korea when they learned that Chosun Christian Federation was violently murdering Christians and ministers who did not support communism. As North Korean communist troops entered Seoul, they were warmly welcome by underground communists already there. Unfortunately, there are records of Christians who volunteered to locate and arrest other Christians during the war. When Seoul was seized, Uk Kim, a member of Gyeongdong Church, hung a signboard reading "Christian Democratic Federation" on the YMCA building in Jongno, Seoul. He spread the word that he was preparing for a welcome party for Il Sung Kim and he was calling other Christians to join him.

Pastors and elders, who did not manage to escape Seoul before it fell in the hands of communists, felt extremely threatened when they saw Moon Sik Choi appearing before their eyes. Moon Sik Choi graduated from Pyongyang Presbyterian Theological Seminar

y in 1933 and was ordained as a minister, but he joined communist
s and functioned as one of the key leaders for the railroad labor
strike in Daegu in 1946. Since then he was serving his term in
prison until communists released him upon their arrival in South
Korea. Choi soon took leadership of the Christian Literature Society.
He organized a conference for supporting the Il Sung Kim administration on 21 August and forced other pastors to join in the
conference. In addition, he forced pastors to sign a petition, which
he claimed to send to nations around the world for gaining approval
for a unified Korea. When the pastors did not show him active
participation, Moon Sik Choi got himself involved in a campaign
for identifying and eliminating anti-communist pastors.

As the UN forces successfully executed the Incheon retake and
recapturing Seoul became only a matter of time, North Koreans
felt the urgency of arresting underground pastors. Rev. In Sun
Kim and Rev. Yun Sil Kim were martyred in prison, and most
of other pastors were taken to North Korea. Among those 60 ministers abducted were Presbyterian ministers Chang Geun Song, Hye
ok Namgueong, Young Joo Kim, and Jae Han Yoo, Methodist
ministers Yoo Soon Kim, Joo Sam Yang, Hun Bang, Hee Un
Kim, Sang Mun Cho, Holiness ministers Hueon Myeong Park,
Geon Lee, Salvation Army officers Sam Seok Kim, Jin Ha Kim.
To date, it remains mystery even whether they are alive. This
is indeed a tragedy for their lives, their families and the Korean
church.[552]

---

552 For detaiedl names of those who were captured to North Korea, see

In fact, those whose names are known and remembered are fortunate ones because there are even more who were martyred or abducted without their names known to us. Also numerous were those who were martyred during the war itself; even Rev. Ik doo Kim, who served as the chairman of Chosun Christian Federation for the benefit of the North Korean regime, was shot dead by North Korean communists. During a dawn prayer meeting at Seobu Chapel in Sincheon, Hwanghae Province, communists raided the church and shot dead Rev. Ik Du Kim and six other Christians. Many other pastors who participated in Christian Federation were eventually murdered by communists as well.

There is one more forefather of our faith we need to remember for his martyrdom. Rev. Gyeong Goo Park, the father of Chang Hwan Park who was once a president of Presbyterian Theological Seminary, was pastoring Seobu Church in Jangyeon, Hwanghae Province. Gyeong Goo Park was originally trained as an educator at Soongsil College in Pyongyang and became a pastor later in his life. When Yang Uk Kang threatened him to join Chosun Christian Federation, he resisted until the very end. As a result, at the dawn of the Sunday when the Korean War broke out, Rev. Park was arrested with his hands and feet tied with wires. Later, he was found dead with all his fingers and toes cut off. Bodies of the church members killed along with him were found with

---

Yang Sun Kim, *Hanguk Gidokgio Haebang 10Yonsa* (The Ten-Year History of Korean Christianity after Liberation), 88-89. Th number of those who were martyred and captured was 177. The names of those are in *Annul of Christianity* (1957), 38-40

their mouths filled with dirt and ashes.[553]

Among those martyred in North Korea, we should remember Elder Gye Joon Yoo and evagelist In Sook Baek of Sanjeonghyeon Church, which was pastored by Rev. Kee Cheol Joo. When Rev. Joo was in prison, Elder Yoo financially supported Rev. Joo's family on a continuous basis, and evangelist Baek worked with Juhng Mo Ahn for shepherding the pastorless church. Unfortunately, they were martyred by communists along with Rev. Il Sun Chung.[554]

In Seoul, Rev. Gil Sun Ahn and Rev. Ye Jin Kim of Jungang Church at Sindang-dong were martyred. Rev. Chae Won Joo and many others were killed in Seodaemun Prison, and Elder Eung Nak Kim was martyred in front of Youngnak Church. In North Jeolla Province, among the 75 members of Wondang Church in Mi-myeon, Okgu-gun, 73 were brutally murdered. Rev. Joo Hyeon Kim of Samrye Church near Cheonju was martyred with seven of his family members. When Rev. Seok Hyeon Park of Yangnim Church in Gwangju was martyred, his mother-in-law, his wife and his only son were killed by communists. Among the 180 members of Gyedong Church in Bongsan, Hwanghae Province, 175 were locked within the wooden church building and were burnt to death.

Rev. Yang Won Son's martyrdom is one of the most tragic of all. Having firmly stood against shrine service, he endured violent torture by Japanese and was imprisoned for six years. Although he gained his reputation as a former prisoner, he did not join

---

553 In Suh Kim. *Kim In Suh Jeojak Jeonjip* (Collection of Kim In Suh's Writings) vol. 5. (Seoul: Sinmangaesa, 1976), 508.
554 *Ibid.*, 509.

the faction supporting Koryo Theological Seminary but rather show-cased his deep love for the Korean church by not standing on the side of church division. Born in Milyang, Gyeongsang Province, he moved to Jeolla Province to work as the pastor for lepers at Aeyangwon in Yeosu. When the October 19 Incident took place in 1948, his two sons, Dong In and Dong Shin, were killed by their communist classmates. Then Rev. Son showed his Christ-like love by adopting one of the killers as his step-son. Rev. In Suh Kim wrote an eyewitness of Rev. Son's martyrdom:

During the Korean War, the communist troops detained Rev. Son Yang Won and some 120 others in Yeosu Prison. On the night of 28 September, they tied all of them in one rope and took them to Mipyeong Hill. Forced to walk on pebbled paths for 16 kilometers, their feet were severely wounded and the journey was bloody. Over the night, they tied prisoners in groups of ten. They had them kneel down as they were shot, stabbed and stoned. A few of them survived the night and they told me their accounts. Among them were an 80-year-old pastor, a female assistant pastor, and a young adults group chairman. Wailing of unbelievers and praises and prayers of believers were heard at the same time. Initially there were many voices singing praises and the number gradually decreased down to about ten and then one or two. The voices eventually became silent. The dim moonlight and starlight shone upon cold bodies of martyrs that night.

Rev. Son's body had bullets pierced through his shoulder and two fingers. His mouth was hit by a stone and his teeth were broken. It is very likely that they shot his shoulder and hand as he was praising and that they stoned his mouth as he was praying to God.[555]

Eleven o'clock on the night of September 28, 1950, the saint of great love, Rev. Yang Won Son, went to be with the Lord. Such a remarkable forefather of our Christian history remains as a great inspiration for those following Christ. He is also a yardstick that shows the extent of suffering involved in pastoral ministry.

The Korean War resulted not only in loss of human lives but also in destruction of church buildings: 152 lost and 467 damaged for Presbyterian Church, 84 lost and 155 damaged for Methodist Church, 27 lost and 79 damaged for Holiness Church, 4 lost and 4 damaged for Salvation Army. These numbers are statistics only; we are certain that the damage was significantly more serious than records show.

3. Responses from the Church

(1) Supports by the Church

In the midst of the unprecedented calamity, the church continued to perform its essential tasks, at least in part. When the Korean

---

555 *Ibid.,* 508.

War broke out, the ministers who managed to escape Seoul and the ministers from areas that were yet to be defeated came together and set up "Christian Society for National Salvation of Korea" at Daecheon Jeil Church in July 1950. The Society established some thirty branches across the country including Daegu and Busan. These branches kept in close contact with the Ministry of Defense and the Ministry of Society for involvement in pacification and broadcasting tasks as well as for cooperation in recruitment of volunteer soldiers.[556] When the Republic of Korea forces and the United Nations forces recaptured Seoul on September 28 and continued on northward, churches sent over a thousand pacification workers to the north in active service.

As the Allied Forces advanced all the way up to Yalu River, unification of Korean Peninsula seemed very possible. But there was another turmoil as Chinese Army joined the war and caused the January 4 Retreat. Pushed back to Busan again, church leaders held prayer meetings in repentance of the judgment God allowed for His church and nation. They also set up "United Christian Committee for Wartime Emergency" and sent petitions to President Truman of the U.S.A., General Secretary of the U.N. and the General-chief of the U.N. Forces. Gyeong Gik Han from Presbyterian Church and Hyeong Gi Yoo from Methodist Church were sent to the U.S.A. as representatives of the Korean Church to plea for support of American churches and to promote healthy media

---

556 Hee Keun Chang, *Hanguk Jangno Giohoesa* (History of Presbyterian Church of Korea)(Busan: Asung Press, 1970), 324.

exposure within the U.S.A.[557]

In January 1952, the Korea Christian Association facilitated various denominations in joint reconstruction projects. These projects, covering six major areas of Sunday School education, culture, social welfare, agriculture, economics, and industry, were carried out in cooperation with mission boards within Korea. Thanks to joint efforts of various mission boards, representatives of international Christian organizations, including the Church World Service, the International Missions Association, and the International Christian Committee, visited Korea and their help made it possible for the world Christian community to participate in aids of the Korean church and the Korean people.

(2) Beginning of New Mission Agencies and Relief Organizations

With the Korean War serving as an important pivotal point, a number of missions and relief organizations came into being in Korea. Among them, Team Mission, an evangelical joint missions agency, began its operation in Korea in 1953. Focusing on broadcasting and publication ministries, Team Mission concentrated on helping established churches rather than planting churches of their own. They also ran orphanages and Bible schools. Team Mission's greatest strength was in broadcasting ministry, which established Far East Broadcasting(HLKX) in Incheon in 1956. Far East engaged primarily in missions for the communist bloc using Korean, English,

---

557 Young Hun Lee, *Hanguk Gidokgiohoesa* (History of Christian Church of Korea), 275.

Chinese, Russian, Mongol and Ukrainian as broadcasting media.[558]

World Vision was also one of the mission agencies that were introduced to Korea after the Korean War. World Vision was set up for the purpose of allowing people to live according to the Good News and the Word of God. As the Korean War left many people homeless, World Vision was established in Korea in 1953 with its headquarters in Daegu. It collaborated with established churches and mission boards across denominations. The World Vision Children's Choir, consisting orphans, traveled around Europe and America to showcase their unusual talents and to express the deep gratitude to those who helped Korean orphans during the Korean War.[559]

Compassion Inc. was founded by Rev. Everett Swanson, a famous American revivalist. He once came to Korea in 1952 during the war for a revival meeting for American troops. When he was back in the States, the Office of Chaplains of the Republic of Korea requested him to come to Korea again to hold meetings for Korean soldiers. When he returned to Korea, he saw numerous wartime orphans and decided to run orphanages. Thus he set up Compassion Inc., through which he set up over 190 orphanages across the country and cared for over 20,000 orphans. Compassion Inc. was also involved in helping rural church pastors and in medical services.

Holt Adoption Program was initiated by Henry Holt, an American.

---

558 A. D. Clark, *A History of the Church in Korea.* 5th print (The Christian Literature Society of Korea, 1992), 353-357.
559 *Ibid.,* 359.

Originally a woodwork merchant, Holt witnessed sufferings endured by wartime orphans, especially those mix-blooded, and established the adoption program in 1955. Since then, the program has facilitated extensive adoption of thousands of wartime orphans and ordinary orphans until today.

(3) Beginning of the Military Chaplain System

One of the most significant progress in Korean evangelism history during the Korean War was establishment of the military chaplain system. The issue of dispatching pastors to the military for proclaiming of the Good News among the youths in battlefields of shadows of darkness and for shepherding and guiding of daily walks of existing Christians materialized as the military chaplain system after a lengthy negotiation between the church and the Ministry of Defense. The first form of the chaplain system came into being back in 1948, when Won Il Sohn, Secretary of Republic of Korea Navy, appointed pastors to work as counseling officers in Navy. Later, Yeon Ho Kwon, Ho Joon Yoo of Presbyterian church and Juhng Won Choi of Holiness church obtained permission of Dr. Syngman Rhee to work as military chaplains without any rank since 1952. They were given ranks as officers in 1954.[560] The military chaplain system was given a legal framework in April 1961 by Regulation for Government Office According to Regulation

---

560 *Almanac of Christianity* (1957), 59. In Suh Kim, "Gunmok Jedowa Hanguk Kiohoe" (Organization of Chaplain System and Korean Church), *Sinang Saenghwal* (Christian Life), December 1953.

for Military Chaplain Rank No. 234.[561] Ever since, chaplains have actively undertaken evangelization tasks among military personnel and have reaped abundant fruits in missions among the military.

---

561 *Daehan Yesugio Jangnohoe Chonghoe Je 46(1961)hoe Hoeuirok* (The 46th Minute of the General Assemble of the Korean Presbyterian Church), 291.

Chapter 4

Emergence of Cults in the 1950s

Although the unprecedented catastrophe of the Korean War came to a ceasefire and peace was granted to Koreans, outcome of the war was too much for the nation to bear. Hunger and diseases, destruction of industrial facilities and educational institutes, interruption of roads and communications, unemployment and poverty were problems not just for a specific groups of people but for the whole population of 30,000,000. Even Christians were not exempted from social unrest and persistent insecurity.

So, just as in other times, when the world seemed to be deprived of any hope and the reality presented with absolute despair, Christians began to exhibit their faith at fanatic levels as they cried out to God in acute desperation. In the midst of social unrest, many Christians found themselves unsatisfied with traditional religious activities carried out at established churches. Instead, many were tempted to feed their insecurity through mystic and supernatural events, that is, actual and realistic religious phenomena that are tangible and visible. In this context there appeared various types of cultic movements within the church. Let us consider a few representative ones here.

1. Un Mong Na and Mt. Yongmun Prayer

Mt. Yongmun Prayer was founded by Un Mong Na. Born at Maengjung-ri, Bakcheon in North Pyengan Province in 1914, Na quit his studies in his second year at Osan Middle School and went to Japan. When his plan to further his studies there, he wandered around Manchuria and Siberia and then returned to Korea in 1940. In June that year, Na bought a part of Mt. Yongmun to set up a private school named Aehyangsuk and to start an enlightenment movement. But he had to close the school due to Japanese interference and went to Seoul. In Seoul, he attended Supyogyo Church and was appointed as an elder there.

Upon liberation, he returned to Mt. Yongmun in order to reopen Aehyangsuk. Thus, in April 1947, he turned the mountain into a prayer mountain and while praying, he had mystic experiences of speaking in tongues and so on. Soon, he devoted himself to a full-scale evangelistic movement and undertook three types of ministries based on the "cord of three" in Ecclesiastes 4:12: ① prayer evangelism, ② revival evangelism, and ③ literature evangelism.

However, the established churches identified Un Mong Na's Prayer Mountain as a cult. The reasons were that teachings at Aehyangsuk were unbiblical and that their Gideon Bible School and Gideon Theological Seminary "devised oriental indigenous spiritist philosophy and interpreted the Bible based on it."[562] For instance, the 5th volume of *Guguk Seolgyojip* (Sermons for National Salvation) contains the following statements:

1. Confucius and Buddha were both sent by God as prophets for the Orient. They were of God.
2. In the ages before proclamation of the Gospel, some people were saved through Confucianism and Buddhism.
3. Confucianism and Buddhism existing in harmony with Christianity is heaven.
4. The truth is not in the form but in the character, and the truth is that Confucianism, Buddhism and Christianity are one.[563]

It is more than obvious that established churches would not welcome such statements. Un Mong Na organized a group named Mt. Samgak Prayer Band. Designed with absolute dictatorship, he made each person pray for two other persons and the two persons pray for other two persons each. Thus, the Prayer Band expanded exponentially.

North Gyeongsang Presbytery of the Presbyterian Church assigned an investigation commission to this and the decision was made at the 55th Presbytery in 1955 at Daegu Seomunbak Church that church members should be prohibited from accessing the Prayer Band. Then at the Presbyterian General Assembly met at Saemunan

---

562 Sung Joon Kim, *Hanguk Gidokgiohoesa* (History of Christianity in Korea) (Seoul: Hanguk Giohoe Gioyuk Yonkuwon, 1980), 268.
563 *Ibid.*

Church in September 1956, the decision made by North Gyeongsang Presbytery was affirmed. Thus, the Presbyterian Church officially labeled Un Mong Na and his followers as a group teaching unbiblical doctrines and disturbing the order of the church.[564] Other denominations made similar decisions and therefore Un Mong Na's organization was completely rejected as a cult by the Korean Church.

2. Tae Sun Park and Evangelism Center

The cultic group initially called Evangelism Center and later Cheonbugyo (Religion of Heaven Father) was founded by Tae Sun Park. Park was born in a poor peasant family in Yeongbyeon, North Pyengan Province in 1915. Orphaned early in childhood, he was raised by relatives in Deokcheon, South Pyengan Province. After finishing the elementary education, he went to Japan and graduated from a vocational school there. While working at a factory, he was introduced to the Christian faith and he became a devout believer by reading the Bible. After liberation, he ran a precision machinery factory near Seodaemun in Seoul and attended Namdaemun Church. Then, when Rev. Chi Sun Kim of Namdaemun Church went to pastor Changdong Church (the present Hanyang Church), Park followed Rev. Kim to Changdong Church. Park also trained himself as a preacher as he led worship services for his employees at his own factory. He was ordained as an elder at Changdong

---

564 *Daehan Yesugio Jangnohoe Chonghoe Je 41(1956)hoe Hoeuirok* (The 41st Minute of the General Assemble of the Korean Presbyterian Church), 48, 49.

Church.[565]

In January 1955, by chance he led a revival meeting at Muhak Church in Seoul. Taking that as a start, he traveled to Seoul, Daegu, Busan and other parts of the country to proclaim the Gospel of comfort to the people still crippled by spiritual damages of the war. In particular, the meeting at Mt. Nam was a turning point for Tae Sun Park to be elevated as a prominent revivalist. Organized by Christian Revival Association, the meeting was held in March 1955 at a square at Mt. Nam and had the American revivalist Dr. Swanson as the main speaker and Tae Sun Park as an auxiliary speaker. Crowds of people came from all parts of the country and there were many with different kinds of diseases seeking healing. Dr. Swanson led Bible exposition sessions in the mornings and evenings, and Park clapped and sang praise songs at dawns and in the afternoons to lead in healing and spiritual ministry.

During one of these meetings, Park made people sing praises continuously and led them into ecstasy. And he claimed that fire came down from heaven to burn away all sins of sinners, "releasing the smell of rotten bones burning and that odor suddenly disappeared and there was the fragrance of lilies and dew came down,"[566] and there was light from the sky. He pounded on the pulpit and blackmailed and threatened the people to repent by saying that

---

565 Some *History of the Korean Church* books wrote that Park was ordained at the Namdaemun Church, but this is wrong; he was ordained at Changdong Church.

566 Duk Shin Choi, *Sinheung Jonggio Jibdane Goanhan Yongu* (Study on the Newly Emerging Religious Group)(Seoul: Chambitsa, 1965), 19-20.

they would all fall into hell if they did not repent at that very moment. To this, many people were caught up in the mood. They clapped their hands, stumped their feet, sang loudly and cried out in prayers as they repented of their sins.

Something even more pathetic happened on the fourth evening. Park claimed that pastors who were sponsored were thirsty of God's blessing and that they were blocking free flow of God's blessing for the people. He argued that the pastors needed to be prayed for by laying hands so that the revival meetings could go on in fullness of blessing. And so this weird situation took place where elders laid hand and prayed for the former moderator of the Presbyterian General Assembly Rev. Yeon Ho Kwon and over 100 other pastors.[567] During the remaining sessions, Park collected gold rings, watches, cash and other items from the people by saying that he will build a prayer house for national salvation. Rev. Seon Hwan Kim, then a staff member of the Revival Association, which organized the Mt. Nam revival meeting, testifies that Tae Sun Park embezzled all the money collected during the meetings.[568] We can easily trace the reason for Tae Sun Park's corruption to the extensiveness of support by then key Christian leaders such as Rev. Yeon Ho Kwon and Rev. Chi Sun Kim and by political figures such as Chi Young Yoon.

---

567 Young Hun Lee, *Hanguk Gidokgiohoesa* (History of Christian Church of Korea), 301.
568 Sun Hwan Kim, 'Nanun Geuul Ddara Daniotda,'(I followed him) Kyung Rae Kim, *Sahoeakgwa Sagioundong* (Social Evil and Heresy Movement)(Seoul: Kimunsa, 1957), 163.

However, history teaches us that such abnormal form of faith cannot last long. The 65th Gyeonggi Presbytery of the Presbyterian church met at Sindang-dong Jungang Church in November 1955 and the Interim Presbytery met at Seungdong Church in March the following year both ordered Changdong Church, where Tae Sun Park was a member, to dismiss Park as an elder. The most crucial of the unbiblical doctrines Park taught was the so-called "blood separation" doctrine. Claiming that he "received the precious blood of Jesus, the blood became his, and he was distributing the blood to others," he taught: "Archangel Michael, fallen as the serpent, committed adultery with Eve and because of that serpent's blood, and all Eve's children including Cain carried the original sin. Therefore one can sanctify one's blood by having intercourse with Park because his body is blessed and sanctified. And the one with separated blood can sanctify others by having intercourse with them. This doctrine of orgies was used to forge mental and spiritual unity among his followers."[569] Moreover, he called himself "the righteous one of the east and the Olive tree of the East" mentioned in Isaiah 41. He claimed that he was sent by God from North(from his hometown in Youngbyon, North Pyengan Province) to save Korea.

The General Assembly of the Presbyterian Church in 1956 classified his movement as a cult by stating, "His teachings are unbiblical; they are not only contradictory of Presbyterian doctrines but also

---

569 Sung Joon Kim, *Hanguk Gidokgiohoesa* (History of Christianity in Korea), 274.

cause great commotion among churches. Therefore it is appropriate to classify him as a cult."[570] Later in July 1957, the National Council of the Churches also classified the Evangelism Center as a cultic organization.

Some time later, Park created self-contained villages at Sosa, Deokso and other places in Gyeonggi Province as a means to building the so-called 1000-year city. He lured many innocent Christians by preaching that 144,000 people will become a holy nation and go up to heaven according to Revelation. Those who believed him liquidated their possessions and cut off their family relations to live in the villages, only to be exploited in harsh labor for producing factory products. These products were then put on compulsory sale at the Evangelism Center for achieving commercial gains. The sect went through a series of internal conflicts and disputes. Park eventually created Cheonbugyo(Religion of Heaven Father) and presented himself as a God. But his death brought about natural dismissal of the sect and so we see another example of cults in their typical cycle.

Tae Sun Park and his Evangelism Center movement were just like any cultic organization we can see in unstable society after a war. Park's movement grew so quickly mainly because some church leaders supported him and guided him in the wrong direction. Another important factor is that existing Christian leaders were unable to fully satisfy spiritual cravings of Christians at the most

---

570 *Daehan Yesugio Jangnohoe Chonghoe Je 41(1956)hoe Hoeuirok* (The 41st Minute of the General Assemble of the Korean Presbyterian Church), 46.

crucial time.

3. Sun Myung Moon and the Holy Spirit Association for the Unification of World Christianity

Sun Myung Moon, the founder of the so-called Unification Church, was born as the second son to Moon Gyeongyu in Deokeon-myeon, Jeongju-gun in North Pyengan Province in the first lunar month of 1920. It is thought that he started attending church while studying at Gyeongseong Commerce Vocational School in Seoul. After liberation, he went to Pyongyang and attended Gwanghae Church. This independent church was known for fanatic believers clapping hands and stumping feet during services. In 1946, he spent four months in Israel Monastery founded by Baek Mun Kim. After studying fundamental doctrines, he returned to North Korea.

In August 1946, Sun Myung Moon performed a forced wedding ceremony with X X Kim , who was already married. Kim's husband reported this to police and in May 1947 the North Korean court sentenced Moon to five years in prison and Kim to ten months.[571] When the Korean War broke out and the U.N. forces advanced north, Moon was released from Hamheung Prison in October 1950. During the Retreat on January 4th of the Korean War he crossed over to South Korea. After his unsuccessful factory operation in Busan, he started his own church movement there. In December 1953, Moon managed to get Hyo Won Yoo, a man of same native

---

571 Sung Joon Kim, *Hanguk Gidokgiohoesa* (History of Christianity in Korea), 275-276.

village, to attend his church. Yoo was an Osan Middle School graduate and a Seoul Imperial University Department of Medicine dropout (his studies were interrupted by illness). Yoo wrote *Wolligangnon* (The Fundamental Doctrines) of the Unification Church by organizing the fundamentals taught by Moon.[572] It contained claims that since age of 16 Moon "freely contacted all sages in the paradise, including Jesus, and all spirits that have visited the earth since the beginning of the history in order to find the truth hidden behind the letters of the Scriptures, had intimate fellowship with God Himself in the pursuit of discovering the secret of morals hidden in the bosom of God, and fought bloody battles with billions of demons."[573]

In May 1954, Sun Myung Moon and Hyo Won Yoo officially founded the Unification Church at Cheongpa-dong, Seoul. Moon was the religious leader and Yoo was the association chairman under the common goal of setting up a religion that would unify all world religions, because,

> Christianity and all other religions are divided beyond repair, they have become as weak as they could ever get that there is nothing they can achieve······the Bible became ever more vague······Jesus died without giving light to the world······the cross cannot save us from the original sin······ fundamentals of great depth and width need to embrace

---

572 *Ibid.*
573 *Wolli Haesuhl* (Fundamental Doctrine), 4th ed. (Seoul: Segye Gidokgio Tongil SinYong Hyophoe, 1962), 19.

all religions."[574]

In July 1955, Moon and four other leaders were jailed for three months as a result of an orgy case. This incident resulted in dismissal of several professors at Yonsei University and Ewha Women's University and dozens of students were expelled from Ewha Women's University. In March 1960, when Moon was 41, he married an 18-year-old high school girl as his fourth wife.[575]

Important doctrines of the Unification Church are found in their *Fundamental Doctrines*, which include the doctrine of creation, the doctrine of the fall, and the doctrine of reciprocal balance. Their doctrines are a work of syncretism that uses biblical content as the foundation with active adaptation of oriental theory of changes, Doctrine of the five natural Element of Positive and Negative, and modern science. At the center of their doctrine is fullness of anti-Christian messages and they bluntly reject core doctrines of Christian faith. The most serious of all is that they see the work of the cross by Jesus Christ as incomplete and that the Messiah would come to finish the incomplete work and that Messiah is Sun Myung Moon. Their logic is that salvation is possible through Sun Myung Moon. The Unification Church caused numerous problems, destroyed homes, propagated its doctrines among Christians and non-Christians alike, forced people to buy flowers and other products, and grew into a gigantic commercial entity through its various

---

574 *Ibid.*, 1, 2, 6, 10, 73, 74.

575 Sung Joon Kim, *Hanguk Gidokgiohoesa* (History of Christianity in Korea), 276.

fundraising projects.

It was axiomatic that this group led by Sun Myung Moon in total ignorance of fundamental Christian doctrine would be criticized and rejected by established churches. The Presbyterian General Assembly in 1971 elucidated the church's official stance regarding the Unification Church, and in April 1979 the National Council of Churches in Korea declared that the Unification Church cannot be a Christian church due to seven reasons. In May that year, the Korean Church Commission for Countermeasure against the Sun Myung Moon Group released 16 statements concerning the Unification Church to confirm and declare that the Unification Church was no more than just a cultic sect in Korea.[576]

Tae Sun Park's Evangelism Center Movement and Sun Myung Moon's Unification Church Movement brought about serious ill effects to the Korean Church and the society. Many churches were damaged by them, many homes were destroyed, and many souls were perished. These sects are still operating in power. In fact, they continue to expand their influence in politics, economy, culture and education. It is important for us to prevent emergence of cultic leaders from within established churches.

---

576 Myong Hwan Taek, *Tongilgioeui Silsanggwa Huhsang* (Real and False Aspect of the Unification Church)(Seoul: Kukje Jonggio Munje Yonguso, 1979), 292-293.

Chapter 5

Division between Tonghap(Union) Side and Hapdong(Joint) Side within the Presbyterian Church

The 1950's marked the continuous period of tragic divisions. The Korean War left the country divided into South and North, and the tragedy of civil war was exposed in front of the world. The message left by Korean War was nothing but a country being divided into two. As the country and its people were divided into two, so did the church. It is truly sad that the Presbyterian Church, in particular, were divided three times in the 1950's. In 1951, the Koryo faction (Koryo Presbyterian Church) separated itself, followed by the Ki-jang (Christ Presbyterian Church) in 1953, and finally in 1959, the Tonghap (Union) and Hapdong (Joint) separated into two. The fact that the Church that was unified as one for more than half a century divided three times within less than a ten year period, this can only be seen as the work of Satan.[577]

1. The Cause of Division

As mentioned before when Dr. Gam Boo Yeol (Campbell) resigned as the president of the Presbyterian Seminary that was found in Daegu, the Board of Directors appointed Dr. Hyung Yong Park as the successor in August 1953. As many were relocating to Seoul following the truce, part of the Seminary conducted classes in Daegu while another part began teaching at Namsan (South Mountain) in Seoul. Many people thought it would be meaningful to set up a seminary in Mt. Nam, which used to be a place for Chosun Singung (Shrine worship temple during the Japanese occupation), where the former place of worshiping pagan gods were conducted, but in actuality, the location was not adequate for the number of students.

In searching for an ideal location for the seminary, the Seminary found a suitable location near Mooakjae area in Seoul, past the west side of Seoul. However, the location was too vast for the seminary to occupy alone, so they suggested to the Seoul Women's University to construct a campus for the two schools together. After Seoul Women's University rejected the idea, the Seminary had no choice but to approach the government to negotiate in purchasing the land in Namsan where they were currently using. As the Seminary's officials were contemplating how to approach the government, Mr. Ho Keun Park came into the picture. Park

---

577 There are more than 200 factions by the name of the Jesus Presbyterian Church of Korea. Cf. *Gidokgiodaeyongam*(Almanac of Christianity) (Kidokgio munsa, 2000).

approached the Seminary officials boasting that he knew Jae Hak Lee, Vice-speaker of the House, and Tae Sik In, Secretary of the Treasury, and that he would pursue them to liquidate the land towards the Seminary. Based on the referral from the principal of Seunghee Girl's School that Park had been influential in Seung hee Girl's School obtaining their land, the Seminary asked Park to be in charge of the project. From the beginning, Park asked the Seminary for transportation, communication, entertaining, and various expenses and spent more than 30,000,000 Whan in less than two months.[578] Of course, all expenses were approved by the Seminary's President Hyung Yong Park. Even after spending large sums of money, Ho Keun Park had yet to secure any deal with the government.

As word spread out, the story became a big problem. It was only natural that this became an issued since nothing was done for the Seminary except to deplete large sums of donated funds. This placed President Park in a bind. Some suggested that he should take full responsibility and resign from his post, sell his house to compensate the Seminary as much as he could, and he agreed to do so. On the other hand, others such as Kyu Oh Chung and Chan Mok Park, disagreed and argued that President Park did not embezzled the money himself and had no real hand on the matter, and thus, should not be forced to resign or sell his house to compensate the Seminary.

---

578 The exact amount of the money was 30,162,172 whan. *Jangnohoe Sinhakdaehak 70 Yonsa* (History of 70years of the Presbyterian Theological Seminary) (Jangnohoe Sinhakdaehak, 1971), 137.

However, the Board of Directors met in Daejun in March of 1958 and decided to accept Park's resignation and asked him to stay on as the emeritus professor. Following the 43rd General Assemble, Rev. Jin Hyun Noh was appointed as the interim president and the academic affairs were to be handled by Dr. Il Seoung Kye. Thus, it seemed to be that the matter of the 30,000,000 Hwan Incident would be taken care of.

2. The Kyunggi Presbytery Delegates Incident

Just as the Seminary's land scandal was about to come to a certain conclusion, another incident that completed the matter happened elsewhere. This is the so called Kyunggi Presbytery Delegate's Incident. This is what happened.

In 1959, the election of delegates for the Kyunggi Presbytery to attend the 44th General Assemble of the Presbyterian Church was an important issue. The reason was because the Kyonggi Presbytery had the most number of delegates, and President Park's scandal was to be the main focus of the Assembly. As a result, both the Ecumenical party(later Tonghap) and the NAE (National Association of Evangelicals) party(later Hapdong) focused much of their attention in getting more delegates of each side. Following the delegate election during the Presbytery meeting in May, the NAE party came out as the victor. Thus, among the 28 delegates, NAE had 18 and the Ecumenical had ten. After the Presbytery meeting had concluded, Pastor Kum Chun Hwang, who believed that he should have been chosen as one of the delegates, made others also question the results and the ballots were recounted. As they re-counted the ballot, it was found that pastor Hwang had actually received 80 votes and should have been picked, but his name had been left out.[579] Having felt responsibility, the moderator Rev. Hwan Soo Lee and Secretary Jae Sin Suh resigned. The following month, vice-moderator Shin Myung Kang called for a special meeting, announced the previous list of delegates void and once again held an election to vote for the Assembly's delegates.

However, eventually, from the votes of the delegates of the special meeting, only one pastor and one elder of the NAE party was selected and the remaining delegates went to members of the Ecumenical party. Despite the fact that the re-election was perfectly legal and free from any doubt, the previous moderator Rev. Hwan Soo Lee of the regular meeting of the Presbytery submitted the results of the original vote held during the regular session. In addition, the result from the special meeting held by Rev. Shin Myung Kang was also submitted, thus creating two sets of delegates list. This came about because the NAE party believed that when faced with the two different sets of delegates list, the Assembly would side with them.

In September of 1959, the 44th General Assembly of the Presbyterian Church was held in Daejun Central Church. From the beginning, however, the meeting began with the problem of the Kyunggi Presbytery delegates. Because there were two sets of delegates

---

579 *The Kidokgongbo* (Christian News), June 29, 1959.

for the Kyunggi Presbytery, they could not begin the meeting without deciding on which delegate list they would accept. Finally, they decided to vote on which result to accept. With the voting results of 119 votes for the General Assembly, 124 votes for the special meeting, and 5 votes of abstention, the delegators from the special meeting were able to acquire the majority. The moderator of the General Assembly declared that they would honor the delegates who were chosen during the special meeting.[580]

As the Assembly continued the next day, the previous moderator of the Kyunggi Presbytery Rev. Hwan Soo Lee once again brought up the issue of the delegates, prompting the same arguments again. Then, members of the NAE party Elder Hee Mong Park and Ja Kyong Kim began interrupting the Assembly by shouted that the delegates were "children of Satan" and condemned the Ecumenical party as pro-Communist, liberal theology, and Single Church Movement. Since they were members of his own party, the moderator of the Assembly Rev. Jin Hyun Noh did nothing to stop them. Even though all he had to do was to call an order to the Assembly and continue, but in hopes of implementing the original delegates list that had more of his own party members, the moderator suggested that they discuss the matter in a joint meeting with the ministrial committee and former moderators. Then the former moderators suggested that the Assembly be postponed until November and asked the Kyunggi Presbytery to re-elect its delegates.

Ultimately, following the former moderators' unanimous vote,

---

580 *Ibid.*, October 5, 1959.

the Assembly agreed to postpone the Assembly until November and to adjust Kyunggi Presbytery's delegates by having five representatives from each group and one from each of the missions along with the moderator of the Assembly. Professor Young Hyun Lee describes the meeting at that time as the following:

······even after saying that he will abide by what was decided the day before, the moderator, without asking for re-discussion, even though the Ecumenical party's members' "no" was louder than the 100 NAE members' "yes," announced the passing of the meeting's postponement to November 24. As the meeting came to this point, Pastor Ahn Kwang Kook, who could not stand how the moderator had officiated over the meeting, stood up and shouted, "This is illegal, and therefore, this matter has not passed. We will not follow the moderator and his fellow members who tried to disrupt the assembly in an illegal manner." The crowd rose and loudly cheered of their assent. When the moderator still continued to hesitate, the delegates shouted for him to step down. Only then did the moderator start to pray and end the meeting. At that time, the members of the Central Church entered the meeting room and began to knock down the delegate's chairs, and the custodian began hitting the delegates with a pair of rubber-shoes, thus turning the meeting room into chaos. Nonetheless, as the 150 members stood steadfast and tried to continue the meeting, Pastor Yang Hwa Suk, pastor of Central Church who was a member of the NAE and also the vice-moderator, came in and ordered everyone out saying that he could not allow the church building to be used as a meeting place any longer.[581]

In actuality, this was the moment that the Presbyterian Church was divided. Members of the Ecumenical Party returned to Seoul that night to hold an extraordinary session of the General Assembly and elected Pastor Chang Gyu Lee as the moderator, Pastor Suk Jin Kim as the vice-moderator, and Pastor Gwang Hyun Kim as the secretary. Because the extraordinary session was held at Yundong Church, at times they were referred to as the "Yundong Side." At the opening of their meeting, they proclaimed the following statements:

- We will follow the 75 year legal tradition by continuing the meetings according to regulations and denouncing the formal officials for their unlawful affairs.
- We will continue to honor the creed and politics of the Korean Presbyterian Church.
- We will maintain the relationship with each foreign Mission organization traditionally established in alliance.
- We do not want division and will do everything in our power to unify the General Assembly.[582]

On the other hand, the NAE Party held the General Assembly

---

581 Young Hun Lee, *Hanguk Gidokgiohoesa* (History of Christian Church of Korea) (Seoul: Concordia Press, 1978), 332.
582 *Ibid.*, 334.

in November as they had decided earlier at Seungdong Church, and at times they were referred to as the "Seungdong Side." Of the 280 delegates, 193 delegates attended, but only 95 came from the Dae Jun General Assembly delegates. In addition, Hannam, Choongbuk, Gunsan, Masan, Kyungnam, and Kyungdong sent delegates who did not have the moderator's approval and no missionaries were present.[583] As a result of electing its official during such a meeting, Pastor Hwa Suk Yang became the moderator, Pastor Duk Hwan Nah, the vice-moderator, and Pastor Chan Mok Park was elected as the secretary. The General Assembly also decided to permanently withdraw from the troublesome WCC, and at same time also to withdraw those pastors and evangelists who had personally joined NAE, even though they did not directly cause the General Assembly to become disorderly.[584]

3. Theological Conflicts of the Ecumenical Movement

The scandal surrounding the site of the Seminary took a strange turn. The question of Dr. Hyung Yong Park's responsibility started to deviate from its true nature headed towards a whole new set of controversies. It was so clear to anyone that even his supporters could not deny that Dr. Park was responsible for the mishandling of the funds. Thus, his departure from his post was inevitable. But to Dr. Park's followers and supporters, his departure meant

---

583 *Ibid.,* 337.
584 Jonah Kim, *Chongsin 90 Yonsa* (History of Chongsin 90 Years) (Seoul: Yangmun, 1991), 382.

much more than simply the resignation of an individual. It brought upon the spread of a dialectic argument that his departure represents the retreat of traditional conservative Presbyterian beliefs and, on the other hand, the emergence of a much liberal progression. As such, the issues of the Ecumenical Movement and pro-communist were brought about as Park's supporters believed that those who wanted Dr. Park out of the picture were actually pushing for the removal of traditional conservatism of the Presbyterian Church, in which the liberal and progressive forces within the Church were gaining power.[585] Since the supporters of Dr. Park were against the Ecumenical Movement and most of the anti-Park supporters were members of the pro-Ecumenical Movement, they used it to peg members of the Ecumenical Movement as liberalists or pro-communists.

The first time the Korean Church sent its representatives to the WCC (The World Council of Churches), the heart of the Ecumenical Movement, was in 1948 when Pastor Kwan Sik Kim attended the 1st General Assembly that met in Amsterdam.[586] When the 2nd meeting took place at Evanston, north of Chicago, pastors Hyun Jung Kim, Shin Hong Myong, and Ho Joon Yoo were sent as the Korean Church's representatives. As the relationship with WCC and the Presbyterian Church grew, some began to question the fundamentals behind WCC, claiming that WCC was pro-communist, single church movement, and liberal theology. Pastor Hyun

---

585 *The Kidokgongbo* (Christian News), October 5, 1959.
586 *Daehan Yesugio Jangnohoe Chonghoe Je 33hoe(1948) Hoeuirok* (The 33rd minutes of the General Assembly of the Presbyterian Church of Korea), 9.

Jung Kim, who served as the secretary of the ministrial committee of the General Assembly, argued that "the WCC is not a single church movement; it respects each creed and facilitates harmonious existence by promoting goodwill and mutual agreement amongst different churches," and that "the WCC is neither pro-communist nor does it have anything to do with the single church movement. It is liberal but only to the extent of Karl Barth."[587]

Despite some objections, the Presbyterian Church joined WCC under the premise that it would be a witness to the Gospel of Christ and work for the betterment of the world, not as an organization that promotes any single church, but as the churches' allied agency, through the fellowship and cooperation among its member churches. Of course, it was always stressed that in the event WCC tried to integrate and join all churches into one single church or if it went against their creed and beliefs, the Presbyterian Church would not hesitate to remove itself from the organization.

As a result, during the 42nd General Assembly, based upon the presentation of the Ecumenical Movement, it was decided that our church would only join the WCC in respect to promoting friendship among churches and achieving synergy effects, and did not agree to the unification of different churches.[588] Because joining the WCC was done based on these reasoning, our churches' involvement with the WCC should not be a matter of criticism.

But the NAE (National Association of Evangelicals) within the

---

587 *The Kidokgongbo* (Christian News), September 13, 1954.
588 Young Hun Lee, *Hanguk Gidokgiohoesa* (History of Christian Church of Korea) (Seoul: Concordia Press, 1978), 323.

Presbyterian Church, thus the members of the conservative "Society of Evangelism" began attacking WCC as progressive and liberal movement.

The NAE was first formed in 1942 in St. Louis and became the Fraternity of World Evangelism in 1951, which developed into an international organization with representative from 24 countries following a meeting in Woodsholon, Netherlands. In Korea, the NAE first started when 51 Chosun(Korea) Seminary students who opposed Prof. Jae Joon Kim's liberal theology in 1948 first created the organization called 'Bokum Dongjihoe'(Friends of the Gospel), then emerged into the Korea NAE during the summer retreat in July of 1952, and then formerly joined NAE in December of that same year through Dr. Erwin Rice, the general secretary of the WEF.

Those who initially joined the movement did so out of pure intentions to be the guardians of traditional faith, but the organization soon became involved in politics and by the time 43rd General Assembly came around, the officials were those who had political motivations. Pastor Hyung Yong Park served as the adviser[589] and was the actual spiritual leader of the group, so it is not surprising that the division of the church was slowly beginning to surface. The result was the division between Pastor Park's supporters, NAE, and those who opposed him, the Ecumenical.

Lead by Pastor Park, the NAE created controversy by bringing

---

589 In Gu Kang, "Hanguk NAEeuie Daehan Sogo" (Brief Survey on NAE in Korea), The Kidokgongbo(Christian News), November 23, 1959.

up things that had nothing to due with the purchasing the land of the Seminary scandal and began attacking the Ecumenical, referring to them as pro-communist, liberal theology, and such. Prior to the 44th General Assembly taking place, the NAE was already in contact with Carl McIntyre, an American fundamentalist who was the leader of ICCC (International Council of Christian Churches), and tried to persuade public opinion that the continuation of Pastor Park's leadership at the seminary was the only way to maintain the conservative tradition of Korean churches. Even Pastor Park himself argued that if the Korean churches are left at the present state, the Korean Church will become ecumenical and "division is inevitable."[590] It is truly regrettable for the Korean Presbyterian Church that Pastor Park, instead of admitting to his mistake and trying to prevent division, focused more on maintaining his position by claiming that liberal theology and the Church cannot co-exist.

One of the NAE members noted of this issue,

> During the Kyungbuk Presbytery in the spring of 1959, the fight to secure more of their party members as delegates at the 44th General Assembly was fierce······In order to outnumber the Ecumenical, the Kyungbuk Presbytery, centered among the NAE side, brought up the issue of WCC being pro-communist as their final weapon, eventually pushing them as liberal theologians and pro-communist.[591]

---

590 Kyoung Bae Min, *Daehan Yesugio Jangrohoe 100 Yonsa* (History of the Centennial year of Presbybyterian Church of Korea) (*Daehan Yesugio Jangrohoe Chonghoe Gioyoukbu*, 1984), 558.

With memories of the Koryo party accusing the remaining church leaders as pro-communist when they separated from the church still fresh in mind, the NAE accused the Ecumenical party as pro-communist in the same manner. How can this not be a truly sad event to witness? Then doesn't that mean that during this entire time the NAE members had worshiped together and shared the blood and flesh of Christ with Communists?

4. The Division of the Presbyterian Seminary and General Assembly Seminary

The division within a church is always coincidental of the division of seminaries. Since the General Assembly was divided, it was a natural course for the seminary to be divided as well. First in October of 1959, the Yundong party's acting president IL Seong Kye held a temporary faculty meeting and decided to move the seminary to Taekwang High School, rent a part of the older building of the school and began classes. With two trucks they attempted to take the seminary's furniture from the Namsan campus, but due to the interference of NAE students, they could not retrieve a single desk or a single book. However, after much complication, the Presbyterian Seminary was later able to retrieve the school register, which was the most important document. The professors were Dr. Il Seung Kye, Dr. Yoon Guk Kim, Pastor Chang Hwan Park, and Missionary Kwon Se Yeol(Francis Kingsler).

591 Jonah Kim, *Chongsin 90 Yonsa* (History of Chongsin 90 Years) (Seoul: Yangmun, 1991), 374.

In the beginning they secured a land at Taeneung, Seoul, but difficult circumstances forced them to liquidate it to Seoul Women's University, and later they purchased 17,000 peong (c. 14 acres) of land at its current site, Sungdong-gu, Kwangjang-dong 353, Seoul. The ground breaking took place on April of 1960 and completed construction in December that year. The following year in February, they were recognized by the Ministry of Education as the Presbyterian Seminary and College.

On the other hand, when the Nam San campus was no longer available, the NAE temporarily moved to Hanyang Church near the Namsan campus. Soon after they received 100,000 dollars from Carl McIntyre of ICCC and purchased a four-story building near Hankang-ro and moved to its current Chongshin University location at Sadang-dong, Seoul, five years later. As the General Assembly and the seminary divided, it was evident that the division between the Ecumenical and the NAE within the Presbyterian Church was a reality.

5. Efforts towards Integration

In the end, the General Assembly and the seminary divided. Following the division, the Presbytery churches also started to divide and the Presbyterian Church as a whole became a quarrel zone. Within the same church, pastors and elders divided, the elders themselves divided, and church members started to divide. This led to the tragedy of pastors and elders suing each other and being judged by non-Christian judges. At Seomun Church in Taegu, the fighting got so fierce that when the pastor went up to preach, someone poured excrement water over his head.[592] The division within the Church was a continuation of tragedies.

Soon the call for a unified church began to surface here and there. In 1960, the Ecumenical side of the General Assembly put together eight parts of a unification proposition.

1. The Korean churches should come together based on the Westminster Creed, acknowledging the faith rooted in the confession of professors of Pyongyang Seminary since 1920. The General Assembly of the Korean Presbyterian Church will continue to honor the creed and politics of 75 years conservative tradition.
2. The unified General Assembly will be held on February 17 at 2 pm at the Seoul Semoonan Church. The preparatory committee members will be Oh Suk Joo, Lee Gi Hyuk, Kang Moon Ho, Lee Kwon Chan, Kim Se Jin, Yoo Jae Han, Ta Johan (John Talmage), Suh Doo Hwa, Gam Eui Do(Campbell), Im Ok, and Kim Sang Dae.
3. The delegates will be the ones that were elected during the Dae Jun General Assembly unless they had either passed away or are too ill to attend. Kyunggi Presbytery will select its delegates under the moderator of the Presbytery prior to the dispute.
4. The Korean Presbyterian Church will sever its ties with WCC due to serious conflicts of ideals and also to maintain peace within the church.
5. The Korean Presbyterian Church opposes any movement even within Ecumenical that is pro-communist, pro-liberal theology, and single church movement.

---

592 *Ibid.,* 386.

6. The Korean Presbyterian Church and any other affiliated organization clearly announce that there is no relation to ICCC.

7. The Board of Directors of the Seminary found on September 24, 1959, must reform the seminary to follow the 75 year old tradition and creed of the Korean Christian Church. The board must select a president to obtain approval of this General Assembly.

8. We ask that in 1960, everyone will focus on bible study and spreading God's word throughout the nation and stop wasting time arguing over many controversies.[593]

The proposition was presented to the NAE and on the morning of the General Assembly meeting in September of 1960, they decided to postpone the meeting until the next morning to give the Suengdong party, who was also at the meeting, one more chance to come together in a joint meeting.

The Seungdong party also put out their own version of propositions. They suggested many items that were difficult for the Yundong party to accept, such as asking the Yundong Party's seminary to withdraw its "illegal" registration of trustees, removing Il Seung Kye as the acting president from the Ministry of Education's register, terminating Chairman of Trustee Ahn Doo Hwa and such.[594] It appeared that unification was impossible from the beginning. Even the Presbyterians from the US and Australia tried to unify the parties. Two leaders from the Southern Presbyterian Mission came

593 *Daehan Yesugio Jangnohoe Chonghoe Je 44hoe(1959) Hoeuirok* (The 44th Minutes of the General Assembly of the Presbyterian Church of Korea), 159-160.

594 *Daehan Yesugio Jangnohoe Chonghoe Je 45hoe(1960) Hoeuirok* (Hapdong Side) (The 45th Minutes of the General Assembly of the Presbyterian Church of Korea), 76.

to Korea in December to bring the two parties together.[595] It was proving much more difficult to unify them than when they had initially separated. Even with the leaders from each General Assembly and the missionaries trying for unification, the possibility of the church becoming one seems further away.

6. Union of the NAE and Koryo Church and the Split

Members of the NAE that separated from the Ecumenial side, called for unification with the Koryo Church, which first separated ten years ago. Because they believed in fundamentally the same theological basis, it was only natural for them to join together. In 1960, the two churches gladly joined and held a combined General Assembly meeting.[596] Here the word "hapdong"(joint) appeared. But there is always a difference between the ideology and reality. The unifying of the seminaries proved to be especially difficult. The argument was that since the General Assemblies have united, the seminaries should also unite, but the Koryo Church insisted that they had to stay in Pusan and unite the seminaries. During the 47th General Assembly, the Board of Directors proposed the following to put the seminary issues to the rest:

······The Pusan Koryo Seminary will remain as a branch

---

595 The entire content of the Proposed Plan for Reconciliation of the three missions is at the *The Kidokgongbo* (Christian News), November 23, 1959.
596 *Daehan Yesugio Jangnohoe Chonghoe Je 47hoe(1962) Hoeuirok* (Hapdong Side) (The 47th Minutes of the General Assembly of the Presbyterian Church of Korea), 35.

school of the General Assembly's seminary, but the student must come to the Seoul campus starting from their 3rd year. In addition, the Pusan campus will not accept any freshmen and the professors will inter-exchange between the two campuses, all budgets will be simplified, and these issues were voted on December 14, 1961, and executed.

There is no argument that the general principle is in unifying the General Assembly, but coming to agreements on specific details was not a simple task. First, the name of the Kyungnam Presbytery; second, conflict of the Koryo Church's leaders' legalistic attitude; and third, Rev. Sang Dong Han's proposal of Keun Sam Lee's professor position, etc. were reasons that forced the Koryo Church to return to Pusan in 1962, and thus once again the tragedy of church division occurred after only a year and a few months of unity of the two churches.

Although some desired for the Koryo Church to go back to its original place, many pastors and churches remained with the Hapdong. Among the most notable churches were the Chunghyun Church (Pastor Chang In Kim), Dongdo Church (Pastor Hoon Choi), Junnong Church (Pastor Hyun Joong Kim), Seoul Namsan Church (Pastor Won Sup Park), and Professor Young Bae Cha and Pastor Yong Joon Ahn. It is believed that of the 600 churches, 200 churches remained with the Hapdong.[597] This also stirred up some controversies within the Koryo Church and ultimately divided

---

597 Jonah Kim, *Chongsin 90 Yonsa* (History of Chongsin 90 Years) (Seoul: Yangmun, 1991), 407.

into two parties, those who wanted to sue those who remained with the Hapdong for their assets and those who did not want to sue by letting the non-Christian courts decide on church issues. In the end, both parties were only left with wounds and the Koryo Church paid much more with their attempt to unify with the Hapdong party. Pastor Hoon Choi, whose church remained with the Hapdong, who said, "any time when there is a group that has strong convictions and lacks understanding of the Bible and theological training, there is bound to be isolation from the outside and more over conflicts and fighting within the group,"[598] should be a poignant message for both parties.

---

598 Hoon Choe, *Hankuk Jaegeon Giohoesa* (History of the Korean Reconstruction Church) (Seoul: Seongkwang Moonhwasa, 1989), 153.

Chapter 6

Change in Churches and Theology from the 1960s to the 1970s

1. Controversy of Indigenization

Ever since the beginning of Christian Missionary, the controversy of indigenization existed. Indigenization is the argument of how Christian missionaries become part of the evangelized culture and grow within that culture. Many Christian scholars have viewed this concept with much interest and depending on the period, many different theories have emerged.[599] Famous Christian scholar of the 19th century Rufus Anderson argued that the missionaries should only spread the Word of God and not force any of the Western culture onto others. He was the first to stress the importance of the indigenous church. This theory gained popularity as ideal coupled

---

599 About the mission theories confer, Charles W. Forman, "A History of Foreign Mission Theory in America," *American Missions in Bicentennial Perspective*, R. Pierce Beaver, ed. (Pasadena, CA.: 1977), 69-114.

with establishing the indigenous church, nurturing the indigenous leaders, and understanding the culture of the indigenous people. But indigenization is not that simple. There is always the question of how far you should take indigenization and the concern of the fundamental Christian creed being modified to fit the indigenous cultures.

The first time indigenization became an issue in Korea was in the early 1960's. Professor Kyung Yen Jun of Hanshin University (Hanguk Seminary) was the first to bring it to light. In his essay "Can an Indigenous Culture become Christian?" he discussed about the faith and culture of Christianity. He argued that the Christina faith cannot be indigenized but culture can. He went further by saying that faith and culture is not one of the same, that the Gospel is God's Word, which is the eternal Truth, and therefore, cannot be indigenized. Culture, on the other hand, is created by humans and differs from locations to periods. Therefore, a Christian culture can be indigenized.[600]

Professor Dong Sik Yoo from the Methodist Seminary opposed such an idea. He claimed,

> I'm of my own unique person. As there are Westerners, there are Koreans. Therefore, there is a Western way of the Christian faith and the Church for Westerners, as there will be a Korean faith and the Korean Church for the Koreans. I believe Korean Christians are not and cannot duplicate

---

[600] Kyong Yun Jun, "Hanguk Giohoewa Sungio," (Korean Church and Mission) *Gidokgio Sasang Gangjoa* (Lectures on Christian Thoughts) vol. 3, 207-213.

the Western Christian faith..... Indigenization is simply to change oneself as it applies in certain historical situations.[601]

Professor Yoo stressed that although God's Word is eternal and everlasting wisdom, when this wisdom comes into a different culture, it must be interpreted and adopted to fit that culture.

As the discussion over indigenization was getting heated, due to the prof Suhng Bum Yoon of Methodist Theological Seminary joined tha discussion, the issue to take a different turn. In May 1963 publication of the *Sasangkye*, Yoon claimed that "Hwanin, Hwanwoong, and Hwan Geum are gods" and attempted to integrate the legend of Dangun into Christian beliefs. Yoon explained that the three gods that appear in the legend of Dangun were actually the Trinity in Christianity. Hwanin is God, the Father; Hwangeum is God, the Son; and Hwanwoong is God, the Holy Ghost. Yoo elaborated by comparing the legend of Dangoon to the incarnation of God. With the permission of Hwanin, Hwangeum, who was in fact Dangoon, came down to the earth at the Sindan tree on Mt. Taebaek carrying three heavenly seals and 3,000 servants with which he ruled the people with 360 divine articles. Yoo interpreted this legend to the Trinity of the Christian belief and Christ becoming man, saying that "Hwan" is "Han," namely that this is God.[602]

Professor Yoon's theory of indigenization of the legend of Dangoon

---

601 Dong Sik Yoo, "Kristogioeui Tochakhwae daehan Eehae," (Understaning on Indigenizaton of Christianity), *ibid.*, 215.

602 Suhng Bum Yoon, "Hwanin, Hwanung, Hwangumeun god Hananimeeda," (Hwanin, Hwanung, Hwangumeun are gods) *Sasangkye* (World of Thought s) (May 1963), 265.

gave quite a shock to the Korean Christian community. The discussion of Yoo's theory continued between the professors Bong Rang Park and Kyung Yon Jun of Hanshin University and Hyun Sul Hong of Methodist University. Some accepted this theory positively, while some negatively. With time, the debate over indigenization diminished, but we have yet to come to any solid conclusions.

The topic of indigenization will have to go through many debates in the future. In some ways this debate is necessary, but in we must also acknowledge that there are certain unproductive elements as well.

2. Dispute over Minjung (People) Theology[603]

Minjung Theology is a movement started by a number of Christian scholars who were persecuted during the military reign of the 1970's in Korea. Minjung Theology is the adherent of Central America's Liberal Theology and was much influenced by J. Molt mann's Political Theology. Moltman claimed that "those who can not defend themselves and are subject to injustice and violence are the poor people. In addition, those who have no resources and have nothing to gain materially and spiritually and have arrived near death's door are the truly poor people."[604] This statement

---

603 In Soo Kim, "Hanguk Sinhak Sajoeui Yoksajeok Baekyong,"(Historical Background of Korean Theological Trends) *Mokhoewa Sinhak*(Ministry and Theology) (August 1992), 34-39.

604 J. Moltmann, "Cheondowa Haebang," (Evanglism and Liberation) *Kidokgio Sasang* (Christian Thoughts) (April 1975), 111.

became the catalyst for the emergence of Minjung Theology.

Professor Kwang Sun Suh of Ewha Woman's University summarized the rise of Minjung Theology in Korea as follows:

···Minjung Theology can be seen as a result of introspection of the experiences of Christians in Korea in the 1970's through their faith. The birth of Minjung Theology came about through the Korean Christians' experience in an era filled with injustice and corruption in Korean society and politics, and their attempt to find ways to correct the situation.[605]

Under President Jung Hee Park's military regime, Korea went through economic and industrial rapid growth. With emphasis on the economic, the Korean government put aside the century-old hostility towards Japan and began developing diplomatic relations. However, a host of problems followed the rapid economic growth: impoverishment of rural communities and increased number of farmers giving up farming, increased poverty in cities, labor issues due to deteriorating working conditions, widening gaps between the poor and the rich, mounting foreign loans, and Korea's dependency on foreign countries.[606]

It is safe to say that the emergence of Minjung Theology is the result of persecutions toward many ministers, Christian educa-

---

605 Kwang Sun Suh, "Hangukeui Minjung Sinhak,"(Korean Minjung Theology) *1980yondaeeui Hanguk Minjung Sinhak Jeonge* (Development of Korean Minjung Theology in 1980s), Hanguk Sinhak Yonguso, ed. (Seoul: Hanguk Sinhak Yonguso, 1990), 39.

606 *Ibid.*, 40.

tors, leaders, and theologians by the military government through surveillance, arrest, dismissal, and imprisonment, etc. Through these experiences, the theologians had encountered firsthand the pain of being repressed and correlated it with evidence from the Bible. The needs of the repressed, persecuted, and isolated people were clearly evident in the Korean history.

But even amongst them, the so-called Minjung theologians have admitted that they cannot define what Minjung Theology is exactly.[607] Having said that, it is safe to say Minjung Theology was a temporary phenomenon that mirrored the efforts of those who tried to revive the human rights of Koreans under military regime. In order for Minjung Theology to mark its stance in Korean theology, it will take tremendous efforts of those scholars who are interested in taking up this challenge.

3. Urban Industrial Mission

One of the most important tasks of a Christian church is mission. A church without mission work is a dead church. The Korean Church, from its early stage, was never idle from the task in various areas. Not only overseas, but also at campuses, rural areas, and internally in the military, the Church has always been active in doing missionary work whenever and wherever it was necessary. With the rapid rise of industrialism and urbanization, the Church started to look towards factory workers as their next prospects

---

607 On the definition of Minjung, cf. Young Hak Hyun, "Minjung, Gonaneui Jong, Heemang," *ibid.*, 11-23.

of the missionary works. Earlier in England following the Industrial Revolution, the Church had begun their mission work towards the factory workers, and the Social Gospel Movement in America began. This movement gained popularity as more industrial mission work focusing on poor working conditions, insufficient pay, and issues of child labor started around the country.

The Urban Industrial Mission started with Mr. R. Urquhart of the Presbyterian Church in 1957, and the Korean churches also joined in. That same year, the General Assembly of the Presbyterian Church decided to create an Industrial Mission Committee. The Methodist churches also joined in with the Presbyterian churches, starting with Rev. G. E. Ogle's mission work in Inchon in the beginning of 1960. In the late 1960's, local chapters were located in Youngdongpo, Daejun, Daegu, Busan, Kwangjoo, and Inchon. There they created local Industrial Mission committees that devoted their time in researching the needs for each respective area.[608]

The need for Industrial Missions increased as Korean society became more industrialized. The churches around factories naturally took interest in such work. In August of 1969, Missionary H. White from the United Methodist Church in the US came to Korea and opened the "Institute of Urban Problems within Yon Sei University." Dr. Jung Hyun Noh, who was the professor of the university, became Head of the Institute. The Institute focused on studying urban problems and rearing the much needed personnel. However,

---

608 *Daehan Gidokgio Jangnohoe Chonghoe Je 52hoe(1967) Hoeirok* (The 52nd Minutes of the General Assembly of the Christ Presbyterian Church of Korea), 53-55.

because Industrial Missions always take on the role of advocates for the workers, they became natural enemies of factory owners and large corporations and even to the government, which was doing everything to industrialize the country. It was said that "wherever Industry Missions enter, the factory or company will be ruined." Therefore, the companies did everything they could in order to prevent the mission works from entering their factories. About this, Rev. Myung Jin In, General Secretary of the Yongdongpo Industrial Mission, lectured at the "Hearing for the Building Policies for the Industrial Missions" that was convened by the General Assembly of the Presbyterian Church of Korea and insisted that there was no evidence to support that factories or companies would become ruined wherever Industry Missions entered.[609]

When Jung Hee Park's military regime proclaimed an unconstitutional law, a so-called "emergency measure" restricting the right s of Koreans, the measure was used to regulate many of the Urban Industrial Mission works and resulted in arrest and imprisonment of many mission workers and others in support of the movement. The government condemned the Industrial Mission as if the mission workers had urged factory workers to break the law in revolt against the government and instigated class consciousness and class conflict.[610] In 1975, the Presbyterian General Assembly got together to summarize their stance adopted from the "Policies of Industrial Missions"

---

609 *Jangno Hoebo* (Bullentin of Elders), April 1, 1983.
610 "Sanup Sungioe Daehan Jungbu Ipjang" (Position of the Government on the Industrial Mission) *Bokuem Sinbo* (The Gospel Newspaper), September 9, 1797.

announced by the Central Committee of Urban Industrial Mission. The principles are as follows:

1. The theology of Urban Industrial Missions must be conducted in the manner of the Trinity set forth by the eternal Gospel.
2. Training and education for the Urban Industrial Mission workers should be reinforced.
3. Urban Industrial Mission work must be conducted as a church collaboration under the guidance and assistance of the local presbytery.
4. The local presbytery and General Assembly will consider Industrial Mission as the priority mission works for newly established industrial corporations.
5. With regard to Urban Industrial Mission works, labor and management issues should be dealt as secondary in evangelism missions.[611]

The Church re-emphasized that industrial mission is part of the church mission and that not only laborers but also owners are objects of the mission. Industrial mission is a necessary and natural choice of mission works for present-day churches as modern society becomes more industrialized and urbanized. However, it is also true that it brought about some confusion within the church regarding the methodology of the missions. Industrial mission slowly gained its place as realization of the rights of workers deepened as the laborer's awareness increased and the government's attitude towards them changed.

---

[611] *Daehan Jesugio Jangnohoe Chonghoe Je 60hoe (1975)Hoeirok* (The 60th Minutes of the General Assembly of the Presbyterian Church of Korea), 95-96.

4. Confession of Faith of 1967 and Theological Dispute

Confession of faith is confessed by individuals or the churches based on their situation and period in time. Therefore, it is only natural that confessions will vary depending on the church's tradition or circumstance. Historically, there are many different creeds, like the Apostle's Creed that our church follows, the Nicene Creed, the Chalcedon Creed, the Westminster Creed and many more that churches follow and confess to. Thus, if a certain church confesses its faith based on a certain situation, then we can consider that as its confession. If the confession does not match with our own church's position, than we can simply choose to ignore it. The matter becomes complicated, however, when we have a deep relationship with that church in which we cannot sever.

In the late 1960's, the Korean Church faced yet another turmoil stemming from the so-called "confessions of 1967." This confession of faith is called "The 67-Confessions" because it was announced by the United Presbyterian Church in the USA in 1967. When this confession was announced, the Korean Church began to show nervousness on such a liberal confession from the United Presbyterian Church with which we had missional relations. The first group that expressed rejection was the Presbyterian churches(Hapdong side). They issued a proclamation by the name of their moderator of the General Assembly rechecting the confession.[612]

---

612 Criticism of Hapdong side, Position of Tonghap side, and other scholarly pro-con controversies on the '67-Confession,' cf. Hee Keun Chang, *Hanguk Jangno Giohoesa* (History of the Presbyterian Church of Korea) (Asung

The confession caused much controversy within the Korean churches. The main focus of the controversy was the fact that the creed put much emphasis on the humanity of Jesus Christ. In addition, the creed encouraged secularization of the church, pushing the church to weaken the transcendental God's providence and focus on the historical aspects of Jesus Christ. It must be pointed out that although this confession was sufficient in explaining the responsibilities of the present church, it did a poor job on emphasizing the fundamental Christian doctrine of individual repentance of sins, importance of born again, and the ministry of the incarnate Jesus. Rather than accepting this confession simply as the confession of another church from another country, although it is arguable that this confession did have direct impact on the Korean Church, the Church was being overly sensitive in acting as if this confession was our own. The fact that the Korean Church wasted valuable resources and time attacking each other only serves to prove that the Korean Church had far more growing up to do. This serves as a valuable lesson that reminds us that even though a confession of faith is confessed based on a given situation and given period of the church, it should never deviate from the fundamental doctrines of Christianity.

5. Japanese Churches' Apology to the Korean Church

Japan's heartbreaking brutality towards Korea began in 1895

Press, 1970), 440-473.

with Empress Myungsuhng being assassinated in her quarters and dragging into the woods to torch her body with gasoline until nothing was left but a few bones and continued with 35 years of colonization. The numerous crimes committed by the Japanese up until their defeat in World War II in 1945 cannot be forgiven, even if they repent and claim indemnity for several million years. Neither the Japanese government nor Japanese churches have yet to apologize for their sins, even 20 years after our independence from them. However, during the national assembly of various Japanese Christian churches held in Tokyo on September 5, 1965, the representatives sent an apology letter to President Jung Hee Park and Speaker of the House Hyo Sang Lee along with the Council of Korean Churches. The contents of the letter are as follows:

1. We apologize for the crimes and brutality committed by the Japanese towards Korea and the Korean churches during the colonization of Korea.
2. Japan is embarking as a peaceful country and will strive to maintain it.
3. We believe that a strong relationship between the churches of Japan and the churches of Korea will lead to a strong relationship between the two countries and will work toward achieving such a relationship.[613]

---

613 *Daehan Jesugio Jangnohoe Chonghoe Je 61hoe(1976) Hoeirok* (The 61st Minutes of the General Assembly of the Presbyterian Church of Korea), 139.

As a gesture of good will, the Japanese Church reconstructed the Jaeamri Church building in Suwon, which was the location of the most gruesome brutality towards the Korean Church and its followers at the March 1st Independent Movement in 1919. Following the leadership of Pastor Oyama, the Committee of Apology for the Jaeamni Church raised 8,000,000 yen and completed the restoration in 1969.[614]

It is hard to even comprehend the crimes committed by the Japanese Church towards the Korean Church during the colonization by forcing Korean Christians to support its Imperial government and worship their emperor as a present living god. It is hard to ignore the fact that even after 20 years later, they have not officially apologized. Moreover, some claim that Korea is where it is now only because Japan had provided the foundation for modernization. The fact that after 20 years the Japanese Church has issued such an apology seems a bit late in retrospect. But their apology, as late as it seems, must be accepted in the name of Jesus Christ, and we must forgive them as they are our sisters and brothers in Christ. We will forgive in the name of Jesus Christ, but we can never forget.

6. Mission Campaign - Thirty Million Souls for Christ

The movement to spread the Gospel has always been imbedded within our Church's history. As far back as 1909 with "A Million

---

614 "Jaeamri Church," *Encylopedia of Christianity* (1986).

Souls for Christ," the Church has always focused on evangelism whenever the country and its people faced difficult times. In 1952, the Ten Million Evangelism Movement emerged in the midst of the Korean War with the intention of "reconstructing the three thousand churches······Let the Holy Spirit instigate the Ten Million Evangelism."[615]

Some ten years later in 1965 marked the historical year as it was the 100th anniversary of the first Korean Protestant martyr Pastor Thomas who was killed near the Daedong River in Pyongyang and the 80th anniversary of the first missionary arrival. With this historical importance in mind, the leaders of the Church agreed to launch a nationwide evangelism and create a committee to oversee the project with various denominations. The main player of the movement was the Headmaster of Ewha Women's University Helen Kim. What started with the Protestant churches, with the joining of the Catholic Church, the movement became an interdenominational movement. The committee decided to invite several international revivalists and held revivals throughout the country. They invited Chinese Revivalist Se Kwang Cho and held many successful revivals. Among the Korean revivalists, Pastor Kyung Gik Han, Helen Kim, Pastor Gi Hyuk Lee, Pastor Sang Geun Lee, Ms. Ok Gil Kim, Pastor Dong Jin Cho, Pastor Won Yong Jee, Pastor Won Yong Kang and many other well known Christian leaders were chosen. The effects of the revivals that went on over a one year period were soon evident in many areas.

---

615 *The Kidokongbo* (Christian News), January 28, 1952.

With over 400 revivalists and over one million people involved, it was the single largest movement in the Korean Christian history.[616] The fact that the churches and denominations that were once divided could come together through this movement was one of the most rewarding aspects of this movement. The mere fact that the Catholic Church joined in what Christians started and that conservative churches, which were skeptical that this might become an ecumenical movement started by the NCC, joined in was a testament that even if the churches can be divided based on theolo-gical differences, when it comes to spreading the Gospel, there cannot be any division.

7. Churches in Search of Unity

(1) Efforts toward Unity in the Presbyterian Church

The Korean Presbyterian Church boasted itself as being the oldest Christian body but has a shameful history of having more disputes and fights than any other church in Korea. As time passed, efforts to unify the Church began to emerge slowly. On September 16, 1972, moderators and secretaries general of the four parties of the Presbyterian Church, namely the Koryo side, Tonghap, Hapdong, and Christ side, got together at the Bible Society's office to hold a prayer and discussion session. During the meeting, they prayed for the Conference of South and North Korea's Red Cross, mission

---

616 *Ibid.,* November 27, 1965.

works in North Korea, and unification of the Presbyterian Church. In addition, the leaders agreed on praying together for the benefit of open dialogue and establishing a permanent organization for the purpose of the churches' common issues and announced the following joint statement:

Agreement between Moderators of the Four General Assemblies

1. We wish for the leaders of the Presbyterian churches to meet regularly to pray together.
2. We wish to establish a permanent organization for keeping the Presbyterian Church faith traditions and collaborate in corresponding objectives in missions.
3. We wish to confirm Bible education in various Presbyterian schools and to secure the authority of churches in the relationship between Church and State. In addition, various national activities on Sunday should not interfere with the freedom of faith.
4. We wish for our sincere prayers to be answered so that our Presbyterian Church can be united as one and passed down to our descendent s as a proud tradition, and the Presbyterian churches are to be the driving force for the evangelism of Korea.
5. We hope that our wishes and prayers are equally shared by the entire Presbyterian Church members and ministers throughout the country.

Signed by: Each Moderator of the General Assembly
Attended by: Secretaries General[617]

---

617 *Ibid.*, September 23, 1972.

With this event, efforts slowly emerged to unify the Presbyterian churches that were once united as one that went through complete division after liberation from Imperial Japan. However, there are many obstacles to overcome in order for this to become successful.

(2) Unification of the Methodist Church

Korea Methodist Church, which had been divided into several different groups, held a joint conference from November 30 to December 1 of 1978 at Jungdong Jaeil Church. The church inaugurated the Bishops Ji Gil Kim (Middle District), Kyung Jae Lee (East), Woo Hee Park (South) and Jae Hwang Kim (Central), and elected Pastor Ji Gil Kim as the Chief Bishop of the Annual Convention. In addition, they became one body in both name and reality by unanimously passing the introduced Constitution and official revised regulations. As over 400 delegates and audiences watched, the joint conference was lead by Bishop Chang Hee Kim. The main focus of the conference was the approval of the laymen's three proposals, which was passed with the approval of an eight member committee (four pastors and four elders). The agreements are: ① all committees will have equal numbers of pastors and laymen; ② the Planning Committee will give their recommendation of the staff and the affairs of the sessions; ③ the Personnel Committee will be formed in each class, and members of the committee will consist of those who are elected into the class.

With passing of this agreement, the elders' involvement in church affairs became more definite, and the unanimous passing of the regulations resulted in the Chongriwon (Headquarters of Annual Conference) to subsist to the Methodist Headquarters and the General Assembly to the Central Annual Conference, and it also limited the Chief Bishop's term to two years. Also, each district Bishop will execute the Chief Bishop's business to rotate every six months, and the Bishop will elect the General Secretary with its term for two years. With this, the division of the Methodist Church that continued for many years finally came to an end. This was the answer to many laymen's efforts and prayers for unification.[618]

(3) Unification to Oppose the Withdrawal of US Troops

When President Jimmy Carter, who held strong beliefs in Human Rights, took office, the USA pressured those countries that violated human rights to adopt a policy to respect human rights. Since President Park's regime issued a so-called "emergency measure" and arrested anyone who criticized the government, it was only natural that Korea became one of President Carter's target. As a consequence, the Carter Administration put pressure on Korea with the threat of the withdrawal of US ground troops from the Korean Peninsula. Since this announcement had direct impact to our fate as a nation, the Christian leaders could not just sit by and watch. The withdrawal of US troops translated into a weaker defense, giving North Korea the opportunity to invade South Korea once again, and the leaders of the church who clearly remembered

---

618 *Ibid.*, December 9, 1978.

the tragedies of the Korean War took it upon themselves to deal with the situation.

With plans for a demonstration opposing the withdrawal of troops from Korea, followed by an official plead to the US Government to terminate its plan of withdrawal, the leaders held a prayer session to oppose the US plans to remove their troops from Korea on May 22, 1977, at Saemunan Church.[619]

The Presbyterian Church (Tonghap) held a prayer session at Youngnak Church with over 20,000 Christians in attendance on May 25 and prayed for the survival of the Church and the people of Korea. During the service, the Church adopted a message to the President of the United States, the Speaker of the House, and the Chairperson of the Senate. The message emphasized the importance of the US ground troops' presence in Korea in terms of national security of Korea and the wellbeing of its people. They also stressed that in order to maintain peace in Korea and in Asia in general, the continuous presence of US ground troops was necessary. The message also reminded the US that the 38th parallel line, the Korean War, and the Armistice Agreement were all done entirely by the US Government and therefore the US had the moral obligation to maintain peace in Korea.[620] The Presbyterian (Tonghap) sent delegates to relay their opposition to the withdrawal of US

---

619 *Ibid.*, May 27, 1977.
620 "Juhanmigun Chulsubandae Gioleuimun" (Statement Against the Withdra wing of US Forces), *Daehan Jesugio Jangnohoe Chonghoe 62hoe(1977) Hoeirok* (The 62nd Minutes of the General Assembly of the Presbyterian Church of Korea), 119.

troops from Korea. Pastors Sang Keun Lee, Jong Sung Rhee, Jo Joon Park, Hyung Tae Kim, Sun Chuel Cho, and Ms. Hwang Kyung Ko went to the US to deliver their message to various churches and political leaders of the US.[621]

The decision of the General Assembly of the United Presbyterian Church in the USA to accept our Church's plea and to send a proclamation of opposition to the withdrawal of US troops to the US Government was true testament of our brotherly love within God. The General Assembly of the Presbyterian Church (Southern Presbyterian Church of the United States) also decided to send a message to President Carter to reconsider the withdrawal of US troops from Korea during their General Assembly held in Nashville in June of 1977. The Church, which always stood against and faced hardships head on in matters of national security, again was in the forefront displaying more passion than any other organization of the nation. Through God's love for us, the plan to withdraw US troops from Korea was cancelled. We need to remember and reflect on what Pastor Jong Sun Shin of the Christ Presbyterian Church, Sungnam Church said during the anti-withdrawal prayer service held at Saemunan Church. He said, "I'm afraid that we neglected human rights and democracy." The Church should seriously bear in mind that if the withdrawal of US troops was matter of life and death at the time, regressing on human rights and democracy is just as an important matter, if not more.

---

621 *Ibid.*, 116-117.

(4) Prayer Meeting of the Protestant Church and Roman Catholic Church for the Prisoners

The establishment of relationship between Protestantism and Catholicism, which had more of a conflicted relationship rather than a cooperating one, started with the Catholic Church's 2nd Vatican Council's new stand towards Protestantism in 1962. In other words, the Catholic Church, who once considered the Protestant Church as a pagan-like religion that separated from Catholicism, now changed their position and began to refer them as their "Separate Brethren" and began accepting Protestantism as their brotherly church.

In order to prolong their regime and in hopes of holding onto power indefinitely, Park's military regime declared a state of emergency in 1972 and adopted the Constitution for Revitalization Reform. With the so-called "emergency measure," Park's regime violated the rights of many innocent Koreans. When priests, pastors, professors, university students, and social leaders opposed to such ruling, Park's regime retaliated with ruthless suppression. The true union of Protestantism and Catholicism came about during these trying times. On September 22, 1974, they held a joint prayer service at the Myung-dong Cathedral to pray for those who were jailed for speaking out against the government. The prayer service was attended by 1,600 Catholics and Protestants. Following the Catholic sermon, the service continued with prayers by male and female representatives for the imprisoned. They presented "Our Procreation" with statements such as, "We believe that God is the owner of our history. Human race must respect each other's opinion and should not impose their belief onto someone else."

The organizing party announced that they would form "The Korean Christian Social Justice Realization Committee" with those youths of Korea who got together for this purpose. The organization that joined the committee were the Korea Catholic Young Labor Workers' Association, the Korean League of Young Christians, YMCA, the Korean League of Catholic Students, the Christian Industrial Mission, the Anyang Labor Union, the Urban Mission of Seoul and Suwon, the Association of Modern Ecumenical Missions, and the Mission for Special Metropolitan Areas, etc.[622]

The reason Catholicism and Protestantism could come together in support of the social issues was because both believe in the same God and had faith based on confessing Jesus Christ as their Savior. This event showed all of us that if Catholicism and Protestantism could overcome their difference in their creed, than both can come together as one under God.

(5) Publication of Gongdong Buhnyok (Co-Translated) Bible

On April of 1977, material evidence of cooperation between Catholicism and Protestantism surfaced. It was the publication of a co-translated Bible that both churches use. In 1968, the two churches agreed to form the "Joint Biblical Translation Committee" and began the process so that nine years later, they were able to publish a co-translated single book of the Bible that was 3,430

---

622 *The Kidokongbo* (Christian News), September 28, 1974.

pages long and included the Old Testament, New Testament, and Apocrypha. This task of combining the two books was first in the world and the first Bible ever published in the history of Korea.[623] This version of the Bible went through much revision following many debates amongst the Catholic and Protestant scholars and was eventually translated into easy-to-read Korean. In addition, they included running commentaries to make it easier for the first time reader of the Bible. The Bible accommodated the Catholic Church by inserting the Apocrypha between the Old and New Testament.

The publication of a co-translated Bible was a good example of the two churches existing in harmony under one God and set forth a path of cooperation under the Ecumenical spirit.

(6) Publication of a Tong-il (Union) Hymn

As Korean churches used different Hymns depending on its denomination, leaders of each church got together and formed the "Unified Hymn Committee" to create a unified Hymn for all churches to use in 1976. In April of 1981, the leaders who had copyrights to the Reformed Hymn and New Hymn came together to formally form the "Society of Korean Hymn."[624] The assembly delegated the task by creating committees for lyrics, music, and Responsive Reading and worked towards completing the Hymn by Easter of 1982. The assembly chose 529 songs recommend

---

623 *Giohoeyonhap Sinbo* (Church Union Newspaper), April 17, 1977.
624 *Ibid.*, December 18, 1983.

by the Division of Music committee and agreed on a total of 545 pages. The reason for the Hymn having more pages than the actual number of hymns is that there are different versions of the same songs.

The project of a unified Hymn was the most important project commemorating the centennial years of Mission in Korea. After eight years of tireless effort, it was finally completed in December of 1983 with a total of 558 pages of Hymns and 76 Responsive Readings. With the publication of this Hymn, eight million Christians who believed in one God, one Christ, and one Holy Spirit were finally able to praise God from the same Hymn.[625] The Tongil Hymn was first of its kind in the history of Christianity in Korea and is sure to set a good example for future collaboration between different sects of Christianity. This proved that our Church, which was used to fighting amongst ourselves, is capable of uniting for a common cause and that all sects can continue to put their efforts in working towards common goals.

8. Rapid Growth of the Church

(1) Movement to Convert the Entire Military

Every Korean young man has obligatory military service. The time spent during military service is often trying, lonely, and arduous for many. Because many young men face hardships, it is also

---

625 *The Kidokongbo* (Christian News), December 17, 1983.

an opportunistic time to introduce them to the Gospel. Pastor Kyung Jik Han once said, "In order to catch lots of fish, you must go fishing where there is a lot of fish." The military is certainly a place where there are many people to catch.

The movement to convert the military population began during the early 1970's. It began when the 1st Army Commander General Shin Han ordered his troops to start to believe in a religion after discovering that the power behind Israel's strong army was their strong belief in Judaism. He believed that allowing the Korean military to have a religion would strengthen his army. The Office of the Chief Chaplain of the 1st Army saw it as the perfect opportunity for evangelism and launched a movement to convert the entire military.

The churches throughout the nation supported the movement and started raising funds for a church building construction at Nonsan Military Training Camp that could hold up to 1,500 people in order to provide a place of rest for the servicemen. The Bible Society donated 460,000 Bibles and delivered them to Chief Army Chaplain Joon Sup Han. The director of the Gideon International Henderson also pledged to donate Bibles for the three million members of the Army Reserve. To aid in their evangelism work, the aid association donated 150 motorcycles to chaplains so they could conduct their affairs more easily.[626]

Following the start of the movement, a new form of baptism called "Mass Baptism" began to be held throughout military camps.

---

626 *Ibid.*, November 11, 1972.

This phenomenon continued in military camps that did not even have their own chaplain and where a private officer was able to preach the Gospel. On October 28, 1972, 17 commissioned officers, 56 Petty officers, and 449 privates for a total of 500 some officers were baptized in a mass baptism. At the 3rd Military Academy, 1,132 cadets and 473 privates for a total of 1,605 were baptized in a mass baptism held at the drill field on November 10, 1972.[627] As mass baptism gained popularity, the most notable baptism was when 3,200 were baptized at the same time. At the Army's 7528 Squad on October 29, 1973, a nighttime mass baptism of 3,200 was held at the drill field. This event was undeniably a very rare incident in the entire church history. In just four years, the number of Christians grew from 88,000 at the beginning of the movement in 1970 to 178,000 in 1974.

Since the start of the movement, the Bible Society had donated 461,000 of specially produced Bibles by the end of September of 1972.[628] The Gideon International also donated 180,000 to 250,000 Bibles every year to each squad throughout the country, and organizations such as the Asia Gospel Mission donated 200 Bibles for the commanders. The donation of Christian newspapers was just as active with the delivery of 7,000 copies of *Christian Bulletin*, 2,000 copies of *Christian Newspaper* every week along with the distribution of 200,000 copies of Home Literature Mission and many other Christian publications. Thirty thousand copies of "What

---

627 *Ibid.*, November 3, 1973.
628 *Ibid.*, February 23, 1972.

is Christianity?" written by Kyung Jik Han and 10,000 copies of "Who is Jesus Christ?" were distributed as well.

We cannot deny the fact that mass baptism that started with the movement to convert the military had played a major role in converting many non-Christian servicemen. At the same time, it is regrettable that there was no control in making sure that those who were baptized had received proper education and truly understood and accepted God. In some instances, many were forced to participate against their will. It also created much confusion for those who wanted to be properly baptized after their discharge. Even with these side effects, it is undeniably the most successful campaign of missionary work of the Christian Church of Korea.

(2) Massive Revival Campaign

The 1970's was marked with a period of rapid growth for the church. This rapid growth can be attributed to massive revival cam paigns that were held jointly regardless of the different denomi-nati ons within the church. The first of such meeting was the Revival Campaign of Dr. Billy Graham held in May of 1973. This campaign marked the single most participated campaign with the participation from the Salvation Army of Korea, the Korean Methodist Church, the Korea Evangelical Holiness Church, the Assembly of God of Korea, the Christian Pentecostal Church of Korea, the Korea Natio nal District Church of the Nazarene, the Anglican Church of Korea, the Presbyterian Church of Korea(Koryo faction), the Presbyterian Church of Korea(Tonghap), the Presbyterian Church of Korea(Hapd ong), the Jesus Methodist Church, the Holiness Church, the Church of Christ of Korea, the Presbyterian Church in the Republic of Korea, the Lutheran Church of Korea, the United Pentecostal Churc h of Korea, and the Baptist Convention of Korea, etc.

Prior to the main meeting, many pre-meetings were held throughout the nation, and the number of volunteers exceeded 1,200,000 and those who decided to convert went over 16,703. The main event took place on the evening of May 30 covering around 100 acres of the Yoido Plaza with an estimated of 516,000 attendees under the presiding of Pastor Kyung Jik Han. The service started with a choir of 6,000 singing "My Only Wish is Christ." Dr. Graham told the crowd, "Of the 50 some countries that I had visited, the Korean service is the most memorable and historical evangelical event in the 2,000 years of Christian history, and Korea is most inspirational in many spiritual aspects."[629] After his sermon, when Dr. Graham asked those who were ready to receive God to stand up, over 20,000 stood resulting in a climatic end to the first day. During the introduction under the slogan "50 Million to Christ," Pastor Han told the crowd that "through this historical event, we, the 50 million Koreans, should pray for the Holy Spirit to help us love one another, and create a pure and beautiful united country." During his visit, Dr. Billy Graham visited President Jung Hee Park and presented him with a Bible. He suggested that he pray for President Park, and they prayed together for about three minutes. The number of new Christians from this campaign is

---

629 *Ibid.*, June 2, 1973.

recorded to be estimated at about 37,000.[630]

In August of 1974, the Campaign of Explosion (the 3rd Holy Spirit Explosion) was held at the Yoido Plaza, sponsored by the Campus Crusade for Christ of Korea. With the slogan of "Jesus Revolution—the 3rd Holy Spirit Explosion," President Bill Bright of International Campus Crusade for Christ, along with many notable speakers, was invited to speak at the event. The campaign was attended by over 3,000 people from 90 different countries. What set this campaign apart was that this was not meant to be a one-time event, but rather this event served as an introduction to the missionary training that followed.

In August of 1977, the "Campaign of" 77 National Evangelization" was held at Yoido Plaza. The planning committee had worked on this event for three years and had held some 70 district campaigns. For the first time, a choir of 10,000 plus were organized for the campaign. The initial idea came following Dr. Graham's Campaign in 1973 and the Explosion Campaign in 1974 with the realization for the need of a national evangelization planned and executed by Koreans. Under the leadership of the Council of Revivalists of Korea (President Pastor Hyun Guen Shin), they planned to hold the event on the 70th anniversary of the Great Revival of 1907. Over 800,000 showed up on the first day, and 300,000 stayed overnight praying for the nation and people.[631]

The result of these massive campaigns of the 1970's had positive

---

630 *Giohoeyonhap Sinbo* (Church Union Newspaper), June 10, 1973.
631 *The Kidokongbo* (Christian News), August 20, 1977.

impacts on the growth of the Korean churches. According to the Institute of Korean Religions, among the population of 37 million, 80% (29,180,000) had a religion and of these 80%, 7,014,000 were Christians, which accounted for 28% of the total population by the end of the 1970's. Within the Christian population, 47% (2,870,000) were Presbyterian.[632]

No one can deny the impact of these massive campaigns on the growth of the Korean church. However, criticisms of these events were also prevalent as much as the supporters of the events. Some argue that the reason why millions of people gathered was to voice their discontentment with the current church, government, and social issues.[633] Since the events were held with the approval of the military regime, the real issues were never addressed nor were the main arguments voiced. The events were criticized because it did not speak out against the current government and it ignored those who were repressed by the government for speaking out. It only preached God's Word and did little to help those with real needs. Dismissed professor Chan Kuk Kim criticized the event by saying, "Although God's Words were preached at the May 16th campaign, the campaign in whole totally ignored the real issue on hand. Furthermore, the event ignored those who were in jail for fighting for human rights and little if nothing was done to either pray for them or collect any donations for their benefit."[634]

---

632 *Ibid.*, June 28, 1980.
633 *Giohoeyonhap Sinbo* (Church Union Newspaper), June 10, 1973.
634 Chan Kuk Kim, "Yoido Daejiphoewa Keumyo Gidohoe,"(Great Gathering at Yoido and Prayer Meeting on Friday), *The Kidokongbo* (Christian News),

There must be an analysis of the reasons behind the rapid growth of the Church in the 1970's. Professor Kyung Bae Min points out two things as the main reasons. The first reason was the strong participation of public affairs, and the second reason was the numerical growth of the conservative groups through the Evangelical Charismatic Movement.[635] In other words, when mass communication and universities could not carry their social responsibilities, the Church took it upon itself to fight for human rights and social injustice under the military regime, even risking imprisonment. It was only natural for the public to "develop a certain moral fascination of the courage, discernment, and foresight of those intellectuals, and the churches were able to accept the Christians who were serving as assistants in the intellectual communities as the new power within the church."[636]

The other reason was as people became more materialistic with the economic growth, people began searching for ways to fulfill their souls and minds that could not be filled with material things. It was just as Dr. Billy Graham had told President Park, "No matter how much you have materially, if you have no peace in your soul, you are truly poor and unhappy." Many people began searching to fill that void and found religion as the answer. It is safe to say that the Church had perfect timing.

It is true that the churches lacked the resources to educate the increasing numbers of their believers. The Catholic Church had

---

March 1, 1980.
635 *Ibid.*, December 22, 1979.
636 *Ibid.*

sharp criticisms in this respect pointing out the fact that "the problem is the quality, not quantity. In order words, there may be an increased number of churchgoers, but the truly baptized Christians are less than half of the total."[637] The quality growth that cannot keep up with the quantity growth is one of the most serious problems of the Korean Church.

9. Resistant against President Park's Regime

(1) Creation of the National Christian Coalition of Justice of Clergies

Since the beginning of Jung Hee Park's military regime, conflict between the regime and the Church grew more over time. The first time the Church and Government came face to face was in 1965 when the Korean Government pushed for a Korea-Japan Conference and the Church opposed it. Things escalated when Park tried to serve as president for the 3rd term by changing the constitution. In order to rule continuously, Park passed the Constitution for Revitalizing Reform, declared an "emergency measure," and began to repress anyone who opposed his government, whether they were regular citizens, students, priest, pastors, or educators. The Church could not sit idly around and do nothing.

The coalition was made up of 321 members from eight different

---

637 Suk Wu Choi, "Hanguk Singugioeui Mannam"(Meeting between the Roman Catholic and Protestant), *Hanguk Gidokgiosa Yongu* (Study on the Korean Church History) (February 1986), 5.

denominations of the Protestant Church in Korea. They held their first meeting on March 20, 1975, at Seoul Yundong Presbyterian Church with 120 clergymen in attendance. The members elected Yundong Church's Pastor Hyung Tae Kim as their leader and Shin Myung Kang, Won Yong Kang, and Gwan Suk Kim as the advisors and Pastor Seung Hyuk Cho as the Secretary General.

In their proclamation, they pointed out that the current regime was abusing their power for the benefit of a chosen few through the use of propaganda and repression and that they would speak out and spread the Gospel to prevent what happened to Sodom and Gomorrah from happening to Korea.[638]

In addition, they concluded that the Church was part to blame in the social injustice as this was result of the Church not fulfilling their purpose of spreading God's Word. They vowed to be friends of those who were persecuted and repressed and to fight for their rights. They also stressed that the clergymen were not the enemies of the politicians, but rather that they were the voice of reason, just as how Prophet Nathan had served King David. Also, if the politicians ignored the advice of the clergymen and continued with repressing the weak, then they would have no choice but to fight in cooperation with society's conscience groups.

The members of this coalition was made up of 80 pastors from the Presbyterian Church of Korea, and 352 pastors from the Methodist Church, Anglican Church, Gospel Church, Salvation Army, Holiness Church, and Lutheran Church, etc. These clergymen, who

---

638 *The Kidokongbo* (Christian News), March 29, 1975.

stood up to set the standards of social justice, became the light of hope during these dark times.

(2) Proclamation of the Presbyterian Church (Tonghap) Manifesto to the Government

In the midst of prayer events that took place for those who were jailed for participating in the Industrial Mission work or while opposing the Constitution for Revitalizing Reform, the Presbyterian Church held their own prayer service in honor of their affiliated Pastors Myung Jin In and Young Keun Ko's release at Yundong Church on July 25, 1978. Approximately 200 persons, including 30 moderators of each presbytery and chairpersons of the institutions that belong to the General Assembly, gathered to pray for their release. During the service, they issued a manifesto and the contents are as follows:

1. The present situation that our Church faces has reached a critical point based on national harmony. The current government who places emphasis on the importance of economical growth as the tool for unification of the country has created an unhealthy society in which material greed and competition has reached an unhealthy level. Both the Church and the Government should recognize the need to be more respectable of each other while abiding by the fundamentals of our government and the separation of Church from the State.
2. To preserve the safety and growth of the Church, the Government should allow the Church to deal with those who must be legally

dealt with by allowing indictment without physical restraint and let the denomination handle them on their own terms. This will be a shortcut to achieving unity.

3. Government officials must realize that restricting the work of the Church is the same as confusing the Word of God with words for the preacher and punishing God's Word as violation of the special measure section.

4. We all need to feel the need for a joint committee of Church and State in order to facilitate a healthy communication to settle recent misunderstandings and conflicts surrounding the Church's Industrial Mission works.[639]

The manifesto ended with a request to the government for the release of all human rights activists and religious officials since the August 15th Independence. With this manifesto, the Presbyterian Church sent a clear message of their view towards the government.

(3) NCC's Resolution for Freedom of Mission Work

On May 8, 1975, a national meeting of the leaders of the six denominations of the NCC affiliated was held at the Christian Academy House. During the meeting, they pledged to "Do everything in their power to show a united execution of mission work and to maintain the freedom to do so." Also, the meeting asked to release those restrained ministers who were accused with abusing the mission fund, and announced the following agreement.

---

639 *Ibid.*, July 22, 1978.

Agreement

1. We will notify all of the churches of today's historical meeting.
2. To rid of any misunderstanding and false rumors about WCC and NCC, we will clarify our usual stand and claims.
3. We will submit an agreement to the President and try to arrange a meeting between the President and moderators of the six denominations.
4. We will point out the problems to the Government regarding the arrests of NCC Secretary General Kwan Suk Kim, Hyung Gyu Park, Seung Hyuk Cho, and Ho Kyong Kwon and ask for their release.
5. We will also address the problem of interfering with Sunday worship, especially with the recent event of arresting the presiding pastor 30 minutes before the service time.
6. NCC will send materials regarding the recent arrests of religious leaders and other necessary documents to churches around the nation. In addition, the restraint of NCC Secretary General Kim Kwan Suk and members of the Committee of Special Metropolitan Area Mission will be handled by NCC's Temporary Measures Committee for Freedom of Mission Work.[640]

May 8, 1975

The fact that the churches could voice their opinions toward the government when their religious freedom and the ability to do mission work were threatened meant that the Korean Church did not ignore social issues and did not choose to remain silent.

---

640 *Giohoeyonhap Sinbo* (Church Union Newspaper), May 18, 1975.

10. Feminism Movement in the Korean Church

(1) The Rise of the Korean Feminism Movement

The women of Korea were traditionally oppressed and discriminated against based on the Confucian society which stressed paternalism. Through churches, women's rights improved somewhat and women began to mark their place in society. This, however, was truer in theory than in actuality.

The place where discrimination against women was more prevalent than anywhere else was at the workplace. The movement that opposed such treatment first came about from the Dongil Textile Company. The labor union for the company was first founded in 1946 and by 1960 all labor leaders were men, despite the fact that there were only 200 male laborers compared to 1,300 female laborers. In 1972, the dynamics were disturbed when a woman became the union leader for the first time in the company's history. The main reason why this was possible was through the mission work of female Pastor Hwa Soon Cho from 1966. Pastor Cho brought about change in the mind set of the laborers by including women in Bible study and various group activities.[641]

In addition, the event that marked the beginning of the end of Park's military regime was the "YH Union Incident," which was organized by women laborers. This was one of the most signi-

---

641 Wu Jung Lee, "Hanguk Gidokgio Yeosuhngundong,"(Feminine Movement in Korean Christianity), *Gidokgio Daeyongam*(Alamnac of Christianity)(1986), 76-80.

ficant incidents in the history of the Korean labor movement and marked the beginning of the women's movement in Korea as all of the organizers, Director Young Soon Choi, Deputy Director Soon Joo Lee, and Chief Officer Tae Yun Park, were all female Christians who received training through industrial missions.

The development of women's theology in the West influenced the Korean Church and society by increasing women's historical and social consciousness in the 1970's. This trend showed its formal self in the creation of the "Women's Association of the Korean Church" on April of 1976. The Association was made up of the six denominations, such as the Presbyterian Church (Tonghap), the Lutheran Church, the Methodist Church, and the Salvation Army. The Association began raising its voice in a broad range of issues, such as the end for gender discrimination, racial discrimination in the US and Japan, Nuclear Weapons, and environmental issues, etc.

YMCA also participated by addressing the issue of family law reform, consumer rights, working women's rights, opening classes for working mothers, and many other things that were worthy causes to the women's movement. These series of events helped spark the women's movement in Korea.

(2) Association of Women Theologians of Korea

With the intention of securing a place for women in the world of Christianity that has become male dominated and to change the role of women as a key member of the community from simply being an assistant, the Association of Women of Korean Church held its first meeting of women theologians in January of 1979. It was decided during this meeting to create an Association of Women Theologians of Korea and was created in April of 1980 with Professor Soon Kyung Park of Ewha Women's University as their president. The purpose of this association was for all women theologians to come together to enhance their integrity, form a theology for women, contribute to mission work, and cultivate peace and justice.[642]

The criteria for membership were limited to those who had former theological education or current women religious workers. The association was made of eight committees: planning, education, theology, pastoral, PR publications, PR, society, and finance. The association vowed to concentrate on studying how female Christians deal with the issues of church and society, how they would plan the future, and to educate women so that they can contribute to a future society where freedom, love, and peace exists. The association tried to progress from being a male-centered church operation to bring the creation order of cooperation between male and female towards mission work and volunteer service work.

(3) Realization of the Ordination of Women

Is clergy only for men? Is it impossible for women to serve as clergy? Is it not possible for women to be ordained even as

---

642 *Christian Sinmun*, November 28, 1987.

an elder? These are all arguments that have been ongoing throughout the church's history. The Catholic Church clearly forbids the appointment of women for any type of religious post. But the Protestant churches vary in its stance depending on their denomination. In the US, for example, the Cumberland Presbyterian Church had confirmed Louisa L. Woosley back in 1889 for the first time in the history of the Presbyterian Church. Also in the 1950's, the Northern Presbyterian Church and in the 1960's, the Southern Presbyterian Church have confirmed and allowed women to become their pastors.[643]

In Korea, however, where it is quite different from the US, the issue of women holding a religious post is far more complicated than just biblical and theological implications. It has far more implication as a social issue. Some Korean churches, however, did grant ordination for women as the Methodist Church has done in the 1930's, followed by the Christ Presbyterian Church, the Assembly of God Church, and the Pentecostal Holiness Church. The Episcopal Church also decided to allow religious posts to women during their International Episcopal Church meeting in July of 1988.[644]

The Presbyterian Church of Korea(Tonghap), the largest denomination in Korea, has yet to allow women to hold any ordained

---

643 In Soo Kim, "Yeosuhngwa Yeosuhng Ansooeui Eehaeeudaehan Giohoesajeok Gochal,"(Study on the Female and Female Ordination), *Gioyokwa Yeosuhng Ansoo* (Ministry and Female Ordination) (Jangnohoe Sinhakdaehak Press, 1992), 27-34.

644 *Gidokgio Sinmun* (Christian Newspaper), September 25, 1988.

post and thus holds the interests of many within the denomination as well as the Christian community as a whole. The Association of Theologians of Women of Korea has held seminars and asked the Presbyterian Church to allow women to hold ordained posts and to reform its discriminating policy. Even the Association of the Women Evangelists of Presbyterian Church(Tonghap) put out a statement asking the Church to change its policy and stressed the urgency of the matter. Finally, these successions of trials and efforts for women ordination bore its fruit. In 1994, the General Assembly of the Presbyterian Church(Tonghap) decided for the ordination of women with absolute majority for the first time in the history of the Church. This issue needed the change of their constitution; therefore, it had to be consented with the majority of each presbytery. Since the majority of Presbyteries consented to the resolution, it was realized at last. This was a meaningful event in the 100 years of the Presbyterian Church history. It provided for the overcoming of gender discrimination and the working together of male and female equally for the church and society.

11. Closing of a Century of Missions

(1) Centennial Anniversary of the Korean Church Mission

The first time a Protestant missionary came to Korea was when the United States' Northern Presbyterian Missionary Dr. Horace N. Allen came to Korea in 1884. If we use this as the beginning of the Korean Church Mission, then 1984 is the 100th anniversary.

Although there were some arguments in using 1884 as the start, but with the majority of the denominations in agreement, it was decided that 1984 would be celebrated as the 100th year anniversary and planned on holding lavish celebrations.

In December 1980, the committee of the 100th year anniversary celebration promotion was formed with the NCC's arrangement, and Pastor Chi Soon Park, moderator of the Presbyterian Church (Tonghap), was elected as the head for the committee. In September of the following year, the formal planning committee was formed and Pastor Park was elected as the chairman and Senior Pastor Kyung Jik Han of Youngnak Church was elected as the president. The committee was attended by representatives of 20 denominations and 25 Christian organizations. The main items on the agenda were:

1) 100th year Commemorative Mission Conference from August 15-19, 1984, at Yoido Plaza
2) construction of a commemorative center
3) holding a commemorative conference, memorial worship for martyrs, art fair celebration, and educational conference;
4) campaign to spread love
5) construction of a commemorative church.

The 100th year anniversary conference opened its historical curtain on the evening of August 15, 1984. The event kicked off with an evening of reconciliation and cooperation for the first day, renewal and the growth of the Church for the second day, evening of peace and unification of Korea for the third day, and finished off with Dr. Billy Graham's sermon of united worship service on the last day.[645] Over 3.5 million people participated and the blood drive that was part of the entire celebration drew 4,000 people. Even though there were some criticisms following the event, the fact that everyone came together as one should be enough to mark this as a successful event.

(2) Centennial Anniversary Joint Service of Underwood's Coming

Horace G. Underwood set foot in Korea as the first Protestant clerical missionary at Easter on April 5, 1885. The five groups of the Presbyterian Church that rooted from Underwood's mission agreed to hold a commemorative service on April 5, 1985, at the Saemunan Church, mother church of the Korean Presbyterian Church. The service was led by Jong Yeol Park of Tonghap, Hoon Choe of Hapdong, Tae Soo Park of Koshin, Gi Soo Park of Daeshin, and Young Chan Lee of Christ Presbyterian Church.[646]

The grandson of Horace Underwood, H. G. Underwood, and 30 of his family members also attended the service. In the sermon titled "Coordinates of 2nd Century of Missions for the Korean Church," Pastor Hoon Choi preached that the direction that the Presbyterian Church should take is reform within its own church, creation of fundamentals for straightforward attitudes toward faith,

---

645 *Hanguk Ilbo* (Korea Daily), August 16, 1984.
646 *Christian Sinmun*, April 13, 1985.

reconsolidation, cooperation, and revival of a fallen public trust.[647] Pastor Jong Yol Park thanked the Underwood family for three generations of devotion toward the Korean Church and its people. In addition, Park pointed out how the Presbyterian Church has been with the Korean people through various schools, hospitals, social works, enlightenment of farmers and reformation of democratic consciousness, the awakening of national identity, and many ups and downs throughout history.

He also reminded everyone of the shameful past when the Church participated in shrine worship during the Imperial Japanese regime and division within the church. Park finished by stressing how the Church should come together in harmony to keep the traditional faith, to prevent the rise of cult movements, to endeavor to evangelize the people, and finally to recover the lost land of North Korea.[648]

Of the 59 Underwood decedents spanning five generations, 30 family members attended and were presented with a plaque in honor of their devotion and work for the Korean Church.

The 100th year anniversary officially ended with a commemorative service for the martyrs on October 14-15 in 1985. The official events continued for the next four years, and cooperation and unity amongst the churches is something that should be praised. There were also some critics saying that the anniversary events only focused on the external side of the church and lacked real substance.

---

647 Daehan Yesugiojangnohoe Chonghoe, *Hangukgiohoe 100Juyonginumsaup Jonghap bogosuh* (Report of the 100 Anniversary Memorial Celebration Works of the Korean Church) (1985), 246-247.
648 *Ibid.*

Especially the fact that the Church did not have a clear direction for the 2nd century of missions was the most urgent issue that the Church needed to solve.

(3) Pope John Paul II's Visit

When the Protestant Churches were busy with the 100th year anniversary of Christianity in Korea, the Catholic Church was busy planning their 200th year anniversary. The main event of the anniversary was the visit of Pope John Paul II to Korea. This was the Pope's very first visit to Korea ever in the history of the Korean Catholic Church. The Pope arrived in Korea on May 3, 1984, for a five day stay. He was greeted by President Doo Hwan Jun and the Catholic Church of Korea. His visit was historical in light of thousands of Catholics who died to lay the foundations for the present Catholic Church of Korea. The message and words he spoke to the Koreans emotionally touched many, and the Pope added deeper meaning to the 200 years of the Korean Catholic Church through the canonization of 103 saints.[649]

The Pope also visited Kwangjoo in hopes of healing the wounds of the past, Sorokdo (island) Leper community, farmers and fishermen, and leaders of other religions. He also met with the leaders of the Protestant Church and confirmed that we are all one in Jesus Christ. His visit, however, also hinted of a political motive as the Catholic Church has always done. The political implication

---

[649] *Christian Sinmun*, May 5, 1984.

of Pope's visit was summarized in the *Donga Daily* newspaper as follows:

> One of the political implications of the Pope's visit was evident in his visit to Kwangjoo where he stressed reconciliation and forgiveness. Although there was no specific mention of who should forgive who, it was clear that the ones to be "forgiven" and "reconciled" was already implied. The visit alone was enough for the government to place a positive spin on everything. The Pope's sneeze on the 3rd evening at Seoul Hae Hwa Dong Catholic University due to the pepper spray used towards student demonstrators was one of the ironic outcomes of the political atmosphere. This surely was the Pope's firsthand experience of our political climate.[650]

Even with all of the criticisms, without a doubt, the Pope's visit was one of the monumental events in the history of the Korean Catholic Church.

---

[650] *Donga Ilbo* (Donga Daily), May 7, 1984.

Chapter 7

Towards the New Century – March towards Unification

1. Beginning of South and North Communication

Following the independence from Japan, our country and people became divided into south and north not by our choice but by the hands of other powerful nations who drew a ceasefire line at the 38th parallel succeeding the Korean War. The different ideology resulted in the split of a single race that shares the same bloodline. Although everyone agrees that we should be united, when asked how, opinions vary. The church(if there is a church in North) can easily come together based on the fact that we all believe in the same God. In other words, the church is the single most ideal organization to come together between South and North.

We have already reviewed that when Il Sung Kim created his communist regime, the "Five Provinces Assembly" that existed was replaced by the communist entity "Josun(Korea) Christian

Federation" and repressed pastors, elders, and many church leaders who refused to join the assembly. With the subsequent abolishment of existing churches, imprisonment and execution of religious workers, it is a well known fact through various channels that there is no church in North Korea.

A historical meeting of the South-North Red Cross Conference was held in 1972 in Pyongyang and Seoul after 30 years of isolation and non-communication. But this event ended as a one time event and talks between South and North ceased again. Then in 1985, a window of opportunity for resuming talks opened again. Both governments agreed to have a talk and decided to visit each other in Seoul and Pyongyang. With this development, church leaders decided that the Church should act along with the government and formed the "Council of Countermeasure for South and North conflict of the Korean Church" where 24 members of the twelve denominations met and agreed to work together on issues regarding Christianity during the South-North talks and elected Pastor Kyung Jik Han as the president and Pastor Jong Yul Park, moderator of the Presbyterian Church(Tonghap), as the chairman and officially came together as a committee.

This committee was supported by the Presbyterian Church (Tonghap and Hapdong, Christ Presbyterian Church), Baptist, Lutheran, Methodist, and Gospel Church along with the Church of Nazareth and many other religious leaders. The committee set forth a mission statement that stated they will "work toward unification of Korea through South-North talks······The church will become one of the windows for the talks······"[651] Although it was commendable that the church took the initiative to take part in the South and North peace talks, it was also pointed out that the committee should have included more denominations and focus on valuing everyone's opinion.

2. Beginning of Discussion on Peaceful Unification[652]

The talk of peaceful unification for our divided country began to arise in the 1980's. The start of this phenomenon began with the creation of the "Institute for Study of Unification Issues" within the NCC during the Korea-German Church Conference in April of 1981. The following year, NCC created the "Institute for Study of Unification," and confirmed the United States' responsibility for the division during the Council of the US-Korea Churches in 1983. These discussions became more detailed during the 1984 "World Council of Churches for Peace in the North-East Asia" that was held at Dojanso in Japan. With representatives from the US, Japan, Korea(South) and many others present, the participants discussed ways the Church could contribute to the peace and unification of Korea. The North Korea Church was supposed to attend, but in the end they could not and sent a congratulatory telegram instead.

---

651 *Christian Sinmun*, April 6, 1985.
652 Won Sik Kim, "Hanguk Giohoeeui Tongil Noneui," (Discussion on the Unification of Korean Church), *Gidokgiodaeyongam* (Almanac of Christianity) (1989), 48-51.

These efforts brought about real results and in September of 1986, the first South-North Christian Conference was held in Glion, Switzerland, sponsored by WCC International. With eleven representatives from both sides, this was the first meeting of Christian leaders since the split. Although nothing solid came out of the meeting, the fact that both sides met, ate, worshipped, and shared the Body and Blood of Christ together was a truly historical event.

Later in April of 1988, the "International Conference of Christians for Peaceful Unification of Korea" was held with 300 representatives from all over the world in Inchon. During this meeting, the participants re-confirmed the initial stands of the NCC and agreed to pray and work together toward a peaceful unification of Korea. Although the Christ Presbyterian Church and the Gospel Church gave their support, the Presbyterian Church(Tonghap) could not come together and form a unified stand.

From this meeting in Incheon, it was decided that rather than relying on external cooperation, it would be more beneficial to communicate directly between the South and North. At the same time, the Government announced the "7.7(July 7th) Proclamation" and the atmosphere was set. As the Gospel Church suggested a joint Christmas service, the "National Pastors Association for the Realization of Justice and Peace" suggested a joint *Chuseok*(Thanksgiving) service. Even the Conservative Association of Korean Youth suggested a joint revival of South and North Korea. But all these suggestions never materialized as North Korea never formally responded. This serves as a wakeup call to all of us as all pieces must be in place in order for peaceful unification to occur.

3. Construction of the First Church in Pyongyang – Bongsoo Church

Even when the ten member delegates of the NCC–USA visited North Korea with an invitation from the North Korean Christian Peaceful Unification Committee and visited Pyongyang and Kyesung, they reported that no church other than the Home Church existed in North Korea. But when the Institute of Religious Social Studies held their anniversary event titled "Great Debate of Korean Religious Issues," Tae Woo Koh, instructor of the University of Foreign Studies, presented that during the 80's North Korea went through change in its policy on religion and that ① North Korea is presenting the visiting foreign Christians with their own version of the Bible and showing them the Home church similar to those in Red-China; ② North Korea started to restore the abandoned Buddhist temples and is showing efforts to present the truth behind Buddhism to visiting Western Journalists and Buddhists; and ③ North Korea has opened communication with international religious leaders.[653]

Pastor Kyung Seo Park, staff of the WCC, delivered shocking news after he visited North Korea that the first church building since liberation was being constructed in Bongsoo-dong, Pyongyang. In addition, he relayed the message that if the South Korean Church would send items for the church through the WCC, North Korea

---

653 *Hanguk Ilbo* (Korea Daily), June 15, 1988.

would accept them. This was confirmed by the Korean-American Pastor Dong Geun Hong who visited North Korea in 1988. Pastor Hong confirmed that there is in fact a red brick stone building in construction at the Mankyungdae area of Bongsoo-dong in Pyongyang City, which will hold about 300 and is scheduled to hold its first service in October.[654]

In addition, he reported that there was also a Catholic Church building that could hold up to 200 located in Jangchung-dong at the Sungyo-ri area in East Pyongyang. Afterwards, the Bongsoo Church building was completed and increasing number of Korean-Americans who visited North Korea reported having attended the service with North Korean Christians.

Although the motives behind these churches were apparent, just the fact that a Protestant and Catholic Church exists in North Korea is a welcoming sign.

4. Assembly of Church Representatives of South and North in Glion, Switzerland

Sponsored by the WCC, a historical meeting of eleven leaders of South and North Korea was held in September of 1986 in Glion, Switzerland. At this meeting, the church leaders of South and North Korea got together to discuss mutual concerns and to

---

654 Dong Keun Hong, "Bukeui Saeyebaedang, Saesuhngdangeul Bogo," (Seeing the New Church Building, New Catholic Church in North Korea) Hung Soo Kim, ed. Haebanghoo Bukhan Giohoesa (History of the Church of North Korea after Liberation), 411.

get to know each other. There was no significant outcome of this meeting other than the fact that the South and North met. The second meeting, also sponsored by the WCC, was held in Glion, Switzerland, from November 23-25, 1988. From the South, eleven representatives attended, including Bishop Sung Soo Kim of the Anglican Church of Korea(President of KNCC), Pastor Yong Sul Cho, Commander Suk Tae Kim of the Salvation Army, Professor Hyo Jae Lee(Ewha Women's University), and Moon Gyu Kang (Chairman of the Board of Directors of YMCA). From the North, seven representatives attended, including Gi Joon Goh(President of the Chosun Christian Federation), Un Bong Kim(Vice-President of the Pyongyang Region of the Chosun Christian Federaton), Pastor Song Bong Lee, Nam Hyuk Kim(adviser of the League), and Hye Sook Kim(translator).

On this day, Pastor Gi Joon Goh said, "We are the only race in the world that speaks the same language, same culture, same bloodline that are separated and cannot meet and attend service together. But to think that, even if we are in a foreign land, we can gather here and have service together brings a lot of things to my mind. We should not pass this tragedy of division to our children and I hope that we can work together as a peace army that creates love and forgiveness in Jesus Christ."[655] During the meeting, representatives of the South and North agreed on a few important issues.

---

655 *Bokum Sinbo* (Gospel Newspaper), November 30, 1988.

1. For the sake of peace and unification of the Korean Peninsula, the churches of South and North will designate 1995 as the Jubilee (Seventy Years) of Unification and honor the Sunday before August 15 as a joint prayer day. We will create a joint prayer especially for this day. In addition, we will ask other member churches around the world to join us and will petition to the WCC.

2. We confirm, based on the "Three Principles of Unification" that consist of "self-determination, peace, and unification of the nation," that the efforts of unification should also consider the preservation of each respective party's ascendant.

3. We confirm that the concerned parties in respect to the issue of unification are the citizens of South and North. As such, we have to eliminate any outside force that interferes with this division and is an obstacle to the process of unification concerning any other matters. Also, we re-confirm that the unification should be executed with the democratic participation of the entire population of the South and the North.

4. The unification of the Korean Peninsula must be achieved for the benefit of peace for Korea and Northeast Asia. Therefore, any form of disguised peace that tries to justify the division of Korean Peninsula must be rejected. In addition, any political measure that supports the prolongation of division should be eliminated.

5. We believe that in order to achieve peaceful unification, both sides must work to rebuild trust. The churches of South-North Korea must create an atmosphere that will facilitate overcoming any lingering hostility and hatred. These efforts should mirror the Ecumenical Principles that the Dojanso Conference adopted for contacts between the South and North. Furthermore, we request for other world churches, including the UN and other international institutions, to assist us

in the process.

6. To reduce military tension that threatens peaceful unification, the large amount of military power and weapons should be reduced. In order to accomplish this, the current Ceasefire Treaty should be converted to a Peace Treaty and the peace of stability of the entire Korean peninsula should be guaranteed and must adopt a Non-aggression Treaty. With this, all foreign troops, including the US troops stationed in Korea, should be removed along with any nuclear weapons pointing towards Korea.

7. The exchange of communication between the ten million dispersed families is the most urgent issue in respect to humanitarianism. But such events are not possible with current military, political conflicts and may even bring despair and weaken the efforts of unification. Therefore, the humanitarianism issues and the matters of communication between the two churches should be executed as one of the methods for unification.

8. WCC will try to continue through cooperating with the Chosun Christians Federation and National Council of Churches of Korea towards Peace and Unification of the Korean peninsula.

November 25, 1988

Attendees of the Conference for Peaceful Unification of the Korean Peninsula[656]

Under this agreement, the two churches accepted the three principles of autonomy, peace, and national solidarity, and the "Proclamation of National Unification and Peace" that was issued by the

---

656 Hanguk Gidokgiosa Yonguwon, ed., '88 Hanguk Giohoesajung (1988) (Situation of the Korean Church in 1988), 187-188.

NCC. Also, the two churches agreed on the year of 1995 as the Jubilee Year and the Sunday before August 15 as the "Sunday of Prayer for Peace and Unification." The two churches strengthened their commitment by agreeing to exchange information and documents through WCC.

Although we could not verify the type of church that existed in the North, the fact that both sides could come together under one God signifies as one of the precursor to what is to come. But when this manifesto was announced, the churches in Korea, not only the NCC members but also non-member churches, expressed strong criticism. Because the manifesto talked about the withdrawal of US troops and other matters that are directly related to the safety of the nation, conservative denominations issued a statement that NCC cannot represent the entire group of Christians in Korea. And the dispute over the manifesto continued for some time.

The third meeting was also held in Glion in December of 1990 and closing the 6th WCC, the General Assembly accepted the political statement titled "Peace and Unification of the Korean Peninsula." With the 22nd General Assembly of WARC, which was held on August 26, 1989, issuing the "Unification and Reconciliation of Korean Peninsula" statement, the issue of unification became a common cause for the churches around the world. When four members of the Chosen Christians Federation attended the 7th General Assembly of the WCC meeting held in Canburra, Australia, in February of 1991 as observers, they showed their desire to communicate with the world Christian community.[657]

5. Creation of Pan-Religious League for Unification

The proposition that divided land and its people must unite is not an issue for specific groups of people, but rather it is shared by everyone. In support of this, from July 2–4, 1988, Catholics, Protestants, Buddhists, and 50 other social groups got together and held a joint campaign called the Peaceful March for Unification.

In the mist of these events, in July 1993, the Protestant Church, Catholic Church, Buddhist, and Won(Circle) Buddhist got together and formed a collective entity called the "League of Religious People for the Nation's Reconciliation and Unification." They held the opening meeting at the second floor of Scoul Yconji-dong Christian Center and elected joint chairmen Pastor Sang Keun Kim, Father Sae Ung Ham, Buddhist monk Sun Ji and Director Hyun Kim. Those who attended were key members from organizations such as the Union of the Korean Christian Society, the Association of the National Ministers for Justice and Peace, the Korean Christian Women Association, the National Catholic Priests Association for Justice, the National Buddhist Association for Practice, and the National Educators of the Won Buddhism for Social Reform. Thus, this also meant the joining of these groups as well.

The reason behind the creation of the league was explained as an effort to revive a civil unification movement that has been

---

657 In Chul Kang, "Hyundai Bukhan Jonggiosaeui Jaeinsik," (Reundersating of Modern North Korean Religious History) Hung Soo Kim, ed. *Haebanghoo Bukhan Giohoesa* (History of Church of the North Korea after Liberation), 211.

weakened due to new government that was leaning towards rather than elimination of the anti-unification force within by restricting any civil unification efforts. In their mission statement, the league pledge to "respect the various approach to unification······and based on this, to help civil efforts to overcome small differences."[658]

We must point out that although it is a good idea to bring about and work with many different people on unification, the efforts should not be only of those few radical leaders and that this has the danger of those few leaders to shift things toward their own opinions.

The NCC continues to honor 1995 as the Jubilee Year and pray for unification while agreeing to participate in various events for the purpose of unification. We will see unification someday. But only God knows when that will happen. All we can do is pray and endeavor that this will happen soon.

---

658 *Hangiorae Sinmun* (Hangiorae Newspaper), July 3, 1993.

Epilogue

Our nation has 5,000 years of history. But the history is filled with continuous hardships through being afflicted between powerful countries by war, invasion, and exploitation. Despite all that, we have endured adversity and survived. At times we fought and at times we retreated, but our national spirit was always strong being passed down, generation to generation, up until today.

We had numerous forms of religion in our history, but none of them made its impact as a national religion. This is the reason why some foreigners refer to us as the nation without a national religion. But this was most fortunate in a sense that this lack of national religion provided an adequate soil for Christianity to come to our land.[659]

It has been two centuries since we have received the Christian Gospel through the divine power of God. The Roman Catholic Church, who first came to Korea and had to face brutal hardships

---

659 Arthur J. Brown pointed out that one of the main reasons for the rapid growth of the Korean Church is that there was no strong established religion in his book, *One Hundred Years*, A Story of the Foreign Missionary Work of the Presbyterian Church in the U. S. A. (New York: Fleming H. Revell, 1936), 421-422.

and persecution and grow strong with the blood of their missionaries, has had a history filled with glory and shame. Although the Protestant came a century later than the Catholics, we were able to establish ourselves by arriving at the same time the country had reluctantly opened its doors to the West. Even though Christians did not become directly involved politically to oppose Japan, but in terms of the anti-Japanese movement, the Church has been in unity with the people in various ways.

Many concerned leaders who worried about our country being behind in culture and science, as well as despaired citizens, flocked to the church and became devoted Christians. This phenomenon helped in the rapid growth of the Church. This was all because God loves our country and has allowed the Gospel to spread in a country that was ignorant of God for thousands of years and worshipped other gods in darkness. The way we were able to received eternal life through Jesus Christ was due to God's divine predestination.

The Church that has provided hope and vision for tomorrow and a place to voice their hardships and wishes had been the best of friends who have laughed and cried with everyone through out the Japanese occupation. Even though there was a time when the Church had abandoned its principles, the fire of faith never died in our hearts and was waiting for a brighter tomorrow. Even during the tragedy of the Korean War and military regime, the Church has maintained its place in society.

Now the Church is in the second century of missionary work

in Korea. The churches of Korea must understand God's wishes for our church and confront the cross that we must carry on. The Church must also spend time repenting for all its shameful deeds of the past and strive to fulfill its destiny with renewed vow. We must believe that God, who has been with our nation and our church, will grant unification in the near future and also pledge to work to fulfill our destiny of the South and North being as one under a unified sky.

The mission of the Church should be to aid Christianity to become our national religion by becoming deeply imbedded in our national and cultural consciousness through directing the nation and its people toward the right path, helping them maintain righteous social consciousness and values, and helping them realize their mission in life. May glory be with God alone. Soli Deo Gloria!

BIBLIOGRAPHY

Books

* Allen, Horace N. *Allen's Diary*. Tr. Kim, Won Mo. Seoul: Dankuk Univ. Press, 1991.
* *Annual Report of the Missionary Society of the Methodist Episcopal Church for 1884, 1885.*
* *Annual Reports of the Federal Council of the Churches of Christian in America*, for the Year 1919.
* Bansoirang, Han, Suk Hee. *Ilje Tongchiwa Ilbon Kidokgio* (Reign of the Imperial Japanese and Christianity in Japan). Seoul: Somangsa, 1989.
* Beave, R. Pierce, ed. *American Missions in Bicentennial Perspective*. Pasadena, CA., 1977.
* Blair, William & Bruce Hunter, *Korean Pentecost and the Sufferings which Followed*. Carlisle, Penn: The Banner of Truth Trust, 1977.
* Blinkley, F. *A History of the Japanese People*. London: The Encyclopedia Britannica Press, 1915.
* Brown, A. J. *One Hundred Years*. A Story of the Foreign

Missionary Work of the Presbyterian Church in the
U. S. A. New York: Fleming H. Revell, 1936.

* Brown, G. T. *Missions to Korea*. The Presbyterian Church
of Korea Department of Education. Seoul: 1962.

* Byeon, Jong Ho. *Lee Yong Do Moksajeon* (Biography of Rev
Lee Yong Do). Seoul: Simuwon, 1958.

————————— * *Lee Yong Do Moksa Seoganjip* (Collection
of Rev. Yi Yong Do's Letters). Seoul: Simuwon, 1958.

* Cha, Jae Myeong. *Chosun Yesugiojangnogiohoe Sagi*. (The
History of the Presbyterian Church in Korea). Vol. 1
Chosun Gidokgio Changmunsa, 1928.

* Chang, Hee Keun. *Hanguk Jangno Giohoesa* (History of Presbyterian Church of Korea). Asung Press, 1970.

* Chang, Hyeong Il. *Hanguk Gusegunsa* (The History of the
Salvation Army in Korea). Salvation Army Korea Territory, 1975.

* *Chinilpa Gunsang* (Gang of pro-Japanese). Minjok Jungkion
Munhwa Yonguwon. Institute of study of national po-
liticeconominy-culture, 1948.

* Choi, Hoon. *Hankuk Jaegeon Giohoesa* (History of the Korean
Reconstruction Church). Seoul: Seongkwang Moonh
wasa, 1989.

* Choi, Seog U. *Hanguk Cheonjugiohoeui Yeoksa* (The History
of the Catholic Church in Korea). Korea Church History
Institute, 1982.

* Choi, Duk Shin. *Sinheung Jonggio Jibdane Goanhan Yongu*

(Study on the Newly Emerging Religious Group). Seoul: Chambitsa, 1965.

- Chosun Chongdokbu Kiongmuguk (Department of Police, Government of Goverer General in Korea). *Chaegune Chosune Chian Sangwhang* (Present Situation of Korean Public Peace). 1938.

- *Chosun Yesugio Jangnohoesagi* (The History of Korean Presbyterian Church) Vol. 1. Chosun Yesugio Chonhoe, 1928. Vol. 2. 1968.

- Chu, Sun Ae. *Jangnogio Yeoseongsa* (The History of Women in the Presbyterian Church). Association of the National Korean Presbyterian Women, 1979.

- Chun, Byeong Ho. *Choi Tae Yongui Saengaewa Sasang* (Choi Tae Yong's Life and Thoughts). Christian Resource Publica-tions, 1983.

- Chun, Taek Bu. *Hanguk Gidokgio Cheongnyeon Undongsa* (The History of Christian Youth Movement in Korea). Seongeumsa, 1978.

——————— • *Ingan Shin Heungwoo* (The Man Shin Heungwoo). Seoul: Christian Literature Society, 1971.

- Chung, Gio. *Daehangyenyeonsa* (The Korean History). The National Institute of Korean History, 1957.

- Clark, A. D. *A History of the Church in Korea*. 5th print. The Christian Literature Society of Korea, 1992

——————— • *The Korean Church and the Nevius Methods*.

New York: Fleming H. Revell, 1930.

* *Daehan Gidokgio Jangnohoe Chonghoe Hoeirok* (Minutes of the Christ Presbyterian Church of Korea).

* Daehan Yesugio Jangnohoe Chonghoe, *Hanguk Giohoe 100 jooyon giniom Saup Jonghap Boguseo* (Collection Report of the Centennial Memorial Works of Korean Church). 1985.

* *Daehan Yesugio Jangnohoe Chonghoe Hoeuirok (Minutes of the General Assembly of the Jesus Presbyterian Church of Korea).*

* *Daehan Yesugio Jangnohoe 100 Yonsa* (The 100-Year History of the Korean Presbyterian Church). Education Depart ment of the Korean Presbyterian Church, 1984.

* Dallet, C. *The History of the Catholic Church in Korea.* Vol. 1. 1990.

* Dawson, C. ed. *Mission to Asia.* New York: Harper and Row Publishing Co., 1966.

* *Doknib Undongsa Jaryojip* II (Resources Book of the Independence Movement Part II).

* Eulyu Editorial Committee of National History. *Hanguksa 16* (The Korean History 16). Seoul: Eulyu Moonhwasa, 1975.

* Fenwick, M. C. *Church of Christ in Corea.* New York: Hodder & Stoughton, 1911.

* Gale, James S. *Korea in Transition.* New York: Laymen's Missionary Movement, 1909.

────────── • *Korean Sketches*. Edinburg: Olimphant Anderson and Ferrior, 1898.

• *Gidokgio Daebaekgwasajeon* (The Christian Encyclopedia). (1985).

• *Gidokgio Sasang Gangjwa* (Lectures on Christian Thoughts). Vol. 3.

• *Gidokgio Yongam* (Almanac of Christianity of Korea). Gidokgiomunsa, 1993.

• Gilmore, G. W. *Korea from its Capital*. Philadelphia: Presbyterian Board of Publication and Sunday School Work, 1892.

• *Gioyukgwa Yeosung Ansoo* (Ministry and Feminine Ordination). Presbyterian College and Theological Seminary Press, 1992.

• Gordon, E. A. *Christianity and the Mahayana*. Tokyo: Maruzen, 1921.

• Gueztlaff, K. *Journal of Three Voyages along the Coast of China, in 1831, 1832, and 1833, with Notices of Siam, Corea, and the Loo-Choo Islands*. London: Frederick Westley and A.H. Davis, 1834.

• *Guhanguk Oegyomunseo* (Diplomatic Documents of the Korean Empire). III, 14. Vol. 20, Legal Documents II.

• Ham, Seok Heon. *Seongseojeok Ipjangeseo Bon Chosunyeoksa* (A History of Chosun in Biblical Perspective). Seoul: Sinsaenggwan, 1961.

• Han, Woo Geun. *Hanguk Tongsa* (Entire History of Korea).

Seoul: Eulyumunhwasa, 1983.

* Han, Young Jae. *Hangukseongseo Chansongga 100 Yon* (100 Years of Korean Bibles and Hymnals). Christian Publishing, 1987.

* *Hanguk Cheonjugiohoesa Yongu* (A Study of the History of Catholicism in Korea). Korea Catholic History Institute, 1986.

* Hanguk Gidokgio 100 Yonsa Pionchanuiwonhoe, *Hanguk Gidokgio 100 Yonsa* (History of Centennial Year of Christianity of Korea). Seoul: Hanguk Gidokgio Jangnohoe Press, 1992.

* *Hanguk Giohoesa* (The History of the Korean Church). Haeseonmunhwasa). 1979.

* *Hanguk YMCA Undongsa 1895-1985* (The YMCA Movement in Korea 1895-1985). Seoul: Daehan YMCA Yonmaeng, 1986.

* *Hangukdongnib Undongsa* (The History of the Independence Movement in Korea). Guksa Pyonchan Wuiwonhae.

* *Hangukgiohoesaui Tamsaek* (Inquiry of the History of the Korean Church). Hangukgidokgiosa Yongu (February 1986).

* Hanguk Sinhak Yonguwon, ed. *Hanguk Minjung Sinhak Jeonnge* (Unfolding of the Korean Minjung Theology in Korea in 1980s). Seoul: Hanguk Sinhak Yonguwon, 1990.

* Harrington, F. H. God, *Mammon, and the Japanese.* Madison: Univ. of Wisconsin, 1944.

- Hong, Sang Pyo. *Gando Dongnibundong Sosa* (A Brief History of the Independence Movement in Jiandao). Pyeongtaek: Hangang Middle and High School, 1966.
- Hudson, W. S. *Nationalism and Religion in America, Concept of American Identity and Mission.* New York: Harper and Row, 1970.
- Hyeon, Seok Mun. *Gihaeilgi* (Kihae Annals).
- Im, Jong Kuk. *Chinil Munhakron* (Treatise on pro- Japanese Literature). Seoul: Piongwha Press, 1986.
- *Jangnohoe Sinhakdaehak 70 Yonsa* (History of 70years of the Presbyterian Theological Seminary). Jangnohoe Sin hakdaehak, 1971.
- Jeong, Jae Mun and Jeong, Jae Seon. *Hanguk Catholic Eojewa Oneul* (Catholicism in Korea, Yesterday and Today). Catholic Publishing Co., 1963.
- *Juhngjo Sillok* (Chronicles of King Jeongjo). Vol. 33. Gyemijo, 11th Month of 15th year of King Jeongjo.
- Kang, Jin Cheol, Kang, Man Gil, and Kim, Jin Bae, *Segiesae Bichun Hangukui Yoksa.* (Korean History Reflected on the World History).
- Kang, Wi Jo. *Iljetongchiha Hangukui Jonggyowa Jeongchi* (Religions and Politics of Korea under the Japanese Rule). Korea Christian Literature Society, 1977.
- Kedulie, Elie. *Nationalism in Asia and Africa.* New York: Ward, 1970.
- Kil, Jin Kyong. *Yeonggye Kil, Sun Joo Moksa Jeojakjip* (Writings

of Rev. Yeonggye Kil Sunju). Vol. 1. Seoul: Korea
Christian Literature Society, 1968.

- Kim, Chun Bae. *Hanguk Gidokgio Sunansahwa* (A Story of
the Tragic History of Christianity in Korea). Seongmu-
nhaksa, 1979.

- Kim, Gwang Soo. *Hanguk Gidokgio Jeollaesa* (A History
of Introduction of Christianity to Korea). Seoul: Korea
Christian Institute, 1984.

——————— · *Hanguk Gidokgio Jeollaesa* (The Origin
of Christianity in Korea). Korea Christia-nity Institute,
1984.

- Kim, Hung Soo, ed. *Haebanghoo Bukhan Giohaesa* (History
of Church of the North Korea after Liberation). Seoul:
Dasan Gulbang, 1992.

- Kim, In Suh. *Kim In Suh Jeojak Jeonjip* (Collection of Kim
In Suh's Writings). Vol. 5. Seoul: Sinmangaesa, 1976.

- Kim, Jonah. *Chongsin 90 Yonsa* (History of Chongsin 90 Years).
Seoul: Yangmun, 1991.

- Kim, Kyung Rae. *Sahoeakgwa Sakioundong* (Social Evil and
Movement of Heresy). Seoul: Kimunsa, 1957.

- Kim, Seong Sik. *Iljeha Hangukhaksaeng Dongnibundongsa*
(The Independence Movement of Students under the
Japanese Rule). Jeongeumsa, 1981.

- Kim, Sung Joon. *Hanguk Gidokgiohoesa* (History of Christianity in Korea). Seoul: Hanguk Giohoe Gioyuk Yongu
won, 1980.

* Kim, Yang Sun. *Hanguk Gidokgiohoesa Yongu* (A Study of the History of the Korean Church). Seoul: Christian Publishing Co., 1971.

─────────── * *Hanguk Gidokgio Haebang 10 Yonsa* (The Ten-Year History of Korean Christianity after Liberation). Education Department, General Assembly of the Korea Presbyterian Church, 1956.

* Kokiobingil. *Chosun Gioyooksago* (Study of the History of Education in Chosun) Seoul: Imperial Regional Administration Conference, 1927.

* Kwak, An Ryeon. *Jangnohoesajeonhwijip* (Compilation of the History of the Chosun Presbyterian History) Vol. I. Chosun Yesugioseohoe, 1917.

─────────── * *Chosun Jangnogiohoesa Jeonhwijip* (Compilment of the History of the Chosun Presbyterian Church). Vol. II. Seoul: Northern Presbyterian Church Mission Board, 1935.

* Latourette, K. S. *A History of Christianity*. New York: Harper and Row Publishers, 1953.

─────────── * *A History of the Expansion of Christianity*. Vol. II. New York: Harper and Brothers, 1978.

* Lee, Chun Young. *Sunggiolkioheosa* (History of the Holiness Church). Korean Christ Holiness Church Press, 1970.

* Lee, Chung Sik. *The Politics of Korean Nationalism*. Berkely: 1963.

* Lee, Gwang Lin. *Chodae Underwood Seongyosaui Saengae*

(The Life of Missionary Underwood). Seoul: Yonsei
Universtity Press, 1991.

* Lee, Jeong Sik, ed. *Hanguk Dongnib Undongsa* (The History
of the Independence Movement in Korea). Vol. 1.
Jeongeu-mmunhwasa, 1983.

* Lee, Jeong Soo, ed. *Hanguk Chimyegiohoesa* (History of the
Korean Baptist Church). Baptist Church Press, 1990.

* Lee, Hyeon Jong, ed. *Hanguk Dongnibundongsa* (The History
of Korean Independence Movement). Vol. 2.

* Lee, Jang Sik. *Asia Godae Gidokgiosa* (Ancient History of
Christianity in Asia). Seoul: Gidokgyomunsa, 1993.

* Lee, Man Yeol, et al. *Hangukgidokgiowa Minjokundong*
(Christianity in Korea and the National Movement).
Seoul: Bosung, 1986.

* Lee, Neung Hwa. *Chosun Gidokgiogeup Oegyosa* (A History
of Christianity and Diplomacy in Chosun). Vol. 1.
Chosun Gidokgio Changmunsa, 1928.

* Lee, Seong Sam. *Hangukgamrigiohoesa* (The History of the
Methodist Church in Korea). Education Department
of the Korea Methodist Church, 1978.

* Lee, Yeong In. *Hangukjaerimgiohoesa* (The History of the
Adventist Church in Korea). Seoul: Sijosa, 1965.

* Lee, Young Hun. *Hanguk Gidokgiohoesa* (History of Christian
Church of Korea). Seoul: Concordia Press, 1978.

* Lim, Jong Guk. *Chinil Nonsul Sunjip* (Collection of the Pro-
Japanese Articles).

* McCully, E. A. *A Corn of Wheat, The Life of Rev. W. J. McKenzie of Korea*, 2nd ed.
* McKenzie, F. A. *Korea's Fight for Freedom*. New York: Fleming H. Revell, 1920.
* Min, Kyoung Bae. *Allenui Seongiowa Geundae Hanmioegyo* (Allen's Missionary Work and Modern Korean-American Diplomacy). Seoul: Yonsei University Press, 1991.

──────── * *Daehan Yesugio Jangnohoe 100Yonsa* (History of the Centennial year of Church of Korea) Daehan Ye-sugio Jangnohoe Chonghoe Gioyoukbu, 1984.

──────── * *Hanguk Gidokgiohoesa* (A History of Christian Churches in Korea. Seoul: Yonsei University Press, 1993.

──────── * *Hangukminjokgiohoe Hyeongseongsaron* (The Study of the Development of the Ko-rean National Church). 1974.

* *Minjoktongilgwa Gidokgio* (The Unification of the Race and Christianity). Seoul: Hangilsa, 1986.
* *Minutes of the Korean Missions of the Methodist Episcopal Church, South*, for 1926.
* Moffett, S. H. *Asiawa Seongyo* (Asia and Missions). Institute of Missiological Issues, Presbyterian Theological Seminary, 1976

──────── * *A History of Christianity in Asia*. Vol. I. San Francisco: Harper, 1992.

Mokhoeyeohwa. Seoul: Hyangryeonsa, 1965.

Moule, A. C. *Christians in China before the Year 1550*. London: Society for Promoting Christian Knowledge, 1930.

Neill, Stephen. *A History of Christian Missions*. 2nd ed. New York: Penguin Books, 1986.

Noh, Pyeong Gu, ed. *Kim, Gyo Sin Sinangseojakjip* (Kim Gyo Sin Christian Writings). Vol. 2. Seoul: First Publications, 1965.

Oh, Yun Tae. *Hanguk Gidokgiosa* (The History of Christianity in Korea). Vol. 4. Hyeseon Publishing Co., 1983.

Paik, Nak Jun. *Hanguk Gaesingiosa* (The History of Protestantism in Korea) Seoul: Yonsei University Press, 1973.

Park, Eun Sik. *Hanguk Dongnibundong Jihiolsa* (The Bloody History of Independence Movement of Korea). Seoul: Dankook University Press, 1920.

Park, Gyeong Sik. *Chosun Samildongnibundong* (The March First Independence Movement of Chosun). 1976.

Quarto Centennial Papers, Read before the Korea Mission of the Presbyterian Church in the U.S.A. at the Annual Meeting in Pyeng Yang; 1909.

Report of the Foreign Mission Committee of the Presbyterian Church in Canada for 1898-1899.

Rhodes, H. A. ed. *History of the Korea Mission Presbyterian Church U.S.A. 1884-1934*. Vol. I. Chosun Mission, Presbyterian Church, U.S.A., 1934.

Robinson, C. H. *History of Christian Missions*. Edinburgh:

Part III · 595

T. & T. Clark, 1915.

* Rockhill, W. W. *The Journey of William of Rubruck to the Eastern Part of the World, 1253-1255*. London: The Hekluyt Society, 1900.

* Ryu, Hong Yeol, *Hanguk Cheonjugiohoesa* (The History of the Catholic Church in Korea). Vol. I. Seoul: Catholic Press, 1990.

* *3.1 Undong 50 Junyeon Ginyeomnonjip* (Fiftieth Anniversary Commemoration Compilation of The March First Movement). Donga Daily, 1969.

* Seo, Myeong Won. *Hanguk Giohoe Sungjangsa* (The History of Church Growth in Korea). Tr. Lee, Seoung Ik. Seoul: Gido-kgyo Seohoe, 1966.

* *Seungjeongwonilgee* (Diary of Seungjeongwon).

* Shin, Yong Ha. *Hanminjok Dongnibundongsa Yeongu* (A Study of the Independence Movement of the Korean People). Euryu-munhwasa, 1985.

* Song, Gil Seop. *Hanguk Sinhak Sasangsa* (The History of Theological Thoughts in Korea). Seoul: Korea Christian Publi-shing, 1987.

* Storry, R. *A History of Modern Japan*. New York: Penguin Books, 1961.

* Tak, Myong Hwan. *Tongilgioeui Silsanggwa Heosang* (Real and False Aspect of the Unification Church). Seoul: Kukje Jonggio Munje Yonguso, 1979.

* *The History of Jeongdong First Church*, 1885-1990.

* Underwood, L. *Fifteen Years among the Top-knots*. New York: American Tract Society, 1904.

──────── • *Underwood of Korea*. New York: Fleming H. Revell, 1918.

* Wells, K. M. *New God, New Nation*, Protestants and Self-Reconstruction Nationalism in Korea, 1896-1937. Honolulu: University of Hawaii, 1990.

* *Wolli Haesul* (Interpretation of the Principle) 4th ed. Seoul: World Unification Church, 1962.

* Yoo, Dong Sik. *Jungdong Cheil Kiohoeui Yoksa* (History of the Jungdong First Church). Committee of Edition of the Jungdong First Church, 1992.

* Yun, Chun Byeong. *Hangukgidokgyosinmun*, Japji 100Yonsa (100 Years of Christian Newspapers and Magazines in Korea). Korea Christian Publishing, 1984. 6.

Magazines and Newspapers

* *The Bokeum Sinbo* (Gospel News).
* *The Bukhan* (North Korea).
* *The Cheollaejiseong* (The Sound of Heaven), 2nd Issue.
* *The Christian Life*.
* *The Christian Messenger*
* *The Christian Newspaper*
* *The Current History Magazine*

- *The Dongyanggi Kwang* (Light of Orient)
- *The Foreign Missionary*
- *The Gidokgio Sasang* (Christian Thoughts)
- *The Gidokgongbo* (Christian News).
- *The Giohoewa Sinhak* (Church and Theology)
- *The Hanseong Sahak* (Hanseoong Magazine)
- *The Hyeondaewa Sinhak* (Modern Time and Theology)
- *The Japan Christian Quarterly*
- *The Korea Mission Field*
- *The Korea Review*
- *The Korean Repository*
- *The Methodist Quarterly Review*
- *The Missionary*
- *The Missionary Magazine and Chronicle*
- *The Missionary Review of the World*
- *The Missionary Review*
- *The Sasangge* (World of Thought)
- *The Seongseo Hanguk* (Bible Korea)
- *The Sinhak Jinam* (Theological Magazine)
- *The Woman's Work for Woman*
- *The Yeonggwa Jilli* (The Spirit and Truth)

Index

B

C

F

G

H

J

K

Myongsung Wanghoo (Queen Min) 108, 124, 140, 186, 187, 190, 197

N

NAE 514
NCC 572
Na, Un Mong 492, 493, 494
NAE Party 506, 507, 508, 510
Nam, Jong Sam 75, 76
Namgoong, Hyeok 329, 330, 372, 373, 481
Namyoungun 79
National Christian Coalition of Justice of Clergies 554
Nestorian Monument 20
Nestorianism 16, 17, 18, 19, 20, 25
Nevius Principles 164, 165, 166, 167, 168, 170, 171, 173, 174
Nevius, John 137, 164, 165, 166, 167, 168, 170, 171, 174, 219
New People's Association (Sinminhoe) 279, 280, 284
Noh, Choon Kyeong 141
Non-church Movement 329, 336, 337, 338, 339, 340, 341, 342
Nongmin Saenghwal(The Farmers's Life) 359
Nongwoohoe (Society of the farmers' Friend) 362
Northern Methodist Church of the United States 129, 152
Northern Presbyterian Church 119, 121, 122, 129, 133, 134, 152, 162, 166, 167, 253, 257, 258, 259, 267, 311, 383, 462, 562

O

Oppert, E. 79, 80

Osan School   280, 290, 398, 399, 400

P

R

S

T

Thomas, Robert J. 96, 98, 99, 114, 271, 312, 536
Tonghap(Union) Side 503
Tong-il(Union) Hymn 545
Tsudasen 108

U

Uchimura G. 336, 340
Underwood, H. G. 111, 120, 126, 127, 128, 129, 130, 133, 135,
137, 140, 142, 143, 144, 145, 147, 148, 149,
150, 154, 157, 158, 159, 164, 171, 176, 179,
181, 182, 186, 188, 189, 190, 191, 192, 194,
195, 197, 215, 226, 241, 253, 255, 261, 264,
397, 565, 566
Unification Church 335, 499, 500, 501, 502
Urban Industrial Mission 528

V

Victoria Presbyterian Church 153
Vinton, C. C. 150, 151

W

WCC (The World Council of Churches) 511, 512, 513, 514, 515,
518, 558, 572, 573, 574,
575, 576, 577, 578
Weltevree, Jan J. 86, 87, 88
Williamson, A. 96, 97, 101
Wolligangnon (The Fundamental Doctrines) 500, 533

Y

Z

판 권
소 유

History of Christianity in Korea

2011년 7월 5일 인쇄
2011년 7월 10일 발행

지은이 | 김인수
발행인 | 이형규
발행처 | 쿰란출판사

주소 | 서울 종로구 이화동 184-3
TEL | 02-745-1007, 745-1301, 747-1212, 743-1300
영업부 | 02-747-1004, FAX / 02-745-8490
본사평생전화번호 | 0502-756-1004
홈페이지 | http://www.qumran.co.kr
E-mail | qumran@hitel.net
           qumran@paran.com
한글인터넷수소 | 쿰란, 쿰란출판사

등록 | 제1-670호(1988.2.27)

값 20,000원

ISBN 978-89-6562-134-8 93230

History of Christianity in Korea

Printed in the Republic of Korea

For information about permission to reproduce selections from this book,
write to Qumran Publishing House, Jongro-gu Ihwa dong 184-3, Seoul.

Tel: 02-745-1007, 745-1301~2, 747-1212, 743-1300
FAX: 02-745-8490
Website: http://www.qumran.co.kr
E-mail: qumran@hitel.net
qumran@paran.com

ISBN 978-89-6562-134-8 93230
Price: U.S. $30